PIMLICO

399

THE KING AND THE GENTLEMAN

Derek Wilson graduated from Cambridge in 1961 and spent several years travelling and teaching in Africa before becoming a full-time writer and broadcaster in 1971. His highly acclaimed and bestselling books include *Rothschild: A Story of Wealth and Power*, *Sweet Robin: Robert Dudley Earl of Leicester*, *Hans Holbein: Portrait of an Unknown Man* and *A Tudor Tapestry: Men, Women and Society in Reformation England*. He has scripted and presented numerous radio and TV programmes. Derek Wilson is married and lives in Devon.

THE KING AND
THE GENTLEMAN

Charles Stuart and Oliver Cromwell
1599–1649

DEREK WILSON

PIMLICO

Published by Pimlico 2000

2 4 6 8 10 9 7 5 3 1

First published in Great Britain by
Hutchinson 1999
Pimlico edition 2000

Pimlico
Random House, 20 Vauxhall Bridge Road,
London SW1V 2SA

Random House Australia (Pty) Limited
20 Alfred Street, Milsons Point, Sydney,
New South Wales 2061, Australia

Random House New Zealand Limited
18 Poland Road, Glenfield,
Auckland 10, New Zealand

Random House (Pty) Limited
Endulini, 5A Jubilee Road, Parktown 2193, South Africa

Random House Group Limited Reg. No. 954009
www.randomhouse.co.uk

A CIP catalogue record for this book
is available from the British Library

ISBN 0-7126-6638-9

Printed and bound in Great Britain by
Mackays of Chatham PLC

CONTENTS

LIST OF ILLUSTRATIONS

INTRODUCTION

The scene has all the stuff of Victorian melodrama: night; a room in the palace of St James's dimly lit by guttering torches. On trestles in the centre an open coffin and, within it, the body of Charles I, head and torso now reunited. Armed guards watch over it. Enter a figure with wide-brimmed hat well pulled down and cloak drawn round the lower part of the face. For several moments the visitor gazes at the features of the dead King. Then, 'Cruel necessity,' he is heard to mutter, before turning and retiring as stealthily as he came. The clandestine, nocturnal visitor is, of course, Oliver Cromwell.

Whether or not this event ever occurred, we have a strong sense that it should have; it accords with the fittingness of things. The main reason why we want the encounter to have taken place is that, although these two men dominated the history of England and her neighbours for a quarter of a century, we have no detailed account of the few meetings between them – no conversation, no impassioned argument, no battlefield confrontation, no exchange of letters. The romantic in us will not allow them to depart into the shades without some display of meaningful, personal contact. Thus, imagination fills the gap left by historical evidence and permits Oliver the gentleman to take his leave of Charles the King.

The tableau is melodramatic and rightly so, for it condenses into a poignant moment of time, one of the most turbulent epochs in our history and one which has never failed to fascinate and intrigue. It poses questions which demand answers: 'Who were these men?' and 'What on earth or in heaven possessed them – literally possessed them – to wade through a nation's blood to so grisly a conclusion?' This book is very simply an attempt to answer such questions. It tells the story of Charles Stuart and Oliver Cromwell, setting them side by side to show how different they were and yet how similar, and why different and why similar, and what moved

1

them, and who moved them, and whether they could have chosen a different fate.

The two tales intertwined in this book have not been told before in this way. That is why I make no excuse for adding another volume to the miles of shelves which groan beneath the weight of books about Parliament, the Constitutional Conflict, the Religious Controversy, Court and County, Local Politics, Anglo-Scottish Relations and every other conceivable sub topic into which the seventeenth-century crisis can be subdivided. The Civil War rages as furiously today as it did three and a half centuries ago, its cohorts cantering into literary battle under such defiantly fluttering banners as 'Whigism', 'Marxism', 'Traditionalism', Grass-Rootism' and 'Revisionism'. They scythe down arguments with finely honed research. They pepper their opponents with snarling invective. They devise novel theories to outflank each other's forces. And in the dust and din of conflict the essential issues are often lost to sight. There is need for chroniclers without academic reputations to establish who can actually *reveal* parts of the enthralling grand design.

And free it from the strangling grasp of 'isms'.

It may help academic systemisers to analyse Puritanism, Anglicanism, Arminianism, Parliamentarianism, Royalism, Republicanism and Radicalism, but such endeavours are of limited value to those of us who gaze from afar at that most violent upheaval in the nation's life and try to make out just what was going on. We long for answers to such questions as 'What was it like?' 'Who made it happen?' 'Could it have been avoided?'. The answers lie not in belief systems, constitutional principles or arguments over taxation; they lie in people. It was not Arminianism or Royalism whose blood seeped into the ditches and ryefields of Marston Moor. It was not Puritanism that thrilled to the battlefield oratory of Hugh Peters. It was not Radicalism and Republicanism that argued the case for the King's death. It was men – and men whose passions and prejudices were the ancestors of our own.

This is not to say that there is nothing to be gained from total immersion in abstract ideas as they appear in sermons, pamphlets, parliamentary speeches and theological tomes. The worlds of the mid-seventeenth and late twentieth centuries are poles apart, most obviously in the centrality of religion to the one and its peripheralisation by the other. Therefore, producing evidence that enables us to adjust our mental focus and see more clearly what the people of that other world thought and believed has a value. But it is not an end in itself and research is not its own reward. History does not belong to the historians. It belongs to everyone and it is the responsibility of those of us who write it to bridge the gap between the archive and the airline lounge, the study and the bedsit.

One way, not of bringing the agitated mid-seventeenth century to life, but of revealing something of that life is through biography. The biographer is constrained to tell a story and, if he is any good, the character of his subject will emerge from the narrative to engage the emotions and imagination of the reader. Studies of real people, great and small, effect real introductions for us to a teeming world of personalities whose problems and relationships touch the great issues of the day at different points. Hugh Trevor-Roper's *Archbishop Laud*; Christopher Hill's book on Bunyan, *A Turbulent, Seditious and Factious People*; Paul Seaver's *Wallington's World* (the life of a London wood turner); Roger Lockyer's *Buckingham* – these are just some of the fine examples that spring to mind. There should be more.

Writing personal histories of the men and women, high and low, who were embroiled in the tumult helps us to understand that tumult and also makes us appreciate something of its vast complexity. There were as many motives for participation in the Civil War, its build-up and its aftermath as there were participants. In conversation with Edward Hyde on the eve of his death at Edgehill Sir Edmund Verney made the well-known observation:

> You have satisfaction in your conscience that you are in the right, that the king ought not to grant what is required of him . . . But for my part I do not like the quarrel, and do heartily wish that the king would yield and consent to what they desire, so that my conscience is only concerned in honour and in gratitude to follow my master . . . to preserve and defend those things, which are against my conscience to preserve and defend: for I will deal freely with you – I have no reverence for bishops for whom this quarrel subsists. [1]

That was one man's confession. Many who fell beside him in battle had different motivations and most of them would have been less able than Sir Edmund to articulate so clearly their thoughts and feelings.

There were, however, two men who knew precisely why they

3

were locked in combat and who believed that it was more than their immortal souls were worth to shun the confrontation. Charles Stuart and Oliver Cromwell were living, breathing icons of those abstractions which their followers grasped with varied clarity. Men and women identified with them, were inspired by them, and for their sakes were ready to become estranged from fathers and brothers, to surrender their family plate, to see their patrimonial fields trampled, to go into exile, to die.

But what motivated Charles and Oliver? Where did they draw *their* inspiration from? To whom did they turn for advice? Why did they stride resolutely down paths at the convergence of which stood a scaffold that one or other of them perforce must mount? My simply stated task in the following pages is to discover what made these two men tick. Yet even that modest objective may require justification. Do we not already possess perfectly adequate biographies of Cromwell and Charles I?

Well, yes and no. It seems to me that existing individual studies of both men have two built-in problems. The first is that they are *individual*. They take us through the life of the King or the gentleman from cradle to grave and are obliged to 'assess' the 'importance' of their subject. Inevitably, therefore, he stands out from his background like an actor before a painted backdrop. The other difficulty is that identified, over a century ago, by E.B. Chancellor in the preface to his *Life of Charles I 1600–1625*:

> It has long struck me as an unfortunate fact, that, notwithstanding so many biographies of Charles I, none have been exclusively devoted to his life during his earlier years, a time which was for many reasons, the most interesting of his chequered career.
>
> Indeed, to my mind, his later history cannot well be understood, except it has been preceded by a study of his life under circumstances so different.[2]

The same holds good for studies of Cromwell. Antonia Fraser's *Cromwell, Our Chief of Men* (and I only cite it as a typical example) devotes forty out of seven hundred and five pages to the first thirty-nine of its subject's fifty-nine years. Such treatment is well and good if we want to know what someone did in his maturity and wherein lies his historical significance; it is less valuable if we would seek to understand *who he was*.

4

Now, for my money, 'who was he?' is a vital question to ask of Oliver Cromwell and of Charles Stuart. It was precisely because of who they were that the history of the nation took the course it did. They were shaped by different material circumstances, family backgrounds, educational systems, cultural influences and friendships. The convictions which impelled them in adulthood were largely formed in childhood and adolescence, so their early years – even where evidence is scarce – must be given due weight by anyone who wishes to stand in judgement on their later actions. Were Charles or Oliver to be placed in the dock today and charged with war crimes, the counsel for the defence would undoubtedly martial an array of social workers, psychologists and psychoanalysts to offer mitigating testimony. We have come to accept the legitimacy of probing family backgrounds and early experiences when seeking to understand later physical or mental disorders and antisocial behaviour and we acknowledge that we are all largely the sum total of our genetic and emotional integers. It is strange, therefore, that psychohistory should be considered not quite respectable by several academics and that, for example, Charles Carlton's excellent *Charles I: The Personal Monarch* should have been received with suspicion precisely because it employed psychoanalytical techniques and explored the king's childhood.

By their own admissions, what gave the lives of Oliver and Charles meaning and purpose was religious faith. So much is universally acknowledged – which makes it absolutely astounding that so little has been written about what the King and the gentleman actually believed. Seventeenth-century historiography is an industry which extrudes books and articles with the eagerness of a manic computer yet J.C. Davis can acknowledge that 'the serious literature on Cromwell's religious thinking . . . has been surprisingly thin'[3] and Charles Carlton can aver of Charles's religious beliefs 'Who shaped them and how they were shaped is a matter for speculation.'[4] The extraordinary lack of texts seriously discussing the religious motivations of Charles and Cromwell does require some explanation. Might it be fair to observe (without opening windows into men's souls) that scholars who lack a faith commitment themselves feel uncomfortable about analysing the religious beliefs of others? Patrick Collinson has asserted that religious history is 'too important to be left to the secularists . . . Those who write from within the tradition, with theological awareness and spiritual sensitivity, have much the better chance of getting it right.'[5]

As one who does write from within that tradition I find so much that is fascinating about the spiritual pilgrimages taken by the King and the gentleman. Both were reared by Puritans within a conformist Calvinism. Both discovered that the religion of their upbringing would not serve their adult needs: one headed in the direction of Counter-Reformation exuberance and mysticism; the other was attracted by the euphoria of charismatic experientialism. These are common phenomena among Christians who reject an imposed formalism in their quest for a personal faith – but none the less fascinating for that. Like many whose spiritual growth involves painful choices and inner struggles, Charles and Oliver were both tolerant of the beliefs of others. Neither wanted to shackle men's consciences, and in that they were both in advance of most of their contemporaries. Yet even for them toleration had limits: Charles could live with Roman Catholics but hated Protestant separatists; Oliver espoused a genuine pan-Protestantism which excluded papists.

Of course, it is all much more complex than that, otherwise unravelling the intricacies of character and circumstance would not have taken up over four hundred pages. This book marks two important anniversaries. In 1999 it is four hundred years since the birth of Oliver Cromwell and three hundred and fifty since the death of Charles Stuart. That may be an appropriate excuse for this re-evaluation but it will only have long-term justification if readers find the conflict of the King and the gentleman as absorbing, stimulating and revealing of fresh insights as I have.

ONE

GENES

Since ye are come of as honourable predecessors as any prince living, repress the insolence of such as, under pretence to tax a vice in the person, seek craftily to stain the race and to steal the affection of the people from their posterity. For how can they love you that hated them of whom ye are come?

James I, *Basilicon Doron*[1]

KING JAMES VI OF Scotland knew the importance of ancestry. He stressed it in the kingship manual he wrote for his elder son in 1599 and it was something he became even more sensitive about when he crossed the border four years later to assume sovereignty over a foreign people. Compared with the Stuarts, who could trace their royal line back into the fourteenth century, the Tudors, who had ruled England for a mere three generations, were upstarts. Yet Henry VIII and his accomplished younger daughter had radiated around their house an impressive aura of glamour and power. Their propaganda machines had successfully created an image which ensured them that affectionate awe of their own subjects and respect of other princes which made their dynasty secure. Genealogists had played no small part in the elaboration of the Tudor myth and few educated Englishmen doubted that Queen Elizabeth had the blood of King Arthur and other legendary heroes coursing through her veins. It was vital for James and his successor to replace this myth with something equally compelling. Therefore to understand the little boy who would become Charles I we need to know about the genetic sap within his family tree and also about the ivy-like *mysterium* which clung to it and grew with it.

What was true for princes was also true for the sons of noblemen and gentlemen. Indeed, it is arguable that heritage mattered more to members of the county squirearchy than to those of the Scottish royal house. Established but ambitious landowning families were,

9

like today's multinational magnates, always in the takeovers and mergers business and habitually behaved with a similar ruthlessness to their modern counterparts. Through purchase, advantageous marriages and royal bounty they sought to add to their estates and fend off the aggression of equally rapacious neighbours. Impressive lineage was important in establishing their standing in local society and in attracting court patronage. It was no mere eccentricity that prompted Oliver Cromwell's grandfather to pay royal heralds to create for him an impressive pedigree and to have his celebrated ancestors displayed in the stained-glass windows of his hall.

Such visual images stimulated the imagination of children and reinforced the stories they were told by teachers, parents and relatives. They influenced profoundly two boys whose birth dates were separated by nineteen months and who grew up in the first decade of the seventeenth century. One was the object of doting parental – especially maternal – love and carried in his person all the hopes of his house. His name was Oliver. The other was brought up at a distance from his mother and father and no one expected much of him. He was called Charles.

Among the stories with which the prince grew up was that of his proud and beautiful grandmother, betrayed by the Calvinist leaders of her own people. He would have conjured up in his mind the melancholy scene on 8 February 1587 when the Queen of Scots mounted a scaffold in the courtyard of Fotheringhay Castle and waved aside the Dean of Peterborough's efforts at consolation with the words, 'Mr Dean, trouble not yourself nor me; for know that I am settled in the ancient Catholic and Roman religion, and in defence thereof, by God's grace, I mind to spend my blood.'

Oliver was no less affected by stories of his grandfather, a Protestant champion who, eighteen months after Mary's execution, had mustered men, horses and arms to see off the threatened invasion of Philip II. In the George Inn at Huntingdon he had stirred his captains with a list of reasons why they should risk their lives in this cause, concluding with the words:

. . . the least of all these considerations is sufficient to draw the most obdurate man of this land to prepare himself in his best strength and to lay aside all malice and privy grudges either between unkind brethren or adverse neighbours and to join hands and hearts together in the united bands of amity and unity, thereby the better to defy those enemies of ours that have sworn our destruction and the utter ruin and subversion of this realm and the sincere religion of Christ . . . instead whereof they purpose to supplant [*sic*] the devilish superstition of the pope.[2]

Young Charles and Oliver were the inheritors, perhaps the victims, of different mythologies. Anecdotes passed down the generations contributed vitally to the sense of identity of young Stuarts and Cromwells. More important than, though complementary to, the conscious inheritance were the 'treasonous genes' which, like Shakespeare's fox,

> Who ne'er so tame, so cherished, and locked up,
> Will have a wild trick of his ancestors.[3]

The Cromwells, like the Tudors, were Welsh. In point of fact, they were not Cromwells at all; their family name was Williams and they came from very modest mercantile stock. It was a piece of monumental good fortune which had placed them at the centre of the English Reformation and vastly accelerated their upward mobility. In the early years of the first Tudor king, one Morgan Williams of Glamorgan, like many of his compatriots, followed the victor of Bosworth across the border to 'try that power which erring men call Chance' in the capital and its environs. He set himself up as an innkeeper and brewer at Putney and, subsequently, at Greenwich, where Henry VII had recently turned the riverside house of Placentia into a royal residence. It was during his days in Putney that Morgan Williams married Katherine, elder daughter of tradesman neighbour, Walter Cromwell.

At what stage, one wonders, did Morgan realise that there was something remarkable about his brother-in-law, Thomas Cromwell? Walter's only son was a restless young man of prodigious intellect who early in life dabbled in several careers – soldier, entrepreneur, lawyer, diplomat – and could only adequately be described by the exciting but vague term 'adventurer'. The Cromwell and the Williams families both belonged to a clamouring band of court hangers-on ever anxious to commend themselves to the great men who surrounded the King, but it was the astute and talented Thomas who unexpectedly reached the very summit of power and royal favour. He married the daughter of a courtier, attracted the attention of Thomas Wolsey and, via the cardinal, came to the attention of the King. By the time he reached his mid-thirties Thomas Cromwell was sufficiently wealthy and important to be reckoned a gentleman and, within the family, a role model for his young nephew, Richard, Morgan Williams's elder son.

Richard had already shown himself to be ambitious and capable. Two and a half centuries later a family chronicler wishing to account for the Williams family's rapid rise told the story of Richard's stunning performance at a court tourney. He appeared richly caparisoned in white velvet and so excelled in the sport that the King threw him a jewelled ring with the words 'Formerly thou wast my Dick, but hereafter thou shalt be my Diamond'.[4] Whether or not this actually took place, Richard's progress to the status of wealthy landed gentleman was more prosaic. Even before his uncle entered the cardinal's service he had established impressive City and court connections and these helped him to make a very advantageous marriage in 1518. His bride, Frances, was none other than the daughter of the reigning Lord Mayor of London, Sir Thomas Murfyn. The union brought him impressive property in Cambridgeshire and Richard became a man of consequence there, being appointed sheriff for the first time in 1536. As soon as his uncle achieved the position of principal adviser to the King and manager of government business, vacated by the fallen Cardinal Wolsey, Richard signalled his membership of the great man's clientage by taking the surname Cromwell. As a loyal supporter and a man of consequence in eastern England, Richard was an obvious choice for regional commissioner when Thomas Cromwell embarked upon his wholesale dismantling of the monastic establishment. The dissolution of the lesser and greater religious houses, together with all their conventual buildings, farms, tenements, pastures, barns, churches and parsonage houses, offered a never to be repeated opportunity to property speculators and aspiring landowners. Most of the plums went to major speculators and to the great magnates who were prominent in local society and at court. But the fenland area between Cambridge and the Wash boasted no noble houses. The social and political leaders of the region were the Benedictine abbots of Ramsey, one of the richest monasteries in the country. In the absence of wealthy bidders the imminent confiscation of this house thus offered possibilities of immense wealth and influence to humbler suitors.

12

WILLIAMS ALIAS CROMWELL
Select Pedigree

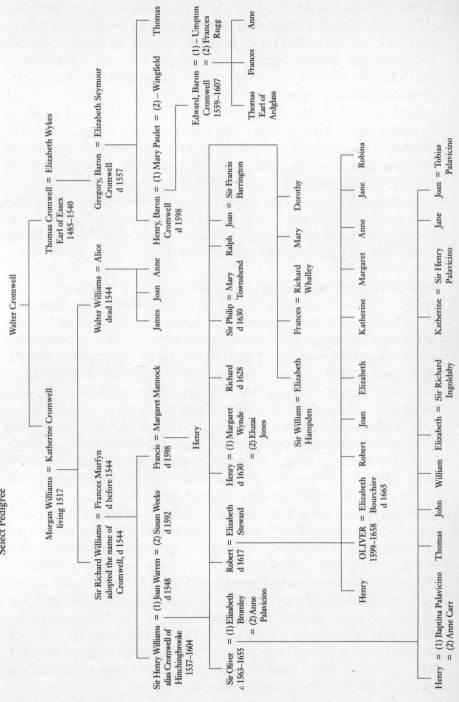

Richard Cromwell firmly set his sights upon becoming the most important man in Cambridgeshire and Huntingdonshire. He was knighted in 1537 and, in the autumn of that year, he was despatched to report on some of the larger religious houses in his area. Faithfully he did what was expected of him; and assiduously he drew his painstaking efforts to the minister's attention:

> Your lordship, I think, shall surely apperceive the Prior of Ely to be of a forward sort by evident tokens, as at our coming home shall be at large related unto you. At the making hereof we had done nothing at Ramsey, save that overnight I communed with the abbot, whom I found conformable to everything as shall at this time be put in use according to your lordship's will . . . As soon as we have done at Ramsey we go to Peterborough and from thence to my house . . . The blessed Trinity preserve your lordship's health . . .[5]

His rewards were not long in coming. The following year he received grant of the small Benedictine nunnery of Hinchingbrooke, just to the west of Huntingdon, with its 'church, steeple, churchyard and house and all lands'.[6] But the Ramsey territorial empire was the prize he most coveted and this he began to acquire in 1540. In consideration of his 'good services' and payment of £4663 4s 2d he received the abbey itself and several of its manors. It was an excellent deal, for the properties in question yielded an annual return of £1987 15s. 3d but the capital and credit involved in this purchase were enormous for a mere knight in the mid-sixteenth century.

As Sir Richard entered his new domain his uncle fell from power, lingered in the Tower for seven weeks, hoping against hope, then went to the block. So far from sharing in the minister's downfall, Richard prospered and became, in effect, the head of the family. Thomas's only son, Gregory – though he married Jane Seymour's sister (thus becoming an uncle of the future King) and inherited his father's barony (but not the Earldom of Essex conferred on Thomas Cromwell in 1539) – was a nonentity. Richard, by contrast had lost nothing of his energy and ambition. He was sheriff again in 1541, sat in Parliament in 1542, was a Gentleman of the Privy Chamber by 1543, and went with the King on the French campaign of 1544. He died in October of that year, perhaps from fever contracted in camp. Throughout his latter years he was avidly consolidating and adding to his fenland estates. By negotiating fresh grants through the Court

14

of Augmentations,* by making deals with London speculators and by exchanging lands with his neighbours, Richard created a Cromwell enclave in the country between Peterborough and Cambridge.

The heir to all these estates, Henry Williams alias Cromwell, was only seven at the time of his father's relatively early death. He was, moreover, an orphan, his mother having died two years earlier. The welfare of the vulnerable members of such an important family was of considerable interest to the government. In 1551 the Council instructed Thomas Cromwell's widow to take Sir Richard's unmarried sisters into her Leicestershire establishment, an arrangement which was not an unalloyed success. Lady Elizabeth complained: 'I have in some cases thought they should not wholly be their own guides, willing them to follow my advice – which they have not taken in good part, nor according to my expectation in them.'[7]

As for young Henry, his lucrative wardship was claimed as a perquisite by none other than the Chancellor of the Court of Augmentations, Sir Edward North. Sir Edward's country estate was at Kirtling, near Newmarket and he was Lord-Lieutenant of Cambridgeshire in the early years of Elizabeth's reign. It was he who charted the course of Henry's early life, modelling it closely on his own. The boy was sent to Queens' College, Cambridge (North had been at Peterhouse) and then to Lincoln's Inn, to acquire that working knowledge of the common law considered essential for those who would control large estates and be prominent in the government of rural England. North arranged an extremely lucrative marriage for his charge and this was duly solemnised soon after Henry came of age in 1558. Like his father, Henry took to wife the daughter of a Lord Mayor of London. Sir Ralph Warren (who died in 1553) had been one of the most successful and wealthy members of the mercantile community, was related by marriage to Sir Edward North and held estates bordering the North lands east of Cambridge. Joan, his only daughter, came to her husband with a considerable jointure, and the prosperous young man lost no time in accumulating the trappings of a man of taste and fashion.

Henry was an ebullient, larger-than-life character. He had no father to impress upon him the need for prudence and could scarcely

*The government body set up to handle the sale of ex-monastic property.

wait for his majority before starting to spend his fortune. Ramsey, where his father had made his principal dwelling, was deep in the fen and notorious for its dampness and impassable roads during the winter. Henry, therefore, decided to transform the nunnery at Hinchingbrooke (previously let to tenants) into a magnificent principal residence. The new house was a commodious, rambling mansion, noteworthy more for its incorporation of everything that passed for 'mod cons' in the Elizabethan age than for its overall architectural style but, as well as providing comfort and luxury for the family and their guests, it also powerfully asserted its owner's importance. Not the least aspect of this was its proclamation of Henry's lineage. The heraldic stained glass of his splendid hall windows told a story that was as impressive as it was spurious. It proclaimed Henry's descent from one of William the Conqueror's barons, the lord of Cardigan and Powys. Henry continued to use the name Williams as well as Cromwell, and his coat of arms, a silver lion on a black ground, was that of his supposed Welsh ancestors and not that of the newly armigerous Cromwells and, in 1602, towards the end of his life, Henry paid York Herald to furnish proof of his noble progenitorship. Like a royal couple on progress, Henry and his wife (when she was not experiencing one of her almost annual confinements) passed back and forth between their two homes and when the Lord of Ramsey and Hinchingbrooke was feeling in a more than usually expansive mood, he scattered silver pennies to the tenants and estate workers who lined the road to pay their respects.

By 1564 Hinchingbrooke was ready to receive its most important guest. Elizabeth I and her court stayed there during their summer progress in that year and so delighted was the Queen with Henry's lavish hospitality that, before she left she dubbed him knight. Henry's rule in Huntingdonshire and Cambridgeshire was almost precisely coterminous with the reign of his sovereign and he took it on himself to replicate in the shire the glittering household of the Queen. Men called him the Golden Knight because of his cultured extravagance. More importantly, he represented royal government to the local farmers, labourers and burgesses. He was sheriff of Huntingdonshire four times and sat for the county in all the early parliaments of the reign. With other leaders of East Midlands society he presided as a magistrate and was the first point of reference in disputes and matters of regional concern.

16

One of the other prominent families with whom he was closely connected was the St Johns, whose seat at Bletsoe was some twenty miles cross-country from Hinchingbrooke. Oliver St John was a close contemporary, came of a family distantly related to the Tudors and was raised to the peerage as first Baron St John at Elizabeth's coronation. His lordship became an intimate friend of Sir Henry and a valuable supporter at court. It is very likely that he stood godfather to Henry and Joan's first-born son who was christened Oliver.* Relations remained close when John St John succeeded his father in 1582. Six years later, in the Armada year, when St John was Lord-Lieutenant of Huntingdonshire he warmly commended his Muster Master to the Council:

> I am further to commend unto your lordships particularly the great willingness and careful endeavours of this gentleman, Sir H. Cromwell, in this service, as well for his furtherance in the general advancement hereof in the shire, as for his own private charge in furnishing of a very large number of horsemen in most serviceable manner to his great cost and expense. The which if it may please your lordship . . . to procure her majesty to take knowledge thereof, which gracious liking it will procure him to persevere and draw others to follow his good example.[8]

Though Sir Henry never held a household office he was among those who enjoyed access to the royal court and he introduced his eldest son there. Oliver followed in his father's steps at Queens' and Lincoln's Inn and became very much a chip off the old block. He was among the athletic and elegant young bucks whom the Queen liked to have around her, a man who dressed fashionably, patronised scholars and artists such as the musician John Dowland but who could also acquit himself well in the tiltyard. It was at court that Oliver met Elizabeth Bromley, the daughter of Sir Thomas Bromley, the Lord Chancellor. Both sets of parents satisfying themselves that the union of their families was acceptable, the couple were married about 1585 and Oliver took his wife to Godmanchester, to the immediate south-east of Huntingdon.

Joan and Henry were a fecund couple. Eleven of their children – a fairly remarkable number by sixteenth-century standards –

---

* This uncommon Christian name, derived from the chivalric Song of Roland, became traditional in the St John family.

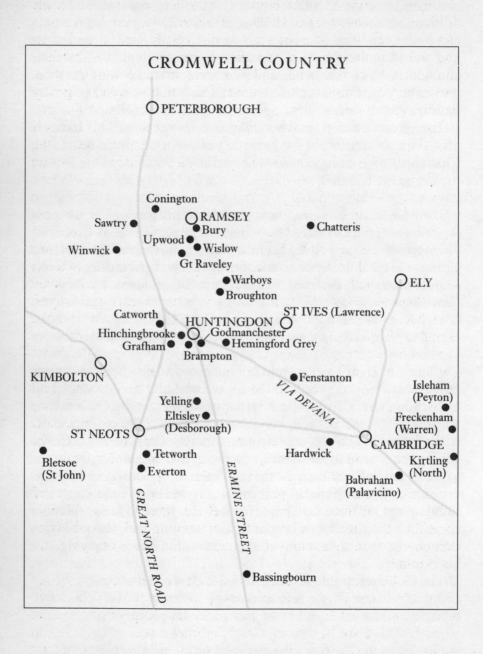

CROMWELL COUNTRY

○ PETERBOROUGH

Conington ●

○ RAMSEY
Sawtry ●   ● Bury
Upwood ●   ● Chatteris
Winwick ●   ● Wislow
Gt Raveley

● Warboys
● Broughton

○ ELY

Catworth ●   ST IVES (Lawrence) ○
Hinchingbrooke ● HUNTINGDON ○ Godmanchester
Grafham ●   ● ● Hemingford Grey
            Brampton

○ KIMBOLTON

● Fenstanton

Isleham
(Peyton) ●

Yelling ●
Eltisley ●
(Desborough)

Freckenham
(Warren) ●

ST NEOTS ○

○ CAMBRIDGE

● Tetworth   Hardwick ●
Bletsoe
(St John) ●   ● Everton

Kirtling
(North) ●

Babraham ●
(Palavicino)

VIA DEVANA

GREAT NORTH ROAD

ERMINE STREET

● Bassingbourn

survived infancy. Theirs was, therefore, a large household (which was increased when Joan's mother came to live with them after the death of her second husband). They all enjoyed an enviable lifestyle and gave every evidence of being a close family content with their position in fenland society and even to being dominated by their ebullient father. When the children were married none of them moved very far away: they all settled as husbands or wives of gentry families in Huntingdonshire and neighbouring counties.

The proudest and most memorable day for all of Henry's offspring occurred on 27 April 1603. For the last few years, the Cromwells, like all England's leading families had speculated about the future with a certain amount of anxiety. As the Virgin Queen drew near the end of her days without nominating a successor those who had enjoyed Tudor favour faced the prospect of a different regime and the necessity of building up new connections. Not until the name of the next sovereign was known could men of Sir Henry Cromwell's rank make plans to draw themselves to his attention. As soon as Elizabeth died and the accession of James was confirmed Hinchingbrooke became an anthill of industry. Henry and Oliver, who had now assumed the management of the estate and the execution of his father's duties, hired extra staff and, heedless of expense, set carpenters, painters and gardeners to flurrying activity. Cartloads of food and drink trundled up the road from Cambridge and even from London, where the Cromwells also sought out and hired the most accomplished actors and entertainers. This hectic activity had been preceded by no less eager importuning of members of the Council. The object of it all was that the Cromwells should be among the first of James's subjects to receive him under their roof as he travelled southwards from Scotland. Hinchingbrooke was excellently placed for this purpose. It lay between Edinburgh and London, not far from the Great North Road. It could boast splendid sport for a king who was known to love hunting and, should James ever choose to make a return visit, it was within a day's easy ride for his entourage.

The Golden Knight intended to live up fully to his reputation. All along the route hosts and hostesses were pawning plate and mortgaging lands in order to put on a lavish display for their sovereign, and the squire of Hinchingbrooke was determined to outdo them all. On 16 April Sir Robert Cecil, Elizabeth's secretary, stayed at the house on his way northwards to meet the King.

Evidently he was pleased with all the preparations that had been made and eleven days later Sir Henry and his son rode out in their finest court clothes to meet James Stuart among cheering crowds.

The lavishness of Cromwell hospitality on this great occasion was long remembered. The King later claimed that it would never be 'blotted out of my mind how at my first entry into this kingdom, the people of all sorts rode and ran, nay rather flew to meet me . . . their hands, feet and all the rest of their members in their gestures discovering a passionate longing and earnestness to meet and embrace their new sovereign'.[9] And yet at Hinchingbrooke he discovered such a welcome 'as the like had not been in any place since his first setting out of Scotland'.

> There was such plenty and variety of meats, such diversity of wines, and those not riff-raff, but ever the best of their kind, and the cellars open at any man's pleasure. And if it were so common with wine, there is little question but the butteries for beer and ale were more common, yet in neither was there difference; for whoever entered the house, which to no man was denied, tasted what they had a mind to, and after a taste found fullness, no man . . . being denied what he would call for.

All the locality were invited to share in the celebration of the new reign:

> As this bounty was held back to none within the house, so for such poor people as would not press in, there were open beer-houses erected wherein there was no want of bread and beef, for the comfort of the poorest creatures. Neither was this provision for the little time of his Majesty's stay, but it was made ready fourteen days, and after his Highness' departure distributed to as many as had mind to it.
>
> Also Master Cromwell presented his Majesty with many rich and respectable gifts, as a very great, and a very fair wrought standing cup of gold, goodly horses, fleet and deep mouthed hounds, divers hawks of excellent wing, and at the remove gave fifty pounds amongst his majesty's officers.[10]

Sixty years later Thomas Fuller could still write of the Hinchingbrooke celebration: '. . . it made all former entertainments forgotten and all future to despair to do the like.'[11] Henry and Oliver were able to present to their liege lord, not only the members of their own family and the leading men and women of the county, but also the spokesmen of the Cambridge colleges, for James, despite his love of learning, had decided against a stay at the university on this occasion. Thus, to Hinchingbrooke

> . . . came the heads of the University of Cambridge in their scarlet gowns and corner caps, when Mr. Robert Naunton, the Orator made a learned Latin oration, wherewith his majesty was highly affected. The very variety of Latin was welcome to his ears, formerly almost surfeited with so many long English speeches made to him as he passed every corporation.[12]

The Cromwells' investment paid handsome dividends. There is no doubting the extent of James's appreciation of their extravagant display of loyalty or of the affection he conceived for Hinchingbrooke and he was not slow to give tokens of his approval. The King made Oliver a gentleman of the Privy Chamber and, at the coronation, dubbed him a Knight of the Bath. The heir of Hinchingbrooke was a mighty hunter before the Lord and therefore a man after James's heart. He was appointed keeper of the game in 'the forests of Weybridge and Sapley, Gaynes and Ramsey and elsewhere in Cambridgeshire and Huntingdonshire and within five miles of Babraham'. He received by royal warrant the privilege of hunting wherever it pleased him in the royal forests. Sir Oliver travelled in virtually aristocratic splendour around the royal hunting lodges, ensuring that there were sufficient animals for the royal sport and Oliver was then permitted the ministrations of his own chaplain.[13] When he was at court he frequently displayed his athletic prowess in the tiltyard. Thus, for example, on Twelfth Night, 1606, he was among the knights contending for Opinion against Truth in Ben Jonson's *Masque of Hymen with Barriers*.[14]

Closeness to the King enabled Sir Oliver to sue for very tangible rewards. He was awarded a pension of £200 per annum out of Crown lands at the beginning of the reign and exchanged it in 1609 for a one-off payment of £6000.[15] But he was always competing with other courtiers and certainly could not take the King's favour for granted. When he offered a 'large sum' for the royal manor of Somersham, north-east of Huntingdon, in order further to consolidate his land holdings, this particular plum went to someone else.[16]

It may be that the King or his close advisers had decided that the Cromwells had already done well enough out of the royal bounty, for Sir Oliver had only recently received a very substantial grant of land. To see how this came about we have to go back to 1600. In that year Elizabeth Cromwell died. The widower wasted little time grieving for his wife. Rather, he grasped the opportunity vastly to increase his wealth. Only days before his bereavement another death had occurred. Everyone had heard of Sir Horatio Palavicino, reputedly the richest man in England, but Oliver knew him and his family well because of his City and court connections and also because Palavicino's rural residence was at Babraham, just south of Cambridge. It was there that this extraordinary man breathed his last.

'Shrewd merchant', 'fraudster', 'banker', 'grasping moneylender', 'thief', 'miser', 'government agent' and 'spy' were all terms used about Sir Horatio Palavicino. Of a Genoese mercantile family, he had settled in England in the middle of the sixteenth century where he obtained the farm of papal taxes during the reign of Mary Tudor. With the Queen's death and the final renunciation of all Roman jurisdiction Palavicino simply pocketed the revenues he had gathered, speculated with his vastly increased fortune and became moneylender to several European governments. At one stage Elizabeth owed him so much that the crown of England might be said to have been in pawn. Inevitably, his loans brought him influence as well as usurious interest. Much to the frustration of Lord Burghley and the Council the Queen took Palavicino as her economic guru, listened to his advice on all matters – not only financial – and used him as an unofficial diplomat and spy in foreign courts. In his personal habits Palavicino was antisocial and frugal, the stereotypical rich miser, and it was widely (and correctly) believed that he had an immense hoard of personal wealth. When, in July 1600, he died, a wit composed this epitaph:

> Here lies Horatio Palavazene,
> Who robbed the Pope to lend the Queen;
> He was a thief. A thief? Thou liest,
> For why? He robb'd but Antichrist,
> Him death with besome swept from Babram
> Into the bosom of old Abram.
> But then came Hercules with his club,
> And struck him down to Belzebub.[17]

THE CROMWELL–PALAVICINO ALLIANCE

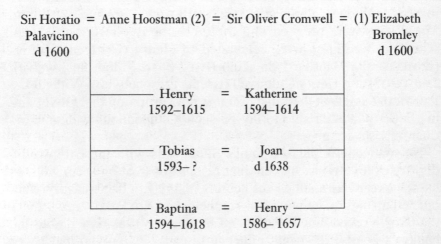

Sir Horatio = Anne Hoostman (2) = Sir Oliver Cromwell = (1) Elizabeth
Palavicino   Bromley
d 1600   d 1600

Henry = Katherine
1592–1615   1594–1614

Tobias = Joan
1593–?   d 1638

Baptina = Henry
1594–1618   1586–1657

Scarcely waiting for a decent period of mourning to pass, Oliver Cromwell paid court to the wealthy widow, Anne Palavicino. Of course, he had his eyes on the immense family fortune but he could also offer Anne and her children a prominent and respected place in the society of court and county. A year and a day after Sir Horatio's death he married Lady Palavicino. There were, however, three loopholes through which gold might still trickle – Anne's children. These gaps were plugged in a triple ceremony on 10 April 1606, when the weddings were celebrated of Henry (fourteen), Tobias (thirteen) and Baptina Palavicino (twelve) to Katherine (twelve), Joan (ten?) and Henry Cromwell (twenty) respectively. With all the Palavicino assets at their disposal it is not surprising that Oliver and his father had been able to lay on such a stupendous welcome for their new sovereign.

No matter how pleased James Stuart was with the Cromwells' display of loyalty, he had another reason for treating them well, as he discovered as soon as the secrets of the English treasury were opened up to him: he was vastly in their debt. On Palavicino's death the Crown owed him £29,000 and this money was now due to the banker's heirs. Preferring influence to cash, Palavicino had never pressed for settlement and Elizabeth, always in need of funds, had opted to pay the interest and not the capital. A couple of years into the new reign Sir Oliver came to an arrangement with the Treasury: in return for liquidating approximately half of the debt he received old chantry lands worth some £5–600 per year.[18] This, added to the income of £2000 per annum Sir Oliver already enjoyed, made him one of the richest gentlemen in England. He would need every penny; loyalty to the Stuarts was to cost him dear.

Sir Henry Cromwell's other sons did not enjoy anything like their eldest brother's standard of living. As was customary, the heir received the lion's share of a father's property. Comparatively modest sums were set aside to provide marriage portions for daughters and to give their brothers a start in life. Younger sons were expected to fend for themselves. Henry's boys all received the education which had become traditional – Cambridge and the Inns of Court. They married girls from moderately well-to-do local families and took their places as MPs and JPs in Huntingdonshire and neighbouring counties. Their sisters found husbands among the local squirearchy and, thus, the matrimonial and clientage network of the prestigious Cromwell/Williams clan extended impressively over the level lands bisected by the Great North Road.

Robert, the brother who had come into the world little more than a year after the first-born, began his married life on about £300 a year, which meant that he was comfortably off by the standards of the day but by no means wealthy. He had gone through Queens' and Lincoln's Inn with his elder brother, then returned home and begun casting around for a marriage that would bring him more property and enable him to boost his income. The woman he had found came from a family whose connections with the Cromwells extended back over several decades. When Sir Richard, in 1537, had reported to Mr Secretary Cromwell that the Prior of Ely was 'forward' (or 'progressive') in outlook he had been referring to Robert Styward (or Steward) alias Wells, a pliant religious who supported the King's spoliation of the Church and was rewarded by being appointed Dean of Ely after the secularisation of the monastic foundation. Steward, who obligingly amended his religious opinions on the accession of Queen Mary, ensured that his family did well out of the Dissolution: they had a grant of former monastic lands and Robert's elder brother became hereditary steward of the cathedral's remaining properties. By the end of the sixteenth century these lucrative responsibilities had devolved upon Sir Thomas Steward who, trading upon the similarity of his name to that of the prospective heir to the throne traced a connection with the royal house of Scotland. It was Elizabeth, niece of this Thomas Steward, whom Robert married about 1591. She was already the widow of a certain John Lynne of Bassingbourn, near Cambridge and brought to her second marriage a jointure of some sixty pounds a year.

Robert and Elizabeth set up home in a comfortable house on Huntingdon High Street, made available by Sir Henry, which had started life as part of the Hospital of St John, run by Augustinian friars. The couple were as successful as Robert's father and brother in the conceiving and rearing of children. By 1599 their family consisted of three daughters and a son, named Henry after his grandfather. Unfortunately, the boy died around the turn of the century.* On 25 April 1599 Elizabeth's fifth pregnancy culminated in the birth of another son, named for his uncle, Oliver. After this,

---

* It is a curious point of comparison between Oliver Cromwell and Charles Stuart that both were second and only surviving sons of their parents and that each had an elder brother named Henry.

Robert and Elizabeth had five more children but had to wait ten years for another boy (Robert) and he died within months. With all those daughters to provide for and only one son to take over the family property the Cromwells may well have considered themselves unfortunate. In 1593 Robert was MP for Huntingdon and, in 1600, was appointed a JP and bailiff in the town. He was a trustee of the local free school and a commissioner for sewers. With income from his own and his wife's lands, with their network of 'respectable' kindred (Thomas Steward was knighted in 1603), with their established social position and with the backing of the powerful Cromwell name they faced with confidence life under the new regime. They were loyal to the Crown and true to the religious settlement. In short, they were unremarkable but vital elements in the social and political structure of Protestant England.

For two generations before the future Protector was born there had been certain persistent and dominant influences brought to bear on the framers of family policy: Cambridge, the Inns of Court, the London mercantile community, the royal court, Parliament and the fellowship of local gentry. When Oliver's father and uncle went up to Queens' in the mid-1570s the university was far from being a quiet enclave of academic study: it would be scant exaggeration to call it an ideological battlefield. In 1570–1 the Lady Margaret Professor of Divinity, Thomas Cartwright, 'the head and most learned of that sect of dissenters then called puritans'[19] had been deprived of his chair and then his Trinity fellowship. This was a *cause célèbre* which set all Cambridge by the ears and whose ripples rapidly spread outwards to be hotly discussed in churches, alehouses and all meeting places where men were interested in religious issues (and few educated people in late Tudor England were not). The essential conflict in what we might call the 'Elizabethan Non-settlement', lay between the ecclesiastical establishment and the 'evangelicals' or 'precisionists' or 'puritans' who wanted further reformation on the Genevan pattern. This involved increased personal spiritual discipline and greater freedom in the conduct of worship. Specifically, Puritans objected to the retention of such 'papistical rags' as the surplice and the Book of Common Prayer. In academic circles, and in Cambridge *par excellence*, these matters were debated long and fervently. Rival preachers thundered at each other from city and college pulpits. Thus Marmaduke Pickering of Corpus Christi condemned Calvin as a heretic and the wives and

26

children of priests as 'whores and bastards', while William Clark of Peterhouse asserted that 'bishops, archbishops, metropolitans, patriarchs and popes were introduced into the church by Satan'.[20] Fellows circulated scurrilous pamphlets about each other and defied university authorities. Accusers and accused appealed beyond their own community to the Chancellor, Lord Burghley, and beyond him to the Queen and Council. As a result of the conflict with Cartwright, which split the university into pro- and anti-establishment factions, new statutes were introduced designed to curb the power of college fellows. This, predictably, threw more fuel on to an already vigorously blazing fire. Scarcely a term passed without trouble in one college or another as individuals claimed liberty of conscience and academic enquiry and the university heads countered that such men were concerned 'only to molest and disquiet their governors; their drift, as it is well known, being nothing else but to procure themselves a licentious liberty'.[21] While Oliver and Robert Cromwell were in residence in 1576 it was the turn of their college to be in the spotlight. Edmund Rockrey, BD, one of the fellows of Queens', was deprived for refusing to wear ecclesiastical habit or the university cap. His case had dragged on for four years and he had only survived as long as he had thanks to the backing of Lord Burghley. In 1579–80 William Browne (founder of the Brownists, the first English nonconformist sect), a fiery, unordained preacher, enjoyed a twelve-month reign as pulpit king. Crowds flocked to St Benet's church to hear him denounce the 'woeful state of Cambridge, whereunto those wicked prelates and doctors of divinity have brought it'.[22] Unsurprisingly, Browne was deposed by episcopal ban at the end of 1580.

Junior college members, little more than children, were not involved in university politics but they could not avoid knowing about these contretemps in the little world of the university – and, as is the way of students in all ages, most of them were partisan. The sons of local families might be more involved than most, for their fathers were often close friends of the dons – friends and supporters. In 1573, when Thomas Aldrich, Master of Corpus, was in trouble with the university authorities, one of the complaints made against him was that 'he made himself too much acquainted with the gentlemen of the country'.[23]

Men like Sir Henry Williams/Cromwell took an almost proprietorial interest in *their* university and the relationship was symbiotic. Their sons received instruction from some of the country's cleverest men and this added lustre to their own cultured image. For their part, the academics, as well as enjoying the financial benefits of the association, found it useful to have influential friends. Propaganda was important to both parties. Gentlemen who felt themselves responsible for the moral and spiritual wellbeing of their tenantry, and held the advowsons of local livings, looked to their university friends to suggest godly ministers to serve their parishes. At one time as many as half of the parishes in a fifty-mile radius of Cambridge were staffed by graduates many of whom valued their contacts with the Puritan theologians at the university. Cambridge Puritans, intent on carrying the Gospel into the countryside, especially where the regular preaching was substandard, toured churches where the pulpits were open to them, held classes for local clergy, or were paid to deliver regular sermons or weekday exegetical lectures.

Sir Henry Cromwell was a supporter of this evangelistic and didactic enterprise. By the 1570s a Puritan lectureship was established in Huntingdon and it, or something very like it, survived for several decades. It could not have flourished as it did without support of the leading local family. Sir Henry believed in sermons and godly lectures. Mustering the country gentry in 1589, when there seemed to be the threat of a second Spanish invasion attempt, he charged them:

> It behoveth us . . . to reform ourselves in that we have been both slack and negligent in coming unto [God], to hear his word, and now before it be too late earnestly to embrace the same lest for our contempt he suffer us to be carried away captives.[24]

Sir Henry may have felt particularly strongly about the need for divine aid in warding off evil because he was personally involved in a current witchcraft investigation. A family by the name of Samwells of Warboys were feared and hated by their neighbours who accused them of casting malign spells. At one point Sir Henry's second wife personally admonished the Samwells and soon afterwards she succumbed to an illness (of which she died in 1592). Lady Susan was convinced that the Samwells were the cause of her afflictions and this doubtless influenced her husband when, in 1589, the clergy of Ellington and Warboys brought Mr and Mrs Samwells and their daughter before the bench. Then he sanctioned, and doubt-less took part in, the verbal bullying and physical torture which elicited confessions of sorts from the unfortunate trio and brought them to the Huntingdon scaffold. These events and especially the plight of his wife affected Sir Henry deeply and part of his reaction was to endow an annual sermon against witchcraft to be preached in Huntingdon by one of the fellows of Queens' College.*

Enthusiasm for sermons, close involvement with the life of the university and the harrying of supposed witches and papists (activities which were pursued with particular ardour in the crisis years 1588–9) do not of themselves constitute proof of party membership. Sir Henry and his sons would have disavowed the name 'Puritan' which, during the last three decades of the sixteenth century was but slowly evolving in meaning from a term of abuse applied to allegedly self-righteous troublemakers to membership of a very loose alliance of men who were determined to preserve biblical doctrine and ecclesiology either inside or outside the Church of England. Sir Henry's advocacy of sermon-tasting did not prevent him enjoying a self-indulgent lifestyle, revelling in the nickname of the Golden Knight, or siring at least two illegitimate children. Not everyone was capable of or even desired a strict holiness regimen but this did not stop them supporting and sympathising with the earnest advocates of profound personal spirituality or (in an age when every educated man was an amateur theologian) taking a lively interest in the debates kept alive by their Cambridge friends.

The theological and institutional conflicts which disturbed the calm of university life in the 1570s were by no means resolved when the first generation of combatants were silenced by intimidation, deprivation or death. There was a continuous flow of ardent young Calvinists into college fellowships just as there was an unfailing supply of men who aggressively defended the *status quo* and the *media via*. The doctrinal and personal *casi belli* shifted from decade to decade but the underlying tension was always between the magnetic force fields of ecclesiastical authority and biblical mandate, as interpreted by the fashionable radical teachers and orators of the day. Thomas Goodwin, who was an undergraduate contemporary of Oliver Cromwell, reflected in later years, 'As I grew up the noise of the Arminian Controversy . . . and the several

---

*The custom was observed until 1814.

opinions of that controversy, began to be every man's talk and enquiry and possessed my ears.'[25] And the Arminian controversy (on the relationship between free will and prevenient grace) was but the latest manifestation of a conflict already two generations old (see pp. 269f).

When Sir Henry's sons moved from Queens' College to Lincoln's Inn they did not escape the atmosphere of intense religious debate. The man appointed regular preacher there a few months before their arrival was that William Clark who had been expelled from Peterhouse for asserting that bishops and their ilk were of the devil. At the same time the Reverend Walter Travers, sometime fellow of Trinity, Cambridge, became a lecturer at the Temple, thanks largely to the patronage of Lord Burghley. Chark and Travers rapidly emerged as leaders of that Protestant element – later to be called Presbyterians – proclaiming from their pulpits, 'the present government of the Church of England being . . . Antichristian, the only discipline and government of Jesus Christ . . . by pastors, doctors, elders and deacons should be established in place of the other.'[26] These thundering orations were, no less than the plays and other diversions at the theatre built by Richard Babbage in 1576, a regular part of the entertainment available in London. Merchants, lawyers and gentlemen's sons training either to be lawyers or rural administrators, crowded into the churches and chapels to listen to the passionate entreaties and denunciations of the preachers, especially after the moderate Richard Hooker was appointed Master of the Temple. Then they enjoyed the spectacle of Hooker mounting the pulpit in the morning to attack 'the new fancied sceptre of lay presbyterial power', and in the afternoon Travers from the same platform answering the master point for point.

Religion was a recurring leitmotif in parliamentary debates throughout Elizabeth's reign, and by their membership of the House of Commons Sir Henry and his sons remained close to the thinking on this and other issues current in government and 'opposition' circles. The skimpy nature of the records provides us with no clues as to their oratorical and voting contributions to the life of the lower chamber but we do know about the activities of one of their kinsmen. Thomas Cromwell, grandson of Henry VIII's minister, was a thoroughly committed parliamentarian. For the first three decades of the reign he kept one of the earliest journals of proceedings, probably at the behest of William Cecil, Lord Burghley. Thomas was his eyes and ears in the Commons and one of the important agents the Council used to handle Parliament. He was an assiduous recorder of important speeches and an increasingly active member of committees. As well as his industriousness Thomas commended himself to Burghley, Walsingham, Leicester and their friends as a man of Puritan convictions. As far as his Huntingdon relatives were concerned, Thomas Cromwell provided yet another link to the centre of power.

The family was represented in all of the 'war parliaments' (1585, 1587, 1589, 1593, 1597, 1601) summoned by the Queen in her growing desperation to raise revenue under the strain of the struggle with Spain. Faced with England's first major conflict since the days of Henry V, the government needed the substantial men of the shires to raise money, recruit and equip fighting men and to generate propaganda. The Cromwells did not fail in their duty to engender Protestant nationalism in the area under their control. On the religious issue they found themselves under pressure from two directions. The Puritan clergy were particularly strong throughout East Anglia and the Midlands where they met regularly in regional classes or conferences to organise, among other things, a national campaign for ecclesiastical reform. They influenced elections, bombarded MPs with literature, organised deputations to parliament and did everything in their power 'to stir up gentlemen of worth and godliness to be zealous for reformation'.[27] On the other hand, the Queen made it vehemently clear on several occasions that she would countenance 'no motion of innovation, nor alter nor change any law whereby the religion of the Church of England standeth established'.[28]

Whatever clash of loyalties to Crown and pulpit the Cromwells may have felt declined after 1588. The Armada heavily underscored the need for national unity, and the death of the Earl of Leicester removed the leading Puritan champion. The government declared that it would proceed with equal severity against both Catholic and Puritan disturbers of the *status quo*. The last regional Puritan conference was held in Cambridge in 1589 and thereafter religious extremists urged their loyalty: 'We are no schismatics, no libellers, rebellious or disordered persons . . . We desire that by a preaching ministry all the people of your kingdom may be taught to obey and serve your highness.'[29] From this time 'precisionists' and 'gospellers' hoped less for reform and more for toleration and those

31

who had no such hope began to drift across the sea to congenial havens in the Low Countries. Many who stayed drew their spiritual succour from secret worship in one another's homes.

What occupied the minds of MPs more than religion as the century drew to a close – and with it, inevitably, the Queen's reign – were government revenue and the succession. As long as the war lasted gentlemen of England, with surprisingly little grumbling, voted taxes and put their hands in their purses over and over again. When Elizabeth had exacted as much as her loyal Commons could be persuaded to subscribe she was still short of funds and had to resort to prerogative levies such as ship money and heavy borrowing. Like his father, Oliver Cromwell was an enthusiastic financial supporter of the government, ready to spend and be spent in royal service. As occasional parliamentarians they were conscious of their identity and common interest with the class of gentry and burgesses on a nationwide basis but they were even more conscious of their duty as subjects and their position in the machinery of government. Issues of 'Crown and Parliament' scarcely occurred to them.

As to father and sons' response to the changes of dynasty, their lavish hospitality to the royal entourage provides adequate evidence of their desire to commend themselves to the Stuart king. They shared the belief that, after years of uncertainty during which Elizabeth had angrily refused to reveal to Parliament her plans regarding her heir, the matter was decided and the Protestant succession secured. They must have been among the first to know that the Crown had been offered to James in order to get in early with their invitation to Hinchingbrooke. We may legitimately imagine their hopes rising more rapidly than their anxieties as news of the royal progress reached them along the Great North Road. Elizabeth had been positively niggardly in the bestowing of honours but James Stuart was reported to be broadcasting knighthoods and other titles like a farmer in the sowing season (he dubbed forty-six new knights at Belvoir Castle before breakfast, and during his first year as King he promoted an astonishing 934 men to that dignity). Sir Oliver had good reason to expect that royal generosity would show itself in a more exalted form than the KB he received in 1603. A peerage or, at least, one of the new baronetcies might have been on the cards, for James quickly developed a love affair with Hinchingbrooke and scarcely an autumn passed without a visit from the royal entourage.

This, then, was Oliver Cromwell's inheritance – the character-istics locked within the genes and the family ethos which cocooned him during his early years. The Cromwells were an extensive, self-assured clan, proud of their ancient lineage and their services to Crown and country. Oliver can have had only the haziest memories of Sir Henry, who died before his grandson reached his fifth birthday. Nevertheless, the exploits of the Golden Knight were firmly embedded in family legend. When Oliver and his parents made the mile-and-a-half journey along a rutted winter road to Hinchingbrooke or (less often) the more elaborate outing to Ramsey they entered a world of ostentatious luxury fit for a king. While the contrast with their own modest home was very humbling, they were proud of belonging to the leading family in the area and one which had such close contact with the royal court. All this gave the young Oliver an innate sense of superiority. He grew up belonging to a breed of men who could say with conviction, 'We are England.'

When Charles Stuart was seven years old he was taken at night with his household and his siblings to watch a solemn and almost clandestine ceremony. A torchlight procession made its way to the great abbey church at Westminster, and came to a halt close to where Henry VII, common ancestor of Tudor and Stuart sovereigns, lay in his splendid tomb. The small cortege had come to watch another interment. King James I had brought his mother's remains from Peterborough to place them – not where she had always wished, in Scotland, but in the royal mausoleum of that kingdom whose crown she had claimed in vain. The child's tutors had already begun to teach young Charles about Mary Queen of Scots and, inescapably, he had inherited characteristics from his grandmother. Some of them would contribute to his sharing of her fate.

The Stuarts were foreigners – aliens in some eyes. Scotland, traditionally and until very recent years an enemy and a harbourer of enemies, was widely regarded as a barbarous land whose lawless people feuded among themselves and made frequent cross-border raids. Instability was certainly a distinguishing mark of the Scottish royal house. While the Tudors had been successfully stamping their authority on the temporal and spiritual nobility, their counterparts north of the border had been quite unable to emulate them. Effective power was seldom lodged in the wearer of the crown as princes of the blood engaged in intrigues with native magnates and foreign ambassadors for control of government. Misfortune added to the problems of the dynasty; it was not only death in battle that prematurely terminated several reigns, ensuring that, between 1371 and 1542, seven heirs ascended the throne as minors.

At about the time that Morgan Williams, Oliver Cromwell's great-great-grandfather, set himself up as an English businessman, Charles I's great-great-grandfather, James IV, grabbed the Scottish throne from his father. He was fifteen and had been put at the head of a rebel army by a group of powerful malcontents. The two forces met on 11 June 1488 at Sauchieburn, scarcely a mile from Bannockburn, the site of Scotland's greatest victory over the 'auld enemy'. But this was to be no glorious clash of arms. Early in the battle the dispirited royal forces were overwhelmed following the flight of their king. Immediately afterwards James III was murdered in mysterious circumstances. Later legend told of his revealing his identity to an old crone who betrayed him to a man at arms who, coming to the King in the guise of a priest, cut him down with a single sword blow.

James IV began his reign in pawn to the great nobles who had engineered its premature beginning but he rapidly established himself as a vigorous, charismatic autocrat. He was a man of strong enthusiasms and passions. He could with equal application seduce the wife of a courtier and retire to a monastery for spiritual exercise. The scale on which he sired illegitimate children was lavish even by the standards of the day. Like Henry VIII a few years later, he came to the throne as a young man succeeding an unpopular father, determined to reverse earlier trends and policies and show himself as an energetic and enlightened ruler presiding over a scintillating court. He created an image of himself as a warrior king by building a well-equipped army and navy. His flagship, the *Michael*, built in 1511, was, at a thousand tons and with twenty-seven great canon, the maritime wonder of the age. He courted Habsburg and Valois rulers and they were happy to reciprocate, for Scotland always held value as a potential irritant to England. Because much of James's kingdom consisted of islands and mountain regions difficult of access, where local lords enjoyed virtual autonomy, he had to be much on the move if he was to assert his authority but by force of personality and extravagant building schemes he established Edinburgh as a permanent seat of government and at least made a serious beginning to the creation of a centralised state.

THE STUARTS

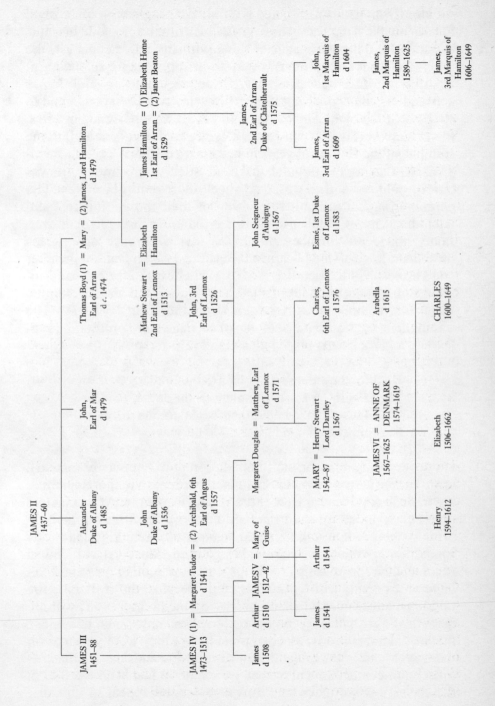

JAMES II
1437–60

Alexander
Duke of Albany
d 1485

John,
Earl of Mar
d 1479

Thomas Boyd (1) = Mary = (2) James, Lord Hamilton
Earl of Arran   d 1479
d c. 1474

James Hamilton = (1) Elizabeth Home
1st Earl of Arran = (2) Janet Beaton
d 1529

John,
Duke of Albany
d 1536

Mathew Stewart = Elizabeth
2nd Earl of Lennox   Hamilton
d 1513

James,
2nd Earl of Arran,
Duke of Châtelherault
d 1575

John,
1st Marquis of
Hamilton
d 1604

James,
2nd Marquis of
Hamilton
1589–1625

James,
3rd Marquis of
Hamilton
1606–1649

JAMES III
1451–88

John, 3rd
Earl of Lennox
d 1526

James,
3rd Earl of Arran
d 1609

JAMES IV (1) = Margaret Tudor = (2) Archibald, 6th
1473–1513   d 1541   Earl of Angus
                                                           d 1557

John Seigneur
d'Aubigny
d 1567

Esmé, 1st Duke
of Lennox
d 1583

James
d 1508

Arthur
d 1510

JAMES V
1512–42

Mary of
Guise

Margaret Douglas = Matthew, Earl
of Lennox
d 1571

Charles,
6th Earl of Lennox
d 1576

Arbella
d 1615

Arthur
d 1541

MARY = Henry Stewart
1542–87   Lord Darnley
                 d 1567

CHARLES
1600–1649

James
d 1541

JAMES VI = ANNE OF
1567–1625   DENMARK
                     1574–1619

Elizabeth
1506–1662

Henry
1594–1612

James's ministers negotiated possible marriages with other royal houses but the King was in no hurry to rush into wedlock. In his mid-twenties he fell passionately in love with his latest conquest, the Lady Margaret Drummond, whom he set up in some splendour at Linlithgow. Theirs was a very serious relationship and James alarmed his advisers by speaking of matrimony. They put an end to such nonsense by having the lady and her sisters poisoned in 1502. Plans were already in train for an alliance with England and, in the summer of the following year, James married Henry VII's thirteen-year-old daughter, Margaret. Like all such arrangements, it was purely political and designed to meet short-term objectives. The neighbouring states remitted nothing of their mutual mistrust and latent hostility. Within a decade this broke out again into open war. James made an alliance with Louis XII of France against his brother-in-law and led his army across the Tweed. On 9 September 1513 almost half the Scottish force was cut down in furious hand-to-hand fighting on the field of Flodden. Among the slain were nine earls, four senior clerics, fourteen lords and King James IV. The traumatic effects of that brief hour of carnage were profound, long-lasting, and took their place in Lowland minstrelsy.

> Dool for the order sent our lads to the Border,
> The English for aince by guile won the day;
> The Flowers of the Forest that fought aye the foremost,
> The prime of our land lie cauld in the clay.[30]

However, the blame for the Scottish defeat by an evenly matched army cannot be put down to Sassenach trickery; a major element in the tragedy was the character of the vanquished King. At around five o'clock on the morning of the battle Scottish sentries on the high ground where James had advantageously taken his stand saw English troops crossing a narrow bridge in the broad valley below to assume their positions. The King's master gunner implored his general – it is said with tears in his eyes – to order the artillery to fire on the enemy. James adamantly refused – he had given his word to meet the English in even combat on the plain, and honour demanded that he did not take advantage of them before they were prepared for the fray. Much of the romanticism which surrounds the Stuarts is of nineteenth-century invention but we cannot understand the fate of the dynasty if we make no allowance for the appeal of chivalric idealism to succeeding generations. Arthurian legends, *chansons de geste*, and the lays of valorous Scottish heroes performed by courtly ballad singers had, from his earliest days, framed James's concept of the mystique of kingship. The man who received the sceptre from God was subject to higher divine laws than those which applied to ordinary mortals. These were symbolically upheld on the tournament field, in popular pageants and in court masques. They veneered the greed, ambition and rivalry of high-level diplomacy. When Louis XII inveigled Scotland into war in 1513 he offered the lure of the English crown while his wife, Anne of Brittany, begged James to enter the fray as her knightly champion. The Scottish king found both appeals irresistible.

During a decade of marriage James's English wife bore him three sons. Two died within a year of birth. The third, James, was seventeen months old at the time of his father's death and was destined to become the victim of an unseemly and psychologically disastrous tug of war between his mother and John, Duke of Albany, James IV's first cousin and the heir presumptive. Albany, who preferred to live in France, was appointed governor, and devoted his endeavours to maintaining the 'auld alliance'. Margaret did her best to repair relations between Scotland and the country of her birth. Court factions rose and fell as the Queen Regent and her lovers and the governor and his allies by turn gained and lost the upper hand. Fatherless, separated from his mother for long periods, surrounded by flatterers and self-seekers, moved from stronghold to stronghold, threatened with kidnap plots, at least one of which was carried out, and assailed throughout his teens with conflicting advice, it was never going to be possible for James V to grow into the strong, well-balanced ruler Scotland needed. James V possessed the vices of his forebears without their redeeming qualities. Cultured tastes masked viciousness. He tried to re-establish sound royal government after two decades of chaos but only succeeded in alienating many of the clan leaders. In his search for affection he took a succession of mistresses and sired a clutch of natural children, each of whom had to be provided for out of the treasury. Yet he produced no male heir. Obsessed with visions of glory and honour, he toyed with a grandiose scheme for the conquest of Ireland, which he was quite incapable of executing. He allowed himself to be caught up in French machinations when he married Mary of Guise and this last folly was to provoke war with England.

Long before this, James's tormented childhood was paying sinister dividends. He was prey to a 'melancholy humour' or, as we should say, he was a depressive. In the spring of 1541, history repeated itself when the King's two infant sons died. At the end of that year he unnecessarily delivered a snub to Henry VIII by failing to turn up for a meeting arranged in York, a discourtesy to which James was nerved by Church leaders eager to chastise the English king for becoming a heretic. Listening to them rather than to his more prudent magnates, James authorised an army to cross the border in the autumn of 1542 under the command of a court favourite, Oliver Sinclair. At Solway Moss in November 1542 this force was annihilated while in a retreat led enthusiastically by its own general. Incoherent with grief, James travelled disconsolately northwards to Falkland in Fife and took to his bed. Days later the news was brought to him that his queen had been delivered of a daughter. That seems to have removed the last shred of James's will to live. 'The devil go with it!' he is supposed to have declared. 'It came with a lass and will go with a lass.'* Thereafter he lapsed into gibberish and died on 16 December. He was thirty years old.

Yet again the wheel of doom had come full circle: a long minority, dominated by pro-French and pro-English factions; a weakened central government, which permitted the great lords to exercise a high degree of regional autonomy. But this time there were three added complications. Scotland had a queen, which raised the near certainty of marriage with a foreign prince and a union of crowns. Secondly, that queen emerged as heir presumptive to the throne of England following the death of Edward VI and Elizabeth I's refusal to marry. And over this sensitive situation brooded the Reformation. Evangelical Protestantism had inevitably reached Scotland by the middle years of the century, spreading its way up the social hierarchy until several town councils and noble houses began to apply a stern biblicism to the conduct of their affairs. In other kingdoms rulers adopted or rejected the new doctrines as they saw their own interests affected by them. In faction-ridden Scotland no such clear-cut decision was possible. Only in the late 1550s, a quarter of a century after Thomas Cromwell had begun to overhaul the politico-religious life of England, did a movement for territorial

*The Stuart dynasty had its origins in the marriage of Marjorie, daughter of Robert the Bruce with Walter Stewart.

reformation begin to make itself known. In December 1557 a league of 'Lords and Barons professing Jesus Christ' came together in a 'common bond', the first manifestation of the 'Covenant' philosophy which was to play a prominent part in developing a characteristic Scottish Protestantism for more than a century. The vision of this pious minority was to transform national life by applying 'our whole power, substance and our very lives to maintain, set forward and establish the blessed Word of God and his congregation'. A few months later and in the safety of Geneva, John Knox, the apostle of the Scottish Reformation, published his *First Blast of the Trumpet against the Monstrous Regiment of Women*. In this vigorous response to Mary of Guise's implacable opposition to anti-Romanism, the writer thundered, 'To promote a woman to bear rule, superiority, dominion or empire above any realm is repugnant to nature, contrary to God, and, finally, it is the subversion of good order, of all equity and justice.' It was an unnecessarily offensive and imprudent diatribe, from which other Protestant leaders hastened to disassociate themselves and which raised English hackles after Elizabeth I's accession in that same year. Knox defended himself by insisting that the cause of Christian truth seemed under dire threat at the time of writing: Bloody Mary was sending the faithful to the stake; Mary of Guise was emulating her north of the border; refugees from both countries were flocking to Geneva and other Protestant havens. The effects of Knoxian thinking ran wide and deep. It bred a truculence among the leaders of society who espoused reform, and it planted firmly within the Stuart psyche a loathing of religious extremism.

In 1560 Mary Queen of Scots, while still in her teens lost her mother and her husband. In 1548 she had been despatched to France and espoused to the dauphin. While she grew up as a thoroughly French princess and Mary of Guise ruled Scotland in her daughter's name, the fate of the realm – and possibly of the whole region – seemed settled: France and Scotland would become united under a single crown and, since the Catholic world refused to recognise Elizabeth's legitimacy, Mary would lay claim to England also. All this fell apart with Francis II's sudden death in the last days of 1560, after a reign of only seventeen months. The eighteen-year-old ex-queen was of no further use to that ogress, Catherine de Medici, who dominated the French court; nay, worse, the continued presence of the beautiful young widow might threaten her own position. Mary was, therefore, packed off back to Scotland. There now began the most poignant quarter-century of the long Stuart tragedy, almost, but not quite, challenged by the similar period her grandson spent on the throne of England. Indeed there are striking psychological parallels between Mary Queen of Scots and Charles I. They shared that combination of high principle and fecklessness which was to bring both of them to the block.

Mary began her reign intelligently. Knowing that she could not survive to impose her pro-Catholic policies without temporising in the short term, she sought to balance the political forces operating at central and local level. She toured her country, securing the personal allegiance of leading clans and creating several new earls and knights, and appointed Protestant and Catholic nobles to her Council in equal numbers. Ministers struggled with female rule but courtiers, as in Elizabeth's household, created a new chivalrous mythology around the Queen. Mary brought from France and elsewhere poets, artists, musicians, scholars and wits and, for a few years, made her court a significant centre of Renaissance culture. A pageant performed in Edinburgh in 1566 involved a large painted timber fortress, assailed by armies of lavishly accoutred enemies and a spectacular firework display and outshone anything performed in England, even in the more exuberant celebrations of Henry VIII. One of the verse eulogies proffered in that year credited Mary, in words which now have an ominous ring, with bringing 'peace in our time'. She was, the poet claimed, both the adornment and the embodiment of Stuart kingship. 'The fates will grant you to extend your kingdom,' he prophesied, mirroring Mary's own ambition, 'until all Britons abandon war and learn at last to unite in one realm.' But all this was no more than a tapestry of vibrant colours covering a wall whose weakened masonry permitted the chill draughts of anxiety and discord to blow through.

The two most contentious issues were the same as those confronting Elizabeth – marriage and religion. But, whereas the English queen thickly hedged these matters about with prerogative, within which she maintained an aloof inactivity, her Scottish counterpart allowed her advisers and her own inclinations to lead her into actions and intrigues so scandalous that they sealed her fate. Mary's greatest folly was to rush into wedlock with a beautiful, empty-headed boy, an action which sucked her into a maelstrom of conspiracy and murder. As both a woman and a queen alone in a world of powerful, scheming men Mary longed for a consort. Faced with the same problem, Elizabeth chose Robert Dudley and for thirty years gave him her affection, enjoyed his support and managed to keep his ambition in check. The Scottish queen, lacking her sister sovereign's judgement and finesse, bestowed her favours by turn on three of the most unsuitable men imaginable and allowed them to strut about as cocks of the walk. In 1565 the nineteen-year-old Henry Stuart, Lord Darnley pranced into her life, egged on by his own arrogance and his ambitious mother. He was one of three contemporary male members of the Stuart clan who stood in close succession to the throne but, apart from lineage, good looks and sexual prowess, he was singularly lacking in redeeming features, as the Queen discovered very soon after their wedding. Darnley was arrogant, vulgar, petulant, indiscreet and unprincipled. He swaggered through the streets of Edinburgh with his drunken cronies boasting that he would return Scotland to the true faith but, a few weeks later, struck up a deal with the Protestant lords of the Council. He used his position to score off his family's enemies, and tried to browbeat his wife into sharing executive power with him.

It had taken Mary very little time to realise that Darnley could never be her political confidant and she turned instead to her personal secretary, David Rizzio. The young Italian had been in her service for four years, rising rapidly from chapel singer to valet de chambre but it was not until after her marriage that the Queen looked to him for support against her manipulative councillors and her brutal husband. As royal guardian and, possibly, bedfellow Rizzio became Mary's link with the great men of Church and state. Proud clan leaders and seasoned advisers who had given years of service to the Crown now had to sue for favours from a swarthy little lutenist who ruled the court through an entourage even larger and more ostentatious than Darnley's. Great as the favourite's power was, the Queen determined to make it greater by appointing Rizzio her chancellor, protected by an Italian bodyguard, and fully independent of Council and parliament. Thus buttressed, Mary would, theoretically, have enjoyed an absolutism which would have enabled her to pursue her own policies without restraint. To the disciples of Knox that meant only one thing: a complete return to Roman Catholicism. To prevent this the favourite's growing number of foes acted swiftly. Rizzio had enjoyed semi-regal splendour for less than nine months when, in March 1566, assassins dragged him from the

Queen's supper table in Holyrood Palace into an antechamber where their savagery and injured pride were expressed in fifty-six dagger blows.

A desperate Queen of Scots, more than ever determined to achieve real freedom of action, looked to military might to gain this prize. Her most trusted general was James Hepburn, fourth Earl of Bothwell, and with him she plotted, first of all, the removal of her husband, the last vestiges of love for whom had evaporated when his complicity in the murder of Rizzio was revealed. By this time the twenty-four-year-old Queen had become adept at dissembling. Smiles and fair words disarmed Darnley and the lords of the Council and there was widespread surprise, if not universal dismay, when the royal consort was found dead in the grounds of Kirk o' Fields after Bothwell's accomplices had blown the house up (February 1567). Three months later, Mary and Bothwell were married, a divorce having conveniently removed the obstacle of the earl's existing wife. Now the treadmill on which the Queen had become trapped turned once more its familiar circle. The latest favourite treated the Council with presumptuous scorn and became in succession to Darnley and Rizzio the 'most hated man in Scotland'. The clan leaders were very far from being squeamish about political assassination and were by very breeding inured to intrigue but several of them were now convinced that the regime had indulged a scandal too far. This group, the Confederate Lords as they styled themselves, took arms against the royal pair and, to save her husband's life, Mary sent him into exile. They had been married for thirty-three days.

The victors forced Mary to abdicate in favour of her thirteen-month-old son who was now crowned as James VI. But the Queen's spirit was not broken. According to the French ambassador she raged about her chambers, tearful and dishevelled and talking of nothing but 'hanging and crucifying' her enemies. Her escape from captivity in the spring of 1568 plunged her country into five years of civil war during which the combatants divided largely along religious lines. Mary herself fled into England where she lived as a prisoner for nineteen years, a constant embarrassment to Elizabeth and the focus of Catholic plots until her execution at Fotheringhay Castle on 8 February 1587. It was a few months short of a century since her great-grandfather had been murdered after Sauchieburn and in all that time no Stuart sovereign had died in bed in peaceful possession of the crown.

King James was scarcely less a prisoner than his mother. Throughout his childhood his daily routine was controlled by the tutors appointed by whichever noble faction had the upper hand in the Council. For the most part they were earnest Calvinists like George Buchanan, who imparted to the young King a strict morality and a love of learning. These admirable but narrow life guides had to stand James in the stead of loving parents. He never knew his father or mother and so had no role model to follow when he had children of his own. Similarly, he grew up with no pattern of regality. There was no way that he could absorb unconsciously the firmness coupled with tact, graciousness and éclat that made up kingly style. Everything he discovered about the parts he would later have to play in the drama of royal government and family life had to be learned from books and from the admonitions of tutors and preachers. It is significant, that when he attempted to instruct his heir in the mystique of kingship he did so by writing books – *Basilicon Doron* and *The True Law of Free Monarchies*. The King who emerged from this regimen was bookish and gauche, 'an old young man' as one courtier observed or, as a French diplomat considered:

He is wonderfully clever, and for the rest, he is full of honourable ambition, and has an excellent opinion of himself. Owing to the terrorism under which he has been brought up, he is timid with the great lords, and seldom ventures to contradict them; yet his especial anxiety is to be thought hardy and a man of courage . . . He dislikes dances and music and amorous talk, and curiosity of dress and courtly trivialities . . . He speaks, eats, dresses and plays like a boor, and he is no better in the company of women . . . his gait is sprawling and awkward; his voice is loud and his words sententious . . . He is prodigiously conceited . . . he is idle and careless, too easy, and too much given to pleasure, particularly to the chase, leaving his affairs to be managed by [ministers].[31]

On 22 August 1582, James and his suite were riding near Perth when a posse of armed horsemen bore down upon them and forced them to hurry northwards to the Earl of Gowrie's castle at Ruthven. This affront to the young King's dignity brought home to him just how much the Crown was still in pawn to the great nobles. The coup was a Protestant protest against the men who had recently grasped the power over the royal household, Esmé Seigneur d'Aubigny (later

Duke of Lennox) and James, Earl of Arran. These distant relatives of the King were next in line to the throne and the chief hopes of the pro-French faction. They had encompassed the downfall and death of the previous regent, the Earl of Morton, and d'Aubigny made a lasting impression on the young King with his elegant sophistication and his flouting of the conventions of the Protestant sobersides. It was Esmé who initiated James into homosexual love. Now Lennox and his colleagues were to be toppled in their turn. James was well treated at Ruthven but devastated by the loss of Esmé and appalled when he was obliged to denounce 'popish schemes' and to outlaw Lennox and Arran. But he had now reached his seventeenth birthday and strongly resented being deprived of companions and mentors whom he loved and trusted. In June 1583 he escaped. It was too late to bring back Lennox, who had just died in France, but the King did reinstate Arran and, with this friend at his side, he began to be king in more than name and to become adept in those aspects of politics in which his fractured upbringing had tutored him – guile and manipulation through intermediaries. Instead of allowing himself to be used by competing-interest groups, he attempted to use them. He became a political puppet-master; in his hands he held the golden strings of sovereignty, which still commanded widespread respect and awe, and to them were attached the favourites, parliament and general assemblies he moved – now in synergy, now in combat – to play out the drama of effective centralised government. He became very good at it – in Scotland.

The prize on which his eyes were set was the English throne but it was not altogether clear at whose hands he was most likely to receive it. Queen Elizabeth would die, as she had lived, a virgin queen. The Scottish king was next in line and he was Protestant. The majority of councillors in Westminster and Edinburgh were in favour of a union of the crowns and some were, by the 1590s, actively laying their plans to bring it about. James only had to maintain good relations with the southern kingdom and his accession was inevitable. But his mother's execution in 1587 had provoked outrage in France and Spain and who was to say that a Catholic reaction might not succeed in sweeping away the heretic Queen of England and replacing her with a more compliant James Stuart? It would be as well to keep lines of communication open with Paris and Madrid and maintain a religious balance within his own council.

Then there was the problem of the Church. The Scottish Kirk was governed by the General Assembly, dominated by Lowland ministers most of whom favoured a Presbyterian form of government but there was an episcopal opposition and the two parties were locked in ongoing argument. 'Ye have fathered on the Scriptures the superiority of pastors over pastors!' an outraged divine roared in 1580 when an opponent presented biblical evidence for the office of bishop. 'And ye have mothered on the Scriptures equality of pastors, which is anabaptistry!' came the angry response.[32] James was in no doubt where his sympathies lay. A Presbyterian church was as effective a brake as the feudal baronage on royal power, as its leading advocate, Andrew Melville, made clear in a celebrated interview with the King in 1596: 'Thair is twa kings and twa kingdoms in Scotland. Thair is Christ Jesus the King, and his kingdom the Kirk, whose subject King James the Saxt is and of whase kingdom nocht a king, nor a lord, nor a heid, but a member.'[33] It became very clear to James that monarchy and Presbytery agreed as well as God and the devil. The problem was that Melville and his friends enjoyed the support of those Puritan elements in the English court and government upon whom James relied for support.

The answer was simple but it demanded patience and cunning. Until he had secured the English crown James courted the Presbyterian party. He transferred power and privileges from the bishops to the General Assembly. He used parliament to transfer ecclesiastical property to the Crown. He used the Protestant clergy and nobles to undermine most of the remaining centres of Roman Catholic activity. Through John Maitland, his chief minister from 1586, he maintained good relations with the ultra-Protestants. This 'softly-softly' approach did not always come easy to the young King and it was during these years that he developed an almost pathological antipathy towards 'arrogant' ministers who did not know their place and who presumed to challenge the authority of God's anointed king. However, he could always console himself with the thought of how pleasant it would be to turn the tables once he was King of Scotland *and* England.

In one matter he refused to be dictated to. He needed a wife and the availability of appealing and acceptable princesses was limited. However, once he had made his choice of a Danish princess, there was no moving him. Anne was a Lutheran which, to many Calvinists, was little better than being a Catholic. The pro-English party was not happy with the proposed union but James was determined. He took the unprecedented step of travelling to Copenhagen in person to press his suit and there, in 1589, the marriage was duly solemnised between the twenty-three-year-old King of Scotland and his fifteen-year-old Queen. At last James had someone with whom to share the pleasures and burdens of sovereignty.

Anne was a pretty, blonde girl, full of fun, who loved the pleasures of court life and introduced a note of gaiety to the household of her dour husband. For a few years their palaces became lavish baroque settings for elaborate plays, pageants and masques. Poets, musicians and writers were employed to flatter the royal couple in elaborate verse tributes and exuberantly costumed stage presentations. James was apostrophised as another Solomon, Constantine, David and, more frequently as the years passed, as *Arturus Redevivus*, the king who should unite the British people in peace and harmony. The euphoria and excitement reached their climax on 5 April 1603 when James Stuart rode out of Edinburgh to assume the rule over a people and a nation of whom he had virtually no understanding.

Yet, although James Stuart saw himself as a forward-looking monarch, a healer of wounds and even as an arbiter in divided Christendom, he was inevitably shaped by his own and his family's past. On his way south he stopped at Peterborough Cathedral to pay his respects at his mother's tomb and there was an air of triumphalism about a little ceremony he ordered to be performed a few months into his reign. By no means everyone in royal circles was enthusiastic about the new regime. William Dethick, Garter King-of-Arms, was reported to the King for murmuring about the Stuart succession. In August 1603 James selected the dissident herald to perform an act of political canonisation:

On the 14th Sir William Dethick, Garter King-of-Arms, being sent to Peterborough, assisted by many knights and gentlemen, and much people at the time of divine service, laid a rich pall of velvet over the tomb of the Queen Mary of Scots, his Majesty's mother . . . Then the Bishop preached a sermon in that behalf in the morning and made a great feast at dinner, and the Dean preached of the same in the afternoon . . .[34]

TWO

KITH AND KIN

'I HAVE LOST TWO or three children in infancy, not without regret, but without great sorrow.' Sixteenth- and seventeenth-century childhood is pulled into sharper focus by those words of Montaigne. Parents' emotional investment in their offspring was limited by the high incidence of infant mortality. Even in those sections of society which enjoyed sanitary living conditions and a balanced diet, between a quarter and a half of all children died before the age of five. This was far from being an unmitigated disaster. It was nature's way or, as contemporaries would have averred, divine providence's means of keeping families to a manageable size. There were no effective methods of birth control and a healthy woman could expect to undergo numerous pregnancies during the first twenty years or so of married life. Death reduced the number of mouths to feed, educations to provide and dowries to find. Parent-child relations were, therefore, more detached than those pertaining in the twentieth-century nuclear family.

Robert and Elizabeth Cromwell might well in moments of acute economic pressure have welcomed more visits from the grim reaper. Their marriage was as fertile and their offspring as healthy as those of Sir Henry and Sir Oliver but their resources bore no resemblance to those of the Cromwells of Hinchingbrooke. There is no indication that they resented being overshadowed by Robert's brother. All the family's eighteenth-century chroniclers could find to say of them was that they were, 'persons of great worth and no way inclined to disaffection, either in their civil or religious principles, but remarkable for living upon a small fortune with decency and maintaining a large family by their frugal circumspection'.[1] It was a considerable misfortune that the only two of their ten children to die in infancy were boys. Apart from Oliver there were no sons to help around the estate, learn a lucrative profession or make a profitable marriage. On the other hand there were seven daughters to provide

49

THE FAMILY OF OLIVER CROMWELL

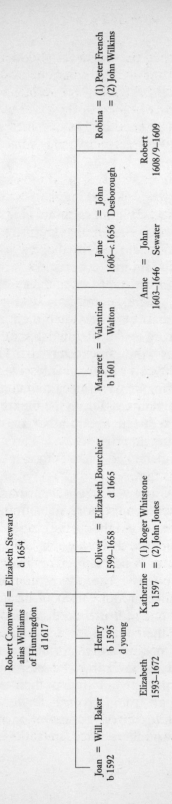

Robert Cromwell = Elizabeth Steward
alias Williams   d 1654
of Huntingdon
d 1617

Joan = Will. Baker
b 1592

Henry
b 1595
d young

Elizabeth
1593–1672

Oliver = Elizabeth Bourchier
1599–1658   d 1665

Katherine = (1) Roger Whitstone
b 1597   = (2) John Jones

Margaret = Valentine
b 1601   Walton

Anne = John
1603–1646   Sewater

Jane = John
1606–c.1656   Desborough

Robert
1608/9–1609

Robina = (1) Peter French
       = (2) John Wilkins

for. Each girl born steepened the Cromwells' downward spiral and made inroads into the patrimony that would be available to Oliver. When husbands were found for Joan, Katherine, Margaret, Anne, Jane and Robina they were not men of the royal court or ministers prominent in government or wealthy London merchants or leaders of the county gentry; they were landowners' sons of the middling sort.

The two dominant realities that shaped Oliver Cromwell's early life and went a long way towards shaping his personality were that he was an only son and that he belonged to the leading local family. As the heir of the Huntingdon household Oliver received the lion's share of his father's attention. He had three older sisters to fuss over him and four younger ones to boss around. As for his mother, the family biographer assures us that, 'Her greatest fondness was lavished on her only son, who she ever partially loved; and to her he was every way deserving of it, he behaving always in the most filial and tender manner to her.'[2] The boy grew up spoilt and by nature egotistical. His visits to the splendours of Hinchingbrooke, particularly when the Jacobean court was in residence, underlined, at least in Oliver's mind, that he was a person of consequence in the district. There was no one in the family to challenge his position as the 'young master' and few to take him down a peg or two when his arrogant self-assertion became intolerable.

Royalist detractors made much of Oliver's wild behaviour in childhood and youth. Most of such stories must be considered very sceptically; authors seeking to win the favour of the Stuart court portrayed the late Protector as a monster, a canting hypocrite and a man of overweening ambition, so it was inevitable that they should seek in his early years evidence of both embryonic wickedness and nascent religious extremism. What they did not invent they based on hearsay and malicious gossip. The temptation for the modern historian is to dismiss all such stories out of hand but it is worth scrutinising them closely to see if there are common elements that can be squared with more reliable evidence. James Heath, an impecunious hack who wrote royalist diatribes in the hope of commending himself to Charles II, had this to say of Cromwell's early years:

> From his infancy to his childhood he was of a cross and peevish
> disposition, which being humoured by the fondness of his mother, made

that rough and intractable temper more robust and outrageous . . . He was very notorious for robbing of orchards; a puerile crime . . . but grown so scandalous and injurious by the frequent spoils and damages . . . committed by this apple-dragon that many solemn complaints were made both to his father and master . . . From this he passed unto another more manly theft, the robbing of dove houses, stealing the young pigeons, and eating and merchandising them.[3]

Heath goes on to inform us that Oliver's parents and tutor could make little impression on the boy's 'obstinate and perverse inclination' and that his school attendance was erratic. Once puberty opened up new possibilities for sin it was inevitable that, in Restoration writings, the young Cromwell should be portrayed as taking full advantage of them. Huntingdon and district were supposedly well provided with little Olivers and Olivias. Late seventeenth-century detractors may have based such tales on a circumspectly anonymous pamphlet of 1650 which asserted that Cromwell was, in the 1630s, renowned as 'the town bull of Ely'.[4]

What is striking about these shocking revelations is that they are not very shocking. Even if we were to take them at face value we would be confronting a picture of a self-willed, rumbustious youngster who preferred scrumping forays to dull lessons but who was far from being a juvenile delinquent. They would speak to us of a character impatient of imposed restraints, impulsive by nature, little interested in book learning and accustomed to imposing his will on others. The child and young man may have got away with misdemeanours because his mother was over-indulgent and because the outraged citizens of Huntingdon were diffident about complaining at the antics of the squire's nephew. Some commentators have claimed that Cromwell later condemned himself with his own pen. In a letter of 1638 to his cousin Elizabeth St John he bewailed the godless ways of his youth and even went so far as to declare himself as 'the chief of sinners'.[5] This pious hyperbole, common in many evangelical circles, indicates that the middle-aged Cromwell lamented his misspent earlier years but it almost certainly refers to unsanctified religious attitudes rather than sins of the flesh (see below pp. 228ff).

As to sexual depravity, for all the allusions to the young Cromwell's libidinous career, no solid evidence was ever produced. By the 1660s 'wronged women', the victims of Oliver's debaucheries, may not still have been around but their relatives and, probably, the now grown-up children themselves would have been. One might have expected royalist pamphleteers to produce them with relish. Their inability to do so is really rather surprising. Society has always been Janus-faced in its attitude towards male pre-marital sex; prudishly disapproving while giving an indulgent nod to young men's needs to prove their virility. Social differences also produced double standards: what was frowned on among the lower orders was winked at when indulged by their betters – partly, at least, because gentlemen could afford to look after the results of their indiscretions. Sir Henry Cromwell left provision in his will for the bastard daughters sired, probably, upon one of his own servant girls. His grandson was in no position to pay for his pleasures. The fact that he married at the comparatively early age of twenty-one into a very respectable mercantile family and thereafter enjoyed a happy domestic life suggests that his sins of youth were such as could very easily be put behind him. He also matured during a period of remarkable disapprobation of carnal sin, an attitude reinforced by Puritan preachers. In the decade 1610–20 sexual licence, measured in terms of illegitimate births, was at a lower ebb than for many years and was declining. Lawrence Stone concluded that in this period 'most men must have exercised extraordinary sexual self-control during the first twelve to fourteen years of optimum male potency'.[6] In the absence of evidence to the contrary we must assume that Oliver Cromwell was not atypical.

What is clear is that the growing young man had considerable energy and that this forced itself to the surface in ways not always acceptable. Even quite late in life he was given to bouts of boisterous horseplay, such as suddenly inaugurating a pillow fight during a serious constitutional debate. He was a victim of mood swings which produced instant hilarity or violent temper. When he was not 'up', Oliver could be very 'down'. A family doctor, chagrined at being several times summoned to Cromwell's bedside in the middle of the night, labelled his patient as 'splenetic' and a hypochondriac who regarded every ache and pain as evidence of imminent death.[7]

There have been many attempts to establish a psychological profile of Cromwell based on the inadequate information about his personal life. Bipolar disorder would explain his mood swings and hypochondria but the most persuasive theory suggests that the future

Protector had a hypomanic personality.[8] Hypomania is defined as 'a minor form of mania, often part of the manic-depressive cycle, characterized by elation and a feeling of wellbeing together with quickness of thought'. Such qualities would obviously serve a battle-field general very well and we know that Oliver possessed tactical brilliance combined with an ebullient confidence that put heart into his men. More interestingly, one characteristic of this personality type is a tendency always to look for the best in people. On the face of it, it may seem difficult to claim this attribute for a man as combative as Cromwell, who could order the indiscriminate slaughter of a townful of 'papists' and pursue a king to death. Yet it does begin to make sense of Cromwell's outbursts of rage against what he saw as the deviousness and downright evil of others if we understand his anger as often stemming from disappointment. As love can turn to hate, so confidence in the good intentions of others can be transformed into disillusionment and an iron determination to trust them no further. In Cromwell's relations with his officers, with other army leaders, with parliaments and ultimately with the King, he invested the capital of faith and goodwill. When it was squandered and returned no dividend he was often driven to profound melancholy or anger. Any perusal of his extant correspondence reveals many more examples of commendation than condemnation and he erred on the side of trust more often than on that of overhasty rejection. Here, too, we may seek illumination on that aspect of Cromwell's policy during his years in power which has puzzled some commentators and drawn grudging praise from his detractors; his extension of toleration to men of wide-ranging religious opinions.

Returning to Oliver's early years, there is another story, this one relating to his performance in a school play.[9] His role was that of Tactus in a morality by an unknown author entitled *Lingua, or the Combat of the Tongue and the Five Senses*. As he made his entrance he is supposed to have tripped over his long robe and immediately ad-libbed to cover his mistake: 'High thoughts have slippery feet; I had well nigh fallen.' Then he moved smoothly into the lines as written:

> . . . this crown and robe
> My brow and body circles and invests,
> How gallantly it fits me. Sure the slave
> Measured my head that wrought this coronet.

> They lie who say complexions cannot change.
> My blood's ennobled, and I am transformed
> Unto the sacred temper of a king.

This tale is likely to be a true incident remembered because later events gave it added significance rather than a fanciful invention; early records note that the play, published in 1607, was first performed at Trinity College, Cambridge and afterwards at the Free School, Huntingdon. It gives us a picture of a quick-witted, possibly precocious, lad who enjoyed appearing in public and had plenty of self-confidence.

This self-assurance did not stem only from the position he occupied in his parents' household. The glittering world of Hinchingbrooke was of immense importance to the growing boy. Chroniclers intent on discovering or inventing links between Cromwell and Charles I told the tale of two infants playing together at Sir Oliver's mansion. They fell to fighting and were not separated before Oliver had given Charles a bloody nose. What matters is not whether the story is true but that it certainly could have been, because Oliver, his parents and sisters had more access to the royal court than most provincial families of modest means.

His uncle and godfather was the complete courtier; cultured but also athletic, maintaining a high level of personal elegance, involved in the ceremonial life of the royal household, accompanying the King on progresses, organising James's hunting expeditions in Cambridgeshire and Huntingdonshire, supporting government policy in the House of Commons (in the assemblies of 1604, 1614, 1623 and 1624) and, above all, being a Stuart loyalist through and through. He was attached, originally, to Prince Henry's household and, in 1617, he was appointed a cup bearer to the new Prince of Wales and, in recognition of his expertise in matters of horsemanship and the etiquette of the tiltyard, he was also made Charles's Master of the Games. Contemporary documents offer us glimpses of him – being placed on the government committee for colonisation in 1607, accompanying Prince Henry to the naval dockyard at Chatham, discussing shipping matters with Vice-Admiral Sir Robert Mansell, participating in tourneys, officiating at the funerals of Henry and his mother, and attending the King on his autumnal forays on to the heathland and fens of Hertfordshire, Cambridgeshire and Huntingdonshire.

Initially, James's decision to revisit Hinchingbrooke must have been a matter of intense pride and satisfaction to Sir Oliver and when the King intimated that he liked the estate and the sport it provided so much that he planned to return often, the courtier knew that he was being uniquely privileged; no other subject entertained James under his roof on so frequent a basis. From the beginning of the reign Hinchingbrooke figured regularly in the court's autumn and winter itinerary. The King was delighted at the quantity and variety of game available for slaughter and was determined to devote several months of the year to the pleasures of the chase. He convinced himself (without, one imagines, any difficulty) that this was good for his health and therefore beneficial to his people.[10] Within months of his accession he exchanged the royal palace at Hatfield with Robert Cecil, Lord Salisbury, for Theobalds near Cheshunt on the edge of the fine hunting country of Enfield Chase. The following year he bought Sir Robert Chester's house at Royston (but never actually got round to paying him) and extended it into a commodious but rambling mansion. He similarly built a hunting box at Newmarket. Thereafter the annual ritual seldom varied. The court left the capital in October and, over the next four or five months progressed in a leisurely fashion via Theobalds, Royston, Hinchingbrooke, Newmarket and Theobalds again back to London. Thus, the royal court used the resources of royal estates – except when staying at Hinchingbrooke.

This regular imposition of the King and his household upon a wealthy subject was quite without precedent. Elizabeth had habitually progressed around royal manors close to the capital and had occasionally been the guest of leading courtiers or councillors; she would not have dreamed of ruining one of her loyal followers by eating him out of house and home every year. This is exactly what James did to Sir Oliver. Feeding, entertaining and accommodating the royal party put enormous strains on the Cromwell finances. In the early years of the reign, as we have seen, the host fared well from Stuart bounty and the settlement of the Palavicino debt, but this gradually changed. Initially, James was intoxicated with his inheritance of a wealthy kingdom, he was profligate with grants and sinecures. When painful experience and the representations of his financial officers brought home to him the true state of his treasury he was obliged to curb his generosity. He still enjoyed showering gifts on a favoured few but Sir Oliver Cromwell was not of their number. Doubtless court gossip and jealousy were partly responsible for this. Moneylenders are never popular and Sir Oliver will have taken over some of Palavicino's reputation with his widow. Then there was the Cromwell ostentation. First impressions are important and Sir Oliver and his father had presented themselves in 1603 as subjects who lived in almost kingly state. As James and his courtiers annually ransacked the Hinchingbrooke larder and cellars they may well have reflected that the Cromwells could afford it. And there may have been another reason why the King became reluctant to offer material reward for Sir Oliver's faithful service. At the beginning of the next reign royal officials were sent to examine the Palavicino deal (see below, p. 181ff). Then, the ugly word 'fraud' was muttered around the court. If suspicions had begun circulating earlier that the financial dealings between the Cromwells and the Crown were not entirely above board James would certainly have been reluctant to pour good money after bad.

Yet, having to provision and staff Hinchingbrooke for the annual pleasure of the cormorant court was not Sir Oliver's only problem: James, quite literally, treated the estate as his own. He made no distinction between Hinchingbrooke and the other residences where he stayed on progress. He regarded as his royal demesne land all the territory he crossed during the autumn and winter months. He was the King indulging ancient kingly pursuits; everything must be ready for his sport and comfort. Warnings went out of dire penalties for anyone caught snaring or shooting game. Farm workers were instructed not to deep-plough their fields because this made hard going for the hunters' horses. Scores of animals and wagons were requisitioned in the localities every time the court moved on. Accommodation had to be found everywhere for the small army of courtiers, servants and hangers-on. A group of Royston citizens once hit upon a novel way of bringing their grievances anonymously to the King's attention. They abducted one of the royal harriers, called Jowler, and released him into the pack during the next day's hunt with this note tied to his collar:

Good Mr Jowler, we pray you speak to the king (for he hears you every day and so doth he not us) that it will please his majesty to go back to London, for else the country will be undone. All our provision is spent already and we are not able to entertain him any longer.[11]

Hinchingbrooke felt the burden of Stuart imperiousness no less than other manors. As early as October 1605 James was keeping such a large store of clothes and chattels there that he had to appoint one William Meredith as 'keeper of the Wardrobe in the Manor of Hinchingbrooke for life'.[12] In July 1620 he had a bridge built in the vicinity of the estate so that his entourage would not be held up by a swollen river.[13] The following year he ordered Sir Oliver to kill pheasants in the outwoods but leave those in the park for his own sport.[14] Small wonder that in 1622 a courtier could report, 'The king is at Hinchingbrooke, which *was* Sir Oliver Cromwell's.'[15]

There must have been some local people who benefited from the regular visits of the court to Huntingdon – merchants, innkeepers, contracted suppliers of meat and grain, and the like – but the dominant reaction was fairly negative. The visitors disrupted farming patterns, turned muddy highways into impossible roads, commandeered bedchambers and made other arrogant demands (150–200 post horses were requisitioned from Huntingdon and nearby villages every time the household moved) and introduced to rural society the lax morals of the court. Yet, more significant than all this was the loss of the Crown's mystique. In and around Huntingdon the ungainly figure of the King was very familiar and it was very difficult for anyone who had seen James Stuart to hold him in awe, especially if he suffered indignities at the hands of some of the King's camp followers. In the crisis of the 1640s Charles I discovered that very few people in the lands where he had hunted since boyhood were prepared to take his side on the field of battle. Prominent among the few who did support him were Sir Oliver Cromwell and his sons, for despite all he suffered at the hands of the Stuarts, the old courtier remained stubbornly loyal to them.

To be fair to James his outrageous exploitation was not the only reason for Sir Oliver's decline. As well as royal favour, the squire of Hinchingbrooke had built his hopes upon the Palavicino fortune. Unfortunately, this goose was not very prolific with golden eggs. First of all the Cromwells had to cope with an expensive lawsuit. On his second marriage Sir Horatio had disinherited Edward, his son and heir by his first wife. The young man now challenged this in the courts and the Cromwells were obliged to agree to an expensive settlement. Sir Oliver continued to enjoy the income from the bulk of the Palavicino estates for several years, until Henry, the elder boy, came of age in 1613 and took over the management of his own inheritance. He died childless within two years and his property passed to his brother. Their sister, Baptina, expired three years later and was followed to the grave by her infant daughter. This left only Tobias. Had he joined his siblings in the afterlife the greater part of the Palavicino fortune would have reverted to his mother. Not only did the young man fail to oblige, he set about running through his inheritance at an alarming speed. He took his wife to London, bought a magnificent mansion and, for a few years, enjoyed to the full an extravagant social life. By 1624 he was driven to the expediency of securing an Act of Parliament to enable him to sell his estates and so meet his mounting debts. Thus, one by one, the Palavicino lands were placed on the market. When all were gone, Sir Oliver had the mortification of having to receive his poverty-stricken daughter, Joan, and her four children back at Hinching-brooke while her husband was confined to the Fleet. The family chronicler later moralised, 'Such is the precarious tenure of wealth in families, especially when gained by injustice, extortion and usury.'[16]

It was a sentiment Oliver Cromwell would have firmly endorsed at a later stage of his life. He became scrupulous in money matters. Once he sought out an old acquaintance in order to repay cash that, in his unregenerate days, he had won in a wager. But in the early years what impressions were formed in his mind by the royal court and by his uncle's way of life? It is scarcely conceivable that he did not spend time with his wealthy Palavicino cousins. Of all the Hinchingbrooke children they were closest to him in age. Their playthings would have been better than Oliver's own; their fine home with its extensive grounds offered much more scope for hide-and-seek and other games than the house in Huntingdon High Street. The annual arrival of the Whitehall circus must have been an exciting and welcome break from the routine of lessons and the chattering of his sisters. Then as he grew up, becoming aware of local resentments, salacious court gossip and the stresses and strains of Hinchingbrooke he began to understand more of the complexities of the relationships between the King and his subjects. How he reacted we have no means of knowing but one fact is very clear: from his earliest days he was familiar with the court and that familiarity did not breed respect.

There were other kindred influences which encouraged him to question the unstinting devotion to the King of the Hinchingbrooke

Cromwells. Not all members of the wider family shared the unquestioning loyalty of the head of the family. Oliver had other uncles, aunts and cousins from whom he heard different messages. When Sir Henry, the Golden Knight, arranged marriages for his daughters he was certainly not looking to ally his family with any caucus of radically inclined gentlemen; his concerns were economic and social. He sought out husbands who were substantial men in the shires and had useful court connections. So it is remarkable that four of his five daughters entered families that were increasingly critical and discontented with Stuart rule and were prominent in the parliamentary opposition in the 1640s. Elizabeth married Sir William Hampden, a very wealthy gentleman of Buckinghamshire, and, in 1594, gave birth to a son, John, who early in life showed evidence of that scholarship and firmness of character which made him one of the lead players in the constitutional crisis of the 1640s and won him the respect of friend and foe alike. The Hampdens were associates and close neighbours of the Ingoldsbys of Lenthenborough, Buckinghamshire, and Cromwell ties with these clans were strengthened when Sir Oliver's eldest daughter, Elizabeth, married Sir Richard Ingoldsby, a loyal gentleman who served as sheriff of his county and was made a Knight of the Bath at Hinchingbrooke in 1617. However, her second son, Richard, who was knighted on the same occasion as his father, later served Parliament in John Hampden's regiment and was among those who signed Charles I's death warrant. Another name to appear on that historic document was that of Colonel Edward Whalley and he was the son of another of Sir Henry's daughters, Frances, by Richard Whalley, a prominent Nottinghamshire gentleman. Oliver's Aunt Mary was the wife of Sir William Dunch of Little Wittenham, Berkshire. Her eldest son, Edward, served as MP for Wallingford in the reign of Charles I and was known as 'a strenuous advocate for the liberty of the subject' who suffered 'very great and severe hardships from the court'.[17] In 1648 Dunch was among those who clamoured for the King's death.

The most influential kith-and-kin group in the early life of Oliver Cromwell was what we may call the 'Barrington-St John Circle'. Of all the marriages the Golden Knight arranged for his children, that of Joan was the most prestigious. Sir Francis Barrington came of an ancient Hertfordshire family and owned extensive Essex estates which he managed from his principal residence, Tofts, in Great

Baddow, near Chelmsford. He was among the first to be honoured by the new King, receiving a knighthood during James's southern progress in 1603. When, eight years later, he was awarded a baronetcy he outranked his brother-in-law, Sir Oliver. Barrington moved in aristocratic circles, being particularly close to the Riches, Earls of Warwick and Holland, who became leaders of opposition to the Crown in the House of Lords. Lady Barrington seems to have taken a great interest in her nephews and nieces and certainly Oliver stayed in her London house at least once during his teenage years. There he came to know his cousins, Thomas and Elizabeth Barrington, who were older than him, and he may well have come into contact with Elizabeth's husband, Sir James Altham, a baron of the exchequer. Altham was another Essex gentleman whose father had surged upwards from the London mercantile ranks to become sheriff of both the City and the county. The younger Altham had carved out an impressive legal career and was one of the first judges to stand up to the King when, in 1610–11, issues of prerogative were raised once again. James, desperate for money, had set his ministers to exploit to the full all possible means of raising revenue by proclamation. On two separate occasions Altham was among the leading justices to challenge these proceedings: 'the King hath no prerogative but that which the law of the land allows him,' they insisted. James was furious, summoned the judges to his presence and made them kneel before him while he lectured them on the law and their loyalty to the Crown. Their nerve broke under this browbeating and all except one humbly confessed their error, but they remembered their humiliation – and so did others. Sir James was considerably older than his wife and, in 1617, he left her a widow. Her second husband was yet another member of the Essex elite, Sir Francis Masham, Bart, of Higher Laver, Harlow.

Elizabeth's brother, Sir Thomas Barrington, served as an MP throughout the reigns of James and Charles and was one of the leaders of parliamentary opposition to the government. As early as 1629 he was summoned before the Council to answer for 'disloyal' words but he continued to make a nuisance of himself and to be at the centre of a growing group of dissident Essex and London noblemen and gentlemen.

After the death of Sir Francis in 1628, Lady Barrington went to live with the Mashams. Their household was a centre of evangelical Christianity. Sir William's chaplain, a certain Roger Williams, recently graduated from Pembroke, Cambridge, came from a London mercantile family and was a distant relative of the Cromwells. More to the point, he was a religious extremist who refused to accept preferments because he disliked Church of England ceremonial. Williams went further: he either believed then or came to believe that the established Church was positively anti-Christian because it imposed upon men's consciences certain practices and articles of faith from which individuals should be free to dissent. In later years Williams became a campaigner for toleration, which he even extended to Jews. This young radical was not the only Puritan minister to enjoy Masham patronage. A certain Hugh Peters (Oliver Cromwell's contemporary at Cambridge) was touring Essex as a travelling preacher and was listened to with approval by Sir William and his friends. As the New Model Army's most ardent chaplain Peters later became one of the most admired and hated men in the land and suffered a barbarous death in 1660 at the hands of vengeful royalists. We can gain some idea of the burden of Peter's preaching in the 1620s from a sermon he preached in the middle of the Civil War. Looking back to the earlier period he averred,

> Those former days . . . were a seed-time of our misery; for most true it is that the seeds of the ruin of estates and commonwealth are sown in the days of their greatest prosperity . . . Oh, call those ill times, when a base messenger from a proud prelate could . . . stop the mouths of the most godly ministers, that the best nobleman here could not enjoy the worship of God freely, and hardly his Bible without reproach.[18]

Peters and Williams, whom Cromwell employed variously in later years, must first have come to his attention through the Masham circle.

Yet there were even closer links. One involved the St John family. Relations between the St Johns and the Cromwells had remained cordial. The Lord-Lieutenancy of Huntingdonshire remained in the St John family, which ensured that Sir Oliver had frequent meetings with the King's representative. It was natural that his nephew should become a close companion of a namesake in the Bedfordshire family who was his exact contemporary. Oliver St John (1598–1673), like Oliver Cromwell, was a poor relative. He belonged to a cadet branch of the baronial family and knew what it was to have to work and study hard with no prospect of a large inherited fortune. He and Oliver Cromwell were undergraduates together at Cambridge and both went on to Lincoln's Inn. (See below pp. 114ff.) St John chose a legal profession and was retained as family advocate by the Earl of Bedford, to whom he was distantly related and who, in the 1640s, became 'the great contriver and designer in the House of Lords' against King Charles.[19] But the lawyer first came to public attention in 1637 when he defended John Hampden in the famous Ship Money case which made a major national issue of the Crown's prerogative right.

In the mid-1620s St John contracted an advantageous marriage. Because of his small estate it was only brought about after much difficult negotiating and the intervention of Lord Bedford. His bride was Joanna, the granddaughter of Sir Francis and Lady Barrington. The marriage was not destined to be of lengthy duration; St John became a widower after about ten years. It was not long before the redoubtable Lady Barrington came to his aid. When her brother, Henry Cromwell of Upwood, had died in 1630 he had left two orphan daughters Elizabeth (fourteen) and Anne (twelve). They were taken into the Masham household and their aunt shouldered the responsibility of bringing them up within the evangelical faith and also of finding suitable husbands for them. Thus it came about that after the death of her granddaughter, Joanna St John, she arranged a contract between Oliver St John and young Elizabeth Cromwell and the wedding was celebrated in January 1638.

Yet, there was one more tie between Oliver Cromwell and the Barrington-St John circle: he met his own wife through it. Elizabeth Bourchier was the daughter of Sir James Bourchier, a wealthy London furrier. He was related to the Barringtons and had an estate near Felsted. Oliver later sent his own sons to Felsted School thanks to the influence of the Mashams and, perhaps, the Earl of Warwick, who was a major patron of that establishment.

It is now clear that the boy who grew up in a modest home in a quiet country town was very far from being isolated from major national events. Through his own family he was familiar with members of the royal household and those who supported and relied on the Stuarts, and through his own family he was in contact with one of the focuses of mounting discontent.[20] On the one side was Sir Oliver, a steadfast member of Prince Charles's entourage. On the other side were Sir Francis Barrington, Sir William Masham, Sir

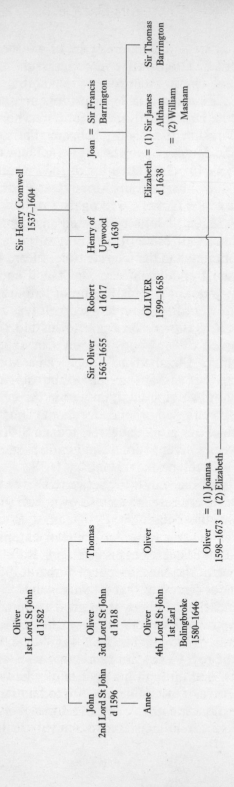

CONNECTIONS BETWEEN THE FAMILIES
OF ST JOHN AND CROMWELL

Edward Hampden and John Hampden who found themselves in trouble in 1627 for refusing the King a forced loan.

He was also, through his Essex friends, in touch with a more momentous movement. Evangelical Christianity in England spanned a wide range of belief and action united in commitment to the Bible, adherence to Calvinist doctrine and abhorrence at what was seen as the moral decadence of contemporary society but differing widely on the divinely ordained way of furthering the Kingdom of God. There was a growing number of men and women who had abandoned all hope of restoring the established Church to anything resembling the New Testament pattern and who brought varying degrees of persecution upon themselves by setting up their own separatist congregations. This movement coincided with the growth of American colonisation. Noble and mercantile backers of settlement schemes had a variety of motives for seeking charters and pouring venture capital into New World enterprises: personal aggrandisement, commercial calculation and fervent imperialism all played their part. However, when the speculators sought reliable pioneers to occupy and develop their overseas concessions it was to earnest, radical Christians that they tended to look rather than to landless and footloose younger sons of the gentry and men who were seeking to put behind them earlier failed business enterprises. Whatever their own convictions (and some were undoubtedly convinced evangelicals), they naturally supported members of the 'elect' whose vision and sense of divine purpose were likely to sustain them through the appalling hardships they would certainly encounter during the early years of coping with an unfamiliar and at times hostile environment.

The leading noble patrons of colonial enterprise were Francis Russell, Earl of Bedford, his son-in-law Robert Greville, Baron Brooke, William Fiennes, Viscount Saye and Sele – dubbed by Clarendon 'the oracle of those who were called puritans in the worst sense and steered all their counsels and designs'[21] – Robert Rich, Earl of Warwick and his brother Henry, Earl of Holland. These were the men to whom religious radicals looked for support when seeking preferment or protection from persecution. In 1640 a friend complained to Archbishop Laud, 'The Earl of Warwick is the temporal head of the Puritans, and the Earl of Holland is their spiritual; or rather, the one is their visible and the other their invisible head.'[22] The motivations of such prominent men in extending patronage to a group of Christians so unpopular at court were undoubtedly mixed. They certainly (Warwick especially) did not allow their association with narrow exponents of holiness to impinge too severely on their private lives, but their support of the vigorous radical minority was reflected in their parliamentary opposition to the Crown; they emerged in the 1620s as the leaders of the anti-court party in the Lords.

At the same time the colonial movement was gathering momentum. The *Mayflower* sailed in 1620 and despite the appalling hardship suffered by the Plymouth settlers other groups of beleaguered evangelicals seriously considered following their example. It seemed to them that episcopal persecution, backed by the King, had almost eschatological significance. One of them, Thomas Dudley, was convinced that 'God will bring some heavy affliction upon this land' and that he had provided New England 'to be a refuge for many whom he means to save out of the general calamity'. In August 1629 a group of Lord Saye and Sele's protégés, including John Winthrop, Thomas Dudley and John Cotton met at Cambridge to plan a transatlantic venture. The result was the Massachusetts Bay Co. which, the next year, despatched to America the largest contingent of colonists who had yet left English shores. Lord Saye and Sele pulled out of the venture because he had no liking for the company's egalitarian constitution. Instead, he turned to his aristocratic friends and with them floated two other projects. With Lord Brooke, John Hampden and others he obtained a patent for a colony on the Connecticut River, to be named Sayebrook, and appointed John Winthrop Jnr as its first governor. He also joined the Providence Island Co. to populate Rhode Island. His fellow patentees included Lord Warwick, Lord Holland, Lord Brooke, Lord Bedford, Sir Thomas Barrington, Oliver St John and John Hampden. In 1630 Roger Williams crossed the Atlantic to seek a more congenial and tolerant environment. He did not discover it until 1635, when, having upset the authorities in other colonies in the area with his extremist views, he joined the growing settlement at Providence. With all these connections it is not at all surprising that Oliver Cromwell should seriously consider emigration as a possibility, as we know he did on at least one occasion.

By 1620 profound changes were affecting the social and political life of Huntingdonshire. New men were being advanced to positions of authority. Old families were fading away. The previous year the old custom of having two Lords-Lieutenant was revived so that one of the King's favourites could be given an extra dignity. Esmé Stuart, Seigneur d'Aubigny and his elder brother, Ludovick, were the sons of James's erstwhile friend, and on their father's death the Scottish king had taken personal charge of their welfare. After James's accession to the English throne they were brought to reside at court and were showered with lands and offices. Among the perquisites which fell to Esmé was marriage to a rich heiress, Katherine Clifton, whose family lands were at Leighton Broms-wold, a mere six miles from Huntingdon. It was he who was made Lord-Lieutenant alongside Baron St John (who continued to do the bulk of the work connected with the office).

This intrusion of court life into rural affairs was not popular locally but it did not have to be borne for long; Esmé died suddenly in 1624. The man who took his place was the head of one of the new families. Sir Henry Montagu was a leading figure in Northamptonshire and a London judge who had succeeded spectacularly in the scramble to win the favour of the new King at the beginning of the reign. He received his knighthood within months, was an MP for London in 1604 and enjoyed a meteoric rise through the professional ranks. In 1606 he entered Huntingdonshire life with the purchase of Kimbolton. One of the in jokes about the court at the end of 1620 was that wood was dear in Newmarket, for it was there that Montagu received from James his staff as Lord Treasurer, an office for which he paid £20,000. Not surprisingly, in the developing constitutional debate he showed himself to be a king's man through and through and was a trusted adviser to both Stuart sovereigns who, by degrees, raised him to the earldom of Manchester (1626). By purchase and royal grant the family added to their landholdings in Huntingdon-shire and Cambridgeshire and his elevation to the Lord-Lieutenancy signalled to the local populace that a new era had arrived.

Another sign was the decline of the Cromwells. For some years Sir Oliver had been selling parcels of land in a bid to maintain his position in court and county. This was now falling from his grasp. The Montagus were casting covetous eyes on Hinchingbrooke and Sir Oliver's appeals to the King went unheeded. Possibly his family connections with disaffected gentry soured his relations with the King. Perhaps in a changing political situation the government wanted to have effective and loyal servants in the administration of the shires. Whatever the reason for Sir Oliver's change of fortune it was obvious that the reign which had begun so splendidly for the Cromwells was destined to end in their humiliation. This was a state of affairs which profoundly affected the generation just emerging into maturity – the generation to which Oliver Cromwell belonged.

The most obvious difference – and perhaps ultimately the most important – between the families of Oliver Cromwell and Charles Stuart was size. Charles had no network of aunts, uncles and cousins, no blood relatives of the same age with whom to play and become involved in childhood escapades, no other Stuart homes where he might stay and absorb different influences or discover confidants with whom to discuss those matters a young man cannot talk about with his parents. His early years, like the rest of his life, were spent amongst servants and favourites, men and women who were not his equals and whose position depended on maintaining the goodwill of the prince. Charles did have an older brother and sister and he loved both of them dearly. When he was twelve years old they were both taken suddenly from him, one by death and the other by marriage. He did have two younger siblings, Robert and Mary, but they died in infancy before Charles had the chance to form any kind of relationship with them. The survival rate in the Huntingdon household was better than that in the royal nursery. Death was no respecter of princes and princesses. Charles inherited the self-concentrated loneliness that for generations had been part of the Stuart spiritual treasury.

He was born on 19 November 1600 and throughout his early years it was feared, even expected, that infant mortality would claim him as it had already claimed one elder sister. He was put to a wet nurse and his day-to-day care entrusted to chosen guardians while his parents got on with their social and political responsibilities. When James, his wife and their other children travelled to London in the spring of 1603, Charles was left behind. He was not far short of his fourth birthday when he was eventually brought south to be reunited with his family. He apparently suffered from rickets during his first years, for a doctor's report in 1604 stated that he had difficulty standing and walking because he was 'so weak in his joints and especially his ankles, insomuch as many feared they were out of joint'.[23] So low was his constitution that he frequently suffered from fevers and was a prey to whatever viruses were around.

The care of a sickly royal prince was a heavy responsibility and we can be in no doubt that Charles was treated with nervous care by those who had charge of him, as though he were made of fragile Venetian glass. The boy was not starved of affection. After his parents' departure he was brought up in the household of Alexander Seton, Baron Fyvie, a grandfatherly figure whose three marriages had resulted in nine surviving daughters and one son. It is interesting to note that, like Cromwell, Charles knew what it was to live in an all-female household. Doubtless the young Fyvie girls fussed over their baby 'brother' while their parents took all available advice about the boy's wellbeing, from old wives' tales to the seldom more efficacious latest medical theories. However, nothing could make up for the lack of parental love in these crucial months. Charles knew that the mother and father whom he could scarcely remember were away in another country which might as well have been another planet, and reports sent to London told of his longing to be reunited with them.

It is not surprising, given the child's physical and emotional problems, that he was a slow developer. By the age of three and a half he could neither walk nor talk properly. A doctor appointed by King James and wishing to put the best gloss on the prince's constitution reported that he had walked the length of Dunfermline Castle's great hall unaided. Charles's bones were still brittle and this fact impeded his growth. In manhood he stood no more than five feet four inches. That was not tiny by the standards of the day but it certainly did not allow him to exert authority by sheer physical presence. His speech defect was dysphemia – stammering or stuttering – a disability he never fully conquered. At the close of the twentieth century clinicians still disagree about the causes of this disorder. Four hundred years ago conventional methods of treatment ranged from exorcism to cutting the tongue's chord (a drastic remedy favoured by James) but then, as now, progress in overcoming the defect lies primarily in the determination of the sufferer.

Willpower was something Charles never lacked and its seeds were sown in his earliest years. Sir Philip Warwick, who knew the future king in later life, observed, 'though born weakly yet came [he] through temperance and exercise to have as firm and strong a body as that of most persons I ever knew.'[24] Some of his guardians regarded the young prince as stubborn and self-willed. There were instances of him throwing violent tantrums and, as young as three or four, resolutely refusing to allow doctors to examine him. Charles's childhood experiences bred in him an inflexible resolution and self-discipline. Embarrassing afflictions often have that effect. Charles was neither the first nor the last for whom the desire to conquer a speech impediment has proved the spur to a prominent public career. His developing view of himself and the world was of a cosmos in which he was the centre of attention (especially from doctors), in which no one dealt firmly with his fits of petulance, in which he had to work especially hard to do many of the things natural to children of his age and in which, despite having a corps of carers, he was essentially on his own. Long before the possibility emerged that he would one day have to rule a kingdom he learned to rule himself or, at least, to practise a rigid self-control in order to achieve the things he desired.

When he was brought to London in the autumn of 1604 Charles was not to find himself embraced within a warm, united and loving family. There were tensions and conflicts which could not be wholly explained by the fact that his father, mother, brother and sister all had their own establishments and lived lives semi-detached from each other. Whitehall Palace was the centre of their existence but it was the mere hub of the Stuart wheel. There James conducted the business of government, received ambassadors and petitioners and caroused with his friends. But he spent several months of the year on tour around royal hunting lodges and the houses of wealthy subjects in the home counties. Queen Anne also enjoyed travelling but the pleasures she avidly pursued differed from her husband's. She was seen by would-be protégés, and saw herself, as the natural successor to Elizabeth, the goddess queen. The cult of Gloriana was developed into a masculine version for the new King but it was difficult to cast the ungainly James in a heroic, semi-divine role, whereas the lovely and vivacious Anne was easily portrayed as Ben Jonson's Oriana. The Queen became an extravagant patroness of painters, dramatists, architects and set designers of court masques. The blossoming of the arts and the profusion of new ideas conventionally labelled 'Jacobean' might more justly be honoured with the name of Queen Anne (and also with that of Prince Henry). The settings for Anne's circle were Somerset House (later Denmark House) which she had completely redesigned, Hampton Court, Oatlands in Surrey where she had a gallery of largely religious pictures, and Greenwich. Her cultural tours extended even further from the capital. In Bristol, for example, after a visit in 1613, she sponsored a company of actors.

Prince Henry shared his mother's love of the visual arts but the ménage he gathered around himself was of quite a different order. His Westminster apartments were at St James's Palace and his favourite out-of-town residences Richmond (where he planned to build, but did not live to carry out, the first new royal palace since the days of Henry VIII), and Nonesuch the Renaissance extravaganza of Henry VIII which inspired the prince's architectural vision. In these settings Henry settled to the serious business of training himself to become both an ideal Protestant king and an *uomo universale*. He acquired the second-best library in England, surrounded himself with scientists and littérateurs, experts in navigation and cosmography, drawing masters, mathematicians and theologians, while to St James's Park were brought a variety of exotic birds and animals.

Until December 1608 Princess Elizabeth was even farther removed from her family. Her upbringing was assigned to John, Baron Harington and his wife, Anne, who created for her an establishment at Coombe Abbey, near Coventry. Here the princess was tutored in those skills necessary for her future role as a foreign queen: languages, the arts and courtly graces. When, at the age of twelve, she became eligible for the marriage market she was allowed to rejoin the royal household and was given her own quarters at Whitehall. But, like Henry, she too had to be provided with her own residences and mini-court. Thus she spent most of the summer and autumn months each year at Kew or in her own suite at Hampton Court.

However, the rifts within the family were emotional as well as topographical. There was, indeed, nothing odd about the farming-out of children of royal and noble households. Placing sons and daughters in other families to learn the refinements of upper-class life was quite customary and in the case of princes and princesses it made sense from the point of view of security – and James was, understandably, paranoid in his fear of assassination and kidnap. The fragmentation of the family would not by itself have created strident disharmonies. Anne and James had a relationship that had broken down and was, in fact, only rendered tolerable by their long periods apart, even though they kept up appearances in public. There must have been many reasons for their growing alienation, as there are for the failure of any marriage. Husband and wife had changed since

1589 when James, a dashing suitor, had rushed impulsively to Copenhagen to bring back in person his teenage bride. Having fulfilled his responsibility in siring sons, James allowed his homosexuality to reassert itself, so that the emotional side of the relationship rapidly cooled. Personality traits, ignored in the early days, had become mutually irritating with the passage of time. Each partner had the necessary wealth and freedom to develop separate interests. As love waned, James and Anne were less disposed to compromise for the sake of marital harmony and even deliberately engaged in behaviour they knew would irritate the other. The Queen's extravagance was a constant irritation to her husband. So was her religion. Brought up as a Lutheran, Anne found Scottish Calvinism abhorrent and the liturgy of the Church of England scarcely less so. Whether or not she was accepted into the Roman Catholic faith remains an unresolved question, though she certainly renounced it on her deathbed. What is beyond dispute is that for most of her married life she maintained with the religion abominated by most Englishmen a relationship which went well beyond 'flirtation'. She kept a mass priest at Oatlands, refused to worship with her husband, attempted to engineer Catholic marriages for her children and frequently interceded on behalf of 'papists'. As for James's conduct, by the age of fifty, he was almost totally lacking, not only in regal dignity, but also in finesse. By turns pompously censorious and vulgarly buffoonish, he was regarded by many as a figure of fun. He had become bored even with the semblance of marital fidelity and took no trouble to conceal his preference for young men.

After the birth in 1606 of Princess Sophia, who survived only a few hours, sexual relations between James and Anne came to an end. It is unlikely that this abstinence was agreed upon out of consideration for the Queen's health. Seventeenth-century wives were expected to be available to their husbands at all times and to go on bearing babies as long as they were able to do so. If a woman died as a result of childbed complications it was usual for the widower to replace her with as little delay as possible to increase the chance of the line's survival into the next generation. It was around this time that James formed an attachment for Robert Carr, a comely young man of about nineteen, newly returned from France, who possessed that combination of Scottish forthrightness and Gallic refinement that James found particularly attractive. Carr's appeal also rested on the fact that his family was close to that of Esmé Stuart. No one now could forbid James the company of a friend and lover and the recklessness with which he threw himself into the relationship with his new favourite suggests a gesture of defiance against Fate for depriving him of d'Aubigny. Carr's achievement of wealth, titles and influence over the King was rapid. By 1616 he was Viscount Rochester, master of wide estates and the virtual arbiter of royal policy. No marriage could survive such an intrusion unimpaired.

It is impossible to disentangle cause and effect in the disintegration of this relationship but one tap root that can be identified is Anne's frustrated maternalism. The first major dispute between Anne and James occurred before they left Scotland and was over the custody of Henry. James entrusted the prince to the care of John Erskine, Earl of Mar. Anne was distraught at the prospect of his being sent away and, as soon as her husband left on his journey to London, she demanded that Mar hand her son over and became so agitated by his refusal that she miscarried. She vented her spleen to James in writing, accusing him of preferring his favourites to his own queen. His eirinic reply reveals a patient husband trying to calm a highly strung wife:

> God is my witness I ever preferred you to all my bairns, much more than to any subject; but if you will ever give place to the reports of every flattering sycophant that will persuade you that when I account well of an honest and wise servant for his true faithful service to me, that it is to compare or prefer him to you, then will neither you or I be ever at rest [or] peace . . . [25]

It seems they seldom were. Anne was quick to take offence and James seldom slow to give it. Poor Henry sometimes became caught in the crossfire. In 1509 the sixteen-year-old prince was only too painfully aware of the clashing temperaments of his parents:

> According to your Majesty's commandment I made your excuse unto the queen for not sending her a token by me, and alleged your Majesty had a quarrel unto her for not writing an answer unto your second letter written from Royston when your foot was sore . . . Her answer was either she *had* written or dreamed it . . . I durst not reply that your Majesty was afeared lest she should return to her old bias, for fear that such a word might have set her in the way and made me a peace breaker . . . [26]

In the walking-on-eggshells atmosphere of the royal household the children's sympathies and affections tended to lie with their mother. Inevitably, there was animosity between the heir to the throne and the King's favourite. As Carr's influence grew, Henry's household at St James's took on the appearance of a rival court. Even before Carr's appearance there had been little love lost between father and son. Henry found the moral tone of James's court offensive. The prince was passionately committed to an extreme form of Protestantism and espoused strict moral values. His attendants were expected to listen to sermons regularly and were fined if they swore in his presence. Those who hoped for great things when the prince should succeed to the throne often repeated the ditty:

> Henry VIII pulled down abbeys and cells
> But Henry IX shall pull down bishops and bells.

He found himself increasingly at odds with his father both because of the behaviour James encouraged at court and the hostility he showed to Puritans. Henry loved court revels and masques and enthusiastically joined in these elevated amateur theatricals, as did his siblings. What embarrassed and outraged him was the excesses that often accompanied them, such as his mother being made up as a blackamoor with breasts almost completely exposed, his father incoherent with drink, the entire court throwing food about like ill-behaved children and indulging in orgiastic behaviour quite *unlike* children. The King, for his part, was jealous of his son, for Henry – tall, athletic, assiduous at study, if not of high intellectual calibre, and enormously popular – was always being contrasted with himself, making him feel like an understudy on stage with the star waiting in the wings.

James was ever the hectoring schoolmaster to his children and, having had no fatherly role model himself, experienced the greatest difficulty in relating appropriately to them. A Venetian visitor to the court reported the following contretemps between James and his twelve-year-old heir.

> . . . one day the king, after giving him a lecture, said that if he did not attend more earnestly to his lessons the crown would be left to his brother, the Duke of York, who was far quicker at learning and studied more earnestly. The prince made no reply, out of respect for his father;

74

but when he went to his room and his tutor continued in the same vein, he said, 'I know what becomes a prince. It is not necessary for me to be a professor, but a soldier and man of the world. If my brother is as learned as they say, we'll make him Archbishop of Canterbury.' The king took this answer in no good part; nor is he overpleased to see his son so beloved and of such promise that his subjects place all their hopes in him; and it would almost seem, to speak quite frankly, that the king was growing jealous; and so the prince has great need of a wise counsellor to guide his steps.[27]

Such parental behaviour scarcely made for good relations between the royal brothers. The taunt that Charles was more fitted for an ecclesiastical career (probably true in historical hindsight) seems to have become a standing, cruel joke with Henry, for the only anecdote related about the boys tells of an occasion, a couple of years later, when Henry grabbed Archbishop Abbot's square cap from his head and plonked it on Charles's curls, saying that he would have his brother for archbishop when he was king.[28]

The contemporaries at the English court who observed and recorded the life of the royal family were, for the most part, foreign ambassadors and others who saw little more than the outward show put on for their benefit by the King and Queen and their children and who placed their own gloss on what they saw. Some of them stressed the emotional distance between Anne and her offspring and made much of those irritated outbursts which all mothers, particularly neurotic mothers, are prone to make from time to time. But the balance of evidence is that she was very fond of her children and found it difficult to take a back seat when important decisions about them were being made. For their part, they loved her. Her natural exuberance was infectious and they became Anne's willing confederates in planning entertainments. In one very particular respect the Queen had a considerable influence on both of her sons – she collected pictures. The fact is worthy of note because Anne was the first member of the English royal house to do so. Earlier sovereigns had bought and commissioned portraits to emphasise the importance of their ancestry and connections. They hung devotional works in their chapels, until the Reformation. Anne's collecting activities went beyond such utilitarianism. The walls of her homes were decorated with still-lifes, landscapes and allegorical scenes as well as portraits and religious subjects. Her delight in painting as in all the arts was complete and she passed it on to Henry and Charles, both of whom became connoisseurs and patrons. The few letters that survive give evidence of a warm, relaxed, good-humoured relationship between Charles and his mother. He called her his 'worthy mistress' and she him 'my little servant'. This relationship was much closer than the dutiful respect with which Charles approached his father.

James's attempt to hold up his younger son as an exemplar to Prince Henry probably signalled to the older boy that Charles was his favourite. Although not true in the sense that the King gave more of himself emotionally to Charles, the impression conveyed cannot have helped fraternal relationships. There was a gap of almost seven years between Henry and Charles, so that while the former was going through adolescence the latter was only his 'kid brother'. Add to this the fact of their long periods of physical separation and it becomes obvious that they never really got to know each other well. Charles's impressions of Prince Henry came as much from the idealised pictures painted by tutors and courtiers as from direct knowledge, and we can observe this adulation in the panegyrics of poets and the heroic paintings of the prince *à la chasse* or in martial pose. The result was that Charles idealised his brother and wanted nothing more than to model himself on him. The slights he received, or fancied he received, from Henry such as the taunt about being more suited to be an archbishop, drew from him bitter tears of humiliation and rejected affection. 'Sweet, sweet brother,' he wrote as a ten-year-old, 'I will give anything that I have to you, both my horses and my books and my [handguns] and my crossbows, or anything that you would have. Good brother, love me . . .'[29] At about the same time Henry's entourage abandoned the French style of dress in favour of the Italian, which the prince regarded as more modest and less prone to the rapidly changing dictates of fashion. Charles immediately ordered his suite to adopt the Italian mode also.

'Good brother, love me' – that heartbroken cry of a little boy is the key to the deeper recesses of Charles's personality. He had a desperate need for approval, recognition, affection. When he failed to find them he locked his vulnerability away in a steel-grey casket of reserve. Thereafter, he found relationships difficult, preferring to sublimate his emotions with works of art and intensely personal religious devotion. When he did find someone who seemed to value him, such as Buckingham or his queen, he clung to that someone with pathetic abandon. As king he wanted his people to love him and looked eagerly for proofs of their loyalty but when subjects rebelled against him he was so inured to rejection that he saw no necessity to ask himself what he might have done to alienate them.

The feelings on the other side – of Henry towards his brother – are best summed up in the one word offered by Sir Francis Bacon: 'indulgent'. Since he was the centre of so much adulatory attention, the focus of men's hopes for the future, and since no one took much notice of little Charles, the Prince of Wales could afford to adopt an attitude of affectionate tolerance. In two ways the brothers were very alike. The first was their taciturnity. Probably in reaction to the father who was brash and forever seeking to impress others with his wisdom, Henry and Charles were reserved about airing their opinions and also about showing their emotions. Their devotion to animals and to beautiful objects was the obverse side of their remoteness from people and their difficulty in making friends.

The second similarity lay in a striking exception to the first: there was one person to whom both boys were very attached – their sister. Elizabeth was two years younger than Henry and scarcely less popular. She represented for many the feminine side of idealised royalty, almost Henry's twin, and contemporaries noted the great bond between them. But Elizabeth also had affection for her younger brother and acted as a link between the two boys. There was much of Anne in Princess Elizabeth; she had her mother's fair hair, vivacity and strong passions. She was very happy with the Haringtons, whose son was Henry's dearest friend and constant companion, but found the diversions of the court equally enjoyable after her re-admission to her parents' circle at the end of 1608. She was able to spend her early teenage years in cultured idleness, charming all who came within her ambit and taking a keen interest in the young men from the royal houses of Europe who arrived to sue for her hand in marriage. The decision, of course, would not be hers. There were many suitors to choose from and many considerations, political and financial, to be borne in mind. Elizabeth's mother argued long and hard for a prestigious union with Philip III of Spain. Henry just as vigorously opposed any Catholic match. To the rival camps in Europe an English alliance was a valued prize and one fraught with weighty significance. To Elizabeth it was all a game of pageants and firework displays to be watched, and tourneys in which courageous young men did mock battle resplendent in heraldic blazon and proud plumes, and gifts of stunning jewels to be gasped over – and masques to be planned and participated in.

The masque, which reached its zenith in the early Stuart court and became a vital vehicle for projecting the mythology of Stuart kingship, was sycophancy raised to an art form.

> Melt earth to sea, sea flow to air,
>   And air fly into fire,
> Whilst we, in tunes, to Arthur's chair
>   Bear Oberon's desire;
>   Than which there nothing can be higher
> Save James, to whom it flies:
> But he the wonder is of tongues, of ears, of eyes.
>
> Who hath not heard, who hath not seen,
>   Who hath not sung his name?
> The soul that hath not, hath not been
>   But is the very same
>   With buried sloth and knows not fame,
> Which doth him best comprise:
> For he the wonder is of tongues, of ears, of eyes.

The panegyric from Jonson's *Oberon, the Fairy Prince*, presented and starred in by Henry in January 1611, is typical of the sentiments conveyed in this kind of Arcadian drama, the message being reinforced by luscious music, sumptuous costumes, vividly painted scenery and revolutionary stage effects achieved by elaborate machinery after the Italian fashion. The Queen and her children entered fully into these entertainments and Charles was, doubtless, involved as soon as he was able to perform a simple dance. The first reference to him as a 'masquer' dates from 1610 when he appeared as Zephyrus attended by a troop of diaphanously clad naiads in the celebrations marking Henry's induction as Prince of Wales. These family and court occasions were among his happiest early memories and were rendered especially poignant after the loss of his mother and siblings. Charles never abandoned his love of the masque.

Performed only for the royal family, the court and invited guests (except for the rare occasions when performances were staged on progress in noble houses), the masque was symptomatic of the

exuberant, luxurious but closed world in which Prince Charles grew
up. Critics regarded such divertissements, especially when they
degenerated into mayhem and licence, as signs of decadence and
conspicuous consumption. Francis Bacon, reluctantly including a
consideration of them in his collected essays complained, 'These
things are but toys, to come among such serious observations. But
yet, since princes will have such things, it is better they should be
graced with elegancy than daubed with cost,'[30] and he went on to
counsel economy and taste.

But they were more than costly amusements. The drama, in
various forms, had for half a century been a medium through which
leading courtiers and influential groups of citizens such as members
of the Inns of Court and the Corporation of London offered their
praises to the Sovereign and also made thinly veiled comments on
current political issues. What the Stuarts did was take over this art
form and use it for their own purposes. James arrived in England
with an exalted vision of two nations united as one (Britain) in
his person. Just how emotionally charged that vision was he
demonstrated in addressing his first Parliament:

> The second great blessing that God hath with my person sent unto you,
> is peace within, and that in a double form. First, by my descent lineally
> out of the loins of Henry the Seventh, is reunited and confirmed in me
> the union of the two princely Roses of the two Houses of Lancaster and
> York, whereof that king of happy memory was the first uniter, as he was
> also the first ground-layer of the other peace . . . But the union of these
> two princely houses, is nothing comparable to the union of two ancient
> and famous kingdoms, which is the other inward peace annexed to my
> person . . . What God hath conjoined then, let no man separate. I am the
> husband, and all the whole isle is my lawful wife; I am the head, and it
> is my body; I am the shepherd, and it is my flock; I hope therefore no
> man will be so unreasonable as to think that I that am a Christian king
> under the Gospel, should be a polygamist and husband to two wives;
> that I being the head, should have a divided and monstrous body . . .
> And as God hath made Scotland the one half of this isle to enjoy my
> birth, and the first and most unperfect half of my life, and you here to
> enjoy the perfect and last half thereof; so can I not think that any would
> be so injurious to me, no not in their thoughts and wishes, as to cut me
> asunder the one half of me from the other.[31]

A nationalistic House of Commons did not see things the same way. To the gentlemen and burgesses of England Scotland was still a foreign country and James a foreign king very much on approval. If they pinned their hopes more on the son than the father it was partly because of Henry's innate qualities and partly because of their belief that he could be thoroughly anglicised. For years James harangued and cajoled his parliaments. He commissioned books and set up preachers to disseminate his own ideas about kingship and union. They made little impact. But in the confines of his own court James could and did ensure that the Stuart way of empery was proclaimed as ardently and colourfully as possible. The overlapping circles of the royal households constituted a closed world where the young Charles, like a seminarist, was largely shielded from outside influences and, whether at work or play, fed an intellectual diet of paternalistic absolutism.

The man who had charge of Charles's upbringing in the early years was the pushy and self-important Sir Robert Carey. As the seventh son of a baron, Carey had been obliged to make his own way in the world. This he did by persistence, self-advertisement and the cultivation of influential men. By 1603, when he was in his early forties, Carey had become one of the principal members of the government of the Northern Marches. As soon as he heard that Queen Elizabeth's health was declining he sped south as fast as hired nags could carry him. Immediately the Sovereign had breathed her last, he was back on the Great North Road. Thanks to his foresight in arranging for fleet post horses, he reached Holyrood in sixty hours and was the first to bring James the news he had been longing for. His bold initiative was almost a serious miscalculation. He was castigated by the Council for conduct 'contrary to such commandments as we had power to lay upon him, and to all decency, good manners and respect'.[32] But someone as insensitive and ambitious as Robert Carey was not to be put off by a slap on the wrist by disgruntled councillors. By selling some of his lands he raised enough money to stay at court where he worked hard at pulling strings. He was not the kind of man to whom others readily warm but his wife was of a more kindhearted and outward-going disposition. Queen Anne took such a liking to her that she entrusted Charles to her keeping on the prince's arrival from Scotland. Charles took to Elizabeth Carey very readily and, trading on this, her husband engineered for himself the appointment as governor of the prince's household, in February 1605.

It is a testimony to Charles's loyalty and also to his poor judgement of character that he consistently supported Carey and rewarded the care he took over his upbringing. In 1611 the growing prince was allotted an increased entourage, one befitting a young gentleman, rather than a child. This involved a reshuffling of those who had attended him hitherto and Lady Carey ceased to have daily charge of the boy. Prince Henry took this opportunity to try to have the self-seeking Sir Robert removed from close attendance on his brother and to see him replaced by his friend, Sir James Fullerton. But even Henry was no match for so seasoned an intriguer as Carey. Charles was prevailed upon to ask for the retention of his old governor and Sir Robert became Chief Gentleman of the Bedchamber while Fullerton had to be content with a lesser position. Six years later, when Charles's entourage was reviewed on his becoming Prince of Wales, Carey once again had to fight for his position. This time Anne joined her son in supporting Sir Robert, as he smugly remarked in his *Memoirs*: 'Then did God raise up the Queen to take my part.'[33] He was now appointed the prince's chamberlain, with the title of Baron Leppington to support the dignity. One of Charles's earliest acts on becoming King was to reward Carey with the earldom of Monmouth and various valuable perquisites. In his favour towards this tedious, self-seeking nonentity (Carey devoted some of his increased leisure to composing his *Memoirs*), Charles showed himself to be very different from his father. James's neglect of faithful servants who did not naturally appeal to him was one of the often heard complaints in the corridors and anterooms of Whitehall. The case of Lord Harington provides an excellent contrast. His care of Princess Elizabeth brought him to financial ruin. Her extravagance regularly carried her expenditure beyond the limits of her allowance and Harington had to make up the difference. When he travelled on the continent with Elizabeth's suite after her marriage his expenses were never refunded and money worries contributed to his death in 1613. Harington lacked Carey's brazen importunity but there were probably other reasons for the King's outrageous neglect: the family was resolutely Protestant and was very close to Prince Henry. Sir Oliver Cromwell was not the only sufferer from James's pettiness.

Loyalty to friends and faithful servants was one of the most often remarked characteristics of Charles Stuart. It endeared to him many men and women, even some who did not share his political and religious views. Yet, when it came to *making* friends Charles was remarkably lacking. His shyness and diffidence prevented him taking the initiative in creating relationships. His awareness of being surrounded by flatterers made it difficult for him to repose complete trust in his companions. Men and women were admitted to Charles's confidence very much on his own terms and if his demeanour inspired devotion in some it certainly alienated others. His respect for the judgement of his parents and the awe in which he held his brother inclined him to accept their recommendations concerning those who should be admitted to his company. Everything we know about the prince's childhood and teenage years supports the view that his family was everything to him and that most of his time away from them was spent in solitary pursuits – study, collecting, horsemanship and mastering the arts appropriate to a royal prince like dancing, fencing and running at the ring. All reports of Charles's early years affirm such qualities as studiousness, solemnity, courtesy and emotional restraint. Yet many observers were aware that this was a mask. So little of his real thoughts and feelings did Charles reveal that royal watchers despaired of penetrating the enigma. 'He is either an extraordinary man or his talents are very mean,' the French ambassador reported. There is a world of difference between the quiet, well-behaved prince and the roisterous country boy plundering apple orchards with his friends.

Indeed, we are hard put to it to discover any bosom companions of Charles's early years or close associations which had their origins in childhood. James I seems to have made no serious attempt to anglicise his younger son, for the prince's household, like the royal court was well stocked with Scots. The young man who was deliberately brought in as a companion for Charles was William, the nephew of his tutor, Thomas Murray (see below p. 118). The two boys were close contemporaries and, throughout childhood and teenage, they studied and played together. They became close friends but Murray was later to find his sovereign's trust an oppressive burden. Like his uncle, Murray had strong Presbyterian sympathies. Through his family he had important connections with Church leaders in Scotland and it was natural that Charles should use him as an envoy. By this time Charles's episcopalianism had become indelibly stamped on his character but he did not understand that the ideological differences between himself and his friend made

Murray an unsafe repository of secrets. King Charles, who set so much store by his own conscience, had real difficulty in appreciating that someone else also had an ethical self which he should not be asked to compromise. Among other Scots who were at the centre of the royal entourage, the family of Esmé Stuart, Duke of Lennox, James's old flame, were very close to Charles. Three of Esmé's grandsons eventually gave their lives for their distant cousin in the Civil War but none of them was of the right age to share Charles's boyhood adventures; James, Esmé's oldest grandson, being born in 1612. James's young sister, Elizabeth, was a favourite of Charles, who became her guardian after her father's death but she rewarded his affection by marrying, without his permission, the Earl of Arundel's son.

Men with whom Charles, from his mid-teens onwards, shared a passion for art, such as Philip Herbert, Earl of Pembroke, Thomas Howard, Earl of Arundel and Sir Dudley Carleton (later Viscount Dorchester) were all older than the prince and their shared connoisseurship never blossomed into friendship. When, in 1615, a new chaplain, Dr George Carleton (not related to Sir Dudley), was brought into Charles's entourage he was appalled at what he discovered: courtiers feuding and scrambling for preferment. But that state of affairs lay beyond the traumatic events of 1612–13.

By the spring of 1612 Princess Elizabeth's fate had been decided; she was to be married to Frederick V, Elector Palatine, leader of the Protestant League of German princes within the Holy Roman Empire. It was a popular match with everyone except Queen Anne, who petulantly raged against it. The Protestant camp throughout Europe welcomed it as an indication that England was once again taking up the leadership of anti-Catholic forces. Elizabeth approved, even more so when she met her bridegroom, an athletic and well-favoured young man of exactly her own age. Prince Henry was, of course, delighted and James was exceedingly pleased with himself, for the marriage was part of an even-handed scheme which included the espousal of the Prince of Wales to a Catholic princess which would put himself in the position of peacemaker of Europe. What the King did not know was that Henry was plotting to travel to Europe with his sister and brother-in-law's party after the wedding, there to select for himself a bride of acceptable religious credentials.

Frederick arrived in England in October to begin the long process of diplomatic formalities and celebrations leading up to the marriage ceremony. The first indication many observers had that there might be a spectre at the feast was the fact that when Frederick descended from the royal barge at the Whitehall watergate he was met not by James's elder son but by Charles, Duke of York, who made a pretty speech and conducted the Elector to his father in the great chamber. Henry, it was explained, was temporarily unwell and unable to perform his ceremonial duty. The Prince of Wales later roused himself and even played tennis with his designated brother-in-law but he was obviously feverish and had to return to his bed. Doctors were summoned and prescribed all manner of treatments and nostrums to no avail. Henry went into delirium. On 1 November his family came to his bedside. Charles carried his greatest treasure, a small bronze horse by Giambologna, the finest Florentine sculptor after the death of Michelangelo. He pressed it into the hands of his delirious brother and hero. He never saw Henry again. The Prince of Wales, in whom a whole nation had reposed such hope, died on 6 November, thirteen days before Charles's twelfth birthday. His last coherent words were 'Where is my dear sister?' Elizabeth had desperately tried to gain admission to the sick room, against her parents' orders, even donning disguise in the hope of slipping past her brother's attendants. But deep as was her mourning, it was not greater than Charles's. As part of his coming to terms with grief he persuaded himself that his brother had been poisoned, a conviction he never abandoned. On 7 December he walked as chief mourner behind Henry's funeral chariot from Whitehall to Westminster Abbey through streets thronged with wailing bystanders.

On 14 February 1613 he was prominently involved in ceremonial of a different kind. He escorted a radiant and bejewelled Elizabeth through the interconnected chambers and anterooms of the palace to the royal chapel at Whitehall for her marriage. Afterwards there were pageants, masques, fireworks and chivalric feats in the tiltyard, in several of which events Charles played the part that would have fallen to his brother. In mid-April he accompanied the newly-weds on their slow progress from London to Margate where they were to join the *Prince Royal* for their Channel crossing. He said farewell to his dear sister at Canterbury. He never saw her again.

Thus, in the space of a few weeks, Charles was wrenched out of childhood and thrust into a series of responsibilities for which he had been quite unprepared. His inauguration as Prince of Wales did not take place until three years after Henry's death (and even then

Anne could not bring herself to attend) but his serious training began immediately. He was involved alongside his father in state cere- monial, in meeting ambassadors – and in encountering Parliament. He attended the formal opening of the brief session of 1614 (the 'Addled' Parliament) and dutifully schooled himself in the political issues of the day by listening to the debates of Lords and Commons.

There was a world of difference between the attitude prevailing in the court of the new Prince of Wales and that of his brother. For one thing Charles lacked Henry's self-assurance. His investiture as Prince of Wales in November 1616 was a very subdued affair. It was held indoors because 'the sharpness of the weather and the prince's craziness did not permit any public show'. Charles even shrank from the procession from Whitehall to the Guildhall, scheduled to follow the ceremony, which puzzled one correspondent: 'how it was mis- taken or shifted they went not'.[35] The same reporter was not very impressed either with the first masque presented by Prince Charles on the next Twelfth Night: 'There was nothing in it extraordinary, but rather the invention proved dull. Mr Comptroller's daughter bore away the bell for delicate dancing, though remarkable for nothing else but for the multitude of jewels wherewith she was hanged, as it were, all over.'[36] Charles knew that in everything he essayed he was being compared with his late, lamented brother. It was unnerving – not less so for the fact that he too was probably comparing himself to Henry. The new Prince of Wales lacked both the wit and the will to make his court that of a king-in-waiting. He presided over no semi-independent establishment with a clearly defined set of religious and political ideas informing the develop- ment of what would one day be the basis of government policy. He deferred to his father on appointments to his entourage and the influences to be brought to bear upon his own education. Men who wished to commend themselves to the future king, whether to advance themselves or their convictions, therefore, went about achieving their objectives by the time-honoured methods of palm- greasing and toadying to the current royal favourites.

Charles's extended household was the silken ladder to wealth and influence which men with an eye to the future scrambled to climb. Men like Sir Henry Vane, who boasted, 'I put myself into court and bought a carver's place by means of the friendship of Sir Thomas Overbury, which cost me £5000.'[37] In 1617 he induced Sir David Foulis to sell him his office of Cofferer to Prince Charles, a position which placed him next in rank to the Comptroller of the Household. By a similar financial transaction he became Comptroller in 1629 and Treasurer ten years later. Closeness to the prince and, later, the King proved well worth the investment. Charles bestowed on him lands, offices, sinecures and, in 1630, a Council seat. But a career based on avarice rather than loyalty led Vane into the parliamentary camp in the 1640s.

One young courtier rapidly rising in the King's favour was James, Marquis of Hamilton, who had the twin advantages of his family's proven loyalty to the Crown and widespread popularity in Scotland. King James gave him various household appointments, brought him on to the Council in 1617, conferred an English peerage (Earl of Cambridge and Baron Ennerdale) on him in 1619 and employed him to good effect as High Commissioner to the Scottish Parliament in 1621. Court gossip even suggested that Hamilton had been considered as a possible husband for Princess Elizabeth. The marquis was too valuable to be assigned to the Prince of Wales's entourage but James did ensure that Charles took advantage of Hamilton's counsel whenever possible and Hamilton was, in part, responsible for one of the most intriguing appointments to the prince's occasional staff – that of John Preston (see below pp. 123f).

James was determined to surround the future king with earnest upholders of Protestant piety. His Queen and her Catholic-inclined friends were just as committed to advancing men of a contrary persuasion to his service. Three such whose company Charles came to enjoy were Sir Toby Matthew, Francis, Baron Cottington and Sir Kenelm Digby. Matthew was an example of that well-known phenomenon, the vicarage rebel. His father was no less a person than the Archbishop of York and, by all accounts, an admirable example of a caring, energetic and erudite ecclesiastic. Toby, the eldest son, fell out with his parents' austere Protestantism and, as soon as he was able, escaped to the continent where the culture and religion of France and Italy particularly appealed to him, and when in Rome he converted. In 1614 he was admitted to the Roman Catholic priesthood. This would have made his return to England very dangerous had it not been for his many court connections and his genius for friendship. He was a witty, effeminate exotic and became the greatest court gossip of the age – the sort of man it is possible to like and disapprove of at the same time. This certainly seems to have been true of King James, who banished Matthew from

86

the realm in 1619 and four years later knighted him ('For what service, God knows!' a contemporary remarked). An outraged pamphleteer described him as 'a man principally noxious, and himself the plague of the king and kingdom of England; a most impudent man, who flies to all banquets and feasts, called or not called, never quiet, always in action, a perpetual motion, thrusting himself into all conversations of superiors, he urgeth conferences familiarly that he may fish out the minds of men'.[38] Sir John Suckling made a passing reference to Matthew in his *Session of Poets*:

> Toby Matthews – on him, what made him there?
> Was whispering something in somebody's ear.

And Walpole later dismissed him as 'a trifling courtier, affected to be a politician'.[39] However, several men and women about the court found him an amusing, engaging companion and for that reason, however much he was denigrated as a papal spy, the prince's favour protected him from his enemies.

Francis Cottington was a congenial companion of quite a different stripe. Where Matthew was ebullient, Cottington was quiet and grave; where Matthew joked with skill and verve, Cottington's humour was dry and subtle; where Matthew sliced reputations with deft rapier sweeps of caricature, Cottington preferred the concealed stiletto thrust of satire. However, he was equally well travelled, having spent several years as a diplomat in Spain. He, too, had become a Catholic at some point although in order to secure court preferment he concealed his religion. Charles enjoyed the company of this urbane and sophisticated courtier and appointed him to be his secretary.

Despite the fact that his father had been executed for complicity in the Gunpowder Plot and that he made no secret of his Roman Catholicism, Kenelm Digby was immediately received into the prince's entourage when the two men met in Madrid in 1623. He was much closer in age to Charles than most of his other companions, having been born in 1603, but shared their well-travelled sophistication. He had spent the previous three years in France and Italy, and wherever he went cultivated the friendship of men of taste and erudition. He was one of those young men who seemed to have everything – good looks, a modest fortune, charm, a lively and enquiring mind and a host of friends. Charles took him back to England with him, introduced him to his father and requested for his new friend the honour of knighthood, which the King readily conferred, though his trembling hand and pathological fear of naked steel caused him almost to put Digby's eye out in the process. All this took place at Hinchingbrooke and will have had its place in the gossip going round the Cromwell family.

It is not surprising that the prince, passing through the years of teenage experimentation and search for individuality, should have been attracted by widely travelled men of cultivated taste; bold independent spirits who espoused a forbidden religion. The contrast with his insular, Protestant mentors could not have been more marked. Charles maintained a devout, almost fawning obedience to his king/father, a respect embedded deep in his unconscious by all those masques and encomiums he had attended since childhood. Nothing reveals the awe in which he held his parent so much as a pathetic letter written in the aftermath of his mother's death. This occurred in March 1619 when Charles was eighteen. He was present for the Queen's last distressing hours at Hampton Court and was chief mourner at the funeral which was delayed for thirteen weeks while her effigy was made. In Anne he lost the last member of his family circle to whom he was bound by ties of simple love. However, sad though his mother's passing was, Charles did not lack the presence of mind to persuade her to make a will nominating him as principal legatee. This so far infuriated James that his son was obliged, in the most grovelling terms to beg the Marquis of Buckingham, the current royal favourite, to intercede for him:

> . . . I pray you to commend my most humble service to his majesty, and tell him that I am very sorry that I have done anything [that] may offend him, and that I will be content to have any penance inflicted upon me, so he may forgive me, although I had never a thought, nor ever shall have to displease him; yet I deserve to be punished for my ill fortune . . . [40]

Mention of Buckingham brings us to the man who had the greatest impact on the life of the young prince. It was in August 1614 that the King's eye 'ever ralling after any stranger', lighted upon the twenty-two-year-old would-be courtier, George Villiers. Robert Carr, Earl of Somerset, the reigning favourite, had already begun to alienate the King's affections by his arrogance and his genius for making enemies. Those enemies were not slow to dangle before James pretty boys who offered the excitement of new sexual adventures. Within months Villiers was installed among the King's closest attendants and when Carr's headlong ambition carried him a scandal too far the see-saw of royal favour plunged him down and lifted Villiers up. Godfrey Goodman* recollected that young Villiers 'was the hand-somest bodied man in England; his limbs so well compacted, and his conversation so pleasing, and of so sweet a disposition . . . that he was as inwardly beautiful as he was outwardly'.[41] Since to his physical attributes he added athleticism and the graces of a skilled courtier, his advancement was characteristically rapid. Within two years he was a viscount with an £80,000 estate and the leading influence in govern-ment policy. In January 1617 he was created Earl of Buckingham and, in 1623, he became the only duke not of the blood royal.

Charles's first reaction to the new favourite was one of resentment: Villiers not only received the affection of James which his son never enjoyed, and adopted an attitude of boisterous familiarity towards the heir to the throne, but he also possessed many of the attributes Charles had admired in Henry. The fifteen-year-old prince showed his animosity by such pranks as turning a water jet on Villiers, but James was determined that the two should be friends and it was certainly in the interests of his favourite that it should be so. In March 1616, after a contretemps at Royston during which Villiers had in exasperation lifted his hand to Charles and met with the shocked response 'What! My Lord, I think you intend to strike me,' the courtier made a supreme effort to win the boy over. He threw a great feast for the royal family and bent over backwards to ensure that Charles enjoyed himself. One biographer sourly noted that the King 'made himself, as usual, very ridiculous' but the stratagem seems to have worked.[42] Certainly, prince and favourite were soon bosom companions though Charles's change of attitude may have owed more to his parents' persuasion than to Villiers's scheming. One characteristic that emerges from a study of Charles Stuart's close relationships is that they seldom, if ever, came into being spontaneously, but relied on the urging of others and his own mature reflection.

Buckingham made a deliberate effort to bring Charles out of

* Bishop of Gloucester 1625–56, he was a friend of Queen Anne, whose pre-dilection for the church of Rome he shared.

himself by involving him in various diversions and encouraging his first, faltering adolescent romances. In May 1620 the favourite married Catherine Manners, daughter of the Earl of Rutland, who in order to secure so prominent a husband temporarily abandoned her Roman Catholicism. Thereafter, the Villiers, together with the Duchess of Lennox and Prince Charles, were often to be seen together enjoying the delights of the capital and other locations when the court was on progress. It was the first time since 1611 that Charles had been able to feel part of a 'family'. If his new companions were not blood relations, they were certainly surrogate elder siblings in whose company Charles could relax, cast off some of his inhibitions and enjoy revels and entertainments with a degree of abandon. By Christmas 1619 he was frequently taking a lead role in court masques, presiding at banquets given for visiting dignitaries and acquitting himself well in the tiltyard. At last Charles was beginning to emerge from the gaucherie of an introverted teenager, and the transformation was largely Buckingham's work.

One of the shortest routes to the Prince of Wales's heart lay through his love of art and it was not out of purely aesthetic considerations that Buckingham began to assemble, about 1619, one of the first major English collections. He had agents such as Sir Dudley Carleton, Toby Matthew and the French-born Balthazar Gerbier scour the continent for paintings and sculptures, and in a short time could display an assemblage of fine pieces which rivalled those of genuine connoisseurs like the Earl of Arundel and the Earl of Pembroke. Together with others of taste and discernment such as Endymion Porter, one of Charles's grooms of the chamber, these men were the founder members of the Whitehall Group, the first coterie of collectors outside mainland Europe. At this stage Charles lacked both the funds and the experience to compete but he delighted to talk with members of this elite club, to be shown their latest acquisitions and to receive gifts from them. Charles was becoming a member of a cultured intelligentsia – something which would set him apart from ordinary mortals just as surely as divine kingship.

THREE

MENTORS

... cherish no man more than a good pastor, hate no man more than a proud Puritan: thinking it one of your fairest styles, to be called a loving nourish-father to the Church; seeing all the churches within your dominions planted with good pastors, the schools (the seminary of the church) maintained, the doctrine and discipline preserved in purity, according to God's word, a sufficient provision for their sustenance, a comely order in their policy, pride punished, humility advanced, and they so to reverence their superiors, & their flocks them, as the flourishing of your church in piety, peace, & learning, may be one of the chief points of your earthly glory: being ever alike ware [i.e. on your guard against] both the extremities; as well as ye repress the vain Puritan, so suffer not proud papal bishops.[1]

SUCH WAS JAMES VI's advice to Prince Henry as he expressed it in *Basilicon Doron*. The charge of nourishing sound religion and pure scholarship fell in turn to Charles Stuart and Oliver Cromwell and both would have endorsed, in broad terms, James's priorities. Oliver, to be sure, would not have subscribed to the King's animosity towards Puritans but when in power he had his own 'proud' and 'vain' extremists to contend with. Nevertheless, like his predecessor, he paid more than lip service to the proclamation of God's unvarnished word, the good order of the Church and the rearing of children and young people to be loyal and godly citizens. Of course, when the King and the Protector used such terms, they meant different things by them. Their understanding of education and Christian faith was largely the result of their own early intellectual and spiritual training. What, then, do we know of their teachers and guides?

The man under whose eloquence and rod Cromwell sat for several years in the Grammar School of St John the Baptist, Huntingdon, was Thomas Beard MA.* This pedagogue is conventionally regarded as an 'uncompromising Puritan'[2] and the man who set Oliver on the road to Nonconformity. The truth is not quite so straightforward. Beard was a graduate of Jesus, Cambridge, who made his first appearance in Huntingdonshire church life in 1595. He appears to have enjoyed valuable patronage, for his presentation to the living of Kimbolton was at the hands of the Lord Keeper of the Great Seal, Sir John Puckering. Beard's ambition seems to have made him restless, for in less than three years he exchanged Kimbolton for Hengrave, Suffolk, where the patronage was held by the wealthy Bourchier family (into which Oliver married). Then, in 1605, he transferred to Huntingdon, which was probably his home town,[3] where he served as master of St John's Hospital and School. After ten years he was looking for another move, for he approached one of the county's most distinguished gentlemen, the scholar and antiquary, Sir Robert Cotton, suing for the rectory of Connington, near St Ives. He was, he claimed, tired of 'the painful occupation of teaching'.[4]

Are these facts the bare career bones of a dissatisfied religious extremist ever seeking a more congenial billet? Almost certainly not. Sir John Puckering, who first set Beard's foot on the ladder of preferment, was no friend of Puritans. Only four years earlier he had presided at the trial of the religious polemicist, John Udall, and sentenced the defendant to death for seditious libel. Although the execution had not been carried out, Udall had died as a result of his imprisonment and was claimed as a martyr by the members of his religious party. Sir Richard Cotton, although a supporter of Parliament in the constitutional fracas of the 1640s, was no patron of Puritans. On the death of Tobias Bland BD, the burgesses of Huntingdon were very pleased to give over into Beard's hands the care of the ancient foundation of their hospital. For Bland was a troublesome fellow. He had almost got himself thrown out of Corpus Christi, Cambridge, for composing a libel against the master, Robert Norgate. But he enjoyed the patronage of one of the Lords-Lieutenant of the county, Sir Henry Cromwell's friend, John, Lord St John, and, doubtless, more than a nod and a wink passed in 1599 between John's brother and heir and Robert Cromwell, one of

* He is thus signified in the presentation records, though he later proceeded to BD (1602) and DD (1614).

the Huntingdon bailiffs charged with filling the vacancy at the hospital. Once ensconced, Bland had devoted much of his time to penning obscure and eccentric treatises and had badly neglected his responsibilities. Beard was someone Huntingdon folk knew and they looked to him to reverse the disastrous trend which the late incumbent had allowed to develop.

Things certainly changed for the better with the arrival of Thomas Beard, as a contemporary testimonial asserts:

> All the said parishes and town of Huntingdon were, for a long time before the said Thomas Beard became master of the said hospital, utterly destitute of a learned preacher to teach and instruct them in the word of God; but sithence the said Thomas Beard became master of the said hospital, being admitted thereunto by the presentation of the said bailiffs and burgesses, the said Thomas Beard hath not only maintained a grammar school in the said town, according to the foundation of the said hospital, by himself, and a schoolmaster by him provided at his own charges, but hath also been continually resident in the said town, and painfully preached the word of God in the said town of Huntingdon on the Sabbath-day duly, to the great comfort of the inhabitants of the said town.[5]

The remainder of Beard's career can be quickly outlined. To his hospital responsibilities he added the rectorship of two Huntingdon parishes, St John's (1610–25) and All Saints, the town's principal church (1611–19). On resigning the latter he was presented by Sir Oliver Cromwell to the parish of Wistow, which he held until his death in 1632 and where he employed a curate to carry out liturgical duties. From 1612 Beard also derived income from a prebendal stall in Lincoln cathedral. He was a very prominent Huntingdon citizen and when he was not about his ecclesiastical duties he was to be found on the magistrates' bench, in the council chamber or in his study writing anti-Catholic polemic.

So far we have a picture of a conscientious minister, who had found for himself a very comfortable niche; a man of academic turn of mind who continued his studies and appreciated being close to the intellectual stimulus of Cambridge but did not much like teaching children; a clergyman of the established Church who gave no sign of rejecting its rituals and formularies; a citizen who aligned himself with the rural elite in local government and the maintenance of law and order; and a protégé unlikely to provoke his patrons by conduct, such as radical preaching, which might provoke dissent. It is certain that he was a frequent guest at Hinchingbrooke and that he was, from time to time, required to preach before the royal court. Charles I later referred to Beard as 'late chaplain of our dear father'[6] and Sir Oliver Cromwell's house is by far the most likely place where the minister can have come to the attention of the King. This does not suggest a religious extremist, a male Jean Brodie filling the minds of his charges with revolutionary ideas.

Beard's writings and pulpit performances enable us to be more positive about the beliefs he was propagating. In 1597 he published what was to be his most successful book, the lively *Theatre of God's Judgements*, a runaway best-seller. This was a translation from the French of a treatise on the core Calvinist doctrines of the sovereignty and providence of God, to which Beard added some three hundred anecdotal examples of divine intervention in the affairs of men. It was aimed at a wide market and was highly successful, running to four editions over fifty years. What *The Theatre of God's Judgements* offered the reader was a kind of supplement to the phenomenally popular *Acts and Monuments* (though without the sensationalising woodcuts which were a feature of Foxe's martyrology). Beard emphasised that, though the lot of Christians was often hard and the enemies of the righteous appeared to flourish, yet God was not mocked; he visited his vengeance upon the enemies of the saints not only in the next world but also here and now. Such a solemn message was not without an element of humour:

> . . . One Burton, the bailiff of Croyland in Lincolnshire, who having been a Protestant in an outward show in King Edward's days, as soon as Queen Mary was quietly seated in the kingdom became very earnest in setting up the mass again and constrained the curate by threats to leave the English service and say mass. The blind bailiff not long after, as he was riding with one of his neighbours, a crow flying over his head, let her excrements fall upon his face, the poisoned stink and savour whereof so annoyed his stomach that he never left vomitting until he came home and there, after certain days with extreme pain of vomitting, crying and cursing the crow, desperately he died without any token of repentance.[7]

One feels that his sermons cannot have lacked entertainment value.

In asserting eternal providence and justifying the ways of God to men Beard stood on the firm foundation of Calvin's *Institutes*:

> . . . the Providence of God . . . so moderates and guides all things that it works sometimes by the interposition of means, sometimes without means, and sometimes against all means; and finally, that it tends towards this end: that we may know what care God has for the human race; above all how carefully he watches over his Church, for which he has the closest regard.[8]

The inevitable theological structure built upon this base included all those doctrinal features the enemies of Calvinism found so obnoxious: double predestination, election, irresistible grace and the equality of all people, not only in terms of eternal judgement, but also in their submission to divine truth as expressed in Scripture and expounded by godly preachers. What Beard's book achieved and, doubtless, what his sermons also accomplished was the 'de-intellectualising' of such concepts for the benefit of men and women unskilled in dialectic. In this Cromwell's teacher performed a valuable service, for the issues so eagerly argued by theologians and pulpit orators and which would be instrumental in tearing mid-seventeenth-century society apart were very esoteric and well above the heads of ordinary mortals. Yet, for all that it touched on issues that were socially and politically sensitive, *The Theatre of God's Judgements* cannot be designated a piece of *Puritan* propaganda, any more than *Acts and Monuments* can be so described.

As a term of scorn 'Puritan' stands alongside such cognomens as 'Methodist', 'enthusiast', 'fundamentalist' and 'born-again Christian' in designating, totally without precision, believers who base on the Bible an exclusivist faith demanding personal commitment and a strict regime of piety and morality. At the turn of the seventeenth century most people who employed the word 'Puritan' did so in the spirit of 'I can't define one but I know one when I see one'. English Protestantism was a broad landscape, extending from lush latitudinarian meadows bordering Catholic country, through a variety of liturgical valleys and doctrinal hills, to the craggy heights inhabited by those who preferred to be known as the 'godly'. Even those who recognised themselves and were recognised by others as occupying the less comfortable terrain of religious radicalism were not a united group; quite the reverse. Sectarianism is bred of introspection out of particularism: the more evangelical Protestants applied magnifying glasses to elements of the Christian mystery the more those features were enlarged into potential matters of difference and discord. The diversity of seventeenth-century religious life must, therefore, make us wary, not only of such terms as 'Puritan', but also of such descriptions as 'mainstream Protestant'.

With that proviso three generalisations can be offered. First, the theological rootstock of English Protestantism was Calvinism. The scholars and pastors who gave the Church of England its main intellectual impetus in the reign of Elizabeth were men who had returned from or were in touch with Geneva and other Reformed centres. Their foundation document (before the dissemination of the Authorised Version) was the Geneva Bible, supported by Calvin's comprehensive schema, *The Institution of the Christian Religion* (usually referred to as *The Institutes*). What Church leaders had to struggle with was the inextricable intertwining of the reformer's doctrine and his ecclesiastical polity. The latter could not be superimposed on an episcopal system; hence the demand by some for more sweeping change: 'Is a reformation good for France and can it be evil for England? Is a discipline meet for Scotland and is it unprofitable for this realm?',[9] an appeal to Parliament rhetorically inquired in 1572. Those who were wedded to the old order still, in the main, wanted to adhere to Reformed teaching but found themselves, in practice, adapting it.

Secondly, the 'popular protestantism inevitably tended towards congregational independency'.[10] While parish priests protested and bishops employed spies and *agents provocateurs*, many of the godly, refusing to be denied spiritual sustenance, travelled to churches which had a 'sound' preaching ministry, met in house groups and attended Puritan lectures. Few forsook their own parishes completely but the number of dissidents increased – dramatically so when Church authorities tried to impose discipline. They had both emotional and intellectual motivation. They took offence at clergy who would not or could not preach, who clung to such 'papistical rags' as the surplice and stood on their dignity rather than their piety. Separation from the established Church was the logical conclusion to be drawn from Calvin's doctrine of the Church. If the true Christian congregation was the community of the elect showing forth the fruits of divine grace it was difficult to identify

98

membership with the residents of a given geographical area. Of course, the majority of clergy and laity did not draw this logical conclusion. They feared the fragmentation of society, they were overawed by the local gentry, and all their material interests lay with the preservation of the *status quo*. But the tensions were there: conformity was a glove that fitted but loosely on the Calvinist hand.

The third generalisation is that all Englishmen, except for the very tiny Catholic recusant rump were anti-popery. In religious terms, King James's subjects defined themselves much more by what they were not than by what they were: they were not Catholic. Since long before anyone could remember England had stood firm against Rome and Rome's secular arm, imperial Spain. And everyone *could* remember at least one highly dramatic event which justified this hostility. Oliver's father must have told him exciting tales of the great Armada and its miraculous destruction. He was six when news reached Huntingdon of a heinous Catholic plot to blow up the King as well as his own uncle and several family friends gathered in Parliament. He was a young man in 1623 when the whole nation went mad with jubilation because plans to marry Prince Charles to the Spanish infanta had come to naught. And in 1641, he heard with anger and horror exaggerated stories of the Catholic rebellion in Ireland when it was reported that tens of thousands of Protestant settlers had been butchered. In addition to these alarms, events on the continent kept the anti-papal pot boiling. In 1618 religious war broke out and was to embroil Europe for a generation. The conflict touched England closely, for it swept James's daughter and her husband, Frederick, from their throne and obliged them to live as exiles in the Low Countries. This was but the beginning of a series of tragedies for Elizabeth, the 'Queen of Hearts' as she was romantically known, every one of which roused her supporters in England to demand action. If James was not prepared to don the mantle of Protestant champion, at least he ought to go to the aid of his own flesh and blood, they argued.

In 1625 Thomas Beard added his contribution to the library of anti-Catholic polemic with *Antichrist the Pope of Rome or the Pope of Rome is Antichrist*. In this he set out to prove from Scripture and history that the occupant of St Peter's chair was the agent of Satan raised up in the last days, now manifestly come, for his final battle with the saints. There was nothing new or extreme in any of this, save that England had just acquired a Roman Catholic queen which gave added point to Beard's argument. Ever since Henry VIII had replaced the Pope as head of the English Church the idea of the Pope as Antichrist had steadily advanced, and every overt or covert attempt by Catholic agents to recover lost ground was taken as proof of plots to overthrow the Protestant state. At the time that Beard wrote, the situations causing alarm were the growing number of Catholics at court, their attempt to achieve toleration for their co-religionists and the appointments of Arminians (widely assumed to be crypto-papists) to the episcopal bench. In his latest treatise Beard was only voicing the mounting concern of those who believed that the English Church and state were under threat.

Beard's preaching was obviously popular with his parishioners. This may call in question just how pungent and challenging it was; did the good doctor, we wonder, ever reflect on his master's words, 'Woe unto you when all men shall speak well of you, for so did their fathers of the false prophets'?[11] For some years there had existed a combination lectureship in Huntingdon: local clergy took it in turns to preach an open-air sermon on market days. When Richard Neile was appointed Bishop of Lincoln in 1614 one of his early acts was the suppression of this tradition. Neile, who boasted that he was 'a great adversary of the Puritan faction', hated public lectures, which he considered potentially detrimental to good order, but the burgesses of Huntingdon outwitted him. They were not to be deprived of their weekday exhortation and set up a new lectureship which they offered to Beard. This is a significant indication of his popularity. The town fathers had other talented preachers they could have approached, particularly at nearby Cambridge. Beard filled the post to the end of his days and preached in All Saints every Sunday and Wednesday morning in addition to his addresses during divine service.

However, Richard Neile was not someone who took kindly to being thwarted and in his eyes Beard was now a marked man. The bishop was the leader of what was becoming known as the 'Arminian' faction (see below pp. 269f) and was well launched on an enthusiastic career of disciplining clergy who refused total conformity with canon law. In May 1614 he overreached himself by making a violent attack on the House of Commons for their presumption in questioning the royal prerogative. He was obliged to make a tearful apology to Parliament for this indiscretion but his fervent advocacy of royal absolutism increased his popularity with the King and ensured him rapid preferment. He spent less than four years at Lincoln before being translated to Durham and, finally, to York.

It was probably three years after his trial of strength with the Commons that he found an opportunity to vent his spleen on Dr Beard.* One of the most conspicuous and prestigious preaching events in London took place every Easter at the Spittal Cross in the courtyard of St Mary's in Vintry, where impressive buildings had been erected for prominent citizens to hear sermons:

> time out of mind, it hath been a laudable custom, that on Good Friday in the afternoon, some especial learned man, by appointment of the prelates, hath preached a sermon at *Paul's* Cross, treating of Christ's passion: and upon the three next Easter Holidays, Monday, Tuesday, and Wednesday, the like learned men, by the like appointment, have used to preach on the forenoons at the said Spittle, to persuade the article of Christ's resurrection . . . At these sermons so severally preached, the mayor with his brethren, the aldermen, were accustomed to be present in their Violets at *Paul's* on Good Friday, and in their Scarlets at the Spittle in the holidays.[12]

The man put up to preach the Good Friday sermon in (probably) 1617 was William Alabaster, rector of Therfield, Hertfordshire and a protégé of Neile's, whose theology was decidedly individualistic. He had twice converted to Roman Catholicism and twice returned to the Protestant fold. Alabaster was undoubtedly a clever and talented man, a keen student of cabala and no mean poet[13] but his views were not such as to commend him to the orthodox. Dr Beard, who was appointed to preach one of the sermons at Spittal Cross, considered Alabaster guilty of rank popery and was all set to contradict him. At this point, Neile summoned Beard before him and instructed him on

---

* The precise dating is difficult. We only know of the event from Cromwell's Commons speech. He placed it within the episcopates of Neile at Lincoln (when he was Beard's diocesan) and Felton at Ely but these two did not overlap; Felton was not appointed to Ely until March 1619. I have assumed that Cromwell's memory played him false and that Beard's appeal to Felton occurred during the period when he was jointly Bishop of Bristol and Master of Pembroke, 1617–19. If this reasoning is correct the sermons at the centre of the controversy must have been preached during the Easter of 1617.

no account to take issue with the Good Friday preacher. Beard, who had obviously been selected as a champion of anti-popery and was expected to answer Alabaster effectively point-by-point, was in a quandary. He was not just faced with a choice between obedience to his conscience or his Ordinary. His reputation was on the line: for someone of his known views to refuse the challenge presented by Alabaster would have been embarrassing in the extreme. His reaction was to seek a friendly and sympathetic ear. Nicholas Felton, Bishop of Bristol and Master of Pembroke, Cambridge, was one of the most respected senior clergymen of the day. He was known as a wise, learned, non-partisan churchman. He had been teaching in Cambridge for over twenty years, in fact since Beard's own student days and the events of 1617 suggest that the two were good friends. Felton now advised the younger man to go ahead and preach from his heart, which Beard proceeded to do. The result was another summons to Neile's presence and an angry episcopal reprimand. But beyond that the bishop was powerless to go. He may well have wanted to stop Beard's Huntingdon lectureship but the popular minister enjoyed the support of Sir Oliver Cromwell and the leading townsfolk and he was *persona grata* with the King. Neither Neile nor his Archdeacon of Huntingdon (1615–21), William Laud, the later scourge of evangelicals, was able to find sufficient cause to dislodge Beard. Laud had to wait until 1633, when he was Archbishop of Canterbury and Beard was dead, to put a stop to the lectureship. There can be little doubt that Neile and Laud between them would have ousted Beard if they could have charged him with extreme doctrines or refusal to comply with canonical norms of dress and liturgical practice.[14]

Thus, the man responsible for giving Oliver Cromwell his basic education was, if we dare risk a label, a conforming Calvinist. Thomas Beard was firm in his evangelical Protestant convictions and his hatred of Rome – attitudes which would have been generally acceptable to many of his fellow countrymen. He was active in the town and popular. He was on good terms with his patrons, the Cromwells – sufficiently intimate, indeed, with Oliver's father to be a witness of his will – who, presumably, were happy with the general tenor of his preaching and were quite comfortable about him performing before the King. Nothing we know about Sir Oliver enables us to put him into the category of a patron of 'Puritans'. In 1644, when Parliament ordered the examination of all parish clergy that were 'scandalous in their lives or ill affected to the parliament of fomenters of this unnatural war or that shall wilfully refuse obedience to the ordinances of parliament'[15] only twenty Huntingdonshire priests were dispossessed. Among them was William Baker of Wistow who had been presented to the living only months before and who had in that space of time offended the existing regime to such an extent that he was imprisoned in Huntingdon jail and 'barbarously treated'.[16] His patron was Sir Oliver Cromwell.

The formal education of Sir Oliver's nephew and namesake was dominated by his energetic and conscientious teacher. On weekdays the boy learned to read and write in English and Latin under the stern gaze of a man of academic bent who, by his own admission, found it irksome to din information into children. Later the pupil moved on to study arithmetic, geometry, logic, rhetoric and the more demanding classical authors. On Sundays there was no escape from Mr Beard, since Oliver and his sisters had to sit with their parents in their prominent family pew and listen to a sermon lasting an hour or more. Judging by Beard's written works he must, literally, have put the fear of God into his charges. Although some of his anecdotal illustrations may have been played for laughs, there were many more which dealt with the outworkings of divine retribution in exceedingly gruesome detail.

It goes without saying that Beard's pupils were brought up to study and become very familiar with the Bible. But the teacher also drew upon his considerable knowledge of Greek and Latin history and mythology in spinning yarns that would captivate his hearers and, hopefully, drive home the morals he attempted to draw from them. He was far from being an unimaginative pedagogue, beating knowledge into children with a verbal cudgel at one end and a birch at the other. He varied his teaching methods, for example by writing brief plays for his pupils to act. Thus, while Charles Stuart was participating in the latest court masque, dancing in sumptuous velvets and silks, upon a vivid stage set designed by Inigo Jones and reciting elegant lines composed by Ben Jonson, Oliver Cromwell, draped in makeshift costume, stumbled through the text provided by a provincial pedagogue in his own dusty schoolroom.

Like all children, Oliver developed both positive and negative reactions to his early training. He was no scholar and, if popular legends are to be believed, often felt Beard's heavy hand. There is a suggestion in a letter he wrote to one of his own sons in 1650 that he found the anecdotal method of teaching tiresome. 'Recreate yourself with Sir Walter Ralegh's *History*,' he writes. 'It's a body of history and will add much more to your understanding than fragments of story.'[17] Ralegh's book was published in 1614 to immediate acclaim and the young Cromwell was, therefore, among its earliest readers. There can be little doubt that when he wrote his letter to Richard he was contrasting the ex-courtier's *History* with Beard's *Theatre of God's Judgements*. Both books, though very different in style, had the same objective: to show God's hand in the human story and particularly in the punishment of evildoers.

This sense of God's involvement in the world became fundamental to Cromwell's thinking. The supreme arbiter, he was convinced, was constantly moving in judgement, sometimes through his saints, sometimes even against them:

> And give us leave to say, as before the Lord, who knows the secret of all hearts, that, as we think one especial end of Providence in permitting the enemies of God and goodness in both kingdoms to rise to that height, and exercise such tyranny over His people, was to show the necessity of unity amongst those of both nations, so we hope and pray that the late glorious dispensation, in giving so happy success against your and our enemies in our victories, may be the foundation of union of the people of God in love and amity; and to that end we shall, God assisting, to the utmost of our power endeavour to perform what may be behind on our part, and when we shall, through any wilfulness, fail therein, let this profession rise up in judgment against us, as having been made in hypocrisy, a severe avenger of which God hath lately appeared, in His most righteous witnessing against the Army under Duke Hamilton, invading us under specious pretences of piety and justice.[18]

When this deep-rooted belief became bonded to a sense of his own divine call there could be for him no backsliding, no seeking of an easier path, no flinching from hard decisions and acts of determined violence. His own mind being well-stocked in youth with horrifying visions of divine wrath and the no less draconian deeds of Antichrist, Cromwell the soldier saw himself as engaged in a cosmic struggle against satanic error for the possession of men's souls, a struggle which must not be abandoned out of any squeamishness about blood-letting. In Ireland he was to make this crystal-clear to his enemies.

I shall not, where I have power, and the Lord is pleased to bless me, suffer the exercise of the Mass, where I can take notice of it. 'No' nor 'in any way' suffer you that are papists, where I can find you seducing the people, or by any overt act violating the Laws established; but if you come into my hands, I shall cause to be inflicted the punishments appointed by the laws . . . As for the people, what thoughts they have in matters of religion in their own breasts I cannot reach; but I shall think it my duty, if they walk honestly and peaceably, not to cause them in the least to suffer for the same. And shall endeavour to walk patiently and in love towards them, to see if at any time it shall please God to give them another or a better mind. And all men under the power of England, within this dominion, are hereby required and enjoined strictly and religiously to do the same . . .

And having said this, and purposing honestly to perform it, – if this people shall headily run on after the counsels of their prelates and clergy and other leaders, I hope to be free from the misery and desolation, blood and ruin that shall befall them; and shall rejoice to exercise utmost severity against them.[19]

There was, of course, one book above all on which Cromwell was reared and to which in later life he devoted intense study. We scan his letters and speeches in vain for quotations culled from classical authors but the words of Scripture appear again and again by allusion or direct citation. Passages conned by rote in the classroom, proclaimed from St John's pulpit and, in later years, meditated upon in the study and campaign tent permeated Oliver's very being. In the letter to Richard quoted earlier, he adjures his son:

Seek the Lord and His face continually: – let this be the business of your life and strength, and let all things be subservient and in order to this! You cannot find nor behold the face of God but in Christ; therefore labour to know God in Christ; which the Scripture makes to be the sum of all, even life eternal. Because the true knowledge is not literal or speculative; 'no,' but inward; transforming the mind to it. It's uniting to, and *participant of*, the divine nature (2 Peter, i.4): 'That by these ye might be partakers of the divine nature, having escaped the corruption that is in the world through *lust*. It's such a *knowledge* as Paul speaks of (Philippians, iii.8–10).* How little of this knowledge is among us![20]

* I count all things but loss for the excellency of the knowledge of Christ Jesus my Lord.

What is significant here is Cromwell's insistence on the 'inwardness' of knowledge. Intellectual understanding of the Bible is not enough. This is good Calvinism: 'We can obtain nothing by only hearing the word of God, without the grace of his Holy Spirit,'[21] wrote the reformer. God is not only the originator but also the interpreter of the Bible to those hearts wherein he has begun a work of grace. That beginning occurred for Cromwell long after he had left Dr Beard's tutelage and it is likely that behind this exhortation to Dick to follow the same path lay the reflection that Oliver's early mentor had only been able to offer him a knowledge that was literal and speculative.

Beard's greatest gift to Oliver was the ability to think. It was his brilliance in assessing battlefield situations which made him an excellent tactician. His ability to grasp issues quickly and to see through verbiage made him impatient in debate. When he was guilty of being brusque, argumentative and abusive it was in part due to the fact that his own assessment of situations was so clear and his own convictions so solid (particularly when they had been arrived at by prayer) that he found the muddled arguments of opponents intolerable. Cromwell's letters and speeches enable us to see how his mind worked. His written style is devoid of artifice and elegance, sometimes it is convoluted, but it is by no means drab. The man whose life overlapped with that of Shakespeare, Jonson, Donne and Milton is not without some share in their literary genius. There are moments when his prose verges on poetry and certainly has about it the cadences of the Authorised Version:

> . . . your 'union'. By the grace of God, we fear not, we care not for it. Your covenant . . . is with death and hell; your union is like that of Simeon and Levi. Associate yourselves, and you shall be broken into pieces; take counsel together, and it shall come to naught. For though it becomes us to be humble in respect of ourselves, yet we can say to you, God is not with you.[22]

Not infrequently passion breaks through and the strict logical flow is lost, yet this adds to rather than detracts from the effectiveness of the whole.

> You know how untowards I am at this business of writing, yet a word. I beseech the Lord make us sensible of this great mercy here . . . Oh, His

mercy to the whole society of saints, despised, jeered saints! Let them mock on. Would we were all saints. The best of us are (God knows) poor weak saints, yet saints; if not sheep, yet lambs, and must be fed. We have daily bread and shall have it, in despite of all enemies. There's enough in our Father's house. . . . I think, through these outward mercies (as we call them), faith, patience, love, hope, all are exercised and perfected, yea, Christ formed, and grows to a perfect man within us.[23]

And when Cromwell became an orator, a man who could put heart into fearful troopers on the eve of a battle and cower recalcitrant parliamentarians, did his style owe nothing to that pulpitry of Thomas Beard to which he had listened, week in and week out, for so many years?

You have been called hither to save a nation – nations. You had the best people, indeed, of the Christian world put into your trust, when you came hither. You had the affairs of these nations delivered over to you in peace and quiet; you were, and we all are, put into an undisturbed possession, nobody making title to us. Through the blessing of God, our enemies were hopeless and scattered. We had peace at home; peace with almost all our neighbours round about . . . These things we had, few days ago, when you came hither. And now? – to have our peace and interest, whereof those were our hopes the other day, thus shaken, and put under such a confusion; and ourselves rendered hereby almost the scorn and contempt of those strangers who are amongst us to negotiate their masters' affairs! To give *them* opportunity to see our nakedness as they do: 'A people that have been unhinged this twelve-years day, and are unhinged still,' – as if scattering, division and confusion came upon us like things we desired: '*these*' which are the greatest plagues that God ordinarily lays upon nations for sin![24]

In those classroom days Oliver cannot have been the easiest of pupils – boisterous, unwilling, spoiled *and* the squire's nephew. However, as the boy grew into manhood his relationship with his former teacher seems to have been cordial enough. It was when Oliver was a Member of Parliament in 1629 that he told the story of Neile's brush with Beard, obviously approving of the minister's opposition to the bishop. When the contretemps took place Oliver was no longer under Beard's tutelage; he had moved on – to Cambridge.

It has become customary to scrutinise Cromwell's brief months at university for religious influences and much has been made of the controversy raging in high academic circles during the first decades of the seventeenth century. There are two objections to this: the extremely meagre information available about Cromwell's undergraduate days offers no suggestion of any tendency towards thoughts of holiness, and the clashes of authority over such matters as the wearing of the surplice in college chapels seldom involved junior members of the university. Oliver's tutor described him as not 'so much addicted to speculation as to action'.[25] We know that he played football, a game which had not changed since Sir Thomas Elyot condemned it as 'nothing but healthy fury and extreme violence'.[26] One of his royalist detractors described Cromwell the student as wholly given over to 'football, cudgels or any other boisterous sport or game'.[27] Sir Philip Warwick informs us that 'the first years of his manhood were spent in a dissolute course of life, in good fellowship and gaming'.[28] All this receives convincing, if vague, confirmation from Cromwell's own confession that he 'loved darkness' and 'hated godliness'[29] and we do not need the oral tradition of tales such as Oliver's leaping on to his horse's back from a first-floor college window to see the young man as the stereotypical 'hearty' undergrad, liberated at last from the constraints of family discipline and the morality of provincial society, determined to enjoy himself and exercising his right to pay little attention to the earnest preachers to whom he was obliged to listen in chapel or university church. But this is not to say that he was unaffected by the intense religious atmosphere of Cambridge.

Oliver entered Sidney Sussex College in April 1616, two days before his seventeenth birthday, not to be trained as a scholar, nor with any thought of taking a degree, but to complete that education considered appropriate to a gentleman. He was above the average age of intake but might well be recognised from Henry Peacham's description of adolescent students:

These young things of twelve, thirteen and fourteen that have no more care than to expect the next carrier and where to sup on Fridays and fasting nights; no further thought of study than to trim up their studies with pictures and place the fairest books in openest view, which, poor lads, they scarce ever opened or understood not; that when they came to logic and the crabbed grounds of art, there is such a disproportion

108

between Aristotle's *Categories* and their childish capacities, that what, together with the sweetness of liberty, variety of company and so many kinds of recreation in town and fields abroad . . . they prove [as able to] gather sand as to attempt the difficulties of so rough and terrible a passage.[30]

Parents were well aware of the temptations ready to swoop – 'like buzzards upon lapwings'[31] – upon their tender offspring at university and that is why many of them favoured strict, even Puritan, tutors for their sons. John Preston, the radical preacher, was described as 'the greatest pupil-monger in England . . . having sixteen fellow commoners (most heirs to fair estate) admitted in one year in Queens' College, and provided convenient accommodation for them'.[32] Oliver's tutor, Richard Howlett, was not in that mould. To those who knew him well he was a 'moderate' man not disposed to be quarrelsome and 'far from Dr. Ward's rigidity in his ways'.[33] Howlett received moderate preferment in the Church, ending his days as Dean of Cashel Cathedral, Tipperary. The 'Dr Ward' with whom Howlett was compared, was Samuel Ward, Master of Sidney Sussex, a man of Puritan convictions and intense personal piety. His reflections upon the life of the university and his own soul's health (he took his spiritual temperature every day) are recorded in his diary. Therein subtle satanic ploys – 'my intemperance in eating plums', 'my little pity of the boy who was whipped in the hall' – were recorded alongside items of university politics – 'Observe two plots laid to bring our college to the wearing of the surplice. 1 Dr Goodge hath prescribed it to be worn in Magdalene College; 2 Dr Montagu hath also appointed it to be worn in Sidney College* . . . There is no way of escape for anything I can possibly discern. Our trust is in the name of the Lord.'[34]

In a small college humble undergraduates had fairly close contact with the fellows and even with the master and it has readily been assumed that something of Ward's intense and radical piety may have rubbed off on Cromwell. Ward undoubtedly set the tone of his college and, although Oliver was only at Sidney Sussex for little more than a year, this must have made a conscious or unconscious impression. But not necessarily a positive impression. A fun-loving and extrovert young man may not have been disposed to take

* Ward was at this time a fellow of Emmanuel.

seriously Ward's diatribes in the college chapel against such prevailing ills as drunkenness.

> Seer, art thou also blind? Watchman, art thou also blind or asleep? Or hath a spirit of slumber put out thine eyes? Up to thy watchtower! What decriest thou? Ah, Lord, what end or number is there of the vanities which mine eyes are weary of beholding? I see men walking like the tops of trees shaken with the winds, like masts of ships reeling on the tempestuous seas. Drunkenness, I mean, that hateful night-bird; which was wont to wait for the twilight, to seek nooks and corners, to avoid the hooting and wonderment of boys and girls; now as it were some eaglet to dare the sunlight, to fly abroad at high noon in every street, in open markets and fairs without fear or shame, without control or punishment, to the disgrace of the nation, the outfacing of magistracy and ministry, the utter undoing (without timely prevention) of health and wealth, piety and virtue, town and country, church and commonwealth.[35]

However, the point needs to be made that Ward was no militant Puritan. While bewailing the days around the turn of the century when his party had been inspiringly led and dominant in the university hierarchy, he took no stand against the changes enforced by the liberalising Vice-Chancellor and heads of colleges. Though unhappy, he conformed.

One question that presents itself regarding Cromwell's university career is 'Why Sidney Sussex?' His family had a long connection with Queens' and his friend, Oliver St John, had started there only a few months before Cromwell's arrival at the newer college. The answer that most readily suggests itself is fashion. The latest Cambridge foundation had come into being in accordance with the will of Frances, Countess of Sussex (d. 1589) and the prime mover in carrying into effect the benefactress's instructions was Sir John Harington – courtier, scholar and master of the Princess Elizabeth's household. Harington's sister married into the Montagu family which enjoyed great favour with James I and were considerable benefactors of the new college. Henry Montagu, who acquired Kimbolton and was created Earl of Manchester by Charles I, and James Montague, who followed an ecclesiastical career and ended his days as Bishop of Winchester, were both Harington's nephews. It was James who was appointed the first Master of Sidney Sussex.

In 1603, when the new King paid his famous visit to Hinching-brooke, his reception of James Montague was carefully noted:

> Here one might see the king (passing over all other doctors . . . his seniors) apply himself much in his discourse to Dr Montagu, Master of Sidney College. This was much observed by the courtiers (who can see the beam of royal favour shining in at a small cranny) interpreting it as a token of his speedy preferment, as indeed it came to pass.[36]

The Master brought to the college some of his own nephews and three grand-nephews and encouraged many friends in high places to send their sons. This patronage and the King's interest ensured that, for several years, Sidney Sussex was *the* college for scions of established and aspiring courtier families to attend. The Montagus' new prominence in Huntingdonshire gave the Cromwells added incentive to support the foundation with which they were so closely involved. During his brief stay in Cambridge, Oliver Cromwell, a gentleman's son of modest means, mixed with some of the elite of Jacobean society, men destined for carers at the royal court.

While he thus roistered, loving 'darkness' and hating 'godliness' and, doubtless, poking fun at solemn-faced preachers and pious fellow students, he may yet have been aware of the religious controversies which continued to reverberate through the world of town and gown. Thomas Goodwin, who went up to Christ's in 1614, remarked of his student years, 'As I grew up the noise of the Arminian controversy . . . began to be every man's talk and enquiry, and possessed my ears.'[37] The term 'Arminian' became a portmanteau word indicating one who rejected the stricter tenets of Calvin, institutionalised grace, thus elevating the importance of sacraments and the priesthood, and looked to other authorities than Scripture in matters of Church order, discipline and liturgy (see below, pp. 269ff for a fuller discussion of the Arminian controversy). It provided theological respectability to those who had a profound distaste for Puritanism and Roman Catholicism and was heartily welcomed by James I; it offered a middle way belief system between the two extremes he abhorred – 'vain Puritans' and 'proud, papal bishops'. Inevitably, most English Protestants did not see it that way. Arminianism was the postern gate through which popery was re-entering the English Church and men like Neile, Laud and Richard Montagu (no relation of the Kimbolton Montagus), the

111

leading High Church controversialist (later Bishop of Chichester), were those who were holding it wide open. In the autumn of 1617, only weeks after Cromwell's departure from Cambridge, Edward Simpson, a fellow of Trinity, was in hot water. In a sermon before the King at Royston he had ventured criticism of the Arminian view of grace. James was furious, demanded action from the senior members of the university and did not stop till he had obtained a recantation. This controversy was the molehill which would grow into a mountain over the next three decades.

It is doubtful whether these nice points of theological debate meant much to the young Oliver but some more localised issues did touch his undergraduate life. He found the hortatory fare on offer in Cambridge rich and varied after a dozen or so years of listening to Dr Beard twice or thrice a week. Undergraduates were required to pack into Great St Mary's on Sunday morning and afternoon *and* take notes of the sermons preached in rote by senior members of the university. Some of them must have been pretty turgid and it is little wonder that hundreds of students turned instead to the radical eloquence of John Preston at Queens' or the Sunday lecturer at Holy Trinity, where extra galleries had to be installed to cater for the swollen congregations. As everywhere, the lectureships in Cambridge were controversial.

It was only a few months since Richard Sibbes of St John's had been banned from the pulpit at Holy Trinity and deprived of his university post because of his Puritanism (he was soon provided with a lectureship at Gray's Inn by a sympathetic patron). Sermons and sermoneers were news and the subject of gossip in the taverns where students argued passionately and essayed witticisms as they excitedly manoeuvred towards individuality through the minefield of ideas.

Not a few experienced conversion in the intense atmosphere of the university town. Cromwell's contemporary, Thomas Goodwin, was impressed by Sibbes's preaching but found himself confused and unedified by the St Mary's sermons of 'the great wits of those times striving who of them should exceed each other' and was lured into 'the lusts and pleasures of sinning, but especially the ambition of glory and praise'. His crisis came when he heard a funeral sermon at which the preacher enlarged on the theme that 'every man had a time in which grace was offered him and if he neglected it 'twas just with God it should be hidden from his eyes'. The young man was stunned: 'I thought myself to be as one struck down by a mighty Power,' he later explained. At the age of nineteen he joined the ranks of the godly.[38] Cromwell's conversion did not occur during his time at Cambridge but he was certainly exposed to passionate, evangelical preaching of a kind which he had seldom encountered before and he struck up friendships among the more radical members of the university.

Oliver's undergraduate days were brought to a sudden end by his father's death. Robert Cromwell was in his late fifties when, in May or June 1617, he took to his bed. On 5 June he knew that he was dying and summoned a group of relatives and friends to witness his will. The document was dictated (very probably to Dr Beard) and attested, among others, by Robert's brother, Richard, and his nephew, John. The will's preamble is couched in terms of conventional Protestant piety. It bears no trace of that assurance of salvation to which members of the elect laid claim in such testaments. Robert informs those who shall survive him that he sets his affairs in order:

> being taught by long experience in others that man's life in his sound and perfect health is like a bubble of water and being at this present sick in body but of sound and perfect remembrance and finding such weakness that by course of nature I cannot continue long in this world, to that end, (being disburdened of all wordly affairs) I may during the residue of that time God shall suffer me to breathe, the more freely address my self wholly to the meditation of divine and heavenly things . . .[39]

Clearly, Robert Cromwell was no Puritan. He was buried on 24 June.

Robert's testamentary dispositions do not suggest that he reposed overwhelming confidence in his only son. He left the bulk of his estate exclusively to his wife for the term of twenty-one years with the proviso that Oliver might, during that time enjoy 'so much thereof as my said wife or his assigns in their discretion shall think meet'.[40] This arrangement obviously provided security for Elizabeth as a widow and made her an attractive proposition for remarriage and it safeguarded the marriage portions of her daughters. As for Oliver, it offered him a choice: he could make his own way in the world or he could take over the running of the modest Cromwell estate but under the guidance and supervision of his mother. Either way, he could not be certain of entering his full inheritance until he was thirty-eight. This caution of Robert's adds weight to the stories of Oliver's wild youth. The terrible example of Toby Palavicino cannot have been far from his mind. Oliver may not have been as licentious and dissolute as his cousin but, in the opinion of his parents, he still had a lot of growing up to do.

There is an aggravating paucity of evidence about the next stage of that process. Insistent tradition asserts that Oliver followed the family pattern of attendance at Lincoln's Inn and the alternative suggestion has been made that he studied at Gray's Inn.[41] Neither institution has any record of his membership. Cromwell's earliest biographer states, *en passant* that, 'his parents designed him to the study of the common law' but that 'he dived not over deep into this study'.[42] Another early account locates Cromwell securely at Lincoln's Inn which he attended 'that nothing might be wanting to make him a complete gentleman'.[43] A third testimony comes from an anonymous account of 1659: 'He came to Lincoln's Inn where he associated himself with those of the best rank and quality, and the most ingenious persons; for though he were of a nature not averse to study and contemplation, yet he seemed rather addicted to conversation and the reading of men and their several tempers than to a continual poring upon authors.'[44] Restoration writers accepted the general opinion of Cromwell's sojourn at the law schools but stressed his failure to achieve anything and his return to the fleshpots of Huntingdon.

It is not difficult to reconcile most of these fragments. It is very likely that Robert and Elizabeth hoped their son would follow the law. It was a path well-trodden by the younger sons of gentlemen. Oliver had an uncle (Richard) who was a lawyer resident at Lincoln's Inn. Oliver St John, who found himself in a very similar position to his friend's, went from Queens' to Lincoln's Inn in 1619 and there laid the foundation of a prominent legal and parliamentary career. But Cromwell lacked St John's staid and rather humourless application to study. We know enough of him by now to realise that he was an active, energetically minded young man impatient of book learning. Oliver Cromwell has sometimes been compared with the young Winston Churchill as someone with a mind too lively and an intelligence too keen to become bogged down in second-hand ideas; a man with a sense of destiny but no clear vision of what that destiny might be.

The Inns of Court offered gentlemen like Oliver a second best: if they could not complete a legal training, they could acquire that smattering of law which would enable them to fulfil their responsibilities as landlords and JPs. For some portion, then, of the next three years Cromwell was in London doing some growing up, insofar as his temperament allowed, before returning to Huntingdon to help his mother look after the family's rural and urban property. How one would love to know of Cromwell's life in the vibrant life of the Jacobean capital. Across the river Shakespeare's plays were still frequently staged along with those of the 'moderns' – Jonson, Fletcher, Ford, Webster, Middleton. City pulpits reverberated to the no less dramatic performances of Donne, Preston, Sibbes and Thomas Adams. Daily, parliamentarians, lawyers, merchants and noblemen met in St Paul's, walking up and down the aisles to discuss the latest news and scandal. At street corners the sellers of satirical ballads and news-sheets stood, ready to run when the constable's men appeared.

There were common themes treated of in all these forms of popular entertainment and debate; corruption at court, for example. Ben Jonson lampooned the beribboned fop and whipped the easy virtue of ladies who preferred abortions to child-bearing or chastity:

> Is it the pain affrights? That's soon forgot.
> Or your complexion's loss? You have a pot,
> That can restore that . . .

> What should the cause be? Oh, you live at court:
> And there's both loss of time, and loss of sport
> In a great belly . . .

> Write then, on the womb,
> Of the not born, yet buried, here's the tomb.[45]

The balladmonger was more direct in naming names:

> They say Sejanus* doth bestow
> What ever office doth befall
> But tis well known it is not so
> For he is soundly paid for all . . .

* 'Sejanus' is Buckingham; Digby is John Digby, chief negotiator of the Spanish match, who became Earl of Bristol in 1622; Yelverton is Sir Henry Yelverton, imprisoned in the Tower in 1620 for opposing royal policy.

> When Charles hath got the Spanish girl
> The Puritans will scowl and brawl
> Then Digby shall be made an Earl
> And the Spanish gold shall pay for all . . .
>
> When Yelverton shall be released
> And Buckingham begin to fall
> Then will the Commons be well pleased
> Which day hath long been wished of all.[46]

And on the same theme Thomas Adams, 'the prose Shakespeare' of Puritan theologians* inveighed from his pulpit near St Paul's:

> Your gallant thinks not the distressed, the blind, the lame to be part of his care: it concerns him not: true, and therefore heaven concerns him not: it is infallible truth, if they have no feeling of others' miseries, they are no members of Christ: go on now in thy scorn, thou proud royster: admire the fashion and stuff thou wearest: while the poor mourns for nakedness: feast royal *Dives*, while *Lazarus* can get no crumbs: Apply, *Absolom* thy sound, healthful limbs to lust and lewdness, while the same blind, maimed, cannot derive a penny from thy purse, though he move his suit in the name of Jesus; thou givest testimony to the world, to thy own conscience, that thou art but a *Judas*.[47]

Cromwell could not have lacked for intellectual stimulus in the London of 1617–20.

Nor companions. Oliver had several friends and relatives at the Inns of Court in these years – Oliver St John, Edmund Waller, Henry Cromwell, Robert Barrington, Edmund Dunch, Robert Waller. And among other contemporaries were men with whom he was later very closely associated – Robert, Lord Rich, John Claypole, John Glynne, Henry Lawrence and John Jones. Beyond this circle there were a dozen or more trainee lawyers who were to feature prominently as parliamentary opponents of Charles I. Indeed, the area bounded by Holborn, Chancery Lane and the Strand, might almost be considered the nursery for England's revolution.

These cannot have been easy years for a man of Cromwell's enormous energy. Before he had come to terms with his own identity

* Robert Southey.

116

he had been thrust into adult responsibilities. Torn between the diversions of the city and his concern for his sisters and widowed mother; needing to prove himself to himself and to his family; seeking and not finding a meaningful role – all these created tensions which must have contributed to that emotional instability which was a part of his personality a few years later. It was only natural that he should seek the comfort and support of family and friends. This would certainly have included his uncle and his uncle's associates at the royal court but it also embraced that circle of Essex-London gentlemen and merchants to whom he was related through his aunt, Joan Barrington. This in turn led to his marriage, on 22 August 1620, to Elizabeth Bourchier. Her father, Sir James Bourchier, the furrier, had an impressive town house in the City, an estate near Felsted and was closely involved with the Barringtons and Riches through marriage alliances, through business dealings and through a common dissatisfaction with the court and policies of James I.

A large question mark hangs over this union between Oliver and Elizabeth, which turned out to be so happy and successful: why did a wealthy, upwardly mobile merchant consent to the marriage of his daughter with the heir to an exceedingly modest estate? Sir James was very nouveau-riche, having received a grant of arms as recently as 1610, and, if at all typical of his class, would have seen his children and the portions settled upon them as the means of buying into the 'ancientry'. The fact that the wedding was announced shortly after Oliver came of age might suggest that it was a love match but such were very rare in the propertied classes where parents and relatives tended to be much more hard-headed than their romantically inclined children. We know about one side of the financial arrangements connected with this Bourchier-Cromwell liaison. No record of Elizabeth's portion has survived. It was, presumably, not large for it seems to have made no serious difference to the resources of the Huntingdon family. Oliver, on the other hand, was under a massive legal bond of £4000 to one Thomas Morley, a colleague and in-law of Sir James, to make a jointure on his wife of 'all that parsonage house at Hartford with all the glebe lands and tithes in the county of Huntingdon'.[48] The terms of this agreement suggest a considerable degree of caution on the part of Elizabeth's family. Legend has it that the marriage was brought about by the urging of the Barringtons. If this was the case there was an interesting sequel three or for years later. As we have seen, when Oliver St John wanted to marry Joanna

Altham it was the Barringtons, the girl's maternal grandparents, who had to be talked round, on this occasion by the Earl of Bedford. In both cases kinship finally counted for more than riches – kinship and, perhaps, shared ideology. One fact is beyond dispute: Oliver's character was acceptable to Sir James Bourchier. Any youthful wildness must, by now, have been put behind him.

> . . . since ye must be *communis parens* to all your people, so choose your servants indifferently out of all quarters; not respecting other men's appetites [i.e. 'preferences'], but their own qualities.
>
> . . . prefer especially to your service, so many as have truly served me . . .[49]

It was no small part of Charles I's tragedy that he attempted to follow the contradictory advice laid down by his father. He tried to like men his parent approved of; or perhaps it would be truer to say he tried to approve of men his parent liked. His selection of advisers and companions was governed, not by discernment, but by a set of prejudices – and even they were not his own.

The mentors of the prince's early years were, of course, chosen by James. For all his faults, the King was a fair judge of character. Certainly his evaluation could be thrown out of kilter by a well-turned calf or a boyish smile but his assessment of intellectual ability was seldom at fault. It is to his credit that he did not only choose scholars of his own persuasion for the households of his children; the trust he reposed in men like Harington and John Preston is proof of that. He showed the same broad-mindedness when he appointed Thomas Murray as tutor to the five-year-old Prince Charles.

Murray was a member of a Lowland clan which had been conspicuous in its opposition to Mary Queen of Scots and its support for her young son. The Murrays were convinced Presbyterians, determined to preserve the independence of the Kirk, and Thomas's younger brother, William, was a minister at Dysart, Fifeshire. The family thus represented that section of humanity whom, above all other, James loathed. They were,

> very pests in the church and commonwealth: whom no desserts can oblige, neither oaths or promises bind; breathing nothing but sedition

118

and calumnies, aspiring without measure, railing without reason, and making their own imaginations (without any warrant of the world) the square of their conscience. I protest before the great God . . . that ye shall never find with any Highland or Border thieves greater ingratitude and more lies and vile perjuries than with these fanatic spirits.[50]

On more than one occasion Thomas Murray crossed swords with the Archbishop of St Andrews, the man charged by James with bringing the Scottish Church under ecclesiastical discipline. His grace feared that Murray's closeness to the heir to the throne would prejudice the maintenance of royal and episcopal authority north of the border. But with the Stuarts personal considerations almost always outweighed principles, or it might be truer to say that support for favourites and loyal servants became a principle of first resort. Murray, who was much of an age with James, had grown up along-side him in the Scottish court and had been an intellectual sparring partner for as long as James could remember. Thc King had a high regard for Murray's learning and wisdom and as soon as his younger son reached the age when he required daily lessons he appointed him to the post of tutor with a pension of two hundred marks a year for life. This was only one of many perks which came Murray's way in recognition of his services and, in addition, James put on record his gratitude for

the pains and travails employed by you, not only in the careful education of our dearly beloved son, the prince, and instructing him in all kinds of good learning according to the capacity of his tender years, but also in penning and framing his missive letters in divers languages, directed either to ourself or foreign princes.[51]

Murray obviously did his job well because everyone who knew the growing prince witnessed his developing skills and his application to his studies. 'I must praise his accomplishments,' George Carleton, the newly appointed chaplain, recorded in 1615. 'He has more understanding than the late prince at his age and is, in behaviour, shy, grave, sweet in speech, very admired, without any evil inclinations, and willing to take advice.'[52]

Such fulsome asseverations should not be taken completely at face value. Members of the prince's household were sure to present themselves and their charge in the best possible light, particularly when reporting to a parent who prided himself on his intellectual accomplishments and hoped that his second son, unlike his first, would grow up a scholar. Charles had not and never would have striking intellectual capacity. He lacked the imagination which enables the mind to rise above the mere assembling of facts. What he did possess was application and a desire to please a parent who was more a schoolmaster than a father. The bills for schoolbooks submitted by Murray suggest an education that was both broad and deep. Charles readily acquired the habit of self-discipline necessary for success in the classroom as well as at the tiltyard, riding school, fencing salon and tennis court, but there were certainly times when he found his tutelage hard and some of the childhood experiences he was obliged to undergo built up unconscious resentments.

One such occurred when the prince was ten years old. His father's admiration for logic-chopping academics bordered on the obsessive. When disputations were staged for his pleasure at the universities James loved nothing more than to enter the fray himself and impress the audience with his verbal swordplay. In 1610 this pushing father decided to initiate young Charles into the delights of public debate; it would build up the boy's confidence and help him to overcome his speech defect. So, a theological disputation was staged and Charles was obliged to engage in contest with some of the King's chaplains before an admiring court. It is not difficult to imagine what an agonising ordeal this must have been for the withdrawn, stuttering child. The legacy of such experiences was complex. Within a few years Charles was able to attend the House of Lords and speak there in debates. Yet, he never lost his distaste for dialectics and, as King, could not accept the equality implicit in the discussion of principles. As for his relationship with his father, it was inevitable that the mould into which James forced his son would one day break.

Something else lay behind this particular exercise: Charles's mind was much more open to varied influences than his brother's and, as we have seen, both parents attempted to stuff it with their own religious ideologies. Just as Catholic and Protestant dogmas had competed for dominance in James's Scottish youth, so now his son was subjected to the same bombardment. George Carleton's appointment was one of several made to counter Queen Anne's Romanising influence. At about the same time Thomas Murray was promoted to the post of secretary.

After the Prince of Wales's death the indoctrination of the new heir assumed much more importance and the pressure on Charles's religious development was stepped up. Several members of Henry's establishment were transferred to his brother's entourage and, in addition, two sober divines were 'placed with him and ordered never to leave him'. They were Dr George Hakewill and Dr Thomas Winniffe, earnest Puritans in their thirties who had been friends ever since their days as fellows at the warmly Calvinist Exeter College, Oxford. Hakewill was a fearless preacher and disputant who had close contacts with Calvinist churches on the continent, later wrote (among other works) *An Apology . . . of the Power and Providence of God in the Governance of the World* and devoted much energy to controversy with the Romanising Bishop Goodman. Of Thomas Winniffe it was said 'Nothing was more mild, modest and humble, yet learned, eloquent and honest' than he. He shared Hakewill's convictions but not his constancy. Winniffe's misfortune was that while his character glistened like gold it also had the malleable quality of that metal. He had a talent for annoying people by his public denunciations and then failing to earn their grudging respect by at least standing firmly by his words. In 1621 he was involved in a fracas with highly placed Roman Catholics but, twenty years later, he so infuriated the Puritans that a mob burned down his London house.

The very fact that James found it necessary to ring-fence the heir to the throne with so many 'safe' Protestants is an indication of the potency of Anne's religious ideas in her son's life and we may be sure that Thomas Murray kept the King informed of every Catholic encroachment into his son's daily routine.

The household gathered around Charles at St James's Palace was, in its early years, a continuation of Henry's earnest Calvinist academy. It was a close-knit community whose members took very seriously their responsibilities to one another and especially to the prince. When, in 1616, Hakewill wrote a refutation of the views of Benjamin Carier, an erstwhile royal chaplain turned Roman Catholic, he declared in the dedicatory epistle that he had based his treatise on certain works written by the King and that he intended it as a source book from which Charles could learn how to refuse the insidious propaganda of the papists. Sycophantic this may have been but it certainly indicates clearly the purpose for which Hakewill and his colleagues knew themselves to have been appointed.

The Calvinist tone of the prince's household was securely established and James could be sure that those who had charge of his son would guard him against other influences. At the same time the King encouraged ecclesiastical diversity in his own court and it was inevitable that Charles would be increasingly exposed to it as he grew up. James liked to hear rival sermons, to arbitrate in doctrinal disputes and to watch the power struggles of different factions. Ambitious clerics and clerics pursuing party agendas sought to ingratiate themselves with the Sovereign, usually by obtaining the patronage of royal favourites. The man who became the most successful ecclesiastical *éminence grise* was the Puritan-hater, Richard Neile. At the very beginning of the reign he was appointed Clerk of the Closet and his duties involved the maintenance of worship in the royal chapel. Despite the string of other preferments which came his way, Neile retained the clerkship until 1632 and he used it to ensure that the King was only served a fare of beautified Prayer Book rites. Neile controlled the preaching rota and, though he could not exclude the more extreme Calvinists from the royal pulpit, he laboured to restrict the influence of evangelicals. And he had other ways of exercising influence. Over the years he applied the water-on-the-stone method of turning the King against Puritans by playing on his fears of disorder and rebellion. He gradually brought more and more men of his own stamp into the household, most notably his chaplain, William Laud, who first preached before the King in 1609. (He almost failed in his efforts to advance Laud, for James neither liked nor trusted the argumentative little man and Laud, growing despondent of ever gaining promotion, had to be persuaded to stay.) Some of Neile's other tricks were more subtle. One was to distract the King's attention from the sermon: 'When any man preached that had the renown of piety' he would lean across from his chair in the royal closet and 'entertain the King with a merry tale . . . which the King would after laugh at and tell those near him he could not hear the preacher for the old bishop'.[53]

Factions and personalities were constantly at play in the Jacobean court but the King maintained control, certainly as far as regulating the direct influences brought to bear on Charles was concerned. Nothing demonstrates that more clearly than the sequence of events which brought two strong but violently opposed characters into Charles's life. In March 1615 James took his son on a visit to Cambridge. One of the entertainments laid on for the King's especial delight was a philosophical disputation with the arcane motion 'Whether dogs can make syllogisms'. Two young graduates particularly attracted James by their wit and subtlety, John Preston of Queens' whose name has already appeared in these pages, and Matthew Wren of Pembroke, who will emerge later as a persecuting bishop. Experienced bystanders remarked the favourable impression made by the protagonists and prophesied bright futures for them but no royal preferment came their way immediately. Wren grew familiar with the court through being appointed as chaplain to the saintly Lancelot Andrews, Bishop of Ely, royal councillor and constant adviser to the King. Wren had in common with his patron the love of ritual, of the adornment of churches and the commitment to episcopacy as the very *esse* of the Church. What he did not share was Andrews's wisdom and toleration of other viewpoints.

While Wren remained within the wide ambit of royal favour, Preston, it seemed, forfeited all possibility of preferment. He took holy orders and shortly afterwards became Dean of Queens' and was soon the intellectual leader of the Cambridge Puritan establishment. He became the star preacher of the university, 'the greatest pulpit-monger in England in man's memory', as a royalist divine later described him. In Cambridge (the Cambridge of Oliver Cromwell's undergraduate year) Preston drew such crowds of town and gown to Queens' chapel, Sunday by Sunday, that the fellows had to elbow their way through the throng to reach their stalls. James Hamilton, himself inclined to Presbyterianism, suggested that a preaching place might be found at court for this rising celebrity, but James had decidedly gone off the skilled debater now that his Puritan colours were being so prominently displayed. The King's suspicions appeared justified in 1620 when Preston had a brush with episcopal authority. The numbers of students attending the Holy Trinity lectures and neglecting Great St Mary's had reached such alarming proportions that the university authorities put Holy Trinity out of bounds. Preston responded by starting his own series of addresses in St Botolph's immediately after the university sermon. Establishing yet another vocal exercise of zealous high Calvinism was not what the Vice-Chancellor and his ecclesiastical friends had in mind. The local representative of the diocesan chancellor, Robert Newcome, turned up one Sunday and provoked a near riot by barring Preston's ascent to the pulpit. In the ensuing enquiry Preston was disciplined by the Vice-Chancellor and that might have been the end of the matter. However, news of the fracas had reached the court and Puritan sympathisers there were anxious to obtain preferment for this outstanding man. Hamilton continued to sing his praises and he was joined by no less an advocate than Buckingham. James agreed to hear Preston again and ordered the Dean of Queens' to preach before him on his next visit to Hinchingbrooke. It would be very satisfying if one had a scrap of evidence to place a young Oliver Cromwell and a young Charles Stuart in the congregation at this occasion when so prominent an orator was performing at the Cromwell mansion. In its absence we can only claim it as 'possible'. After this test piece James was not disposed to change his opinion of Dr Preston but Villiers, who was taking an increasingly independent line, and had his own reasons for wooing the Puritan party in court and parliament, argued the preacher's cause vigorously. 'He saw ... that King James approved not his siding with him; yet was he more express than ever in his affections to him and freer with him.'[54] Buckingham had no leanings whatsoever towards the godly but he was a pragmatic politician and he knew the value of having friends in both opposing ecclesiastical camps. Furthermore, since Preston was a man who could not be ignored it made sense to the favourite to have him on his own side. He also recognised that this Puritan was not like most of his colleagues: while fearlessly denouncing sin at all social levels, he possessed the gracious manners of an accomplished courtier. Placed in high position, therefore, he might be a valuable ally. Villiers persuaded the King to appoint the young Puritan as Chaplain-in-Ordinary to the prince. But James was just as skilled at stratagems. A few months later, he provided Charles with another chaplain – Preston's ideological opponent, Matthew Wren.

We can only speculate on the rival sermons Charles must have had to listen to in his private chapel from these two men whose subsequent troubled careers diverged so widely. For a few years Preston enjoyed widespread fame. With Buckingham's backing he became preacher at Lincoln's Inn (just too late for Cromwell to be among his regular congregation), Master of Emmanuel, Cambridge, and Holy Trinity lecturer. With positions at court, in the City and in the university, no Puritan was more influential, and he used his contacts to advance radical ideas at the centre and to support provincial activists such as Arthur Hildersam, an intransigent Nonconformist who in a ministry of forty-four years was suspended no less than six times on episcopal authority. A man as partisan and uncompromising as Preston could not last for ever in the Stuart court. Although he relied on Buckingham's support, he opposed the favourite's policy of being all things to all men: he preached 'against the mingling of religions and mixing truth with falsehood and showed how impossible it was to mingle truth with error or make up one religion of theirs [i.e. Catholics] and our own'.[55] He was already out of favour when he died in 1628, probably of cancer, at the age of forty-one. At that date Wren, though his opinions were well formed, had yet to embark on his career as scourge of the Puritans. As a diocesan in the thirties he was widely hated for his persecution of the godly and his closing of lectureships. He was arrested by Parliament in 1640 and spent most of the next twenty years in the Tower.

The ministrations of such rivals can scarcely have helped Charles cope with the confusions of adolescence. His self-concept was largely modelled on the remembrance of the brother he had idolised. His Calvinist mentors encouraged him to be the Elisha to Henry's Elijah and to assume the mantle of the godly prince so cruelly plucked from his sibling's shoulders. Charles was constantly regaled with anecdotes by Henry's former tutors and companions and doubtless suffered the younger brother's fate of being compared with the first-born. But Charles was not Henry and he had to escape from the dead prince's shadow. This was a slow and painful process, very probably tinged with an element of guilt. The young man became even more turned in upon himself so that courtiers and diplomats found it difficult to understand what he was really thinking. The same problem faces the historian seeking to chart Charles's development from dutiful Calvinist youth to aggressive Catholic maturity.

The propulsion of those years came from a unique combination of teenage rebellion and filial duty. As well as discovering and asserting his own identity, Charles had to try to understand just what it was his King and father wanted of him – and that was far from easy. Looking back on the years 1618–23 when his own convictions on matters of faith were formed (and from which sprang so many of his later woes), Charles claimed, 'Among all [my father's] cares in my education his chief was to settle me right in religion.' Throughout his son's childhood and early adolescence James's principal concern was the simple one of making sure that the boy grew up a good Protestant, but after 1617 this became complicated by the imperatives of foreign policy. That was the year the King opened negotiations with Madrid to marry his heir to the Spanish infanta. James shared quite sincerely the nation's abhorrence of Roman Catholicism but this did not prevent him pursuing his plans for a Habsburg marriage alliance, which would, at a stroke, solve all the Crown's money problems and enhance his role as Europe's peace-maker. If he gave any thought at all to his son's future domestic bliss he may have believed that, just as he contained the activities of Anne and her household, so Charles would be able to control his wife. Perhaps his financial problems were so pressing that he did not properly assess the pros and cons of a policy which alienated the greater part of the political nation. His parliaments and most of his councillors were thoroughly alarmed and followed the on-off negotiations of subsequent years with anxiety; to them a Spanish alliance would be the not-so-thin edge of a monstrous Roman Catholic wedge. Those who had any contacts with the Spanish court knew that King Philip and his religious advisers were as committed to the reconversion of England as their predecessors had been at the time of the Armada.

For Charles's household – and, of course, for Charles himself – the conflict between the King's private instructions and his public policy was especially disturbing. At an emotional level the prince was already struggling with the grey earnestness and simplicity of his Calvinist instructors. He was discovering in himself a love of those arts which accentuated colour, voluptuous shapes, luscious melodies, amusing yet instructive mythologies and the seductive delights of the flesh. When he attended worship in his father's chapel, with its vividly painted religious images and its large silver crucifix he found it more to his taste than the austere ritual at St James's. By 1621 the prince's mentors were distinctly alarmed that they were 'losing' him. Presenting a book of his sermons to Charles, Hakewill intimated that the young man was in danger of turning his back on all that he had learned 'now that your frequent presence with his Majesty enforceth your often absence from your Family [i.e. the household at St James's]'. In the following text the chaplain pulled no punches and roundly attacked the 'Romanised' worship of the royal chapel: 'The Ark and Dagon will not stand together: neither can a crucifix ordained to such an use, and Christ himself well dwell together under the same roof.'[56]

The development of Charles's religious convictions was, doubt-less, gradual but 1619 seems to have been a crisis year for him. In

March his mother died. One aspect of Charles's grief was a warming to those things Anne had loved and this, in part, lay behind the unseemly squabble between father and son over her will. At the same time her passing removed the principal Catholic influence from Charles's life and with it the imperative of maintaining a strong Calvinist barrier to that influence. Then, within weeks, and before his late queen could be buried, James, too, fell desperately ill. He lay at Royston doubled up with excruciating pain from bladder stones, his face a mass of ulcers and his body throbbing with fever. His senior bishops, realising that they faced an unknown future should the Crown pass to Charles while he was still a minor, made their anxieties known and Lancelot Andrews bewailed to James the fact that the prince was surrounded by Scots who properly understood neither the liturgy nor the doctrine of the Church of England. Richard Perrinchief, royal hagiographer, champion of the Anglican establishment and enemy of all toleration, represented the sick King as making a solemn vow that 'if God should be pleased to restore his health, he would so instruct the prince in the controversies of religion as should secure his affections to the present establishment'.[57] Like many sickbed promises this one lost its urgency once the crisis had passed. However, it was from about this time that the King took a personal hand in his son's instruction and important changes were made to the prince's entourage – but only after a showdown which occurred in 1621 (see below).

The more important result of these traumatic events was that it brought together the triumvirate which would rule the Stuart dominions for the rest of the reign. As Charles and Buckingham stood by the King's bed in Royston, James urged his son to protect the Church of England, respect its bishops and be guided in all things by the favourite. Then, even before Charles could accustom himself to the changed pattern of his life, it was Villiers's turn to be at death's door. He took to his bed in June and the royal father and son visited him almost daily. This bewildering succession of events impacted heavily on the seat of Charles's emotions. He had to grapple with his feelings for his father and his new friend, face up to the prospect of his own coming responsibilities, acclimatise himself to the possibility of marriage to a Roman Catholic princess, weigh the opinions of the Neile circle which were now pressed upon him at every opportunity *and* listen to the contrary urgings of his own household officers. Small wonder that he kept his own council and that, as the Venetian ambassador observed, 'before his father he always aims at suppressing his own feelings'.[58]

The crunch came two years later. Murray and his colleagues could not avoid taking an interest in government policy, particularly as it affected their young charge. The fact that the basic values of Whitehall and St James's seemed to be drifting further apart made it very difficult, at times, for men of principle to know how to act. The King, like his son after him, was sublimely indifferent to the fears and prejudices of his people and saw no need to explain the apparent or real inconsistency between his religious beliefs and his political actions. The men who were tutoring Charles and preparing him for his future role could not encourage this compartmentalisation, particularly when the prince seemed to be being drawn into dangerous courses. In the autumn of 1621, when the marriage negotiations were enthusiastically revived, Murray, Winniffe and Hakewill had secret talks with Archbishop Abbot and other prominent men concerned about the drift of policy. They decided that a confidential approach to Charles was justified and Hakewill wrote a treatise explaining the dangers of the Spanish match for presentation to the prince. When he nervously handed it over he begged Charles to be discreet: 'If you show it to your father I shall be undone for my goodwill,' he is reputed to have said. He did well to be afraid; Dr Sampson Price, a colleague at St James's, had just spent a spell in the Fleet for an injudicious sermon preached to the court at Oatlands. Charles promised to keep the secret – and within two hours passed the manuscript to the King. A furious James gave the offenders a dressing-down and temporarily banished them from the court.[59]

Two of the conspirators left Charles's service soon after this event and may not have been sorry to do so. Hakewill returned to his Oxford college and passed there most of the rest of his days. Thomas Murray, a man widely esteemed for his straightforwardness, had been tutor and, later, secretary to the prince for almost seventeen years and now that the young man's formal education was over he was minded to seek a position removed from the centre of national life. In 1617 James had promised him the provostship of Eton but this was blocked on suspicion of the candidate's Puritanism. The position fell vacant again in 1622 and this time, with the support of Buckingham, Murray's application was successful, though not before the Bishop of Lincoln had, once more, raised religious doubts about him.

Winniffe seems to have learned nothing from these events. Six months after the Hakewill fracas he preached a sermon against the Spanish match. In it he castigated Philip III's ambassador, Diego Gondomar, and likened General Spinola, the Catholic conqueror of the Palatinate, to Satan. James was furious at this slight to a government whose friendship he was actively courting and had Dr Winniffe unceremoniously hustled off to the Tower. The poor doctor was terribly shaken by this display of royal wrath. He hastened to pen a grovelling apology and send it to the Spanish embassy. Gondomar interceded for the repentant cleric, who was released after a few days. His submissiveness ensured Winniffe his pupil's continued favour. He remained a royal chaplain and Charles ensured that subsequent preferment did not take him far away from the court and capital.

This train of incidents provides us with the first recorded indication of Charles's untrustworthiness. In the years to come other royal servants as well as opponents of the King would learn the unreliability of Charles Stuart's word. His betrayal of men who had served him faithfully for years also indicated that the prince was coming to a clearer understanding of his priorities. It was time to think seriously about the duties that lay ahead and as he prepared himself for kingship he looked increasingly to his father and his father's ministers for guidance.[60] The fact that the King now showed a more open interest in him was of great emotional significance to the young man. His father was the only family Charles now had and he grasped eagerly at any moments of intimacy. The King's new involvement in his son's training would have been enough in itself to surround with an aura of reverence those bombastic utterances to which James treated him but his father's obviously failing health added a poignancy to their meetings. James was prone to a complex of disorders whose symptoms were carefully noted by his physician.

The liver . . . is liable to obstructions and generates much bile . . . He often swells up with wind . . . Sometimes he is melancholy from the spleen in the left hypochondrium exciting disorders . . . he becomes very irascible . . . often his eyes become yellow but it soon passes off; he glows with heat and his appetite falls off; he sleeps badly; he readily vomits and at times so violently that his face is covered with red spots for two or three days; he sometimes has difficulty in swallowing . . . Vapours from his stomach precede illness. The alvine discharge is uncertain . . . He sweats easily owing to his delicate skin. He often suffers bruises from knocking against timber, from frequent falls, rubbing of greaves and stirrups and other external causes which he carefully scrutinises and notes in a book to show to his physicians that it was not from an internal disorder and so avoids having to take medicines which he detests. He is of exquisite sensitiveness and most impatient of pain . . .

Arthritis: Many years ago he had such pain and weakness in the foot that it was left with an odd twist when walking. In 1616 pain and weakness spread to knees, shoulders and hands, and for four months he had to stay in bed or in a chair. Three times in his life he was seized with excruciating pain in his thighs . . . which, as if by spasms of the muscles and tendons, most pertinaciously twitched at night. His legs became lean and atrophied due to lack of exercise not calling forth the spirits and nourishment to the lower limbs.[61]

The King frequently suffered from diarrhoea, vomiting and other digestive disorders and found sleep difficult. The father to whom Charles had never been able to get very close and who had seldom shown him deep affection was now an ailing and irascible old man who might not live much longer.

James I has often been presented by historians as a grotesque: a slobbering, incontinent king, fondling boys and presiding indulgently over a sin-ridden court. Insofar as this image has any accuracy, it is a representation of James in his last years. It is based on the indignation of preachers and the ill will of gossiping pamphleteers, whose prose offerings are distorting mirrors in which vices are twisted and bloated into bizarre shapes. If we try not to be overswayed by hyperbole what we see is an old man whose undoubted sillinesses have become exaggerated and who tries to suck youth and vigour from the presence of beautiful and athletic companions. His afflictions, the reminders of his mortality, frightened him and those who valued his favour learned not to allude to them. In October 1617, the great London gossip and letter-writer, John Chamberlain, passing on the latest news to a friend, reported,

The king is now at Hinchingbrooke, by Huntingdon, where he hath sprained his leg in his bed – as he saith – but it must not in any wise be thought to be the gout; so that, unless he amend the faster, it is doubted whether he will be here at Hallowtide.[62]

James kept up his long autumnal hunting expeditions and his court was the scene of boisterous slapstick entertainments which the King enjoyed with the 'lads' of his chamber:

> Sir Edward Zouche, Sir George Goring and Sir John Finet were the chief and master fools and surely this fooling got them more than any other wisdom, far above them in dessert: Zouche his part to sing bawdy songs and tell bawdy tales; Finet to compose these songs. There were a set of fiddlers brought up on purpose for this fooling and Goring was master of the games for fooleries, sometime presenting David Droman and Archer Armstrong the king's fool on the back of other fools, to tilt at one another till they fell together by the ears.[63]

This ad hoc buffoonery – described admittedly by a disgruntled ex-courtier dismissed from royal service for making scurrilous jokes about Scotland, a touchy subject with the King – was typical of the day-to-day cultural menu at Whitehall, Royston, Newmarket or Hinchingbrooke. It reveals James's sublimated sexuality and reads more like the last stages of a rugger club outing than the in-house entertainment of a refined European court – earthy, vulgar and coarse rather than morally reprehensible.

There were several aspects of the King's behaviour which sat very ill on someone who had once charged his heir to 'make your court and company to be a pattern of godliness and all honest virtues to all the rest of the people'.[64] His relationship with his favourites was emotionally, and sometimes physically, homosexual. This handed power to those who should have been servants and encouraged all those vices to which royal courts were, in any case, prone: simony, nepotism, intrigue, damaging rivalries, sexual licence and over-indulgence of all kinds. James, for all that we now know, neither felt nor expressed any shame for the relationships he enjoyed with his closest companions. There was, however, one habit which upset the soberer members of the court and which the King did feel sensitive about:

> He would make a great deal too bold with God in his passion, both in cursing and swearing, and one strain higher, verging on blasphemy; but would in his better temper say he hoped God would not impute them as sins and lay them to his charge, seeing they proceeded from passion.[65]

Prince Henry had fined members of his household for bad language and there is no doubt his father's profanity made Charles wince.

He did not need the tirades of Puritan preachers to be aware of the failings of his father's court.

> . . . neither fornicators, nor idolaters, nor adulterers, nor wantons, nor thieves, nor covetous, nor drunkards, nor extortioners shall inherit the Kingdom of God: This is spoken of kings, as well as of others. And in the Revelation, we find, that the fearful and unbelieving, the abominable, murderers and whore-mongers, and sorcerers, idolaters, and all liars shall have their part in the lake that burneth with fire and brimstone: And this is spoken of the king as well as of the beggar . . .
>
> Nay moreover, great men, noble men, and mighty princes, are not only liable to [Hell], but the greatest part of them shall to the devil . . .[66]

So thundered Henry Greenwood from St Paul's Cross in June 1614, but such fiery evocations of divine wrath were commonplace and many ministers chosen to preach before the court were much more specific in their condemnation of sin in high places. Prince Henry had dared his father's anger by fearlessly criticising the moral laxity of the Whitehall midden. Such teenage rebellion was alien to Charles's nature but he had been too well trained by sober pedagogues not to recognise the immorality his father easily tolerated. Instead the young man reacted *internally* by becoming fastidious to the point of prudery. He ate and drank sparingly and never seems to have been lured into any sexual adventures. There were occasions when he banished licentious courtiers from his presence.

Charles had to try to evolve a personal belief system in a confusing world where refinement vied with vulgarity and worldly vice with the mystique of divine kingship. In any one day he might experience the sophisticated and elaborate formality of a joust, a masque or a banquet for some visiting dignitary, be the unwilling spectator of a lavatorial prank by the King's cronies, hear a fresh piece of unsavoury gossip about the adulterous antics of some household officer, and listen to a sermon about 'the divinity which doth hedge a king'.

His father had laid the theoretical basis of the kind of religion appropriate to a King of England:

> Remember then, that this glistening worldly glory of kings, is given them by God, to teach them to press so to glister & shine before their people, in all works of sanctification & righteousness, that their persons as bright lamps of godliness and virtue may, going in & out before their people, give light to all their steps.[67]

James's religion was of the head rather than the heart. A man fond of argument who prided himself on his cleverness in dialectic, he adhered firmly to the Calvinistic doctrines of the sovereignty of God, providence and election but reached his own conclusions from them. Thus, he could assert with the most earnest radical, 'It is atheism and blasphemy to dispute what God can do: good Christians content themselves with his will revealed in his word,' but then draw an ultra-reactionary moral: 'So it is presumptious and high contempt in a subject to dispute what a king can do.'[68] Where an evangelical Puritan rendered heartfelt thanks and obedience to God for numbering him among the elect, James charged his son, 'Ye have a double obligation; first for that he made you a man; and next for that he made you a little god to sit on his throne and rule over other men.'[69] Divine order was the keystone of James's religion. It was Protestant and biblical but not evangelical. Thus he welcomed the Reformation in Scotland but regretted that it had been carried through by a 'popular tumult' and by men 'clogged with their own passions'.[70] He acknowledged that God called men and women into the community of the saved but rejected the egalitarianism among the saints and the parity of ministries which Puritans inferred from this: 'parity is the mother of confusion and enemy to unity which is the mother of order.'[71] And something he could never stomach was the loving intimacy the godly claimed to enjoy with their Saviour, 'for if a subject will not speak but reverently to a king, much less should any flesh presume to talk with God as with his companion.'[72] James's religion in practice if not in theory was one of moral striving which placed emphasis on the human will and its capacity to achieve divine approbation rather than relying purely on election and irresistible grace. The barrier between him and the Puritans was emotional rather than rational; lacking profound experience of affective religion himself, he resented those who did possess such a faith and who used it as the basis of disturbing theological and political ideals. To counter the elect's assurance of salvation he assented to a relationship with God based upon *his* divine election

133

as King; a relationship which guaranteed order, decorum and the moral rectitude which flowed from the exercise of royal justice.

Rationally James supported his politico-religious system with a rag-bag of ideas and bigoted assertions derived from Gallic absolutism, paranoid hatred of the radicalism he had been subjected to in youth, abhorrence of civil disorder and the need to assert his own authority in church and state; his 'doctrine' of the divine right of kings was composed of rhetoric more than argument. Paradoxically, this autocracy and the levelling tendencies of his opponents were two rivers fed by a common source – Calvin's incomplete theory of kingship. Since monarchs existed by the providence of God they were therefore to be obeyed; such, Calvin recognised, was the clear teaching of Scripture. But this did not imply that unrestrained individual sovereignty was the best form of government. On the contrary, experience and history proved that it all too readily disintegrated into tyranny, corruption and vice: kings 'are so swollen up with pride, they think the world was made for no one but them'. 'They want to be privileged beyond other men: They would like to be outside the ranks of mortals altogether.'[73] The reformer believed that a truly Christian monarch would limit his power in accordance with customary law and divine revelation as mediated through the ministers of the word. James and the Puritans could both claim to stand within the Reformed tradition and both used it, selectively, to bolster their own authority.

Having proved the truth of Calvin's accusation by assuming semi-divine attributes, James took upon his own shoulders the salvation of the national Church and even of the whole of Christendom. Providence had placed him at the head of a Christian body that could look, Janus-like, towards the Catholic and Protestant communions and hold aloft for their inspiration the banner bearing his device, *Beati Pacifica*. At home it was his God-given charge to unify the worship and beliefs of his people. Having imposed episcopacy on the Scots, he now went on to enforce uniformity by relentlessly promoting the Five Articles (episcopal confirmation, private baptism, kneeling for Communion, observance of holy days and private Communion to the sick) between 1617 and 1621. After they had finally been passed by a reluctant parliament James could not rest content; he ordered local magistrates to tour churches to see how well the regulations were being enforced. Inevitably, authoritarianism provoked discontent. Over the years more and more Scots found it easier to identify with the auld Kirk than with their absentee King.

In England James faced a harder task in enforcing unity upon a church in which religious conviction ranged across the spectrum from crypto-Catholicism to scarcely conforming Puritanism. It was the latter whom he regarded as the greater danger and with reason. In many parts of the country the more radical Protestants had effective leadership, organisation and, through lectureships, propaganda. They also had friends in high places – friends whom the ecclesiastical authorities were loath to offend. As early as January 1605 James had summoned Bishop Dove of Peterborough to Hinchingbrooke to charge him with indolence in enforcing conformity. He found the bishop, who was no covert Puritan, to be 'aged and fearful and unwilling to act, pretending sometimes that he has received no express directions'.[74] The major obstacle to any policy of enforced conformity was the inability and, often, the unwillingness of bishops to deliver it. Most of the churchmen who were qualified for appointment to the bench were good Calvinists who understood, even if they did not sympathise with, their more extreme brethren. James did, from time to time, appoint men of a different theological hue, such as the disciplinarian Richard Neile, Samuel Harsnet (Chichester, 1609) who had caused a furore by preaching against predestination in 1584, and John King (London, 1611) who was widely believed to have been received into the Roman Church on his deathbed in 1621. But William Laud (St David's, 1621) only received his appointment on the intercession of Charles and Buckingham and Richard Montagu, an ardent controversialist who asserted that there could be no church without a priesthood, had to wait until the next reign before being appointed to Chichester (1628). In truth King James had as little love for arrogant, power-hungry bishops as he had for reformist ministers. The end result was that he followed no consistent ecclesiastical policy save that of maintaining a balance of parties. His edicts and pronouncements were reactive rather than proactive.

Subjected to his mother's Catholicism, his father's declared but ineffective anti-Puritanism and the rainbow-hued Protestantism of his teachers and chaplains, what convictions had Charles appropriated for himself as he approached manhood? We must leave a discussion of his matured faith and its comparison with Cromwell's to a later chapter. What we should be clear about at this point is that the final stage of Charles's Christianity, when he could say 'I will either be a glorious king or a patient martyr' was not the Christianity of his early manhood; it was a faith honed by experience and suffering. Religious commitment develops and changes. We cannot say of either Charles Stuart or Oliver Cromwell, 'his religious position was such and such' without locating the period of life we are discussing. What emerges from any consideration of Charles the young adult is that he was a puritan before ever Cromwell was, if by puritan with a small 'p' we refer to the inwardness of religion. Charles was a precisionist in his personal life, a man whose daily routine and standards of behaviour were governed by the strict applications of habits and principles learned from others and rigidly applied to himself. This was as true of religious exercise as it was of regular practice in the tiltyard or set hours spent with Virgil or Froissart. Charles practised the regularised devotion of the young man who has been brought up in the habits of worship and meditation rather than having made exciting faith discoveries for himself.

> His exercises in religion were most exemplary. In his own bed-chamber or closet he spent some time in private meditation . . . never failed before he sat down to dinner to have part of the liturgy read to him and his menial servants. On Sundays and Tuesdays, he came to chapel. No one better understood the foundations of his own church and the grounds of Reformation than he did.[75]

Never was the concept of duty as 'stern daughter of the voice of God' more aptly applied than to Charles Stuart. His father had provided him with the catalogue of virtues required of the godly prince; his Protestant mentors had instilled high standards of personal morality; and Charles schooled himself to follow the path laid down by his elders and betters. Add to this his growing aesthetic sense, his love of ritual as exemplified in court entertainments, his reaction against the harsh simplicity of Puritans' worship matched by the uncompromising directness of their preaching and his impatience with the bawdy rowdiness that surrounded his father, and we build up a picture of a prince whose emotional and spiritual need was for a religion of decorum, order and beauty, a trainee monarch whose fervour had to be expressed through the baroque exuberance associated with Catholic courts and not through the restrained taste of most of his subjects, a future head of the Church for whom *mysterium Dei* had more instinctive meaning than *verbum Dei*.

The man who unofficially took over the tutelage of Charles when the apron strings of tutors and chaplains had been severed was George Villiers. The favourite knew or sensed what the still-hesitant and introverted prince needed to bring him out of himself and he certainly knew how vital it was for his own interests to bind Charles to him with strong bonds of friendship and trust. He took to discussing matters of state with the heir, often without the King's presence or knowledge. Charles became a member of the Council in 1621 and often went to listen to parliamentary debates when the Houses were in session. He reported his impressions to Steenie (James's pet name for Villiers) orally when he was at court and by letter when he was not:

> ... my opinion is that the king should grant them a session at this time, but withal I should have him command them not to speak any more of Spain, whether it be of that war or my marriage. This, in my opinion, doth neither suffer them to encroach upon the king's authority, nor give them just cause of discontentment ...
>
> The lower house this day has been a little unruly; but I hope it will turn to the best; for, before they rose, they began to be ashamed of it. Yet I could wish that the king would send down a commission here, that (if need were) such seditious fellows might be made an example to others, by Monday next, and till then I would let them alone. It will be seen whether they mean to do good, or to persist in their follies; so that the king needs to be patient but a little while ...[76]

For the Sovereign, Parliament had always been an unfortunate necessity. The Tudors had known how to manage it – by packing it with royal servants, by manipulation of business, by making gracious concessions or by overawing the assembly with sheer force of personality. James's relationship with the Lords and Commons was not all that less satisfactory than his predecessors'; he had, in fact, managed to do without Parliament for almost seven years (1614–21). But he never grasped the necessity of 'handling' the assembly. He behaved as though he were a schoolmaster and the members of the Commons merely children – and dim, ill-behaved children at that. This attitude Charles was quick to assume.

It is an attitude which explains the events of 1622–3 which would otherwise seem bizarre in the extreme. The prelude to those events was proclaimed in a letter written in the closing hours of December 1621 by Lord Digby, James's ambassador extraordinary to Spain, currently on home leave, to Lord Zouche, Lord Warden of the Cinque Ports:

> My very good Lord,
> His majesty was pleased, for some particular reasons, to give licence to Mr Toby Matthew to return to England, who, being landed at Dover, he understands he is there stayed by your Lordship's office. His majesty hath, therefore, commanded me to signify his pleasure to your Lordship that you give present orders that he may be forthwith freed, and have liberty to make his present repair hither, to attend his majesty . . .'[77]

James's summons to the exiled Catholic recusant puzzled and alarmed royal officials. It was one piece of evidence among many that signified to anxious observers a Romeward lurch in royal policy. Only days before, relations between the King and his latest Parliament had come to an abrupt end when the Commons had urged their 'ancient and undoubted right' to discuss foreign war and the marriage of the Prince of Wales and James had sent them packing and torn the record of their protestation from the journal of the House. Protestant fears were encouraged by the prevailing mood in inner court circles. Catholicism was in fashion among the smart set. It was a cultured cosmopolitan faith which set its adherents apart from the 'bourgeois' Commons and the provincial squirearchy. Porter, Cottington and others of Charles's household were covert or open papists, as were members of Buckingham's family. The duke's wife had only made a show of conformity to the established Church on her marriage and, with the aid of the Spanish ambassador, enjoyed the ministrations of priests of her real religious persuasion.

The running tide of suspicion and ill will was irresistible but James did his best, Canute-like, to resist it. In January he ordered Buckingham and his family circle to receive Church of England Confirmation. And he wrote a poem. It was entitled *The Wiper of the People's Tears, the Dryer-up of Doubts and Fears* and it expended a hundred and seventy lines of excruciating verse on denying evil rumours and defying their authors. How dare people suggest that he was contemplating conversion?

> Why do you push me down to hell
> By making me an infidel

His subjects should stop dabbling in matters which were not their concern:

> Hold your prattling, spare your pen,
> Be honest and obedient men.

And, ominously, he threatened:

> Be war what may befall,
> I must do more
> . . . to keep all in obedience.[78]

Such varied tactics were necessary to remove obstacles from the Spanish alliance to advise on which Matthew had been brought back from exile and which remained his policy flagship. To keep it afloat he relaxed the laws against Catholics and to prevent pulpit broadsides he had his archbishop impose severe restrictions on preaching. James was progressively alienating more and more of his people, but the Spanish match was no closer.

This was the background to the romantic, impulsive, fantastical adventure of Charles and Buckingham in February–March 1623. The mad dash of the two friends to Madrid was a wild speculation by gamblers who believed, against all the odds and against all the advice of experienced councillors and diplomats and against all the instincts of the political nation, that they could bring off a coup which would, at one stroke, solve the government's most pressing problems. They convinced themselves that if the prince arrived, unexpected and unannounced, like some ardent Romeo, to woo the infanta in person, there would be an end of procrastination, Philip IV would call off the campaign in the Palatinate, universal peace would be restored and the princess's dowry would refloat the national finances.

The idea was, almost certainly, Buckingham's but Charles readily fell in with it. It would release a long-repressed craving for excitement. It would repeat the escapade of his father who, as a young suitor, had rushed to Copenhagen to bring back his bride. It would dramatically announce his arrival on the stage of international affairs. It would enable him to see some of the sights that he had for years heard courtiers and diplomats speak about. Specifically, the trip would offer a wonderful opportunity to add some superb paintings to his small collection. Its success would put all the moaning, puritanical greybeards in their place. Above all it would free him from the personality and policies of his father which he was finding increasingly suffocating.

What was obvious to the 'two sweet boys' was far from clear to their 'dear dad and gossip'. When the plan was presented to James he was aghast. The madcap scheme would put at risk years of patient diplomacy, not to mention the dangers to which the journey would expose his son. When he asked the advice of Cottington the diplomat was equally dumbfounded. The Spanish court was notorious for observance of protocol and King Philip would scarcely take kindly to the arrival of a foreign prince in so unseemly a fashion. As for the infinitely subtle Spanish negotiators, they would scarcely be able to believe their good fortune at having been handed a royal hostage on a plate. So far from reducing their demands, they would be in a position to increase them.

James refused. Buckingham raged. Charles sulked. And James gave way. The confrontation highlighted the characters of the three men: the King, weak, emotional, unable to make purely rational decisions where his favourites were concerned; the marquis assertive, secure in the power he held over his sovereign, playing the elder brother to the heir, eager to get Charles to himself for a few weeks and tighten the cords binding him to the favourite; the prince, at last rebelling against parental restraints (but only in order to effect his parent's policy), eagerly accepting Buckingham's tutelage; and tentatively trying on the mantle of kingly authority. The scene in James's private chambers in which the old man threw himself on his bed screaming 'I am undone! I shall lose Baby Charles!', his son shouting that he would never marry if permission for the Spanish trip were refused and Buckingham haughtily lecturing the King on statecraft, is of greater significance than any of the events of the ensuing weeks.

The frolic began on 17 February: under cover of a smokescreen of misinformation to explain their absence from court, the adventurers, disguised as 'Jack and Tom Smith' rode off towards the Kentish coast, and the King reconciled himself to their departure in self-admonitory verse:

. . . The grandsire, godsire, father too,
Were thine examples so to do,
Their brave attempts in heat of love,
France, Scotland, Denmark, did approve,
So Jack and Tom do nothing new,
When love and fortune they pursue.

Kind Shepherds that have loved them long,
Be not too rash in censuring wrong;
Correct your fears, leave off to mourn,
The heavens shall favour their return!
Commit the care to Royal Pan
Of Jack his son, and Tom his man.[79]

The little triumphs and near disasters of the next few weeks probably made up the happiest period of Charles's life to date. At Rochester the unexpected appearance of the French ambassador obliged them to leave the road, leap hedges and gallop across open country. At Boulogne they were almost unmasked by a Newmarket acquaintance and had to put on a great act to convince him. In Paris they gained access to the court and gazed from a distance at members of the royal family. They were overjoyed at the success of their own audacity as Steenie reported to the King: 'I am sure now you fear we shall be discovered, but do not fright yourself, for I warrant you the contrary. And finding this might be done with safety, we had a great tickling to add it to the history of our adventures.'[80] At Bordeaux the travellers aroused the suspicions of the governor and only some hard talking saved them from arrest as undesirable aliens. At Bayonne, finding the Lenten fare of a Catholic country not to their liking, they negotiated with a goatherd for one of his kids. While Buckingham and his man rushed around in an ineffective attempt to catch the nimble creature Charles felled it with a shot from his Scottish pistol.

Their arrival in Madrid on 7 March created the anticipated stir. Buckingham called at the embassy to inform Digby (recently created Earl of Bristol) that the Prince of Wales was waiting in the street outside. The ambassador was furious and wrote immediately to the King to express his displeasure but he had no alternative to accepting the *fait accompli*. He made the necessary introductions at court and the next few days were filled with embarrassed, more-or-less clandestine meetings between the visitors and members of Philip IV's family, while officials hurriedly arranged a suitably splendid ceremonial welcome for the King of England's son. This occurred on 16 March and made a great impression on Charles as well as the populace of Madrid.

> ... The prince was feasted, and served by divers great officers of state, waiting bareheaded. After dinner the king came to conduct his Highness through the town to the royal palace, having prepared all things for the solemnity in the greatest magnificence and splendour. The king setting the prince on his right hand, they rode in great glory, under a canopy of state, supported by the *Regidors* of the town, who were arranged in cloth of tissue. The nobility and grandees of Spain attended by their several liveries, all very rich and costly, went before; and after came the Marquis of Buckingham and the Condé Olivarez, executing their places of Masters of the Horse; after them followed the Earl of Bristol and Sir Walter Aston [resident ambassador in Spain], accompanied with divers counsellors of state, and gentlemen of the king's chamber . . .[81]

Everything seemed to be going swimmingly. Superb gifts exchanged hands. The prince was joined by a modest retinue (though the suite James had sent by sea were soon ordered home) including Cottington, Porter and Matthew. Buckingham received news in May that he had been raised to the highest rank of the peerage. For Charles one of the highlights of the visit was his tour of the great royal and noble art collections. Helped by Endymion Porter and Buckingham and aided by the duke's artistic adviser, he made several purchases and received presents from the young Spanish king (who was also an enthusiastic collector). Charles's taste at this time was for the voluptuous and sometimes erotic Venetians and his acquisitions included fleshy Venuses and classical subjects by Titian and Veronese. These exuberant works precisely match the newly liberated personality revealed in the Madrid adventure, which stands in contrast to the restrained and inhibited prince of earlier years. Although the mission to Spain failed it certainly brought Charles out and its importance in his development can scarcely be exaggerated.

As the heat of the Castilian summer increased so the negotiations cooled. The demands of the two parties were irreconcilable. Philip IV would not marry his sister to a Protestant. Charles would not become a Catholic. It was impossible for Spain to confront its Austrian Habsburg allies over the Palatinate and it was asking too much of England not to go to the aid of James's son-in-law. But it was not just treaty difficulties which dampened the ardour of the adventurers. They found frustrating beyond measure the ultra-formality of the Spanish court and the infinite capacity for procrastination which it covered. Charles was permitted no close access to the infanta and when he attempted to display his ardour by climbing into the orchard where she was gathering flowers she ran off screaming and he was escorted away by outraged officials. The Spaniards had even less appreciation of Buckingham's brash behaviour. Despite the insurmountable cultural and religious differences Charles persevered to the point of making concessions he could not have kept (and probably knew that he could not have kept), including permanent removal of all restraints on Catholics. His pride was involved. Emotionally and psychologically he had invested heavily in the Spanish match and the prospect of returning home empty-handed was terribly humiliating. When he finally came to accept failure it was inevitable that his love of Spain should turn to contempt. On 2 September, he took his leave of Philip IV and, behind the smiles and embraces, he was resolved to be revenged on these perfidious people.

Toby Matthew's arrival in England provided the prologue to this comedy of errors. Words from his pen furnish its epilogue. As the prince's party prepared to leave he wrote a personal letter to Philip IV in a tone of utter dismay:

> . . . if the Catholic subjects of the king, my lord, shall grow liable to persecution or affliction by occasion of breaking this match, through the disgust of the king, my lord, and his Council or through the power which, infallibly, the Puritans, assembled in parliament, will have with him . . . that blood or misery whatsoever [may ensue] may partly be required at their hands who have advised your majesty not to accept of those large conditions for Catholics which my lord the king, and the prince have condescended to.[82]

The success of the Spanish venture would, doubtless, have been politically disastrous. That it was not only a failure but a farcical failure made an impression on Charles that was arguably even more so. Had the amorous advances of this late-developing adolescent been reciprocated and led to both sexual and diplomatic consummation he might, in the words of the Venetian ambassador, have 'burst forth into great and generous [nature]'.[83] The coup would have enabled him to start his reign secure in a warm domestic relationship and in a nation at peace with its neighbours. In the event, he had proffered his heart only to have it trampled on. As a result the beginnings of a personality thaw were followed by an even harder frost. To quote again the carefully chosen words of the Venetian envoy, 'The coldness of his nature even in actions becoming his youth is not, perhaps, a good sign.'[84] He retreated into the repressed safety of a sexually restrained, well-disciplined libido. Outwardly calm, polite and gentle, Charles Stuart, as a recent biographer has suggested, seethed inwardly, 'his stutter being probably the symptom of some boiling subterranean rage'.[85]

The warm welcome he received in England may, paradoxically, have fed that anger. At home, where news of the Buckingham and Prince of Wales's initiative had, in Robert Carey's words, 'made a great hubbub in our court and in all England besides',[86] universal dismay at the prospect of an alliance with the old enemy turned to unrestrained rejoicing as soon as word spread of the enterprise's failure. When the travellers approached the capital the air reverberated to the sound of church bells and the Tower cannon. On every open space a bonfire burned: on the road from the City to Whitehall one observer counted 335. When Charles moved on from London to join his father at Royston his coach was mobbed along the entire route and, in places, had to be carried through the surging throng. Everywhere, 'the people for joy and gladness ran up and down like mad men and none of what condition soever would work upon that day'.[87] The spontaneous public celebration became an official annual holiday in many places and remained so until the outbreak of the Civil War. It was a manifestation of nationwide relief such as had not been seen since the failure of the Gunpowder Plot or the Spanish Armada. As men, women and children cheered and waved and called down heaven's blessing upon him Charles bathed in the adulation of his father's subjects. But did he really understand just what it was they were applauding him for?

FOUR

RESPONSIBILITIES

FOR A FEW months, between the autumn of 1623 and the high summer of 1625 it seemed that Charles had learned something from the celebrated dictum of Machiavelli, 'It is necessary for a prince, wishing to maintain himself, to know how not to be good and to use this, or not use this, according to necessity.'[1] He had returned from Spain very much the king-in-waiting, with clear policies in mind and a determination to pursue them. Immediately leaping into the arena of national and international politics, he showed himself adept at wielding charm, anger, duplicity and the weapons of intrigue to enforce his own aggressive policies against the eirenicism of his father, the parsimony of Parliament, the caution of councillors and the machinations of well-practised diplomats. Seasoned observers were taken aback at the way Charles not only manipulated the various participants in the political process but achieved widespread popularity while doing so.

It was an illusion: Charles was no more able to divest himself of what Machiavelli would have regarded as the clutter of ideas, beliefs, feelings and prejudices than any prince who might have studied the Florentine's most notorious and misunderstood work. What he displayed in the dwindling days of the old reign was a confused mélange of attitudes, some inherited from his father, some instilled by his partner in the great adventure. The brief sunlit interlude ended, as the old clouds of religious passion, foreign policy complexity and the desperate need for government revenue tumbled across a darkening sky. Charles was revealed as even less a master of statecraft than his father. Yet, even if he had maintained the promise of those few months, even if Buckingham had managed to curb his arrogance, and even if fortune had smiled on Stuart foreign policy, events would still have propelled Crown and Parliament along divergent paths.

In the euphoria which greeted the adventurers' return from Spain, *vox populi* had spoken very loudly but neither Charles nor Buckingham, and certainly not the King, heard *vox dei* in the tumult. The motivations of the governing triumvirate had little correspondence with popular sentiment and, anyway, there was no great unity within the triumvirate. James persisted in believing that diplomacy could induce Spain to restore the Palatinate; Villiers had done a 180-degree turn and was now urging war against the Habsburgs; Charles largely inclined to the same view but clung for several weeks to the hope of salvaging the Spanish match.

After a few days at Royston, where the returning 'heroes' were besieged by well-wishing, adulatory and curious crowds, James withdrew his court to the comparative quiet of Hinchingbrooke. Those who attended there on the prince and the favourite cannot have failed to pick up the 'vibes' of rancour and bitter vexation emanating from the homecoming travellers. Charles felt utterly humiliated. He had cast aside his natural reserve and entered into the escapade with wholehearted enthusiasm. He had wooed the infanta with unrestrained ardour; perhaps even fancied himself to be genuinely in love. His sincere commitment had been thrown back in his face and he was convinced that Spanish duplicity was entirely to blame for his humiliation. Yet, because he was deeply moved by the plight of his sister and because his emotions were engaged by his promised bride, he was still prepared to swallow his pride, as he explained to Ambassador Aston: 'I do really intend and desire this match and . . . [if] we may have satisfaction concerning the Palatinate, I will be content to forget all ill-usage and be hearty friends. But, if not, I can never match where I have had so dry entertainment, although I shall be infinitely sorry for the loss of the infanta.'[2] Those brief lines indicate quite clearly Charles's priorities: personal feelings, family concerns and dynastic considerations came high on the list; the manifest anti-Spanish and anti-Catholic prejudices of the people figured not at all in his thinking. Not until late December did he finally acknowledge the unbridgeable gap between London and Madrid and throw his support fully behind Buckingham.

Villiers, ever more pragmatic than his royal patrons, had decided on the summoning of Parliament, believing that he could count on the support of a majority of Lords and Commons for a policy of confrontation with Spain. In order to improve their chances prince and favourite used their patronage in the shires to secure the election of compliant members, although they certainly did not 'pack' the lower house. When, after two postponements because of plague, the assembly met in February 1624 he had to account for the spectacular and expensive failure of the previous year's escapade and recommend the future direction of foreign policy. He addressed a joint meeting of both Houses in the Banqueting House at Whitehall with the prince beside him indicating, by body language, his total support. Buckingham alleged that the Spanish negotiators had really only been interested in the reconquest of Britain by Roman Catholicism. They had, for instance, insisted that any children of Charles and Maria (including the heir to the throne) were to be brought up by their mother. These and other conditions were, of course, as abhorrent to Charles as they were to all the King's loyal subjects. For good measure, Buckingham threw in an accusation against his personal enemy, the Earl of Bristol, who, he said, had urged the marriage so enthusiastically that he had even tried to persuade the prince to change his faith. To salvage the nation's honour and also to aid the Palatinate the King should not only break off treaty negotiations but also declare war on Spain. This message was precisely what most red-blooded Englishmen wanted to hear and, in their subsequent speeches to the Lords, Charles and Villiers so deliberately and skilfully played on their audience's xenophobia and hatred of Rome that they became immensely popular even with seasoned and sceptical politicians.

However, persuading Parliament to vote adequate funds for an adventurous foreign policy was far from being plain sailing. Members might warmly receive Buckingham's speech but many were still cautious about trusting the government, and voting supply without reasonable safeguards was out of the question. The Venetian ambassador judged well the mood of the assembly: 'the parliament seems not only disposed to make war with Spain, but resolved upon it, owing to the desire for something new, natural to the people, their special hatred for the nation and the hope of growing rich at their expense as in the days of Queen Elizabeth . . . provided the people are assured that they will not be deceived by the king's tricks . . . [that, having received money] he will return to the vomit of these negotiations.'[3]

What seems to have made a favourable impression on all observers was the maturity and apparent considerateness of the heir to the throne:

I think never was prince more powerful in the parliament house than he and there doth he express himself substantially so well that he is often called up to speak and he doth it with that satisfaction to both houses as is much admired; and he behaves himself with as much reverence to the houses . . . as any other man who sits amongst them; and he will patiently bear contradiction and calmly forgo his own opinions if he have been mistaken . . .'[4]

Thus the Countess of Bedford reported to the Queen of Bohemia. Though she wrote with conventional exaggeration and wished to impress Elizabeth with her brother's zeal in the cause of the Palatinate, her recognition of the prince's newly acquired maturity was supported by others. It was manifest that the nation was standing on the threshold of a new reign and natural optimism coloured their thoughts about the future. James was, by now, 'a very foolish, fond old man', alternating between oath-supported assertions of royal will and maudlin, tearful appeals for advice from his 'dear boys'. He increasingly took refuge from pain in alcohol and was able to devote less and less time to affairs of state. Charles acted as his deputy, presiding over the Council, instructing ambassadors, posting back and forth between Whitehall, Royston and Theobalds, where the King, when not confined to bed, still devoted himself to the pleasures of the chase, constructing policies that were increasingly his own – or his own and Buckingham's – and assiduously attending Parliament.

Charles was impatient to take over the reins of government. The Spanish expedition had marked the end of his years of tutelage. He was now a fastidious young man, less inclined to be indulgent about the moral tone of the royal court, which deteriorated as James's health waned, and eager to replace his father's timid attitude towards foreign powers with a greater assertiveness. It was as part of this preparation for the imminent future that he allotted time to the one activity he would not be able to engage in after his accession – speaking and listening to the members of the three estates.

The Lords and Commons were flattered by the frequent appearances of the heir to the throne in the Upper House. Even Prince Henry of blessed memory had not paid them this compliment. Any who knew Charles well appreciated that public speaking did not come easily to him and this added to their appreciation of his contributions to debate. If he lacked the presence of a Henry VIII or the oratorical skill of an Elizabeth, he did take the trouble to understand the Parliament men and tune into their mood. Some even called the 1624–5 session the 'Prince's Parliament'. But this did not mean, as Lady Bedford implied, that Charles had developed a new sympathy for the people's representatives. He cultivated the assembly because he had good reason to do so. He needed its support in his efforts to move his father to a warlike stance. Only the King could break the Anglo-Spanish treaty and this was against all his pacific and cost-conscious instincts. James may have become a mere shadow of a monarch but he was no cypher. He had to be manipulated and so did Parliament. Buckingham, more skilled in intrigue, was exploiting faction and personality clashes. He was flirting with Puritan leaders and using the radical preacher-cum-courtier, John Preston, as a go-between to disarm his parliamentary opponents. Charles was more straightforward but he, too, was playing the political game. Within the Council, he chose to work with a cabal of loyal supporters who decided tactics on a daily basis and planned the most effective ways of handling Parliament. The early months of 1624 were a time of vigorous haggling: the Commons offered money for war but wanted to oversee its expenditure and made it conditional on tougher laws against Catholics; the King considered the grant inadequate for effective aid to the Palatinate, would not countenance parliamentary supervision and had no intention of being forced into a religious war. Charles and Buckingham were kept busy brokering a deal and countering the wrecking tactics of the Habsburg ambassadors and their English friends. It was not until late March that a revenue figure of approximately £300,000 (three subsidies and three fifteenths) was agreed upon. The tin cans tied to the tail of this accord were parliamentary accountants as overseers of war expenditure and a royal promise not to relax the recusancy laws as part of any future marriage treaty. Two weeks later James formally informed the Spanish court that the treaty negotiations were finally voided.

What the parliamentary negotiators knew, certainly by the later stages of discussion, was that another marriage, another Catholic marriage, was on the agenda. The possibility of a match between Charles and Princess Henrietta Maria, youngest daughter of Henry IV of France, had been mooted before James had firmly decided on a Spanish alliance. As soon as it was known in diplomatic circles that the marriage with the infanta was unlikely to proceed, the

French court made fresh overtures. Henrietta Maria was not as attractive a proposition financially as the Spanish princess and her father was in no position to force the withdrawal of the army occupying the Palatinate, but a marriage treaty with France would strengthen the anti-Habsburg bloc and facilitate the passage of troops going to the relief of the Elector.

Charles was enthusiastic. Now that he had fully embraced the idea of matrimony he wished to enter into that state as soon as possible. Dynastic and political duty demanded it but, more personally, it chimed with his vision of a new court and a new government. Everything about acquiring a wife and children pointed to the future. His father's attitudes to the responsibilities of kingship had been forged out of his early constitutional struggles in Scotland. The people of England still harked back to a glorious Elizabethan past. What Charles would provide would be a new, young Stuart generation at the centre of a renewed nation.

That decided, the qualities of any proposed bride were of relatively minor import. Charles approached his new wooing with a very different spirit to that which had fired the aborted Spanish match. There was no rushing off to Paris to court his proposed bride in person: the prince had worn his heart on his sleeve once; he would not do it again. This time he acted out of duty, uncomplicated by affection. Henrietta Maria had just passed her fourteenth birthday and if Charles had noticed her at all on his brief incognito visit to the French court, it was not as an object of desire. Months later he still harboured a passion for the infanta. The French match would be entered into coolly, correctly and with due deference to diplomatic conventions. If emotion was engaged at all it was Charles's pleasure in snapping his fingers at the arrogant court of His Most Catholic Majesty.

In the immediate term the French marriage alliance was all about foreign policy and concluding it involved more months of wheeling and dealing and the unavoidable attendant duplicity. Cardinal Richelieu tried to hoodwink the English negotiators, Charles and Buckingham were economical with the truth when reporting to the King, and James deliberately deceived his Parliament. Members of Lords and Commons had to rely on court gossip and diplomatic contacts to find out what was really going on. There was, in 1624, as there always is, a yawning chasm between the realities of international relations as discussed in the tap-room bar and as argued across the conference table. Robert Paul captured the politico-religious xenophobia which informed the simplistic attitude of most of James's subject:

> In the struggle against Spain and the Empire, in the stubborn opposition of the Rochellais to Richelieu and in the victories of Gustavus Adolphus, the English Puritan felt that his own battles were being fought, and when Frederick, the Elector Palatine, was forced into exile, when La Rochelle was forced to capitulate, and when Wallenstein swept through central Europe, the Puritan felt that it was time for all true Englishmen to take a hand . . . When Gustavus fell at Lützen, every Puritan's heart sank within him. It was a cosmic struggle in which all the Powers of Light and Darkness were engaged, and this being so James I's vacillating foreign policy seemed to be criminal folly.[5]

What the government should be doing, in the view of most parliamentarians, was declaring war against Spain and waging it primarily at sea, as in the good old days. The rulers, diplomats and ministers actually engaged in trading treaty clauses and secret codicils were painfully aware of the Byzantine complexities of European politics. Louis XIII feared Habsburg encirclement and wanted defensive alliances that would strengthen France, but without provoking Spain. However, if this policy led to close relations with Protestant neighbours it would give encouragement to the Huguenot 'rebels' who represented his greatest internal problem. The United Netherlands, the masters of the Narrow Seas (their great hero, Piet Hein, lifted eight million ducats' worth of bullion from a Spanish silver fleet in 1628), were prepared to provide ships for joint actions against Spain but wanted land troops to help raise the Spanish siege of Breda. The Stuarts' kinsman, Christian IV of Denmark, was ready to march an army south in the Protestant cause but wanted money. James I was committed to helping the Elector Palatine but terrified of offending Philip IV. He favoured alliances that might force Spain to the negotiating table, failing which he looked for agreements which would involve other people fighting his battles for him. He certainly had no intention of aiding the Protestant rebels based at La Rochelle: while passionate about peace, he was more than willing to help his brother monarch, King Louis, deal with the troublesome Huguenots.

The Anglo-French treaty negotiations occupied almost the whole of 1624, the principal feature (apart from the marriage) being a joint expedition for the relief of the Palatinate to be led by the Luxembourg mercenary, Count Ernst von Mansfeld. Christian IV, subsidised by King James, would also provide forces. This was popular – at last England was taking on the role of Protestant champion – and went some way to sweetening the pill of another Catholic queen. Henrietta Maria was to be allowed her own chapel staff and freedom of worship and was to have the upbringing of any children of the marriage. She brought with her a dowry of £120,000. All this was common knowledge. Not so the *écrit particulier*. In this written undertaking accompanying the treaty, the King and the prince promised to lift all restrictions on English Catholics. It is scarcely surprising that in England virtually no one, apart from James, Charles and Buckingham, was a party to this subsidiary agreement. The King was under no obligation to discuss matrimonial matters and foreign alliances with his Parliament but he knew full well that they would have plenty to say about the details of the secret codicil to the treaty. Indeed, Buckingham was able to use the threat of summoning Parliament when the French tried to exact even more extreme conditions. It could, he warned, wreck all prospects of the match: 'the wit of men could not foresee the dangers that would be cast in by the Spanish party (who would have but too much cause to hope it would be no match) . . . and by the Puritans, who, out of fear that it would prove a match, might, with a just cause, seek to hinder it.'[6] James and Charles ratified the treaty at Cambridge on 12 December 1624.

What was needed to make it tolerably palatable to the nation was a brilliantly successful Palatinate campaign by Mansfeld. Unfortunately, the condottiere's expedition turned into a ghastly fiasco of divided counsels, under-funding, disease and death. In November and December 13,000 impressed men made their way to Dover. Since Mansfeld, whose payments from the Exchequer were irregular and inadequate, accepted no responsibility for them until they arrived in his camp, they could only feed themselves *en route* by pillage. Complaints poured into the Council from outraged householders. Matters were little better when the 'army' assembled on the Kent coast. Louis XIII developed cold feet about allowing the expedition to land in France and link up with his promised cavalry. While the two courts argued through December and January Mansfeld's force dwindled through desertions and became even

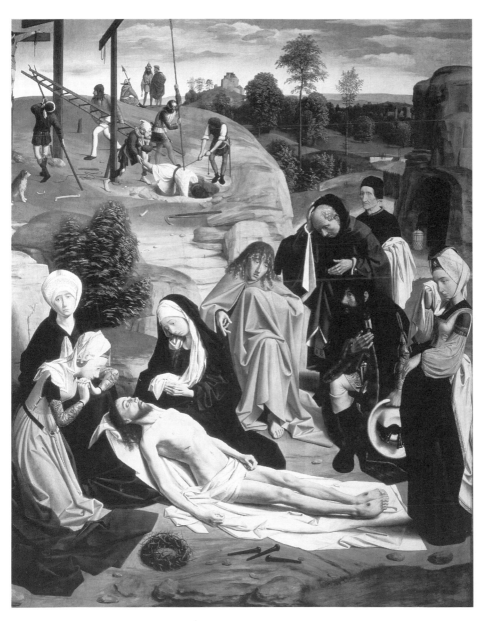

1. *Beweinung Christi* by Geertgen Tot Sint Jans.
Charles's religious sentiments are well expressed in the religious paintings
of his collection. This entombment scene he gave away in preference to
the more sumptuous treatment of the subject by Titian (plate 21)

2. *James I*
by Paul Van Somer.

3. *Anne of Denmark*
by Paul Van Somer.

4. *Robert Cromwell*
Artist unknown.

5. *Elizabeth Cromwell*
Artist unknown.

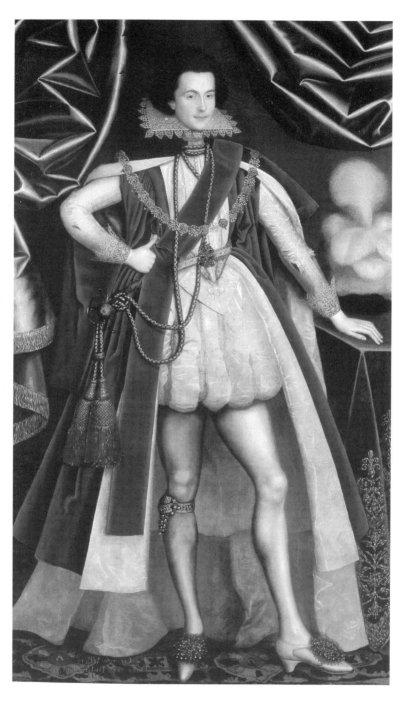

6. The man who brought Charles out of his shell, the self-aggrandising royal favourite. *George Villiers, 1st Duke of Buckingham* by William Larkin.

7. The inheritor of a divine kingship.
Charles I by Gerrit van Honthorst.

8. General Cromwell in his mid-forties.
Oliver Cromwell attributed to Robert Walker.

9. *Elizabeth Cromwell*
Attributed to Sir Peter Lely.

10. An exalted life; an elegant life; a public life – the calm before the storm.
Charles I, Queen Henrietta Maria and Charles Prince of Wales Dining in Public
by Gerrit van Honthorst.

more ill-disciplined through inaction. Charles and Buckingham had to dig deep into their own purses to meet the commander's urgent demands for cash. The expedition finally set sail on 31 January – still with no clear idea where they were going or what they were supposed to do when they got there. In the Netherlands Mansfeld tried to find winter quarters for his men but there simply was not enough food or accommodation to be had. In the harsh winter conditions the troops died in their hundreds. By the time the frost released its grip on the low-lying land there were only about three thousand men left capable of bearing arms. This remnant was finally given a job to do – to go to the relief of Breda. But they were now too few to make any impression and when the city capitulated in May 1625 the brave English contribution to the Protestant cause ended, not with a bang but a whimper.

While this dismal charade was being played out, Charles's life changed monumentally: he lost a father, gained a wife and became a king. For years James I had abused his constitution by eating and drinking to excess and hunting in all weathers. The treatments he had undergone during his varied and increasing illnesses had developed in him a contempt for doctors and he was as likely to rely on old wives' tales and remedies recommended by sycophantic courtiers as on the nostrums advocated by his physicians. His own attitude towards illness was to treat it with contempt and permit it to interfere as little as possible with the pursuit of his own pleasures and, although he appeared to many in the latter part of his life as a feeble old man, the fact that he kept death at bay for more than fifty-eight years betokens a considerable mental and physical stamina. On 5 March, when he took to his bed at Theobalds with a tertian ague (malarial fever), there was no especial alarm. The shivering fits subsided after a week but then returned, at which point James banished his doctors and tried a powder and a plaster recommended by Buckingham and his mother. When the King's condition thereafter worsened, the physicians had a perfect scapegoat and were readily listened to by the favourite's enemies. Charles was now sent for and, after consulting with the medical men, he instructed the Bishop of Lincoln to prepare the King for his end. We may detect a certain symbolism in the fact that the two divines on hand to bring the consolations of religion to the mourners were the worldly Bishop Williams and the Puritan John Preston. The death of James I was accompanied by all the solemn formality which the seventeenth century considered appropriate to the passing of a monarch. On 24 March, attended by his son and all his principal officers of state, the old man received holy communion. Afterwards he was closeted with Charles in private for almost three hours. The end came in the early morning of 27 March. The prince rushed to his father's bed in his night attire and, although James was now beyond speech, he had the consolation of his son's presence when he breathed his last.

To all outward appearances Buckingham was more grief-stricken than Charles. He wept openly, had to be consoled by the new King and took to his bed, weak and exhausted. Charles, by contrast, seemed very composed as he assumed his new duties. One of his first acts was to set his friend's mind at rest: 'I have lost a good father and you a good master,' he told Villiers, 'but comfort yourself, you have found another that will no less cherish you.'[7] He returned immediately to the capital for his proclamation as King and plunged into the policy discussions relating to the continental situation and the making of arrangements for his father's obsequies and his own marriage. The latter was performed in Paris by proxy on 1 May and public celebrations were authorised in England. At his father's funeral, which did not take place until 7 May, and on which no expense was spared, he unprecedentedly took the place of chief mourner (a service he had performed for his brother and his mother). Significantly, in the midst of all these activities, Charles found time to revel in a consignment of paintings acquired in France by his agent, Balthazar Gerbier, who almost salivated in his enthusiasm: 'the most beautiful piece of Tintoretto . . . flint as cold as ice might fall in love with it'; 'a picture by Michael Angelo Buonarotti . . . the most divine thing in the world. I have been such an idolater as to kiss it three times.'[8]

Doubtless Charles mourned in private but his feelings must have been mixed. His distaste for the life of his father's court and his disagreement with James's appeasement policy towards Spain had created friction between father and son during the last months of the reign. Charles had been appalled at the King's lack of enthusiasm to go to the aid of his daughter and son-in-law and his apparent readiness to swallow the insults he and Buckingham had been subjected to over the Spanish match. Towards the end of James's life court watchers, perhaps motivated by a measure of wishful thinking, had reported a cooling of royal favour towards Buckingham. The King had certainly lent a willing ear to malicious gossip that the favourite was planning an assassination attempt. That particular storm passed but when the French negotiations followed the Spanish ones into the quagmire of deceit and mistrust it was Villiers who bore the brunt of the King's wrath for leading the prince astray. 'Where is your glorious match with France and your royal, frank *Monsieurs*?' he thundered at the grovelling duke.[9] Charles took his friend's part in all these contretemps, the young lion ready to show his claws to the old king of the jungle whose policies were dated and whose days numbered.

Yet, against all that we have to set the Banqueting House ceiling. Even before the late King's funeral in May 1625, his successor had authorised Peter Paul Rubens to execute the greatest cycle of pictures ever to commemorate a British monarch. It is true that the scheme had been proposed in 1621 but it was Charles and his artist who were responsible for this stupendous piece of laudatory iconography. Its three main panels depicted James uniting the crowns of England and Scotland, James banishing evil and rewarding good, like an earthly facsimile of the Almighty, and the glorious apotheosis of James. Yet even more remarkable than these blatant expressions of semi-divine monarchy are the bordering panels of animals and putti cavorting among symbols of fruitfulness and plenty. It has recently been discovered that these were intended as a commentary on the Prophet Isaiah's famous vision of the peaceful reign of the King of Kings:

> The wolf also shall dwell with the lamb, and the leopard shall lie down with the kid, and the calf and the young lion and the fatling together and a little child shall lead them. And the cow and the bear shall feed, their young ones shall lie down together, and the lion shall eat straw like the ox. And the sucking child shall play on the hole of the asp, and the weaned child shall put his hand on the cockatrice den. They shall not hurt or destroy in all my holy mountain; for the earth shall be full of the knowledge of the Lord, as the waters cover the sea.[10]

Once this is realised, the whole ensemble can be seen as an apologia and a vindication of the Gospel words James took as his personal motto: 'Blessed are the peacemakers.'[11] Just as only the semi-divine king could inflict war upon peoples and nations, so only he could confer the blessings of universal peace. This had been James's self-imposed mission and he had successfully kept his realm out of the appalling conflict which engulfed the continent. In the last months of the reign Charles had played Churchill to his father's Chamberlain and he would maintain a bellicose posture towards foreign powers. Yet he put splendidly on record James's dreams and achievements and must often have reflected upon them. Charles raised no fine tomb over his father's remains in Westminster Abbey, so much so that they were not identified until the nineteenth century. Instead he dramatically commemorated the idealised kingship which James had represented and this gilded dream of divine monarchy exercised a dominant influence throughout the years ahead. It was not just in painted effigy that James loomed over his son's court. The personality who had dominated the first half of Charles's life would continue to be a real presence throughout the second.

A spectacularly failed foreign policy; an unpopular marriage; an even more unpopular court favourite; massive debts; rumbling religious discord; the inescapable need to summon a parliament that was certain to have difficult questions to put to the government – it would be difficult to imagine a more unpropitious start to the reign. Much would depend on how Charles perceived and handled his new responsibilities.

First among those responsibilities was the one he owed himself. At the age of twenty-four Charles had, at last, the opportunity to develop his own ideas and principles and to project them, primarily, in the routines, personnel and ambience of his court. It was very soon apparent that a new broom was sweeping through Whitehall and the other royal residences.

> The face of the court was much changed in the change of the king, for King Charles was temperate, chaste and serious; so that the fools and bawds, mimics and catamites, of the former court, grew out of fashion; and the nobility and courtiers, who did not quite abandon their debaucheries, yet so reverenced the king as to retire into corners to practise them. Men of learning and ingenuity in all the arts were in esteem and received encouragement from the king, who was a most excellent judge and a great lover of paintings, carvings, gravings and many other ingenuities, less offensive than the bawdry and profane abusive wit which was the only exercise of the other court.[12]

Lucy Hutchinson's account was based on hearsay, for she was only five years old in 1625, but she had relatives at court and was only setting down what was common knowledge among the ruling elite. The Venetian ambassador in his first report on the new regime told the same story:

> The king observes a rule of great decorum. The nobles do not enter his apartments in confusion as heretofore, but each rank has its appointed place and he has declared that he desires the observance of the rules and maxims of the late Queen Elizabeth whose rule was so popular . . . the king has also drawn up rules for himself, dividing the day from his very early rising, for prayers, exercises, audiences, business, eating and sleeping.[13]

The rigid self-control and strict Puritanical piety in which Charles had schooled himself years before was now projected into the regimen of his household. Many established royal servants who were willing and able to adapt were kept on. Sir John Finet, the old King's roistering companion, on his appointment as Master of Ceremonies, abandoned the coarse jokes and lewd songs that had delighted James, and devoted himself to issues of etiquette and protocol in which he became so expert that he wrote a handbook for others who had to deal with the *Reception and Precedence, the Treatment and Audience, the Punctilios and Contests of Foreign Ambassadors in England*. His colleague, George Goring, was attached to Henrietta Maria's entourage, and, as her Vice-Chamberlain (and subsequently Master of the Horse) was able to initiate her into the ways of the English court. He did remarkably well out of the Queen's patronage, becoming Earl of Norwich and the wealthiest, most notorious monopolist in the land. However, no place was found for the third member of the raucous triumvirate, Sir Edward Zouche. And even Buckingham's brother, the mediocre Christopher Villiers, Earl of Anglesey, who had been showered with honours by King James, was dismissed by Charles from his post in the bedchamber for drunkenness.

In regimenting his own life and that of his court the King was creating a controlled atmosphere to facilitate the efficient work of government but he was also evolving a carapace to protect his own insecurity and vulnerability – and to uphold the dignity of his royal person. For example, Charles was alone among Europe's secular rulers in insisting that his meals be presented by servants *kneeling*.

There was an enormous amount of administrative detail to be attended to and by designating set hours for Council meetings and deskwork he hoped to prevent unanticipated events intruding upon the routine of kingly rule. By setting aside one day a week for public audience he reduced the pressure of importunate suitors. By continuing to rely on a cabal of like-minded advisers Charles shielded his mind from argument. Toby Matthew, in a letter to Dudley Carleton, described the King as weighing the comments of all his councillors before reaching a decision. In the sense of bringing important matters to the table, giving due weight to the expressed pros and cons of each case and forming an impartial judgement, this was simply not so. When the Earl of Arundel became the mouthpiece of those councillors who felt themselves excluded from the King's confidence and asked that they be consulted on the complete range of government business, Charles regarded this as a veiled attack on Buckingham – which it partly was – and gave him a short answer. Soon afterwards the earl found himself in the Tower, ostensibly for having aided and abetted his son's marriage to the Earl of Lennox's daughter. Within months the same request was voiced by the House of Lords. Such appeals were counter-productive: the more members of the political establishment campaigned for open government, the more the King retreated behind a barricade of men he trusted to carry out his will.

Ambitious courtiers and ideologues with their own agendas to promote competed for royal favour and positions of influence because that was the way that court life worked. Success depended on attracting the attention of the King, judging his moods and passions and anticipating his wants. This was no simple matter with a monarch like Charles, who, though affable and approachable to the habitués of his palaces, was essentially a private person who protected himself with elaborate protocol rituals and admitted very few people to his friendship. There was, however, one sure route to the charmed inner circle – for those wealthy enough to embark upon it. It lay through membership of the select international band of art connoisseurs. Charles always had time for fellow initiates of the cultural elite who admired his paintings and sculptures, and could discuss them impressively. The surest way to win his affection was to present him with a coveted masterpiece to add to the rapidly growing adornment of his royal homes.

The one area above all others in which the King's tightly wound

160

self-control unravelled completely was collecting. Acquisitiveness is a common manifestation of a domineering personality and in Charles it was an obsession which, immediately upon his succession, became a key element of his statecraft. He spent profligately in his haste to become one of the leading Maecenaces of Europe and it was not unusual for him to hold up ceremonies or keep councillors or ambassadors waiting while he showed off his treasures to the latest visitor. Through and alongside the network of normal diplomatic and political activity, there operated an art-world grid connecting artists, patrons, agents, dealers, speculators and runners. In the upper echelons of English society a very odd assortment of aficionados was intermeshed in this cultural brotherhood. Pembroke, whose treasure chest of a mansion at Wilton Charles adored, and Arundel were the older generation of collectors. Around 1619, Buckingham, whom both men loathed, joined their exclusive club, employing the disreputable Balthazar Gerbier to accumulate as rapidly as possible a selection of representative Renaissance masterpieces which would exalt him to the ranks of Europe's leading connoisseurs. At the beginning of Charles's reign, the agent could with self-congratulation as well as applause for his patron remark, 'I cannot but feel astonishment in the midst of my joy; for out of all the amateurs and princes and kings there is not one who has collected in forty years as many pictures as Your Excellency has collected in five.'[14] Gerbier later became an English ambassador in Brussels, entrusted with secret negotiations which failed, largely because of his inability to keep them secret. Even more bizarre was George Gage, Jesuit priest, painter and wheeler-dealer, who toured foreign courts helping Charles to locate and acquire masterpieces before they came on the open market and who, for no better reason than that James I found him delightful company, was employed as go-between for the Spanish match. Puritans were scandalised by his behaviour and easy access to the King but Gage continued to enjoy generous marks of royal favour right up until his death in about 1640. Another cleric more involved in the quest of beauty than the pursuit of holiness, was the Reverend William Petty, sent by Arundel on an almost permanent basis to scurry around the Mediterranean lands snapping up bargains and to keep one step ahead of Buckingham's agents.

Back at home, a late entrant into the coterie of court collectors was James, third Marquis (and later first Duke) of Hamilton. He was eighteen when, within days of each other, his father and James I died. He was brought to court, where the new King would readily have promoted him because of the young man's important Scottish connections and the love he bore the family. Unfortunately, Hamilton conceived a profound hatred for Buckingham, to whose niece he had been married in childhood, and he retired to his Scottish estates. He returned after Villiers's death and was immediately appointed to the bedchamber staff and given the late favourite's office of Master of the Horse. All seemed set fair for him to take Buckingham's place in other ways. But his first spectacular attempt to vault into the favourite's position flopped badly: he led six thousand men to the Baltic to support Gustavus Adolphus's invasion and lost most of them through disease and mismanagement. It was as part of a calculated campaign to repair his reputation and recover his position that he set about amassing paintings by the Venetian masters whom Charles so greatly admired. In a frenzy of activity Hamilton's agent, the English ambassador to Venice, acquired over five hundred paintings within the space of a couple of years, several of which he presented to the King. He did not always get the better of his rivals and one incident serves to prove that art-world chicanery has a long ancestry. Hamilton's agent found himself in the ring against William Petty for the acquisition of an important group of Titians, Giorgiones, Tintorettos, Bassanos and Bellinis, and triumphantly carried them off for 15,000 ducats. It later transpired that Petty had deliberately upped the bidding on behalf of the vendor, and received three priceless items for his services.

Arundel, Buckingham, Pembroke, Hamilton, Francis Cottington, Dudley Carleton, Endymion Porter and, at a lower level, Gerbier, Gage, Henry Wotton, Nicholas Lanier, Daniel Nys were all whirling planets in a firmament which was as real, and at times more real, to Charles I than the mundane political cosmos where he was obliged to spend so much of his time. If we seek a single image to express the mythology created by and for the King through the media of painting, poetry, music and dance we find it in a large painting at Hampton Court. In 1628 Buckingham brought Gerard van Honthorst over from Utrecht to create an allegorical masterpiece of the liberal arts being presented to Charles and Henrietta Maria. The muses and their attendants, no longer content to dwell in their classical homelands, have come to England. They make their homage to the King and Queen, who as Apollo and Diana are throned on Elysian clouds, while barbarism is banished at spear-point. And the winged messenger, Mercury, who brings the blessings of culture and civilisation to the land is George Villiers.

This was not just monumental sycophancy designed to boost the favourite's standing with his master; it was national propaganda. So was the King's expenditure on works of art. The moment he had access to sufficient funds Charles went on a buying spree. In the spring of 1625 he sent his Master of Music, Nicholas Lanier, to Mantua to appraise, with the aid of Dudley Carleton's agent, Daniel Nys, the collection which the local ruler Ferdinando Gonzaga was obliged to offer for sale. The Gonzaga family treasures were among the finest in Italy and their dispersal offered a unique opportunity for other courts to enhance their prestige by enlarging or, in Charles's case, establishing their own excellent collections. The King of England acquired a hundred and seventy-five paintings of the finest quality for £16,000 at a time when foreign policy adventures, his father's sumptuous funeral and his own, no less splendid, marriage had plunged him well over a million pounds in debt. It was his largest individual purchase but his agents continued to scour the continent for new treasures and he let it be known that he was always in the market. By 1629 Rubens could observe, with only slight hyperbole, 'When it comes to fine pictures by the hands of first-class masters, I have never seen such a large number in one place as in the royal palace and in the gallery of the late Duke of Buckingham.'[15]

Charles was not content with a walk-on part in the drama of Christendom politics. His father's pacifism had been intellectually consistent and had given his people peace but only at the cost of sidelining England in the counsels of European statecraft. The new King was personally a withdrawn and reticent character. Perhaps for that very reason he decked his court and his government in boldness and elegance that demanded attention. He was determined that people should not continue to compare the Stuart regime unfavourably with that of Gloriana, whose poets and musicians, captains and generals had created the legend of the glorious and victorious Protestant champion. The march to the Palatinate was one element of the image Charles wanted to project. The splendour of the royal setting was another. Spain's rulers had the austerely grand Escorial – 'a hovel for a king and a palace for God' as Philip II had described it with pious humility. Louis XIII had the Renaissance exoticism of Fontainebleau, recently enlarged by his father. England had no such architectural proclamation of exalted monarchy and Charles devoted much time and energy in his early years to rectifying this defect. He had Inigo Jones draw up plans for a grandiose new palace complex at Whitehall and set Rubens to work on the recently rebuilt Banqueting House. Although provided with a spur in the impressive extension Buckingham was having done to his town mansion of York House, the grand Whitehall project proved beyond the King's means but he did sanction for Henrietta Maria a work of baroque splendour at Somerset House (see below pp. 203ff) and a contrasting structure of Palladian restraint at Greenwich (the Queen's House). Though unable to effect his Whitehall project, he did join with other enthusiastic patrons such as the Earl of Bedford (who laid out Covent Garden) in adorning the capital. His principal contribution was in renovating and refaçading St Paul's Cathedral (see below pp. 206).

Another project which reflected glory on Charles I and gave expression to his aesthetic sense was his active patronage of the Mortlake tapestry works. Founded some six years earlier by King James, who poached Flemish master weavers with the deliberate intention of rivalling the factories of Brussels, Bruges and Gobelins, the English atelier acquired artistic dominance during the reign of his son and became 'the single most successful entrepreneurial art venture ever undertaken by the Crown in the history of the English monarchy'.[16] The King persuaded artists of the stature of Van Dyck and Rubens to produce designs for the factory and it was on the suggestion of Rubens that Charles brought off one of his earliest art-world coups, the purchase of Raphael's cartoon series *The Acts of the Apostles* which had been designed for wall coverings in the Sistine Chapel. The magnificent work of the great weavers was scarcely less valued than that of Europe's leading painters and the many tapestries hung in Charles's palaces to cover large areas of bare stone or wainscot were statements of royal prestige as well as decorative adornments and practical draught excluders.

The image Charles was projecting was of a new style of English monarchy. He was signalling to his own people, but especially to foreign diplomats, that the Catholic courts of the realm's nearer neighbours held no monopoly of the arts of civilisation. The household of the Stuart king was a microcosm on display – decorous, sophisticated, cultured and Protestant. Charles believed, as tutored by his father, that the King should appear before his people as an icon to be respected and revered, an embodiment of all that was best in the nation. When St Paul's, Covent Garden, the first church built in the capital for a hundred years, was completed, the King had his statue erected in front of it symbolising his headship of the Reformed Church and also his association with all that was culturally excellent. Many, probably the majority, were impressed by royal ostentation but others were alienated. In Puritan circles there was a long-running debate on 'Faith and Art'. There was no dissent from the necessity of outlawing religious imagery but did Christian spirituality leave any room for the enjoyment of representational art? The godly earnestly debated whether portraiture was vanity, and expenditure on needless luxuries poor stewardship of God's gifts. Such thoughts overlapped with the concerns of people who certainly did not regard themselves as members of the godly elite. They disliked arrogant courtiers who swaggered around with hundreds of pounds' worth of silk, jewels and gold embroidery on their backs. Hardworking gentlemen and burgesses wondered just what it was they were helping to fund through taxation. As the crises of the forties drew nearer controversialists based their arguments on theology and constitutional theory but the visual image was always more immediate and more powerful. Charles's cultural elitism appealed to some of his subjects and repelled others. What it could not do was unite them all.

There was a story circulating in France in the early eighteenth century about the marriage of Charles I and Henrietta Maria. A group of English friends were in London and it was suggested that they had a party to celebrate the royal nuptials. One of them held out against the idea for some time before reluctantly yielding to his companions' entreaties with the words, 'Let us enjoy ourselves, by all means, but I fear that this marriage is no matter of celebration for our country.' The dissident voice belonged to Oliver Cromwell.[17] The story may be apocryphal but the sentiment expressed was widespread when, in June 1625, Charles travelled to Dover to meet his bride. England had another Catholic queen and, though the French were considered to be not as fanatical as the Spanish about their religion, it was inevitable that Henrietta Maria and her suite would be regarded as a Trojan horse.

Charles cared nothing for such considerations but he had good reason to be nervous as he entered upon the responsibilities of the married state. His own parents had scarcely provided role models of

165

marital harmony. He had had no close relationship with a woman since the departure of his sister and the death of his mother. Throughout his early manhood he had come to rely for affection on George Villiers. 'Sweetheart,' he once told the favourite, 'all the world shall daily know more and more that I am and ever will be your faithful, loving, constant friend'[18] and those words expressed a depth of feeling which no amount of criticism, scandal or even disagreement was able to remove. Charles had grown accustomed to sublimating his deeper feelings, in chapel and chamber, with beautiful music, paintings and sculptures and the life he lived was a kind of aesthetic monasticism. Henrietta Maria had never known her father, who was assassinated when she was six months old. She was very close to her mother, Marie de Medici, a domineering creature constantly at odds with her son, Louis XIII. Marie doted on her youngest child who grew up, utterly over-indulged in the fun-loving French court. The princess who came to England in the summer of 1625 was a giggling, high-spirited, self-willed, spoilt girl, nine years her husband's junior. She brought with her her own closest friends and companions and, understandably, preferred their company to that of any English courtiers. There can be no doubt that bride and groom came virginal to the marriage bed. Their first night together was at Canterbury, whither the King had conveyed his bride from the coast. After the formalities and the feasting rowdy friends conveyed the couple to their chamber for the traditional ceremony of seeing the newly-weds tucked up together but Charles would have none of this impropriety and forestalled them. As soon as he and Henrietta Maria reached their room he locked the door against the revellers, only emerging in the morning to claim that the marriage had been consummated.

Whether this was true only husband and wife ever knew. Within months Charles was complaining of coldness on the part of his consort. There is no record of what the Queen thought of her introverted spouse's lovemaking. What is on record is that within weeks the couple were quarrelling violently, and that the Queen was not pregnant until 1628. The immediate cause of friction was the emotional immaturity of both parties: Henrietta Maria did not know how to go about winning her husband's affection; Charles could not cope with a frivolous and petulant teenager. The immediate members of the two households did not help. The Queen complained that Buckingham came higher in her husband's affections and that he

166

was poisoning the King's mind against her. Villiers was at pains to deny this but he was certainly guilty at least of giving the impression of hostility. He was smarting at the failure of his pro-French foreign policy and his treatment by the court in Paris. The very fact that he was the recipient of Charles's complaints and was the emissary between the King and the officials of the Queen's household must have made it seem that he was deliberately exacerbating the situation. The King was no less adamant that it was his wife's French attendants who were preventing her from rendering the loving obedience that was his due. They effectively cocooned her from English influence, attempting to create a mini-Fontainebleau around her and running up colossal expenses. More than this, they actually made fun of the customs of Henrietta Maria's adopted country. On at least one occasion the Queen and her ladies deliberately walked, chattering and laughing, through the royal chapel when the sermon was being delivered. Charles complained, probably with justification, that his wife had been instructed not to get too close to him emotionally for fear he should infect her with his Protestant heresy.

Religion lay at the heart of the problem. Henrietta Maria had been devoutly brought up and it had been impressed upon her that she must keep herself pure from religious error. Her mother counselled her to demonstrate in matters of doctrine and worship 'such constancy and determination that you need not fear telling [your husband] boldly and openly that you would rather die than give way on even the slightest point'.[19] Once established at court, her large retinue of priests swaggered about defiantly in their 'Romish garb' – or so it seemed to outraged courtiers. Friction increased when the zealous Frenchmen began proselytising and when Parliament learned of Charles's secret undertaking to relax the recusancy laws.

Behind the growing volume of daily irritants that drove Charles to unaccustomed rage and Henrietta Maria to tearful reproaches was the deterioration in Anglo-French relations. Politics had been the propellant for the marriage both in general terms – Henrietta Maria was potentially both a hostage and an influential agent in the English court – and specifically in terms of cementing the recent treaty. The French had already reneged on their commitments to Mansfeld's expedition; they now outwitted their treaty partners over the loan of ships for helping to reduce La Rochelle. Charles and Buckingham delayed as long as possible in authorising the handing over of the vessels, knowing the criticism that aiding Louis to suppress his Protestant subjects would arouse. Only when news reached London of an agreement between the French king and the Huguenots was the appropriate order sent to the English captain. But Richelieu had tricked his allies: there was no peace with the 'rebels' in prospect. Thus, instead of linking up with French and Dutch ships to menace the Spanish treasure fleets the English vessels were employed to menace La Rochelle. They were only released, months later, when the Rochellais had been forced to sue for peace with their sovereign. Thereupon, Richelieu, instead of making resources available for an anti-Habsburg league, signed a peace treaty with Spain. Charles and Buckingham had been outmanoeuvred and humiliated and would now have to face a furious Parliament.

It is not surprising that relations between Charles and his Queen were close to breaking point by the early weeks of 1626. The storm almost broke in February when Henrietta Maria told her husband that she would not attend his coronation because it was to be conducted by a heretical bishop. So tetchy had Charles become that he began to behave with uncharacteristic pettiness. When, a week later, he opened Parliament on a wet winter's day Henrietta Maria asked permission to watch his procession from her own quarters instead of crossing a muddy garden to join the Duchess of Buckingham's party. Charles grumpily agreed. Then, to please him, and at the suggestion of the French ambassador, the Queen went to Lady Villiers's after all. When this was reported to the King he was so furious because she would do for the ambassador what she would not do for him that he ordered her straight home. When tension was particularly bad the couple communicated through intermediaries. Yet, despite such outbursts, Charles somehow retained his patience and there were calm interludes in the relationship when courtiers detected real affection between the royal pair. Less than a fortnight after Charles's latest explosion Henrietta Maria put on a performance of *Artemice*, a pastoral by the French courtier-poet Honorat de Bueil, Seigneur de Racon. It was the first court masque of the reign and, though it was a deliberate importation designed partly to show the superiority of the dramatic conventions in fashion at Louis's court, the King was pleased with it. However, even here sensitive issued were raised. Parliament was in session and that meant that Puritan propaganda was pouring from the Commons benches as well as City pulpits. Some of the more extreme advocates of social and religious purity inveighed against the theatre as one of the age's more lascivious and corrupting influences and were particularly incensed by the idea of women cavorting on stage. The Queen's performance, therefore, had to be given behind locked doors to a very select audience; an acknowledgement by the King that his courtly elite and the most vociferous element of his people were pulling in opposite directions and that his wife and her entourage were making the situation worse.

It was a provocative public display of Henrietta Maria's religious sentiments that finally crushed the vial of Charles's wrath. Someone drew the Queen's attention to the numbers of Catholics who had been hanged at Tyburn. In the simplistic mythology which was a part of her faith these men were martyrs and, one July morning as she chanced to be driven past the scaffold with its viewing galleries, she ordered her coach to stop, dismounted and paused to kneel in reverent prayer. It is not difficult to imagine the impact of this indiscretion on passers-by or citizens who had come out to the fields for a glimpse of the Queen. The impact on Charles was galvanic: did the stupid woman not know that those she was openly honouring were not simple souls who had died for their faith but convicted traitors, some of whom had plotted the death of their divinely appointed sovereign? Charles was no bigot when it came to respecting the sincere convictions of others but he shared the abhorrence felt by most of his people for Rome-inspired rebellion, and could not tolerate his wife appearing to condone it. This time the mischievous French priests had gone too far in filling Henrietta Maria's head with lies and propaganda.

He immediately sent a message to Buckingham instructing him to send all the Queen's French attendants packing. The favourite demurred, only too well aware of the political repercussions which might result from such draconian action. He prevailed upon the King to lay the problem before the Council. This was done and for a few days it seemed that Charles had simmered down. Then some fresh irritation forced the King to reissue his order. Once again Buckingham counselled moderation but this time Charles would not be denied:

I have received your letter by Dick Graham. This is my answer. I command you to send all the French away tomorrow out of the town — if you can, by fair means, but stick not long in disputing; otherwise force them away, driving them away like so many wild beasts until ye have shipped them. And so the Devil go with them. Let me hear no answer but of the performance of my command.[20]

In fact it was Viscount Killultagh (Edward Conway), another member of the Council, who wielded the verbal scourge three days later. While Charles detained his Queen in a room at St James's Palace, Conway, accompanied by a group of Yeoman of the Guard, collected members of her suite from neighbouring chambers and, amidst terrible screams and imprecations, ejected them. When Henrietta Maria realised what was happening she ran to a window overlooking the courtyard and beat upon it with her fists, breaking some of the glass. The boil had, at last, been painfully lanced and the poison drawn off but soreness remained and would do so for many more months. It would take the advent of children and the removal of Buckingham to create a marriage which could be paraded before the world as an idyll of domestic happiness.

The intensity of the 1625–6 conflicts was a diluted foretaste of the bitter cup Charles would have to drink in the 1640s and it is informative to observe how he coped with it. The first eighteen months of his reign can scarcely have been more disastrous. He was defied by Parliament and humiliated by his French allies. His hopes for the Palatinate were swept aside brusquely when Christian IV was comprehensively defeated in Thuringia and Mansfeld died of a plague in an obscure Bosnian village. His treasury was under constant pressure to meet demands for which the resources simply did not exist. And when he sought escape from all these worries in the intimacy of his marriage he was confronted by a wife who defied his wishes and was too involved in her own diversions and petty squabbles to show any interest in his affairs.

In this situation the King struggled to preserve a kingly front. Through the years of tutelage he had mastered the art of self-control. In a crowded court where his life was lived in full view of personal attendants, advisers, guards, household staff and privileged courtiers he substituted the hail-fellow-well-metness of his father with a dignified reserve. When this came under attack and anger and frustration burst out he could not always ensure that his discomposure was only observed by his tiny circle of intimates. Charles was a man who did not trust his emotions. He used intermediaries to express his displeasure with others and it was his custom to retreat from conflict. Because he shunned argument he was able to resist compromise and thus keep his own convictions inviolate. This emotional and intellectual purdah hampered him when he *did* want to communicate his thoughts and feelings to others. He needed a pragmatist like Buckingham to act as interpreter as well as a buttress to his insecurities. Not until after the favourite's death did he look to his wife for that kind of support.

This lack of personal engagement was immediately evident in the King's dealing with Parliament. Gone was the prince who had assiduously attended debates, listening to the arguments of others and offering considered contributions. As King he took a much more detached view. This was evident even before Lords and Commons assembled in June 1625. Charles and Buckingham made little or no attempt to influence the election of new members or to organise a court party. They were, it is true, preoccupied with arrangements for James VI's funeral, and the King's marriage and the imbroglio of foreign affairs, but they seemed genuinely to believe that Parliament would do its duty, which was to bail the government out of its financial problems. Those problems, they reasoned, were entirely attributable to the anti-Habsburg policy which the last parliament had warmly supported. The corollary to the fact was, as Charles stated in his opening speech, unavoidable: 'I pray you remember that this being my first action and begun by your advice and entreaty, what a great dishonour it were, both to you and me, if this action, so begun, should fail for that assistance you are able to give me.'[21] The assembly was asked to vote supply immediately and to relegate any other matters to a later session. Not until this royal demand met with respectful opposition did government spokesmen even begin to think in terms of negotiation and striking deals.

Was the King's uncompromising stance a defensive blanket for smothering the flames of discontent which Charles knew full well were being fanned by the winds of broken promises and bungled foreign policy, or did he genuinely believe that, just as a wife should obey her husband, so he had the right to expect unconditional loyalty from his parliament? Probably something between the two. He was embarrassed and annoyed by the amendments forced on his policy by his father during the last months of the previous reign, by the duplicity of the French, by the justifiable anxiety caused by the antics of the Queen's religious entourage and by the abject failure of the warlike enterprises he had sponsored. Typically, he wanted to avoid any discussion of these matters and he believed that if Parliament could be bounced into providing substantial sums of money, diplomatic and military failure could be turned to success. Then criticism would dissipate or could be easily dealt with. In the event, in 1625 the Commons voted wholly inadequate taxation, used their procedures to raise discussion of grievances to the top of the agenda and began proceedings for the impeachment of Buckingham. Charles's answer was the same as the one he would apply to Henrietta Maria's household. Despite the urgings of Villiers and the Council he dissolved Parliament after less than two months, while dropping dark hints that there were other ways of raising money.

His intention appears to have been to summon another assembly which, with better management and manipulation, would be more compliant. The reality was a session which 'brought forth nothing but a tympany of swelling faction and abrupt dissolution'.[22] Those beating the drums may have seemed to the King's supporters to be filling the air with a cacophony of sectional interests and wilful opposition in order to drown out the government's reasonable demands for support but those who opposed the Crown, through the time-honoured stratagem of opposing the favourite, believed that they were protecting the nation from continental-style Catholic despotism. They feared creeping papalism and the squandering of taxation revenues to implement policies which advanced neither the security of the realm nor the Protestant cause abroad.

The struggle imposed increasing stress on the King. He was worried about the mounting debts which prevented him carrying through his military schemes, angry at the defiance of the Commons' majority, distressed at the growing attacks on Villiers and humiliated at having to play the political game by Parliament's rules. Only those close to him saw the strain Charles was under. One courtier overheard him in anguished conversation with Buckingham: 'What can I do more? I have engaged mine honour to mine Uncle of Denmark and other princes. I have, in a manner, lost the love of my subjects. What wouldst thou have me do?'[23] His public face was more firmly set and his tone more unyielding:

Now that you have all things according to your wishes and that I am so far engaged that you think there is no retreat, now you begin to set the dice, and make your own game; but I pray you to be not deceived; it is not a parliamentary way, nor it is not a way to deal with a king. Mr.

172

Coke told you it was better to be eaten up by a foreign enemy than to be destroyed at home. Indeed, I think it more honour for a king to be invaded and almost destroyed by a foreign enemy, than to be despised by his own subjects. Remember that parliaments are altogether in my power for their calling, sitting, and dissolution; therefore, as I find the fruits of them good or evil, they are to continue or not to be.[24]

So he threatened the assembled Lords and Commons when he summoned them to appear before him in March. But while the King demonstrated regal authority his favourite was allowed to cajole, explain, flatter and bargain.

The Council was divided between the two attitudes. Some urged the necessity of winning the support of Parliament; the more reactionary advised the King to do away with the troublesome body and rule without it. There was nothing in itself unconstitutional about such a suggestion but it did mean that the government would have to be inventive and resourceful in the extreme to find the resources to meet its commitments. Eventually, it was once again Buckingham's fate which decided the King's action. The Lower House brought a bill of impeachment while in the Lords Villiers's attempts to discredit his enemies provoked counter-charges of treason. Charles tried every stratagem to prevent his friend being condemned: he harangued the Lords in person; he created new peers to change the balance of the house; he demonstrated his support for his friend by appointing him Chancellor of Cambridge University; he arrested two 'contumacious' MPs. But eventually only one course was left to him. When he informed the Lords on 15 June of Parliament's immediate dissolution, four peers, Manchester, Pembroke, Carlisle and Holland – all government men – begged more time to conclude important business. Charles's reply was succinct: 'Not a minute.'

Within two years of assuming the Crown issues of 'responsibility' had, in Charles's mind, resolved themselves into issues of 'power' and 'prestige'. He had been defied by his wife and he had won. He had been defied by Parliament and, for the moment, there was a truce. He had been opposed by foreign princes and, for the most part, had the worst of the encounters. His reaction to these experiences was an increased determination to *be* king in his own realm, to be an important player in world affairs and to preside over the most cultured court in Europe. There was one area of national life where no one could resist his authority. It was largely to impress upon the parliamentarians and their Puritan friends that he was master in his own house that he imposed his will on *his* Church, setting it full-sail upon a perilous course, utterly heedless of the shoals ahead. At the same time he threw himself even more enthusiastically into patronage and the accumulation of collections that would rival those of rulers in Spain, France and Italy. *And* he now changed his stance on military intervention in France.

In pursuing a more aggressive foreign policy he was influenced by Buckingham, who was under no misapprehension about the importance of securing the goodwill of Parliament and who now tacked about in a bid for popularity by proposing a naval expedition to go to the aid of the beleaguered French Protestants. Thus it was that, on 11 June 1627, the King dined in Portsmouth upon his flagship, the *Triumph*, and toasted his captains who were preparing to embark for La Rochelle to succour the Huguenot minority in their struggle for religious freedom. On his return to the capital a week later he promoted to the Council Bishop William Laud, who was to be his agent in enforcing uniformity on the English Church. Meanwhile in his correspondence with Lanier he responded delightedly to the news that his agent had successfully outbid Cardinal Richelieu and other princes for the gems of the Mantua collection. This was a critical phase: it was the time when Charles began to move from reality to fantasy, from calm appraisal to dogmatic assertion, from things as they were to things as he wished and willed them to be.

'. . . it is easy for us to set down in paper ships and money and arms and victuals and men. But to congest these materials together, especially in such a penury of money, requires more time than the necessity of your affairs will permit.'[25] So wrote Sir Humphrey May in October to his fellow councillor, the Duke of Buckingham, who was sitting on shipboard off La Rochelle desperate for supplies. At about the same time Filippo Burlamachi, the King's banker, scribbled the following in the margin of a note from Nicholas Lanier before passing it on to the treasury:

I pray . . . let me know where money shall be found to pay this great sum. If it were for £2000 or £3000 it could be borne, but for £15,000, besides the other engagements for his majesty's service, it will utterly put me out of any possibility to do anything in those provisions which are so necessary for my lord duke's relief.[26]

174

The money Lanier was demanding was the bulk of what was required for the Mantuan collection. Charles was one hundred per cent committed to both projects and for much the same reason in both cases: victory in the art market and on the field of battle would alike add lustre to his crown. Lanier and Daniel Nys were urged on by the King's entreaties, to devote all their energy and guile to outwitting agents acting for the French court and the emperor. As for the La Rochelle expedition, Charles repeatedly assured Villiers of his support and came close to making threats when he told Sir Richard Weston, Chancellor of the Exchequer and *de facto* Treasurer,* that failure would bring 'irrecoverable shame to me and all this nation' and that any who were responsible for that failure would deserve 'to make their end at Tyburn'.[27] What Charles could not or would not acknowledge was that the state of royal finances would not permit him to have both. Although his spending on paintings was only a fraction of what was needed for his military activities it rendered a difficult situation impossible.

The result of his obliging his money men to juggle with their slender resources was that cash and equipment only reached Buckingham in dribs and drabs and after four months' campaigning the English expedition plucked defeat from the jaws of victory. Villiers had begun well; all of the Isle de Ré was soon in his grasp, save for its main fortress of St Martin. He needed only to starve the citadel into submission to secure an impregnable base from which to launch an invasion of the mainland and lift the royal siege of La Rochelle. By the end of September the French garrison were in dire straits and close to surrender. But the invaders were scarcely better off and when a relief expedition with food and munitions forced its way into St Martin, Buckingham's men were too depleted by disease and hunger to stop it. For four more weeks Villiers hung on, waiting for supplies and reinforcements. Then he ordered his dispirited men to break up their camp and embark for home. He set sail on 6 November and off the English coast he met the relief force which had finally been sent to his aid.

Buckingham knew the price that failure would extract. He had done everything in his power to achieve success. He had poured thousands of his own money into the expedition, selling up lands

---

* The *de lege* holder of that office, Lord Marlborough, was seventy-two and incompetent in matters of finance.

and possessions down to the very pearl buttons on one of his coats. He had led the sea and land assault with passing competence. He could honestly claim that responsibility for the dismal outcome lay elsewhere. That was not how most Englishmen saw it.

> And art returned again with all thy faults,
> Thou great commander of the all-go-naughts,
> And left the Isle behind thee? What's the matter?
> Did winter make thy teeth begin to chatter?[28]

So ran a popular song. And a gentleman diarist tartly recorded that Buckingham's 'coming home safe occasioned almost as much sorrow as the slaughter and perishing of all the rest'.[29]

Charles, however, was completely out of step with the prevailing mood. He wrote several letters of encouragement and support, assuring his friend that he was doing all he could to raise the necessary funds – which, short of cancelling the Mantua deal, was certainly true. He was relieved at Villiers's safe return, the more so since alarming news had reached him of an abortive assassination attempt on the duke. He sent his own coach to Portsmouth to convey Buckingham swiftly back to court and on more than one occasion assured him that he attached no blame to the expedition's leader; 'all the shame must light upon us here remaining at home,'[30] he insisted. Yet still he had not learned to cut his coat according to his cloth. Within a year he was negotiating the purchase for £10,500 of another tranche of Gonzaga treasures, including Mantegna's incomparable series of paintings, *The Triumph of the Caesars*.

This new extravagance did not signal a decision to set court embellishment above military endeavour, for King and favourite were both resolved on a new attempt to wrest La Rochelle from the vice-like grip of Richelieu's army. This would need money. Buckingham was not prepared to tolerate a repetition of the previous campaigning season's disaster and when a Council majority urged the King to summon another parliament Villiers's was the loudest voice. He argued that, in the rapidly changing European situation the representatives of the political nation would willingly lend support to aggressive policies. France and Spain had recently signed a treaty and there was alarmist talk of a Catholic invasion of England. But Charles was implacably opposed to inaugurating another assembly which might challenge his prerogatives and launch a further attack on his friend. He had developed an absolute contempt for those who cloaked in parliamentary privilege their rejection of the loyalty and obedience they owed him as subjects and he was not prepared to go cap-in-hand to them for money. As to finance, he had promoted clever men to his government specifically to provide for his and the nation's needs; let them do their job. In January 1628 he appointed a commission to 'enter into consideration of all the best and speediest ways and means you can for raising of monies . . . the same to be done by impositions or otherwise as in your wisdoms and best judgements ye shall find to be most convenient'.[31]

Charles Stuart was a stubborn man. Though often a prey (and increasingly so over the years) to indecision and inner questionings he recoiled from the 'weakness' of appearing to change his mind under pressure. It was, thus, only when Buckingham supported the argument of his fellow councillors that no novel exactions would bring in sufficient funds sufficiently quickly for a successful renewal of the conflict with France that Charles gave way on the issue of calling Parliament. It convened on 17 March and the King made clear his feelings in a brief opening speech in which he demanded supply, once more indicating that he would turn to other means if they refused, and told the members he did not deign to threaten them, 'for I scorn to threaten any but my equals'.

It fell to Buckingham to try to manage Parliament – and the King. His main concern was to obtain the vote of supply. This could only be achieved by dissuading the two Houses from making extravagant demands and by restraining an indignant sovereign from hastening to a premature dissolution. The underlying issues had not gone away and it took all Villiers's stamina and charm to achieve a compromise both sides could live with. In return for taxation amounting to £275,000 Charles accepted a Petition of Right which claimed that freeborn Englishmen should not be subjected to financial imposts without parliamentary sanction, nor arbitrary arrest, nor the billeting upon them of soldiers and sailors, nor the imposition of martial law. When the news reached the streets of the capital there was spontaneous outpouring of public rejoicing: bells were rung and, according to one reporter, more bonfires were lit then than had marked the failure of the Spanish match.

But if the champions of civil liberties thought that they had taken some important steps forward they discovered their mistake on 26 June, the day Charles prorogued Parliament. Alarmed by the public reaction, the King made it clear that the Petition of Right represented not the slightest diminution of his prerogative. He, aided by the judges, was the source of law and Parliament had no power to legislate anything prejudicial to the rights of the Crown. Charles called in fifteen hundred copies of the petition and ordered their destruction. Hope dashed is worse than hope not raised and many were the members who returned to their own homes disgruntled.

Charles now gave all his attention to helping Villiers to assemble and equip the new Rochelle operation. It was vital for the prestige of both men that the 1628 expedition was successful. Charles gave orders that no money was to be paid from the treasury until all Buckingham's needs had been met and the duke remained in London until the last possible moment to oversee the recruitment of men and the equipping and victualling of his ships. By mid-August King and favourite were both in Portsmouth, Villiers supervising final preparations for the fleet and Charles staying five miles away at Southwick to lend his support to the enterprise. The atmosphere was busy and tense and it was not only the commotion caused by soldiers and sailors off to war, chandlers and captains arguing over supplies, and animals being driven to the butchers' yards, which contributed to the feeling of uneasiness and apprehension. Hatred for the duke was running high as he strutted through the town, shouting orders and flaunting his authority. One morning a crowd of sailors surrounded his coach and tried to pull him from it. Buckingham had the ringleader arrested and executed but such firm action did not quell the disaffection. On 22 August a disgruntled soldier, called John Felton, succeeded where others had failed. He stepped forward from the crowd as Buckingham was leaving his quarters and plunged a dagger into the commander's chest.

Charles's reaction to his friend's death speaks volumes. He was at divine service in his chapel when the news was brought to him. He registered no emotion whatsoever and signalled to his chaplain to continue. Then he retired to his chamber and broke down completely. For several days he ordered that no one was to intrude on his private grief. Emerging at last, he arranged for the duke's embalmed body to be conveyed with all pomp to London, there to lie in state before the funeral. The King was determined to mark his loss by a no-expenses-spared ceremony and an elaborate tomb. But wiser counsels prevailed: it would be unseemly for Buckingham to be interred with greater obsequies than those which had attended

James I; the behaviour of the crowd at a lavish public ceremony could not be guaranteed; it would be more appropriate for the money to be spent on settling the deceased's debts. Eventually the coffin was conveyed to Westminster Abbey at night in a torchlight procession, the people giving vent to expressions of joy rather than commiseration as it passed.

Yet again Charles Stuart was deprived of someone he had loved intensely. Once more he was alone, thrust back on his own resources. Buckingham's death was a major turning point. He may have been enormously unpopular and played a significant part in undermining the Crown – but at the same time he filled the function of a scapegoat; government critics could blame the servant for the failings of the master. Above all, by the assassination of George Villiers Charles lost a pragmatic adviser. The duke was by nature a survivor. He understood how to placate enemies, when to stand on principles and when to abandon them. He was the only man who was ever able to persuade a proud and blinkered king to compromise, to bargain, to settle for the possible rather than pursue the unattainable ideal. Without Buckingham to fasten round his shoulders the protective cloak of political realism Charles would confront opponents clad only in the silken purity of honest, haughty autocracy.

This left him vulnerable to the attacks of determined and subtle parliamentarians who, with every return to Westminster, developed new procedures and stratagems to force reform on the government. When members came together in January 1629 it was with a determination to discuss 'abuses' of prerogative and Laudian innovations in religion. In order to prevent the King controlling their debates through the Speaker, a royal nominee, they resorted to the committee system. Since committees chose their own chairmen they enjoyed unlimited freedom of speech. Charles responded by adjourning the assembly and trying to use the Lords to curb the Commons. This tactical battle led up to the celebrated crisis of 2 March. When a further adjournment was proposed, the Speaker attempted to leave his chair. Five members held him in place until they continued their proceedings. For Charles this was the last straw. He ordered the dissolution of Parliament on 10 March and resolved to rule the country without it.

When Oliver Cromwell took his bride home to Huntingdon he went to preside over an all-female household. Besides his wife and his mother there were still three unmarried sisters at home. With a certain abruptness his life of carefree pleasure with friends of his own age had come to an end. In Cambridge and London there had been plenty to do; important and intelligent people with whom to discuss new ideas, evaluate contemporary events at home and on the continent; sermons and plays to attend; gossip to listen to and pass on. Now his time was mostly taken up with administering his modest patrimony, a patrimony of which, thanks to the terms of his father's will, he was not even fully master. His mind was occupied with the concerns of tenants and property, issues of municipal politics and the business of making ends meet. Careful budgeting, under his mother's practised eye, was a necessity, for the family enjoyed only modest means. Oliver's marriage to the daughter of a wealthy merchant seems to have brought little by way of material benefit and his landed income was no more than £100 per annum. All these factors combined to suggest a restricted and restricting atmosphere for a young man whose life to this point had been one of physical, if not mental vigour.

Oliver's financial concerns may have been exacerbated rather than eased by the fact that he had expectations. Two childless uncles had designated him as their heir. Sir Thomas Steward, his mother's brother, held property in and around Ely and Oliver was his closest male relative. Richard Cromwell of Upwood was an unmarried lawyer who lived and worked in London. Oliver must have seen a great deal of this uncle during his years in the capital and it is likely that Richard had occupied the role of unofficial guardian and guide to the young man. The fact that Oliver named his third son Richard (the older boys were baptised Robert, after his grandfather and Oliver) suggests a bond of affection between them. There is a certain frustration in waiting for relatives to die in order to inherit, not to mention feelings of guilt, and as Oliver and Elizabeth struggled to meet the expenses of a growing family (six children were born in their first decade of married life) it cannot have helped to know that they were dependent on legacies for their future security.

The background of Oliver's early married life in Huntingdon was the steady, rapid disintegration of his family's influence in the area. By 1623 his uncle, the head of the clan, was in desperate straits. His creditors were pressing and he wanted to sell Hinchingbrooke in order to clear his debts. He offered the property to James at what seemed to him a fair price ('a penny for a pennyworth') but the King procrastinated – why should he pay for something he could enjoy for free? Thus, Sir Oliver could neither sell the estate nor afford to keep it up. What concerned him even more was the suspicion that others were undermining his standing with the King. He had, he insisted, raised his sons to be dutiful royal servants and had hoped to install them at court, but no places had been found for them and he had had to provide for them himself. Three of them became military adventurers: John, William and Giles travelled to Holland and pledged their swords to the deposed Elector Frederick and his courageous wife, Elizabeth. For several years they were attached to the court in exile and served as officers in the pathetically small cosmopolitan army that fought for the 'Queen of Hearts' and the Protestant faith. Risking their lives for James's daughter was romantic and noble but financially disastrous. Maintaining themselves and their men (whose pay was permanently in arrears) was a drain on their capital and if they hoped that their sacrifice would commend them to Elizabeth's father they miscalculated. Like Sir Oliver they found themselves in reduced circumstances. Once the splendours of Hinchingbrooke had impressed all who visited it or even heard of it. Now its owner's dwindling fortunes spoke just as eloquently of a glory that was past and undermined his position in the county. Even his friends were beginning to believe that he was out of favour.[32]

The truth is that he was. Much as James loved Hinchingbrooke, he had never admitted its master to his inner circle and now his feelings for Sir Oliver cooled much further. The reason for the estrangement was money: someone had planted in the King's mind the suspicion that the Cromwells had swindled him. The principal culprit was Sir Thomas Wilson, Keeper of the Records at Whitehall, a man whose chief claim to notoriety was his malevolent and subtle interrogation of Sir Walter Ralegh in the Tower. After the dissolution of Parliament in January 1622, royal officials were set to explore the King's finances minutely to see where extra revenue might be found. Wilson, an assiduous scrutineer of old documents, pounced on the acquittances signed by Sir Oliver Cromwell and his wife at the beginning of the reign, when the new King had made them a grant of land in settlement of the Crown debt incurred to Sir Horatio Palavicino. The Cromwells, he asserted, had then received property with an annual value of £5–6000 at old rents, 'now worth twenty times as much'. This enormous endowment, Wilson now claimed, had been extracted by fraud. His reasoning was based on the dubious technicality that Palavicino's widow had ceased to be his executrix on her remarriage. From this he triumphantly concluded, 'therefore, the whole affair was a cozenage; if the parties are called in question it will bring the king more money than he expected from Flanders' (the spoils promised to James from a proposed Anglo-Spanish expedition to the Low Countries in 1620).[33] Wilson either accidentally or deliberately exaggerated the value of the land grant which was, in fact, about £500 per annum[34] but even if James realised this, the prospect of reclaiming it would still have been very attractive and the belief that he had been cheated out of it would have rankled. As long as the matter remained unresolved there was certainly no question of pouring good money after bad by buying Hinchingbrooke – particularly as he could continue enjoying its facilities without doing so.

The dispute rumbled on into the next reign and was complicated by becoming entangled with the activities of Toby Palavicino. That rakehell was as desperate for cash as the government and just as adept at employing old documents. As soon as any parental restraining hand was removed by the death of his mother, in 1626, he demanded satisfaction from the corporation of London in regard to a loan which his father had made to Queen Elizabeth in 1583 and for which the mayor and aldermen had stood guarantors. Toby claimed that the debt had only been partially repaid and he now claimed £14,000. If this was not forthcoming, he threatened, he would seize the property of London merchants in foreign ports. This wild ultimatum was taken sufficiently seriously for the City fathers to appeal for aid to the Council. However, nothing came of it and, as we have already seen, Toby died in a debtors' prison. The proceedings regarding the Cromwells' alleged defrauding of the Crown also seems to have dwindled into silence.

These debilitating proceedings added to Sir Oliver's worries. He was now in his mid-sixties and widowed for a second time (though destined to live to the age of ninety-three). He found no place at the court of Charles I and royal visits to Hinchingbrooke ceased with the death of the old King. He had an honoured place at the funeral as a bannarol, a bearer of one of the standards which were draped over the tomb at the conclusion of the ceremony. This appears to have been his last service to the Stuarts. Despite the wrangle over

Palavicino monies and the bad odour caused by Toby's activities, Sir Oliver seems not to have been in actual disgrace but, as far as the new regime was concerned, he was certainly one of yesterday's men. In the early months of Charles's reign a payment of £300 was made to him for 'special services'.[35] It was the last significant disbursement he received from the royal treasury. In July 1627 Sir Oliver and his eldest son, Henry, resigned the park rangerships in Huntingdon and Cambridgeshire, which had brought in £20 per annum, in favour of the Earl of Manchester's two elder sons, Edward, Viscount Mandeville and Walter Montagu. Political power was moving in the same direction. Between 1623 and 1625 the knights of the shire in Parliament were Edward Montagu and Sir Oliver Cromwell. In the election of 1625 Cromwell was replaced by Sir Robert Payne, a friend and protégé of the Kimbolton family. The new order was harshly emphasized two years later by the sale of Hinchingbrooke to the Montagus. Sir Oliver retired to Ramsey and ceased to be a leading social and political figure in the life of Huntingdon. From henceforth ambitious burgesses and landowners would seek the patronage of the new family.

Oliver Cromwell knew the younger Montagus very well indeed. Edward and Walter had been his exact contemporaries at Sidney Sussex and they had shared both revels and studies. A further link was forged in July 1626 when Edward married Anne Rich, daughter of the Earl of Warwick. He was much in the company of his father-in-law's friends and relatives, that London-Essex circle to which Oliver was connected and which would provide several parliamentary leaders in the years ahead. Few families were to be more divided than the Montagus by the coming conflict. The first earl, Edward and Walter's father, was a conventional Protestant and king's man. As Lord Privy Seal and one of Charles's most trusted advisers he applied the law firmly against Puritan and papist alike and worked hard to raise money for the King during the years of personal rule. Edward became a leader of parliamentary opposition to that personal rule. Walter became a Roman Catholic in 1634, was later imprisoned in the Tower by order of Parliament and subsequently exiled. Oliver's feelings towards the family which had usurped his own must have been mixed: humiliation at no longer being part of a powerful clan; friendships with the sons of the ruling house; dependence on the support of the Montagus in many issues of local politics.

As one of the leading burgesses of Huntingdon Oliver still had a part to play in public affairs. In 1621 he helped to elect two Members of Parliament for the borough: Sir Henry St John, and Sir Miles Sandys of Wilberton, between Huntingdon and Ely. Both men are likely to have been among the parliamentary radicals; Miles's brother, Sir Edwin Sandys, was one of the more vociferous opponents in the House of Commons to 'creeping papalism' and a champion of parliamentary privilege, and Henry was a close relative of Oliver St John. Municipal events and family births and deaths were the punctuation marks in a very quiet passage of Cromwell's life. With the passing of King James and the end of regular royal visits Huntingdon slipped back into provincial obscurity. In 1628 Oliver's Uncle Richard died and the modest inheritance helped with the expenses of a growing family. The Cromwell nursery was already a busy, noisy place occupied by five healthy children – Robert (seven), Oliver (five), Bridget (four), Richard (two) and Henry (one).

For someone of Oliver's energetic disposition, the life of a small landowner in a rural backwater was too quiet. Everything about his ancestry, his upbringing and his personality urged him towards finding a more fulfilling role in life. Like many young men for whom their approaching thirtieth birthday points like an accusing finger, Cromwell was anxious to make his mark. This internal stress is obvious from contemporary and near contemporary medical evidence. Oliver was something of a hypochondriac. Being fussed over by mother, wife and sisters made him very introverted about his health, so that, for instance, careless of the quizzical glances of passers-by he frequently swathed his neck in red flannel if the weather was damp. In September 1628 he went to the expense of consulting, in London, the leading doctor of the day. Sir Theodore Turquet de Mayerne had established a fashionable and highly lucrative practice since his appointment as king's physician and he kept case notes on several of his patients. Of Cromwell he observed that the subject was *valde melancholicus*, 'extremely melancholy'. 'Melancholy' was, in the seventeenth century, a necessarily portmanteau word for a variety of mental disorders. George Sandys (brother of Edwin and Miles) called it 'that windy melancholy arising from the shorter ribs which so saddeth the mind of the diseased'.[36] One of the major symptoms of this disorder, which was associated with an excess of black bile, was 'choler' – anger. Sir

184

Philip Warwick in his memoirs (published in 1681) recalled a conversation with the Cromwell family GP, Dr Simcott, which confirms Mayerne's diagnosis:

> ... for many years his patient was a most splenetic man, and had fancies about the cross in that town, and that he had been called up to him at midnight, and such unseasonable hours, very many times, upon a strong fancy, which made him believe he was then dying; and there went a story of him, that in the day-time, lying melancholy in his bed, he believed that a spirit appeared to him and told him that he should be the greatest man (not mentioning the word King) in this kingdom. Which his uncle, Sir Thomas Steward, who left him all the little estate Cromwell had, told him it was traitorous to relate.[37]

The obsession about being the greatest man in the kingdom, if not a 'reading back' from later events, ties in with Oliver's sense of personal destiny unfulfilled, a conviction that he had been born for better things which his current situation prevented him fulfilling. A quest for purpose and meaning would certainly predispose him towards a thoroughgoing evangelical conversion, with its concomitant assurance that God had chosen him and numbered him among the elect and had for him a pre-ordained life plan which would be revealed in the Almighty's good time.

At the beginning of 1628 Cromwell made a determined attempt to break out of obscurity by becoming a candidate for parliamentary election. What lay behind Cromwell's projection into national politics is one of the larger unanswered questions of his career. We can only suggest some of the factors which, to a lesser or greater degree, may have contributed to this pivotal event. It would have been natural for someone whose ambitions extended beyond the parochial horizon to seek to occupy a position held by several of his forebears. His uncle's family, once so prominent, had disappeared from the political scene. He was the eldest male Cromwell of his generation apart from Sir Oliver's first-born, Henry, and much more energetic than his cousin. Oliver's uncle ceased attending Parliament as a Knight of the shire in 1624 and Oliver may have felt it incumbent on him to maintain the family's representation. The opportunity to represent Huntingdon in the new Parliament may have arisen from the Crown's desire to introduce new and potentially more loyal members. It is not clear why Henry St John was not available in 1628 and for two terms Miles Sandys had been replaced by the prominent courtier, Sir Arthur Maynwaring. The government would have been delighted by their exclusion. Sir Edwin Sandys, who also failed to find a constituency for the new Parliament, had been a particularly aggravating thorn in the flesh. Though there is little evidence of extensive packing in the 1628 House of Commons it is inconceivable that royal agents were not at work doing all they could to secure the election of a more docile chamber. At the local level the Earl of Manchester certainly influenced the selection of candidates, and the burgesses of Huntingdon were happy to oblige him by casting their votes for the Montagu 'ticket' – James, the earl's third son, and Oliver Cromwell, a friend of the family. Then, there is the presence of the anti-court party gathered around Warwick and his Essex friends. Oliver was in close contact with the Barrington-Rich-Bourchier circle. Through them and from other connections he was well informed about the animosity between Charles and his first two parliaments and news from Westminster did nothing to calm his choleric nature. The Barringtons, Francis Masham and Edmund Dunch had been among those who refused to pay the forced loan of 1627, as were John Hampden and Oliver St John. It was as an uncomplicated English gentleman, resentful, not so much at government policies, as at the sheer arrogance with which those policies were prosecuted that Oliver Cromwell took his Commons seat in March 1628. This was the man who stood with colleagues below the bar and listened to Charles's contemptuous harangue at the opening of Parliament which concluded with the words 'I scorn to threaten any but my equals.'

Cromwell sat through the stirring events of the spring and summer of 1628 – the drafting of the Petition of Right and the reaction to Buckingham's murder – and that, as far as we are aware, is all he did do. We rely for our knowledge of parliamentary debates at this period on private journals, none of which make any reference until the following February to the Member for Huntingdon. Clearly Cromwell did not take the House by storm: either he had very little to say or what he did say made no significant impact. Even his first recorded speech received scant coverage. As part of its defiance of the Crown the Lower House formed committees to discuss sensitive issues. Such committees were not under the control of the Speaker and the assembled knights and burgesses could therefore express themselves freely on those matters of concern to themselves and their constituents. Oliver joined the committee on religion. In February 1629 the matter under discussion was the growing dominance of Arminian bishops who were encouraging the preaching of heresy and royal absolutism. Inevitably Richard Neile's name came up for censure and, in order to support the criticism, Oliver related to the House the Beard–Alabaster conflict of a decade earlier. The House took note and sent for Dr Beard to present his version of the events at first hand. By relentlessly accumulating evidence the House reached the conclusion that Neile and Laud were among 'those about the King who are suspected to be Arminians . . . and unsound in their opinions'.

Oliver may have made little impact on Parliament but Parliament cannot have failed to make an impression on him. The simmering antipathy between King and Commons boiled over on the very issues of religious error and episcopal tyranny in which he had shown himself to be concerned. Three weeks after Cromwell's modest contribution to the debate there occurred the turbulent scene of Members holding the Speaker in his chair, which was followed by Charles's angry dissolution of the assembly. The ex-Member of Parliament had much to think about as he rode back to Huntingdon.

There he found other things to try his patience. The next couple of years were troubled and unhappy ones in local politics and even more so for the Cromwell family. Faction fighting and Oliver's tendency to become heavily involved emotionally created so much disturbance that he sold up and left the town of his birth and even contemplated emigration. The conflict centred around two interrelated issues: the establishment of a lectureship and the application for a new municipal constitution. Richard Fishbourne, a wealthy member of the London Mercers' Company left a £2000 legacy to his native town. The burgesses of Huntingdon decided to allocate £40 per annum from their invested capital for a lecture to be delivered on Saturdays and repeated on Sundays in the poorer part of the town. Some members of the corporation wanted their colleague, Dr Beard, to be appointed. Others, including Cromwell, did not.[38] Council chamber politics in the seventeenth century were little different from those of today: personality clashes and religious arguments were involved, not to mention financial considerations, but the Fishbourne bequest also raised the old, sensitive issue of lay sponsorship which so exercised royal and episcopal minds. Charles saw pestilential,

Puritan sedition in every pulpit utterance that was not strictly controlled by ecclesiastical authority. Knowing this, the pro-Beard caucus went over the heads of the Mercers' Company and appealed to the Bishop of Lincoln (John Williams) and the King. Charles peremptorily ordered the corporation to install Beard (which must finally scotch any idea that Oliver's old tutor was a rabid Puritan). Understandably, this enraged Fishbourne's brethren and their Huntingdon friends. The Mercers sent a delegation to the King respectfully asking that the burgesses be allowed to make a free choice from a previously agreed short list. We are left to imagine the behind-the-scenes manoeuvring that now occurred, but in the subsequent combat by vote Cromwell and his associates were victorious in securing the appointment of a certain Robert Proctor. But the outwitted Beard faction had not shot their bolt. They filibustered, procrastinated and raised points of order. Williams deliberately hesitated over granting a licence and Proctor was kept from his pulpit for another nine months. The inevitable compromise was reached in the summer of 1631, Beard receiving the not-inconsiderable sum of £40 to salve his bruised ego. The good doctor's Parthian shot in an engagement which had involved the entire local community was a reprinting of *The Theatre of God's Judgement* with a new dedication to the mayor, aldermen and burgesses of Huntingdon who 'stood faithfully for me in the late business of the lecture, notwithstanding the opposition of some malignant spirits'. The messages of the book, he pointedly observed, 'much concern the sins of this town which, being a thoroughfare . . . is subject to many disorders by the baser sort of people'.[39]

The Fishbourne lectureship was the spark which ignited highly flammable divisions among the leading citizenry of Huntingdon and the resultant blaze could only be doused by central government. In February 1630 a majority of the burgesses petitioned the Crown for a new charter, 'for the better governance of the said borough' and 'to remove all occasions of popular tumult'.[40] Hitherto the bailiffs and common councillors had been elected annually. What was now requested was a modern constitution which would give Huntingdon a body of aldermen appointed for life and an annually elected mayor. Whatever the long-term advantages of such an arrangement it certainly reflected the antagonisms of the moment and was a stratagem to exclude more unruly elements from the government of the town. Prominent among those elements was Oliver Cromwell.

The application for the charter was pushed through with commendable despatch or indecent haste (according to your point of view) by a local lawyer, Robert Bernard, and was granted on 15 July 1630. Oliver Cromwell's name was not on the list of founding aldermen, a slight he was not disposed to suffer meekly. He spoke out vehemently in the Council chamber; he canvassed support for a petition against the new charter; he verbally attacked Bernard and the new mayor, Lionel Walden; and he accused the rival clique, now in power, of arranging the terms of the constitution for their own pecuniary advantage. Battle royal raged throughout the summer and into the autumn and when all attempts at conciliation had failed it was referred to the Council. On 26 November Cromwell and William Kilborne, who, as master in charge of the posts, was one of the most important officers of the local administration and had also been passed over, appeared before their lordships at Whitehall. They were bound over in custody for six days and, on 1 December, confronted their accusers in the Council chamber.

> . . . both sides having this day had a long hearing, there appeared much contrariety and difference in the allegations on each side, whereupon their lordships thought fit and ordered, that the examination of the whole business should be referred to the Lord Privy Seal, as well as touching the charter of the said town, as also that his lordship should, in particular, consider what satisfaction were fit to be given to the said mayor and Mr. Bernard for the disgraceful and unseemly speeches used unto them, and should settle and end the differences amongst them, if it may be, or otherwise to make report to the board how the state of these differences stands, together with his opinion touching the same, that such further course may be taken as shall be fit.[41]

The Lord Privy Seal was the Earl of Manchester, joint Lord-Lieutenant of Huntingdonshire, and his colleagues were delighted to hand over to him this tiresome provincial dispute.

Montagu's adjudication shows no sign of having been arrived at with any partiality or malice. On the contrary, he was at pains to heal the breach. He concluded that Cromwell had used 'disgraceful and unseemly speeches' against Walden and Bernard and pressed the speaker to apologise. This Oliver did, acknowledging that his words had been uttered 'in heat and passion', and his retraction was accepted, so that Lord Manchester could claim, 'I left all parties

189

reconciled and wished them to join hereafter in things that may be for the common good and peace of the town.'[42] As to the substantive cause of Cromwell's complaint – the new charter and the corrupt manner in which it had been drawn up – Manchester reported,

> I have heard the said differences, and do find those supposed fears of prejudice that might be to the said town, by their late altered charter, from bailiffs and burgesses to mayor and aldermen, are causeless and ill-grounded, and the endeavour used to gain many of the burgesses against this new corporation was very indirect and unfit, and such as I could not but much blame them that stirred in it. For Mr. Bernard's carriage of the business in advising and obtaining the said charter, it was fair and orderly done, being authorised by common consent of the town to do the same, and the thing effected by him tends much to the good and grace of the town.[43]

In the process of collecting evidence Montagu obtained an affidavit from Thomas Beard to the effect that Cromwell had given his full assent to the new charter when it was presented to the burgesses for their approval, the implication being that Oliver's objection only emerged when he discovered that he was to be excluded from the governing body. It seems that, after a quarter of a century, the relationship between Oliver and his old teacher ended in enmity and bitterness, for Thomas Beard died in the early days of January 1632. Cromwell was not entirely on the negative end of Lord Manchester's adjudication. The earl upheld certain complaints that Oliver had made about the powers enjoyed by aldermen under the new charter and obliged the corporation to place on record certain safeguards of citizens' rights.[44]

The disputants went home, apparently reconciled but Cromwell felt himself broken by the experience. He was depressed by failure, by his lack of status, by the animosity stirred up against him and by the realisation that he would never achieve high office in his home town. Everything seemed to be running against his sense of having been marked out by God for greatness. In the national and the local assembly he had stood up for what he believed right and in both places his adversaries had triumphed. He decided immediately to shake the dust of Huntingdon from his shoes and in six months he was gone.

In doing so he was hastening towards the central crisis of his life.

This small landholder entering his fourth decade was an angry man and he had much to be angry about – his family's situation and the tyranny of men in power, whether king, bishops or local councillors. There is no evidence at this stage of his life that Cromwell's motivation was predominantly religious. He was by nature confrontational and his argumentativeness stemmed not from bigotry but from the uncertainties and insecurities which fuelled an at times unhealthy introspection. However, the upheaval of 1630–31 made a profound spiritual impact and his geographical relocation cannot be separated from that major shift in religious experience and outlook which we will explore in more detail in the next chapter.

It is unlikely that his decision to leave Huntingdon was prompted by the petulance of the spoilt child refusing to go on playing the game because he was losing. Such evidence as we have shows this to have been a very disturbing time for him. Cromwell's influence in and around the town was declining rapidly. Sir Oliver was disposing of many of his holdings and his name also appears on the conveyance of 7 May 1631 which transferred the bulk of his nephew's patrimony in Huntingdon to Richard Oakley of Westminster and Richard Oliver of Middlesex for the sum of £1800. The principal vendor was Oliver's mother, the legal owner of her late husband's estate, and she added her jointure to the transaction, as did Oliver's wife. However, the older Elizabeth Cromwell elected to stay in the town which had been her home for almost forty years. This lends credence to the legend that Oliver was now resolved to emigrate. The months during which he was locked in bitter dispute with his rivals were the months when seventeen ships were bearing across the Atlantic the largest party of settlers yet to venture to New England. The departure of over a thousand men, women and children was one of the major news items of 1630 and it excited several other colonising ventures. Oliver was well informed about the enterprises being planned by Warwick, Bedford, Brooke and Saye and Sele. John Hampden, the Barringtons and Oliver St John had bought into them and it seems highly likely that Cromwell resolved to follow suit, not just as an investor but as a migrant. That would explain his cashing up of all the family's assets and also Elizabeth Cromwell's remaining at Huntingdon. All sources confirm the strong bond which existed between Oliver and his mother and it would have taken a momentous change of circumstances to separate them. But, by now into her fifties, Elizabeth may well have been disinclined to face the rigours of an ocean crossing and the challenge of a new life in an untamed land. Oliver, on the other hand, a man give to impulsive decisions and wild mood swings, may well have decided after his recent experiences, that he had no future in England and that the New World must be the setting for that destiny which he still believed to be beckoning.

Oliver took the tenancy of a farm a mere five miles away in St Ives on land belonging to Henry Lawrence, who was an old friend and later a highly trusted colleague of Cromwell's. If an American move was at least on the cards, St Ives may have provided the family with a haven while they sorted out their future plans but, as we shall see, the town had other attractions.

The five years that Cromwell spent as a grazier in this little town on the Ouse were the most crucial in his whole life. They are also the years about which we know least. Now that he was no longer a landholder or municipal official his name did not feature in local records. We are driven back on the gossipy and often malicious testimony of early biographers but these are not entirely without value. James Heath paints a picture of an unpractical farmer and puts Cromwell's incompetence down to his preoccupation with religion. The tenant, he tells us, called all his labourers together every morning for household prayers, which often went on until past nine o'clock, and sometimes gathered them again after the midday meal for further devotional exercises. As a result, Heath exults, more labour was devoted to the spiritual harvest than the agricultural one.

> And that little work that was done, was done so negligently and by halves that scarce half a crop ever reared itself upon his grounds; so that he was (after five years' time) glad to abandon it, and get a friend of his to be the tenant for the remainder of his time.[45]

The reference to Cromwell's religious exercises is very revealing and we shall return to it later. For the moment we focus on his discharge of his wordly responsibilities. Cromwell was no farmer. At Huntingdon he had managed the family's modest estate and left seasonal husbandry to his tenants. It is hardly surprising if, when he actually had to roll his sleeves up to help with lambing and calving or closely supervise ploughmen and harvesters, he found himself at a loss. Certainly, he made considerable inroads into the £1800 proceeds from the Huntingdon sale (or as much of it as his mother allowed him to get his hands on).

This led to an unsavoury incident related by the violent anti-Cromwellian, Sir William Dugdale: 'Having attempted his uncle Steward for a supply of his wants, and finding that on a smooth way of application to him he could not prevail, he endeavoured by colour of law to lay hold on his estate, representing him as a person not able to govern it; but therein he failed.'[46] This is supported by a reported letter of Bishop Williams of Lincoln to King Charles: 'Your Majesty did him but justice in refusing his petition against Sir Thomas Steward of the Isle of Ely.'[47] It seems that Oliver, being in dire financial straits attempted to anticipate his inheritance as his uncle's principal beneficiary on the grounds of Sir Thomas's alleged physical or mental incapacity but that the old man was neither too infirm nor senile to resist his nephew's importunity and it was he who had the law on his side. Cromwell, never a man to give up easily, travelled to the royal court to appeal directly to the King, doubtless urging his family's long service to the Crown. The fact that Charles turned him down can only have deepened Oliver's conviction that the Stuarts were no friends of the Cromwells.

In the end all this frantic activity was unnecessary. Whatever ill will there may have been between Sir Thomas Steward and his nephew was not sufficient to cause him to disinherit his sister's son. In January 1636, following his wife's death, he made a new will confirming his intention to leave the bulk of his estate to Oliver. Within five months the old man died and Cromwell's fortunes changed dramatically for the better.

By the move to Ely to take up his uncle's position Oliver became, once more, a man of modest wealth and status. Socially, politically and economically the town was dominated by the fenland cathedral and its senior clergy but Cromwell was a substantial and influential figure who held an important place in the local hierarchy. He farmed several parcels of land held on lease from the Church and acted as a steward to the dean and chapter for other properties. In the latter capacity he was responsible for ensuring that those beholden to their ecclesiastical masters for their lands, homes and barns were prompt in the payment of their tithes and other dues. Few can have been more conscious than Cromwell of the gulf separating the comfortable clergy from the families who struggled for a livelihood in the wide waterlogged meadows and the biting winds off the North Sea.

Too much can be made and has been made of the hardships suffered by the people of this bleak region. Throughout England life on the land was not easy for those at the lower end of the economic scale. That said, the men of the fens – the 'slodgers' – were a special case. Traditionally insulated from the outside world within a landscape traversed by few good roads and a myriad causeways known only to the inhabitants, they had a reputation for being secretive, taciturn and boorish. Conventional farming made up only a small part of their lives and they relied heavily on fishing and wildfowling to sustain themselves and their families. When royalists later referred sneeringly to Cromwell as 'Lord of the Fens' they were alluding, not only to his inconsequentiality, but also to his lack of sophistication. Yet if beribboned cavaliers chose to regard Cromwell as an uncivilised fenman it is extremely doubtful whether the slodgers were prepared to regard him as one of themselves. To them he would have been an 'uplander', someone who had come in from outside to make their lives even more difficult. The cathedral steward will have had to cope on an almost daily basis with hard-luck stories, difficult tenants and anti-clerical resentment.

He may well have found it difficult to deal firmly and authoritatively with those over whom he was set. One of his servants later described him as

> . . . naturally compassionate towards objects in distress, even to an effeminate measure. Though God had made him a heart wherein was left very little room for any fear . . . yet did he exceed in tenderness toward sufferers. A larger soul, I think, hath seldom dwelt in a house of clay, than his was.[48]

That eulogy is more than borne out by many incidents in Cromwell's life: his genuine concern for his soldiers; his support for itinerant preachers; his defence of men imprisoned for their radical views; his passionate concern for toleration. The reverse side of Cromwell's sympathy for the outcast and downcast was his indignation at what he considered the misuse of authority. He had always rejected the pretensions of power-seeking clergy but his sojourn in St Ives had thrown him into a situation in which the religious establishment had attempted to suppress the fervent faith of the godly (see below pp. 229ff) and this intensified his mistrust of the ecclesiastical hierarchy. At Ely he found himself representing that hierarchy, sometimes against those who believed themselves oppressed by it. Little wonder that he developed no affection for Ely. He moved on as soon as he had the opportunity and when he sought a Commons seat it was for the constituency of Cambridge and not for the cathedral city.

Since very little is known about Cromwell's life at Ely, the significance of the snippets of information that have survived has tended to be exaggerated. Such is his involvement in the process of land reclamation. A mini-agricultural revolution was inaugurated during the reign of James I with the application of techniques developed in Holland and Germany for the drainage of marshland and coastal and riverain levels. The fenland of East Anglia was an obvious target for improvement and various groups of venture capitalists obtained charters to finance improvement schemes. Some of Cromwell's relatives and friends took part in the 'reclamation boom' and he certainly saw the potential advantage to everyone concerned of providing more land for conventional agriculture. He was also alive to the possible dangers. Like all far-reaching innovations, fenland drainage was attended by greed on the part of developers and Luddism on the part of those who feared for their traditional way of life. As marsh and water meadow disappeared under the plough and streams were diverted the poorer countryfolk saw their ancient fishing and wildfowling rights under threat. When investors enclosed their share of reclaimed land, driving the commoners' beasts from their pasture trouble was sure to ensue. One such confrontation occurred at Holme Fen, Huntingdon in 1637 when the local community, brandishing scythes and pitchforks, turned out to obstruct the developers' agent. The disturbance was duly reported to the Council as was a current rumour that 'Mr Cromwell of Ely' was doing his best to defuse the situation by promising the commoners, on payment of a groat for every cow, 'to hold the drainers in suit of law for five years and that in the meantime they should enjoy every foot of their common'.[49]

We do not see here, as used to be suggested, Cromwell the champion of the little man, so much as Cromwell the responsible member of the squirearchy, concerned for a just resolution of conflicting claims. In this he was following his uncle, Sir Thomas Steward, who had campaigned successfully for a fairer distribution of reclaimed land between developers and commoners. Throughout the 1630s while the King, ruling without Parliament, was distancing himself more and more from his people, the gentleman was deeply involved in the bread-and-butter existence of ordinary people, the realities of provincial politics and the consolations of religion which sustained men and women at all levels of rural society.

FIVE

FAITH

CARL JUNG MADE the point that for many people religion is a substitute for religious experience, and that is a distinction we need to be clear about in assessing the motivations and policies which fired discord in the years leading up to the overthrow of the monarchy. Throughout the 1630s and 1640s religion topped the agenda of every political activist. Preachers and parliamentarians debated ceremonies and episcopacy and the prayer book and the decoration of churches and the location of the communion table and the keeping of the sabbath and a host of other issues which seemed to them of overmastering importance. Without doubt there were those who went into battle because they favoured or opposed a particular form of church order. Every man is free to choose what he is prepared to die for. It is different for those who lead them: without inner conviction of a high order it is utter barbarity for any commander to urge his soldiers to 'death or glory'. That is why right at the heart of this story of two remarkable men set upon paths of tragic convergence there lies the issue of faith. What did Oliver and Charles passionately believe, not about Puritanism or Arminianism or Independency or bishops or presbyters or ceremonies or divine right, but about their own standing before the Almighty, the responsibilities he had laid upon them and the judgement they would rightly merit if they failed in their response to their holy calling?

Charles and Oliver were both slightly acquainted with George Herbert. The poet was a fellow at Trinity during Cromwell's Cambridge days and was later attached to the royal court, particularly on its autumnal peregrinations through the northern Home Counties. Between 1626 and 1630 Herbert lived at Leighton Bromswold, some seven miles from Huntingdon, where James Stuart, Duke of Lennox, was lord of the manor, and, as prebend of Layton Ecclesia, he devoted himself to the restoration of its

199

dilapidated church. This gentle poet-priest was, thus, geographically very close to Cromwell during the years that he was trying to make a success of the family concern and experiencing his altercations with the town council, but spiritually he was far nearer to the King. Herbert loved the 'perfect lineaments and hue both sweet and bright' of the established Church. In a poem dedicated to it he expressed in verse much of what James I had put into stumbling prose about *ecclesia anglicana*'s middle way between Romishness and Puritanism:

> . . . She, on the hills, which wantonly
> Allureth all, in hope to be
>   By her preferr'd,
> Hath kiss'd so long her painted shrines,
> That ev'n her face by kissing shines,
>   For her reward.
>
> She, in the valley, is so shy
> Of dressing, that her hair doth lie
>   About her ears:
> While she avoids her neighbour's pride,
> She wholly goes on the other side,
>   And nothing wears.
>
> But, dearest Mother (what those miss)
> The mean thy praise and glory is, –
>   And long may be!
> Blessed be God, whose love it was
> To double-moat thee with His grace;
>   And none but thee.[1]

It was, of course, an idealistic view but one to which Charles, who seldom set foot inside an English parish church, fully subscribed. He was determined, as his father had charged, to be a 'loving nourish-master' to *his* Church and that involved preserving her distinct identity. For him, as for the poet, the concept of 'church' was, at its most readily accessible level, that of a building gloriously adorned. Outward beauty was the dominant thought in his mind when he reflected on holy things; it was for him the portal to spirituality. Here lies what is possibly the most important psychological difference between the King and the gentleman. In buildings religious ideas became frozen and that process was well under way when Herbert wrote. So starkly contrasted were the whitewashed Calvinist auditoria for the proclamation of the Word and the brash baroque gilded temples for the performance of the transubstantiation miracle, that a visitor might legitimately question whether the same God was worshipped in both. Herbert believed that only the English Church expressed in its purged but dignified chancels the truth of reformed Catholicity. Cromwell's was a religion of the Word and it found easy expression in human words. Charles's faith was an encounter with mystery conveyed through images. It was no less real but it was, by its very nature, less readily communicable. Indeed, the King saw little need to communicate it: what was self-evident to him in the privacy of his chapel demanded no exposition to others. He was enigmatic in talking about his faith and that was frustrating both for those 'on the hills' and 'in the valley'. Puritans were convinced that Charles was a covert papist. Earnest Catholics who laboured for his conversion could not understand why he had no intention of being reconciled to Rome. The same perplexity afflicts the historian who must try to extract the essential elements of the royal religion from a study of the art objects he loved, the spiritual advisers he chose and the policies he instigated or encouraged.

In the 'sale of the century' which followed the death of Charles I, when his 1570 paintings were sold, the Spanish ambassador Alonso de Cárdenas exultantly carried off the prize for his master:

> I can now tell Your Excellency, much to my pleasure, that, thanks to God, I have also purchased the large painting by Raphael of Our Lady, Her Child, St John and St Anne, life-size, and St Joseph, in small, in a perspective, that was valued at 8000 escudos [£2000], which I have had for 4000 escudos, which is half. I do not wish to talk to Your Excellency about this picture for fear of understatement, but in a word I can tell Your Excellency that nowadays it is esteemed as the best in all Europe, and here it is renowned among the painters as the finest painting in the world.[2]

Raphael's masterpiece was known as 'La Perla' because it was, as Cárdenas claimed, agreed to be the finest item in the collection. It was one of the pictures that Charles had acquired in the Mantua sale and one from which he drew great inspiration. The King's taste in masters of an earlier epoch inclined very much towards the humanistic Italians of the High Renaissance. His collection of religious subjects included works by Titian, Giorgione, Raphael, Tintoretto, Correggio and del Sarto – all artists who located the divine story securely in this world of accurately realised figures, buildings and landscape and imparted significance to it by dramatic gestures, flowing lines, glowing colours and daring spatial relationships. For the northern painters Charles felt little. This is somewhat surprising bearing in mind the impetus given to Charles's collecting career by his visit to Spain. In Madrid and at the Escorial the prince would have seen the superb Gothic and Renaissance pictures accumulated by Charles V and Philip II from their northern provinces but he bought none of them and subsequently when he sent the industrious copyist, Michael Cross, to make facsimiles of paintings he admired but could not acquire there were no Flemish items on the list.

It is worth pursuing this theme a little further and we can do so by comparing two treatments of the same subject which passed through the royal collection. In 1636 the States General of the Dutch Republic made a magnificent gift to the King which included an *Entombment* by the late fifteenth-century master, Geertgen tot Sint Jans. Nine years earlier Charles had acquired Titian's *Entombment* as part of the Mantua sale. The two pictorial accounts could scarcely be more different. The Haarlem artist painted death – and not just any death. The two thieves being taken down from their crosses, in the background, and the nails and crown of thorns prominently displayed in the foreground fix the event historically and spiritually. The elongated figure of the dead Christ is the focus of attention and St John invites the ecclesiastical donors of the painting to kneel in reverence. Hard edges, brittle colours and geometric patterns in the folds of cloth emphasise the stark message. The painting is loaded with spiritual significance and compels the viewer to become involved in a frozen moment of the Passion drama. This was the kind of graphic, didactic art that the anguished devotion of Philip II dwelt upon in the seclusion of his great monastery-palace.

The Venetian painting is a study of human mourning. It throbs with movement and we feel that if we turned our eyes away for a moment the disciples would have changed their positions. Our eyes move round the painting, taking in the facial expressions of the bereaved. By contrast Christ's visage is in shadow; his body is certainly not the semi-emaciated cadaver of Geertgen's study; the viewer's attention is not drawn to the wounds; and the crown of thorns, propped against a block of stone, is a more refined affair than the jagged coronet displayed by the northern artist. Cognoscenti would have recognised that Titian had copied the grouping of his figures from Roman sarcophagi reliefs. The lurid sky and dramatic lighting effects emphasise not the spiritual significance of the event, but the human emotions involved in it.

Charles kept the Titian. The Geertgen he gave to his friend, the Duke of Hamilton.

The King's taste in narrative art, whether treating of mythological or Christian themes was for the dramatic and the emotional, as was perhaps inevitable for someone brought up on court masques with their vivid scenery and cunning stage effects, and on barriers – the tiltyard contests which by the seventeenth century had become formalised, highly theatrical affairs and invariably had a mythological or allegorical theme. These were all components of the sumptuous, court culture and divine worship was part of this glorious, glittering world to which the 'common sort' were not admitted and which they would not have been able to appreciate if they had been.

Unfortunately – as it turned out – part of this worship was Roman Catholic. Charles's queen, like James's queen, kept her own chapel staff but whereas Anne of Denmark's religious rituals had always been carried out circumspectly and had been something of an irritation to her husband, Henrietta Maria was permitted the complete and unashamed celebration of the mass. Not only that: she was provided, at considerable expense, with chapels exuberant with baroque splendour. Not only that: the King sometimes joined her for worship, as did other, supposedly Protestant, members of the royal entourage. The Queen's most important chapel was the one which was created for her at Somerset House between 1632 and 1636 by Inigo Jones. One of her Capuchin priests was ecstatic in his praise of this building. Its sanctuary, he exclaimed, was

'a paradise of glory, about 40 feet in height'. There was a great arch, supported by two pillars, about 5½ feet from the two side walls of the chapel. The spaces between the pillars and the wall served for passages between the sacristy and the altar, and the choir, with the organ and other instruments, was on either side over these vacant places. The altar stood outside the arch, and there were six steps leading up to it. Behind the altar was a dove holding the Blessed Sacrament, and forming the centre of a series of separate oval frames painted with angels seated on clouds, most ingeniously contrived, with the aid of perspective and hidden lights, so to deceive the eye and to produce the illusion of a considerable space occupied by a great number of figures. There were seven of these ovals – the outer and large ones consisting of angels playing on musical instruments, the central ones of angels vested as deacons, and carrying censors, and the inner ones with child angels in various attitudes of devotion. Immediately round the dove were cherubim and seraphim in glory, surrounded by rays of light.[3]

When Charles gazed upon the altar, fashioned by François Dieussart, who had recently been brought over from Rome, he reportedly exclaimed aloud that he had never seen 'anything more beautiful and more ingeniously designed'.[4]

Charles was a baroque prince: the work of contemporaries such as Reni, Caravaggio, Bernini and, interestingly, Rembrandt featured in his collection. His queen shared in this patronage of living artists: a *Virgin and Child* by the lesser-known Giovanni Baglione was among her more treasured possessions and hung for many years in her bedchamber. The couple's artistic preferences set them apart from most of their people just as much as did their seclusion within the court. In an age when all art was propaganda of one kind or another, when paintings, sculptures and church decor were used to wage ideological warfare, style and content reflected national and religious consciousness. Counter-Reformation baroque art with its gilded mouldings, melodramatic gestures, theatrical transports and its apparatus of emotional overstatement which, except in the hands of genius, replaced sincerity by sentimentality,[5] did not match the mood of Protestant England. Not only did it represent an alien faith, its style was antipathetic to Englishmen – or certainly to the kind of Englishmen for whom George Herbert spoke. 'The British Church' manifests a dilemma: in an age when virtually all cultural stimuli came from the continent, English religion could only identify itself by what it was not – neither the unimpassioned insipidity of the North nor the South's vulgar lack of restraint.

King and Queen were both conscious of the pressures they were under from over-eager activists. Papal agents and emissaries from the Vatican were constantly at work in the royal court. One cardinal after years of experience of dealing with Charles averred that his motives 'as all who know him at all will admit, are beyond guessing'. There seemed to be two possible routes through the maze of the King's will and intentions: his wife and his art collection. Consignments of paintings arrived from Rome designed to convince Charles that his heart really lay with the people of the old Church. The most gratifying compliment was paid by Urban VIII in 1637 when he made the King a present of a portrait bust by the great Bernini (created with the aid of Van Dyck's celebrated triple portrait of Charles). George Conn, a Scottish-born cardinal who arrived from Rome at about the same time, had several earnest discussions with the King, one of which concluded with Charles's good-humoured outburst 'but I *am* a Catholic', by which he endorsed the official doctrine of the Church of England that it was fully a member of the Holy, Catholic and Apostolic Church, faithful to the ancient creeds and the teaching of the Bible and the Fathers. On another occasion he was heard to regret the Reformation breach most vigorously. 'I would rather have lost one of my hands,' he said, 'than be separated from Rome.'

Such statements and the relaxation of laws against recusants gave Catholics cause for hope and some indulged in premature triumphalism. A painting confiscated during the Civil War showed Charles offering his sceptre to the Queen, who is directing him to present it to the Pope. The indignant discoverer of this piece of propaganda urged Parliament 'to command the picture to London and there permit it to the public view [where] I conceive 'twould very much convince the malignants and open the eyes of all that are not wilfully blind'.[6]

Paintings only expressed to a very limited elite something of the King's religious aspirations. Far different was the project he initiated in 1634 which was meant to display publicly his care for and commitment to the established Church. The fabric of St Paul's Cathedral was in a deplorable state. James I had planned a major restoration but never got round to it and it was left to his son to take in hand this high-profile project. He did so at the urging of his Archbishop of Canterbury, William Laud, who smarted at the taunts of Romanists about the 'heretics'' lack of care for ancient centres of worship. The archbishop set in hand a major rebuilding, canvassed support from the City corporation and livery companies and, when the burgesses showed little enthusiasm, threw his net wider by devising methods of coercion to prise cash from the purses of the wealthy nationwide. In 1634 Charles gave the campaign impetus by offering to pay personally for a new imposing west front. Inigo Jones was put in charge of the operation and work continued well into the next decade. This was a prestige project quite deliberately intended to provide England with an edifice to rival the splendour of St Peter's, Rome and, moreover, one in the latest baroque fashion. Existing drawings and descriptions suggest an Italianate façade lined with massive Corinthian columns, restrained by comparison with some contemporary continental structures but decidedly foreign in terms of native architectural tradition.

Here was a building which might have stirred national pride but spectacularly failed to do so. The King and his archbishop conceived the new St Paul's as a statement about the British Church: its beauty, its permanence, its true catholicity. What many of Charles's subjects saw was, in Milton's words, 'idolatrous erection of temples beautified exquisitely to out-vie the papists',[7] an activity which confirmed their fears about a Romeward drift. When the project organisers committed serious public relations gaffes, private grumbling turned into public protest. Inigo Jones – vain, haughty, dyspeptic and tyrannical – was working on a handful of church schemes and managing to upset parishioners in different parts of London. St Paul's was no exception. The architect had a long-running contretemps with the churchwardens of neighbouring St Gregory's which ended with the church being demolished by order of the King. In such cases Charles's insensitivity sprang from a reality that was, to him, self-evident: the splendour and independence of the native Church should be proudly owned by its members and visibly proclaimed to the world.[8]

Although Charles genuinely regretted the divisions of Christendom, he did not, like his father, consider himself to have a divine call to fuse together the fragments of the European Church riven by the Reformation thunderbolt. What he did believe was that it was his responsibility to restore unity and uniformity to the Church in his dominions. Whereas James had, in his own religion, leaned towards the Protestant side, all Charles's inclinations lay with the culture of the Counter-Reformation. If the direction of events had not been taken out of his hands would the pressures of Queen, queen-mother, court friends and papal agents ultimately have prevailed? One recent historian has described Charles as 'a lazy aesthete short of self-confidence'.[9] That is too easy a dismissal of a character which contemporaries found aggravatingly difficult to read and the biographer must wrestle with the inconsistencies and contradictions of the King's personality. In no area is this more important than religion. Students of the reign continue to debate the extent of Charles's involvement in the Laudian programme of reform: did he languidly leave everything to his archbishop or was he the controlling genius behind the ecclesiastical policies which provoked the civil wars? We must leave a detailed consideration of this to the next chapter but to the extent that Charles's personal faith was the starter motor of the religious policy engine we must preview it here.

Charles Stuart was, as we have seen, impelled by the stern and uncompromising taskmaster, Duty. It was his consciousness of the responsibilities of government that obliged him to organise a detailed routine for himself and his household. He spent allotted periods at his desk, reading reports, petitions and memoranda. He got through the day-to-day business of kingship and no one ever accused him of serious neglect. As an executive head of state he was more efficient than several of his predecessors and certainly more so than his father. But his was the efficiency of a pedant and not of a creative ruler. Habitually he passed on documents to his ministers without comment or with scant marginalia. His attendance at Council meetings where policy issues were thrashed out was sporadic. While Villiers was alive he discussed matters of state within the intimacy of their relationship and was mostly content to let his friend handle the opposition of parliaments and rival ministers.

This was certainly not laziness or the weakness that evades responsibility by hiding behind inferiors. It may not even have been, strictly speaking, a lack of self-confidence. What lay behind the King's reluctance for personal confrontation and explanation was an incapacity for analytical thought and a lack of imagination. To what extent he was *consciously* aware of these shortcomings is beyond discovery but they are abundantly obvious to anyone who troubles to look below the surface of his words and deeds. His religious faith needed the constant stimulus of works of art and sacramental worship. His fascination with the output of painters, dramatists and musicians reflects an awareness that he lacked their imaginative insights. He collected avidly, not because he was a creative genius manqué, but because he could only buy what he was powerless to envisage himself. When he took a few lessons from Van Dyck he became very aware of his obvious lack of talent. This deficiency mattered little in private cultural pursuits but took on immense seriousness when it influenced religious policy. Charles simply could not *imagine* what kind of faith motivated his Puritan subjects. Because his approach to the divine could only be gradualist, sacramental and reliant on the mediation of bread, wine and exquisite ritual he found offensive the very idea of direct access to the Saviour.

What he could not intuitively appreciate he declined to explore intellectually. He had early been put off religious disputation and he lacked his father's passion for sermon tasting. Charles's devotion to the liturgy was, in part, a reaction to his parent's impatience with it; James often marched into his chapel after the office had started and ordered the minister to leave off what he was doing and get up into the pulpit. To his son the reverent performance of the Prayer Book rite was sacrosanct and not even such grave news as that of Buckingham's assassination was allowed to interrupt it. Charles's intolerance displayed itself towards theological debate. The truths of God were deep mysteries, secrets into which mortals had no business prying. He found the warfare of pulpit and pamphlet deeply distasteful no matter what opinions were being propelled into the battlefield. This was basically an emotional reaction but it also reflected his own inability to master the intricacies of doctrinal dialectic. He knew what he believed about the essentials of the faith and the worship of the English Church. On the former he was content to allow his subjects considerable freedom as long as they avoided ardent proselytisation but he was determined not to apply the same toleration in matters of the outward forms of religion. His tragedy – and the nation's tragedy – was his inability to see that inward and outward, private belief and public expression cannot be compartmentalised. Whether the sacrament is administered by a priest from a railed-off altar or by a minister to fellow believers seated around a table are issues which go to the heart of Christian soteriology.

By the time he came to the throne there was a hard core to Charles's faith which could not be eroded by the detrition of Puritan denunciation or Catholic infiltration. In a document entitled *The King of Great Britain's confession of his faith* and dated 3 January

1626, Charles described himself as a 'Catholic Christian' who accepted the teaching of Scripture where it was plain and accepted the interpretation of the Fathers and properly constituted authorities where it was not. He reverenced the Virgin Mary and the saints but rejected any notion of their intercessory powers as he did other Romish dogmas such as transubstantiation, purgatory and the veneration of images. This did not prevent him using pictures, statues and crucifixes as aids to devotion nor attending regular private confession.[10]

The King's religious preferences were encouraged by the friends and spiritual advisers with whom he chose to surround himself. Several of those friends and advisers became serious liabilities. In 1640 the House of Commons passed a resolution for the removal of 'all popish recusants' from the royal court and specifically Walter Montagu, Toby Matthew, Sir Kenelm Digby and Sir John Winter, the Queen's secretary. The existence of a clique of Catholics and pro-Catholics in the entourages of the King and Queen had caused anxiety, mounting for more than a decade and culminating, earlier that year, in the 'discovery' of a plot to overthrow the Protestant state (Endymion Porter's name was also added to the list of 'usual suspects'). The elaborate intrigue, involving secret intelligence channels to the Vatican, money from Paris and Madrid and arms and men from Ireland was largely, but not entirely, a fiction and reveals more about the growing paranoia of the 1630s than about carefully planned espionage activities. However, there were enough unpalatable bones of truth to be picked from the ragout of rumour and hysteria for the stratagems of scheming Antichrist to be taken seriously. Suspicion was not confined to excitable Puritans. In 1637 Archbishop Laud complained to the King in front of the whole Council about the goings-on at Somerset House.

Charles was very clearly embarrassed and irritated by the behaviour of members of his intimate circle. Laud's denunciation arose from the proselytising activities of men and women close to the King and severely upset the harmony the King liked to preserve in his household. Mountjoy Blount, Earl of Newport, was a longstanding companion of Charles and an efficient (if rapacious) Master of the Ordnance. His wife Anne was the sister of Endymion Porter's wife, Olivia. It was members of Olivia's circle who induced Lady Newport to convert to Catholicism in 1637. Blount was furious and demanded that Laud take action against Toby Matthew and Walter Montagu. In the ensuing altercation the Queen, inevitably, took the part of her friends, and Charles was placed in the position of having to side with his wife or his archbishop. According to Viscount Conway, the King showed no hesitation: '. . . the matter was debated at the Council table, where the king did use such words of Wat Montagu and Sir Toby Matthew that the fright made Wat keep his chamber longer than his sickness would have detained him and Don Tobiah was in such perplexity that I find he will make a very ill man to be a martyr.'[11] However, any expressions of displeasure were short-lived. The two Catholics were soon back in favour and remained so until the Long Parliament secured their banishment. As for Newport, he joined the growing ranks of the disaffected and supported the anti-court party in the House of Lords.

The truth was that Charles liked to have about him men of erudition, sophistication and taste and he was not overly concerned about their religious opinions. The most striking example of this trait was his friendship with George Conn, a Highland Scott who had joined the Dominican order and spent most of his life in the administrative and diplomatic service of the Vatican. This much travelled and urbane Catholic spent the years 1636-9 in England as papal agent to Henrietta Maria's household and soon commended himself to the King. Conn was charged with advancing the Catholic cause through the conversion of leading social and political figures and it was his success in the royal court that largely outraged Protestant observers. It was significantly thanks to Conn's charm and refinement that their protests went, for the most part, unheeded. The friar, who had written a hagiographical life of Mary Queen of Scots, made strenuous efforts to reconcile Charles to Rome, even promising that the Pope would come in person to England to receive him back into the fold, but his advances were always couched in good-humoured terms which gave no offence. Charles hugely enjoyed these discussions which usually ended with him pointing out that, though conversion was impossible, he saw very little difference between his religion and the Pope's.

When we consider the men Charles chose as his advisers in things spiritual and ecclesiastical we need to make a distinction between the politicians, like Laud and Neile, and those to whom the King looked for a more detached, other-worldly approach to the problems of Church and state. There were five men who came into this category, five men who, significantly, had a great deal in common. Brian Duppa, John Earle, William Juxon, Gilbert Sheldon and Richard Steward were all Oxford graduates, staunch episcopalians, enemies of extremism, men who enjoyed the respect and even affection of their opponents and who managed to rise above the conflicts in which they were involved. The King appointed, at various times, Duppa, Steward and Earle as tutors to his elder son, advising young Charles to follow his mother's counsel in everything *except religion*. In 'all things concerning conscience and church affairs' he was to defer to his holy mentors.

There is a special solemnity about the advice a father gives a son, especially when, as was the case here, that advice is given against the background of intense family crisis. It involves looking backwards as well as forwards, attempting to draw lessons from experience in the hope that the next generation can avoid the pitfalls of its predecessors. Whether or not Charles consciously reconsidered his own upbringing when counselling his heir, the comparisons are striking. James had surrounded his son with a defensive ring of Puritans to thwart the proselytising sallies of his wife's household. Charles I, for the same reason, provided a stockade of solid and spiritual Church of England men. He had appreciated his own tutors and taken from them a basic pattern of piety without following their theology. Now he hoped that his son would be guided both spiritually and intellectually by those with whose characters and judgement he had come to identify himself in his mature years.

Since they were fighting an intellectual war on two fronts it is not surprising that these apologists for the Church of England defined their distinctive position largely in terms of polity. Against Presbyterians and separatists they insisted on episcopacy as of the *esse*, the identity, of the Church. Against Catholics they proclaimed that English bishops were truly consecrated and linked, through legitimate succession, with the Apostles. In his will (1677) Sheldon described himself as being, 'a true member of [Christ's] Catholic Church, within the communion of a living part thereof, the present Church of England'. He and his colleagues were concerned to establish an authority structure, a defining form. Within that structure they did not wish to define belief too narrowly.

The 'Chillingworth Case' well illustrates the kind of debate going on within academic Church of England circles. William

Chillingworth was a fellow of Trinity, Oxford, and a close friend of Sheldon (who had studied at the same college and became a fellow of All Souls in 1622). He plunged with enthusiasm into the religious controversies of the 1620s and this led him to examine critically the Laudian preoccupation with order. He concluded that mere outward conformity not founded upon a solid basis of doctrine was a sham. Only the Church of Rome could produce such a body of infallible dogma and to this Church Chillingworth converted. Catholic controversialists triumphantly celebrated the capture of such an important scalp, which was a great embarrassment to Chillingworth's Oxford friends, especially as the academic now embarked on an exposé of the Laudian position. Sheldon, recently appointed a royal chaplain, was among those who now entered into vigorous debate and, in 1634, he had the satisfaction of bringing Chillingworth back within the Protestant fold – but not, immediately, the Church of England fold. The scholar had searched for intellectual certainty as a basis for faith and come to the conclusion that this was a chimera. He refused to become a party man or even to accept ordination because he could not in all honesty subscribe to the Church of England's Thirty-Nine Articles of Religion. Since no doctrinal system was valid every Christian had to obey his own conscience in arriving at a system of belief which was consonant with Scripture. In *The Religion of Protestants* (1638) he defended his conclusions in great detail, disassociated himself from the certainty claimed for their systems by Roman Catholics and Puritans alike and averred that he would 'damn no man nor doctrine without express and certain warrant from God's word'. In essence this toleration within well-defined limits was not dissimilar to Cromwell's. When Chillingworth declared a dislike of denominational labels and wished that men would be content to be known as 'plain, honest Christians' he was close in spirit to the general who commended his soldiers for sinking theological differences and observed 'pity it is it should be otherwise anywhere'. *The Religion of Protestants* was an instant best-seller and provoked predictable opposition from extremists of all stamps. The King, however, was delighted with it and offered Chillingworth a benefice. The scholar protested his inability to subscribe to the Articles but his friends pressed him and Laud declared himself happy to accept a modified form of subscription. On this basis Chillingworth was appointed Chancellor of Salisbury diocese and prebend of Brixworth.

Thus the 'Chillingworth Affair' insofar as it throws light upon the religious attitudes of Charles I. It is, however, interesting to record the last sad days in the life of this honest scholar since they illustrate well the passions roused by theological issues at this time. Chillingworth joined the royalist army and fell ill at Arundel Castle, where he was captured at the end of 1643. Here he suffered (in every sense) the ministrations of a fanatical Puritan minister who assiduously cared for the sick man's body while daily assaulting his mind with contentious arguments. When, weeks later, Chillingworth died and was buried, his self-appointed nurse/disputant threw a copy of *The Religion of Protestants* into the grave so that it might 'rot with its author and see corruption'.

Charles was a stranger to the turbulent feelings aroused by religious dogma. Unlike his father, he had no pretensions to being thought of as a theologian but he shared with James an admiration for university-trained apologists. One of the characteristics that attracted him to men of academic detachment was that they, too, stood outside the sawdust ring of vulgar polemic. When they engaged in disputation, whether in the pulpit or on the printed page, it was with reasoned argument and civilised language, that stimulated the mind rather than stirred the blood. When Chillingworth preached before the King at Oxford in the early days of the war he spoke, not to scourge the enemy with verbal vehemence, but to point out the moral failings of both parties.

> [When I see] publicans and sinners on the one side, against scribes and Pharisees on the other; on the one side hypocrisy, on the other profaneness, no honesty nor justice on the one side, and very little piety on the other; on the one side horrible oaths, curses, and blasphemies; on the other pestilent yes, calumnies, and perjury . . . I cannot but fear that the goodness of our cause may sink under the burthen of our sins and that God in his justice, because we will not suffer his judgements to achieve their prime scope and intention, which is our amendment and reformation, may either deliver us up to the blind zeal and fury of our enemies, or else, which I rather fear, make us instruments of his justice each against other, and of our own just and deserved confusion . . .[12]

Charles did not enjoy the cut-and-thrust of debate. He had had enough of that in his earlier years when forced to listen to his father exercising his supposed dialectic skills and occasionally being himself thrust into disputation. Furthermore, he regarded theological wrangling as destructive of good order. He had scarcely been a year on the throne when he issued a proclamation forbidding the writing or preaching of doubts about 'the doctrine and discipline of the Church of England heretofore published and happily established by authority'.[13] Charles was not curious about doctrinal niceties: his duty was simply to uphold the *status quo*. However, he did like to surround himself with members of the intellectual and spiritual elite, men of erudition and unpretentious piety. Sheldon, Earle and Chillingworth were such. They were frequent visitors at Great Tew where Lucius Cary, Viscount Falkland, kept open house to poets, wits, London cognoscenti and scholars from the nearby university. John Earle was a versifier and social commentator of skill and, according to Clarendon, 'a man of great piety and devotion, a most eloquent and powerful preacher and of a conversation so pleasant and delightful, so very innocent and so very facetious [i.e. elegant] that no man's company was more desired and loved'.[14] Laud recognised him as the sort of man the King liked and secured his appointment as chaplain to the princes in succession to Duppa on the latter's consecration as Bishop of Salisbury in 1641. Richard Steward was another who, from the relative obscurity of a rural parish, was brought into the royal household as chaplain and clerk of the closet in 1633. He remained in daily attendance on the King until 1639, when he became provost of Eton. His main attraction to Charles seems to have been his erudite and forthright upholding of episcopacy and his effective disposing of Presbyterian arguments.

But the churchman who enjoyed the King's respect and affection in greatest measure was William Juxon. He was a fellow of St John's Oxford and, in 1621, became president in succession to Laud who had already marked out the younger man as someone who could be useful to him. Juxon was a conscientious and devout clergyman quite devoid of ambition, firm in his judgements on men and policies, modest about expressing them, and lenient in his prosecution of them. Charles said of him that he had never received Juxon's opinion without having had to press him for it but that having received it he had always benefited from it. This quiet man would have been content with his responsibilities in the university and as rector of Somerton, some twenty miles distant, where he regularly resided in vacation time, but as Laud's career surged forward under full canvas he was towed in its wake. At the very beginning of the reign he was nominated a royal chaplain and, in 1633, when Laud was translated from London to Canterbury, Juxon, though already designated for Hereford, was appointed to succeed him. The archbishop was determined to keep his unworldly friend close to the centre of power as part of his policy of increasing the dignity and authority of the Church and he congratulated himself on a major triumph when he secured Juxon's appointment as Lord Treasurer in the spring of 1636. 'No churchman had it since Henry VII's time,' he told his diary, 'and now if the church will not hold up themselves under God, I can do no more.'[15]

The office had remained vacant for a year and during much of that time Laud had pestered the King to appoint Juxon. Charles knew that it would be controversial to put the state's finances in the hands of a reformist cleric. His caution was well founded.

> The treasurer's is the greatest office of benefit in the kingdom, and the chief in precedence next the archbishop's, and the great seal: so that the eyes of all men were at gaze who should have this great office; and the greatest of the nobility, who were in the chiefest employments, looked upon it as the prize of one of them; such offices commonly making way for more removes and preferments: when on a sudden the staff was put into the hands of the Bishop of London, a man so unknown, that his name was scarce heard of in the kingdom, who had been within two years before but a private chaplain to the king, and the president of a poor college in Oxford. This inflamed more men than were angry before, and no doubt did not only sharpen the edge of envy and malice against the archbishop, (who was the known architect of this new fabric,) but most unjustly indisposed many towards the church itself; which they looked upon as the gulf ready to swallow all the great offices.[16]

Well might Laud exult at this battle won and the signal it sent to all observers of his influence over the Sovereign. As for Juxon, he seems to have been genuinely unaware of the jealousy and bitterness his promotion had provoked. Most men who had dealings with this uncomplicated man came to agree with the papal representative to the Queen's household: 'He is little versed in politics and professes no other ambition than the king's advantage and to administer the treasury with clean hands . . . He is very moderate in his views and far removed from any kind of pride or ambition.'[17] A scholar who knew the bishop in his later years tells us that,

215

In his duty this good man went along with conscience in government . . .
Religion was the inclination and composure as well as care of his soul;
which he used not as the artifice of pretence or power, but as the
ornament and comfort of a private breast, never affecting a pompous
piety nor a magnificent virtue, but approving himself in secret to
that God who would reward him openly . . . Never courting, but
always winning people, having a passage to their hearts through their
brain.[18]

For such a man the treasurership posed moral questions on a daily
basis. It was the state office *par excellence* through which great
fortunes were amassed. Ambitious courtiers expected, by means of
bribes, to obtain from him valuable perquisites. Above all, the King,
constantly in need of funds, brought pressure to bear on the Lord
Treasurer to extract money from unwilling subjects and to sell
monopolies and offices. Juxon certainly did not vastly enrich himself from his office and he frequently annoyed others by declining to
enrich them. Resisting the King's demands when he regarded them
as unjust or unwise was more difficult, for Juxon felt a deep
obligation of obedience to God's anointed. His preferred solution
seems to have been to remain silent until his opinion was called for
but then to give it without compromise or equivocation. Juxon
opposed – though usually ineffectually – the farming-out of taxes
and other revenues. He supervised the royal finances with an
efficiency bordering on ruthlessness, chasing up Crown debtors with
the same enthusiasm that he devoted to the withholding of payment
to Crown creditors. He did not originate the extension of ship money
or the other unpopular imposts by which Charles sought to
perpetuate the term of his personal rule but he laboured hard to
ensure that levies, once imposed, were collected as effectively as his
overstretched administration would allow. It seems that for Laud
and, presumably, Juxon the change of treasurership marked a
change in the theory and practice of government. Before 1636 rule
without Parliament was regarded as a temporary state of affairs
which would see the uncooperative members suitably chastised.
Thereafter, it seemed – for a while – that the Laudian vision of
authority vested in King, Council and Convocation might prevail as
a new, permanent policy. What smashed this golden dream was the
King's inability adequately to curb his personal expenditure and his
foolish blundering into war with Scotland.

The build-up to the Bishops' Wars was another issue creating a dilemma for Juxon. Laud's tidy mind determined that the unity of the nation would be enhanced by religious uniformity on either side of the Scottish border. Thus, the Scottish canons were revised to bring them into line with those of the Church of England and a new Scottish Prayer Book was imposed in 1637. Juxon approved the objective but, as Treasurer, was unhappy about the cost of imposing on the King's northern subjects the will of the man they referred to as 'the pope of Canterbury'. When ecclesiological discord turned into military conflict Juxon was appointed president of the Council of War and applied himself with his customary diligence to raising vastly increased revenue and overseeing the disbursement of funds to the army and its provisioners.

Given the bishop's total commitment to the King and to the policies of the archbishop, it is remarkable that he was not earmarked for immediate investigation and punishment in 1640. He certainly did not preserve himself by turning his coat or grovelling to Parliament. On the contrary, in his maiden speech to the Lords in December 1640 he berated Edward Montagu, Lord Kimbolton, for encouraging neglect of the Prayer Book in Huntingdonshire and was obliged to come to the bar of the house to render an apology. Two months later a speaker in the Commons exempted Juxon from the charges of arrogance and power-seeking directed against many of his episcopal colleagues. 'There are yet some,' he insisted with specific reference to the Bishop of London, 'who, in unexpected and mighty place and power, have expressed an equal moderation and humility, being neither ambitious before, nor proud after either the crosier's staff or the white staff'.[19] The attitude of triumphant enemies in not imprisoning Juxon and permitting him to continue as a close adviser to the King is eloquent testimony to the respect in which he was widely held.

Juxon remained in Charles's entourage to the very end and was the friend who was at his side in his last moments. Had the King relied for advice upon his Bishop of London rather than on his Archbishop of Canterbury in earlier crises it is possible that the two men would not have found themselves standing together on a scaffold on a frosty January afternoon. Juxon was no less principled than his King but he possessed qualities that Charles conspicuously lacked. He was warm and sympathetic in human relationships, understood opposing points of view and was able to tread – as perhaps only a theologian can – the narrow path between conscience and compromise.[20]

A degree of independent theological thought might, indeed, have stood Charles in good stead.

> But learn wisely to discern betwixt points of salvation and indifferent things, betwixt substance and ceremonies; and betwixt the express commandment and will of God in his word, and the invention or ordinance of man: since all that is necessary for salvation is contained in the Scripture.
>
> But as for all other things not contained in the Scripture, spare not to use or alter them, as the necessity of the time shall require. And when any of the spiritual office-bearers in the church, speaketh unto you anything that is well warranted by the word, reverence and obey them as the heralds of the most high God: but, if passing that bounds, they urge you to embrace any of their fantasies in the place of God's word, or would colour their particulars with a pretended zeal, acknowledge them for no other than vain men, exceeding the bounds of their calling; and according to your office, gravely and with authority redact them in order again.[21]

When James I gave this advice to his heir he envisaged the future king as being the divinely appointed regulator of things spiritual as well as temporal. This thoroughgoing Erastianism was a doctrine Charles in practice, if not in theory, rejected in favour of a partnership between Crown and Mitre. James's concept also assumed that the King would be theologically educated and, therefore, fully able to spot when some of his bishops were exceeding their mandate in matters of doctrine or ceremony. Charles did not challenge the wisdom of his spiritual advisers. The old King had profoundly mistrusted William Laud and there is no doubt that he would have recognised in the archbishop a 'vain man exceeding the bounds of his calling' but Charles chose to repose complete trust in him, neither weighing the merits of his policies nor observing the disastrous results of their implementation.

William Laud was a man with a mission. He was one of many career ecclesiastics, several of whom had their education in Oxford, and in whom there seethed an utter loathing of those whose sacrilegious and unrestrained zeal was, as they believed, befouling the national Church. These scoundrels who cocked a snook at episcopal authority, played fast and loose with the Prayer Book, encouraged uneducated lay people to preach their bizarre fantasies from parish pulpits and defaced the beauty of God's houses were, of course, embraced within the catch-all term, 'Puritans'. There was nothing new about this establishmentarian, anti-evangelistic, anti-enthusiasm stance, as we have already seen. Many churchmen, including several who considered themselves good Calvinists, were unhappy with religious extremism. What was different about Laud and his sympathisers was that they were Catholic sacramentalists (though, unlike Charles, Laud was chary about owning the unpopular word 'Catholic') committed to the restoration of pre-Reformation episcopal power. Laud was an ecclesiastical politician and he, therefore, set out to win patronage that would bring himself to the attention of the court.

His waspish, humourless, dogmatic personality worked against his ambition and, although he became a royal chaplain in 1614, and was a protégé of Richard Neile, he only advanced slowly through the ecclesiastical ranks. It was the rise of Villiers that enabled him to accelerate his preferment and draw himself to Charles's attention. Laud was among the cavorting pack of courtiers who saw the potential of the new favourite and rushed to fawn upon him. According to Clarendon, Villiers was attracted by Laud's outspoken criticisms of the Puritan group in Parliament. The favourite was eager to gain adherents from men of all parties. At the same time that he took Laud under his wing he was advancing the career of John Preston. Yet even the favourite did not find it easy to gain royal backing for such outspoken advocates. James loved theological controversy as an intellectual exercise but he was very wary of unbalancing the church by filling top posts with extremists. Both Preston and Laud experienced the King's caution as a check on their careers. The King made his reservations very clear in 1621 when Buckingham, who had appointed Laud his own confessor, persisted in seeking a bishopric for him. 'You have pleaded the man a good Protestant and I believe it,' James acknowledged, but 'I find he hath a restless spirit and cannot see when matters are well, but loves to toss and change and bring things to a pitch of reformation floating in his own brain which may endanger the steadfastness of that which is in good pass.' When Villiers persisted James gave way with a particularly bad grace: 'Then take him to you but, on my soul, you will repent it,' he muttered and, according to the report 'so went away in anger using other fierce and ominous words, which were divulged in the court and are too tart to be repeated'.[22] The fact that Charles's father and his friend disagreed about Laud was, in itself, sufficient to make up the prince's mind; he threw his support behind the cleric and, once his favour was offered it was never withdrawn. As soon as he became king he made Laud his trusted adviser in all Church matters and promised him the archbishopric of Canterbury. On the very day George Abbot died, in 1633, Charles, true to his word, elevated his chaplain to the primacy.

The facts stated thus baldly might suggest a close bond between the Monarch and the prelate but they shared no real affection. Charles found Laud useful because he supported his own attitudes towards authority in Church and state and because he was an efficient administrator within his own sphere. Laud, for his part, was happy with a king he could, with care, manipulate and in whose name he could implement his own programme of reform. He was able, steadily, to promote churchmen of his own party, make an impact on conciliar debate, enter fully into palace intrigue and even exercise influence over government appointments. Yet he never felt completely secure in a court which was not his natural milieu. He lacked the wit and cultivated charm that Charles looked for in his close companions and, like all intriguers, was always anxious that he was being intrigued against. An incident as early as 1623 reveals both Laud's concern and his sense of mission. Charles and Buckingham had just returned from Spain when Laud hastened to interrogate Matthew Wren, who had been with the royal entourage, to discover how the prince had responded to months of papist propaganda. Wren was able to reassure him that, although Charles lacked his father's understanding of religious issues, he was firm in his adherence to 'our vision' of the Church. Thereafter, he worked assiduously to realise that vision and he used his relationship with Charles to that end. He became a master of court politics, built up a personal following and maintained a corps of spies and informers.

In large measure the King was a willing victim of the court system. He had grown up in an atmosphere of personal and faction rivalries, of men and women jockeying for power and competing for royal favour. This was the way the clientage system worked. It threw up talented officials, who could serve the Crown well, mediocrities, and ambitious sycophants more interested in their own agendas than in the good of the state. But that was the way things were and to change them would have demanded a higher degree of organisational creativity than Charles possessed.

The extent to which Charles endorsed his archbishop's views has been much debated. The traditional opinion sees the King as a victim: 'the monarchy declined into an instrument of the Laudian minority-group'.[23] More recently, there have been attempts to exonerate the archbishop and also to present the King as a more 'hands-on' monarch, both of which have sought to present Charles as the creator of Church policy.[24] We must return to this in the next chapter. The point to be made at this juncture is that Laud was instrumental in placing about the King clerics who were gentle, erudite Oxford men able to present the acceptable face of episcopal reaction. They could provide any theological justification that Charles might require for the draconian activities of his archbishop – but Charles seldom did require such justification.

The new King displayed his support in the first challenge mounted by Parliament to the Arminian camp. Richard Montagu (no relation to the Earl of Manchester's family) was a Cambridge scholar and the most accomplished apologist of the established Church since Hooker. Determined to 'stand in the gap against Puritanism and popery', he engaged in vigorous controversy with Catholic pamphleteers throughout the second half of James I's reign, effectively drawing on the support of the Fathers and ecclesiastical history to demonstrate that the Church of England and its priesthood were 'valid' and distancing it from the evangelical-sectarian fringe. Montagu was enthusiastically supported by the King, so much so that when George Abbot, egged on by Puritan complaints, remonstrated with the author over the content of a printed sermon, James supported Montagu against his archbishop, declaring 'If that is to be a papist, so am I a papist.' Charles's first Parliament lost little time in censuring the unrepentant polemicist but the new King immediately intervened. He demonstrated his support for Montagu by appointing him a royal chaplain. This did not put a stop to the controversy: pamphlet and sermon warfare rumbled on for years and 'Montagutians' became a term of abuse thrown at churchmen who were suspected of not being sound Calvinists. Charles's reaction was, by the proclamation of 1628, to forbid public theological controversy and, within weeks, to appoint Montagu to the first episcopal see that fell vacant (Chichester).

The Montagu fracas set the tone for the reign. Ever thereafter the

King reacted with mulish obstinacy against all who challenged the distinctive way of his Church. Like many men who lack the inclination or ability to engage in debate with opposing points of view, he only planted his hooves more firmly when others tried to push and pull him. To change the metaphor, the King became a commander-in-chief, appointing Laud and other episcopal field officers to continue the campaign while he remained in his HQ, well behind the lines, occasionally giving thought to strategy while leaving battlefield tactics in the hands of his subordinates.

His own religious perceptions were a compound of loyalty, duty and a sense of the beauty of divine order. He was loyal, first and foremost, to his father's concept of religion and virtuous kingship. Almost his last words on this earth were 'I die a Christian according to the profession of the Church of England, as I found it left me by my father.'[25] James's understanding of royal power had derived from high Calvinism and been strengthened by conflict with high Calvinism. Since God is sovereign it is 'atheism and blasphemy to dispute what God can do'. It followed that the Almighty, having designated kings to rule in his name, 'it is presumptuous and high contempt in a subject, to dispute what a king can do.'[26] James had ordained that episcopacy and monarchy stood or fell together and, in accepting this, his son implicitly accepted all that the Laudians understood as flowing from the ecclesiology of the Church of England. Charles was loyal, also, to his bishops. He supported their judgements and never intervened to moderate the crusade against Puritans. He was loyal to his wife, allowing her the unfettered exercise of her religion, being courteous to her Romanist friends and tolerant of all who quietly practised their Catholicism.

Charles's dutifulness was shown in his strict observance of his private devotions, his conscientious application to government routine and his setting of a high moral tone in his own household. The ethical template devised by James I that monarchs should shine 'as bright lamps of godliness and virtue' was more consistently used by his son. His love for Henrietta Maria and their children was the factual base from which a golden myth was created and propagated through paintings, masques and poetry. Courtiers were encouraged to emulate the sexual purity of the King and Queen and to see their marital fidelity as an exemplar of commitment and harmony. The last of the great court masques, *Salmacida Spolia* (1640) was a glorification of Charles's efforts to bring his people peace and concord. In the final tableau King and Queen were seen together against a perspective backdrop which extended into a radiant infinity inhabited by approving deities.

> If one believed, as those who watched the Stuart masques did, in that complex series of correspondences that governed the universe, spectacles such as this were stating eternal, immutable, truths on royalty by peopling the stage with a succession of tableaux of the Divine Ideas of which the court itself was but the earthly reflection.[27]

And the central image was that of the love shared by King and Queen, apostrophised by the poet William Davenant:

> So musical as to all ears
> Doth seem the music of the spheres,
> Are you unto each other still;
> Turning your thoughts to either's will.
>
> All that are harsh, all that are rude,
> Are by your harmony subdu'd;
> Yet so into obedience wrought,
> As if not forc'd to it, but taught.[28]

It was a worthy image, much more wholesome than that of James I's marriage, not to mention those of contemporary foreign royal households. The tragedy was that in a court equipped with mirrors instead of windows the Stuart entourage was overwhelmed with its own reflected myths. It could not expose to common view its own exalted vision nor see how far removed that vision was from the beliefs and aspirations of the real world.

Inevitably, there was much about the idealised images of the King that was mutually contradictory. He was portrayed as the embodiment of chivalry, an identification he enhanced by embellishing the Garter ceremonies at Windsor and by personally sporting the insignia on every possible occasion. He was martial hero, *imperator*, philosopher king, the epitome of virtue. He could not be all these things and the crisis of war would show him to be none of them. In death another myth took over – that of the martyr king, who dies for his people. This, too, must be rejected; and yet out of all the elements of exaggerated PR it comes closest to the truth. As Erica

Veevers suggests, Charles 'was never popular in the way that Henry had been nor did he have the type of personality that lent itself to heroic myth-making. He did, however, fit the category of "saintly" Kings whose personal life was beyond reproach and whose religious interests were internal and spiritual rather than public or military.'[29] This was the identity he came increasingly to adopt in the last decade of his life, as personal woes and griefs multiplied while his conscience would not permit him to take the easy road out of his troubles by abandoning his principles. It was the image he projected when there were no longer royal image makers to do the job for him; when sycophantic verse and seductive music had fallen silent and elaborate masque scenery was gathering dust in a Whitehall lumber room. Those who were able to observe the King closely in those years, including some of his parliamentary captors (perhaps one should say *especially* his parliamentary captors, for they saw how the king coped with isolation and stress) were impressed by the real Charles. They found a courteous, quiet, fastidious man who valued privacy and used it for prayer, study and contemplation and who was conscious of the needs of those around him. They noticed how he winced at vulgarity so that people in his presence instinctively moderated their language. They realised that he was sincere in his punctilious chapel attendance and in the attention he paid to sermons from preachers whose scholarship and moderation attracted him. The contrast between this gentle soul and the shifty, temporising 'man of blood' denounced by Commons orators and army chaplains must have struck any who had much to do with the royal prisoner and they could not fail to be aware of his readiness to embrace suffering. Had he been concerned predominantly with his own fate he could have taken any one of several opportunities to make a deal which would have restored him to his family and court. It was his inability to relinquish his sacred charge which kept him locked up and closely guarded. Immediately after his death a small book purporting to contain his devotional reflections and his observations on the major events of the conflict years was published. The *Eikon Basilike* was a sensationally effective piece of royalist propaganda and it has never been possible to establish how much of it emanated from Charles and how much was the work of John Gauden, who worked from the King's notes. That said, there are within the book passages which would go far to explaining the devotion and respect Charles inspired in foe as well as friend; for example:

I desire always more to remember I am a Christian than a king; for what the majesty of one might justly abhor, the charity of the other is willing to bear; what the height of a king tempteth to revenge, the humility of a Christian teacheth to forgive.[30]

Such sentiments are far removed from the glorification and self-glorification of the court masques, the adulatory lyrics and the mythologising canvases of the 1630s and may reflect the closer contact with reality which Charles achieved in his captivity years. In themselves there is nothing remarkable about them: exhortations to humility were a constant of court preaching. The Puritan earnestness of his early mentors, his revulsion at the unseemliness of his father's household, his longing for purity in matters aesthetic and spiritual, his learning of rigid self-control, his daily reflection on Christian truth – all these went to the making of a devout character. In the balmy days of the personal rule they were always in conflict with flattery and with the exercise of and belief in absolute power. It needed affliction and the stripping away of worldly pomps to distinguish the holiness from the hollowness.

Yet, he was king as well as Christian and the essential simplicity of the man neither could nor would divest itself of the *mysterium* of sovereignty. To Charles, who possessed the wealth, the leisure and the aesthetic appreciation to enter the realm of divine beauty through ordered worship, music, drama and the contemplation of his growing art collection, it was self-evident that he had been chosen to occupy a semi-divine position, far above the dreary world occupied by ranting preachers and pathetic parliamentarians: He stood upon the threshold of the heaven of heavens and was afforded glimpses of the glories within. His subjects could never share that experience but, if only they would accept his tutelage and the guidance of their spiritual leaders, they would see something of the awesome harmony and magnificence of the Trinity. In that contemplation they would realise how futile was the wrangling of attention-seeking pulpiteers and the presumption of evangelicals who claimed to have entered into a personal relationship with God in the midst of their own drab world of stinking streets and claustrophobic hovels.

This was precisely what Oliver Cromwell did claim. He had come, after years of conscious or unconscious searching, to a vivid and life-transforming experience of the divine, the reality of which, from the moment of his conversion, he never called in question. Carl Jung observed, 'Among all my patients in the second half of life . . . there has not been one whose problem in the last resort was not that of finding a religious outlook on life.'[31] That description fits Cromwell precisely. At some moment in his late twenties or early thirties, during his years at Huntingdon or St Ives, this troubled, unstable, depressive farmer and family man found a religious outlook. This event was his great turning point but, infuriatingly, no precise details about it have survived and generations of scholars have expended considerable mental effort poring over the same meagre pieces of evidence in order to be able to allot a year and month to it. Three of Oliver's letters demarcate the temporal space in which we have to search. On 14 October 1626 he wrote to an old friend, Henry Downhall of St John's College, Cambridge

Loving Sir,
   Make me so much your servant by being godfather unto my child [Richard]. I would myself have come over to make a more formal invitation but my occasions would not permit me, and therefore hold me in that excused. The day of your trouble is Thursday next. Let me entreat your company on Wednesday.
   By this time it appears I am more apt to encroach upon you for new favours than to show my thankfulness for the love I have already found. But I know your patience and your goodness cannot be exhausted by
                    Your friend and servant
                    Oliver Cromwell.[32]

By its complete lack of biblical allusions and its matter-of-fact treatment of a religious convention this note suggests a pre-conversion dating.

Just over nine years later, shortly before his move to Ely, we find Cromwell writing in a very different vein about a Puritan lectureship.

To my very loving Friend Mr. Storie, at the Sign of the Dog in the Royal Exchange, London: Deliver these.

MR. STORIE,
   Among the catalogue of those good works which your fellow-

citizens and our countrymen have done, this will not be reckoned for the least, that they have provided for the feeding of souls. Building of hospitals provides for men's bodies; to build material temples is judged a work of piety; but they that procure spiritual food, they that build up spiritual temples, they are the men truly charitable, truly pious. Such a work as this was your erecting the lecture in our country; in the which you placed Dr. Welles, a man for goodness and industry, and ability to do good every way, not short of any I know in England; and I am persuaded that, sithence his coming, the Lord hath by him wrought much good amongst us.

It only remains now that He who first moved you to this, put you forward to the continuance thereof: it was the Lord; and therefore to Him lift we up our hearts that He would perfect it. And surely, Mr. Storie, it were a piteous thing to see a lecture fall, in the hands of so many able and godly men as I am persuaded the founders of this are, in these times, wherein we see they are suppressed, with too much haste and violence by the enemies of God his truth. Far be it that so much guilt should stick to your hands, who live in a city so renowned for the clear shining light of the gospel. You know, Mr. Storie, to withdraw the pay is to let fall the lecture; for who goeth to warfare at his own cost? I beseech you therefore in the bowels of Christ Jesus put it forward, and let the good man have his pay. The souls of God his children will bless you for it; and so shall I; and ever rest,

Your loving Friend in the Lord,
OLIVER CROMWELL.

St. Ives,
11 January 1636.
[P.S.] Commend my hearty love to Mr. Busse, Mr. Bradly, and my other good friends. I would have written to Mr. Busse; but I was loath to trouble him with a long letter, and I feared I should not receive an answer from him. From you I expect one so soon as conveniently you may. *Vale.*[33]

These epistles provide the markers within which Cromwell's spiritual crisis occurred. The only letter in which he alluded directly to that event was written on 13 October 1638 to his first cousin, Elizabeth, who had just married his friend Oliver St John but was still living in the devout Masham household.

To my beloved Cousin Mrs. St. John, at Sir William Masham his
House called Oates, in Essex: Present these

DEAR COUSIN,

I thankfully acknowledge your love in your kind remembrance
of me upon this opportunity. Alas, you do too highly prize my lines,
and my company. I may be ashamed to own your expressions,
considering how unprofitable I am, and the mean improvement of my
talent.

Yet to honour my God by declaring what He hath done for my
soul, in this I am confident, and I will be so. Truly, then, this I find:
That He giveth springs in a dry and barren wilderness where no water
is. I live (you know where) in Meshech, which they say signifies
Prolonging; in Kedar, which signifieth *Blackness*: yet the Lord
forsaketh me not. Though He do prolong, yet He will (I trust) bring
me to His tabernacle, to His resting-place. My soul is with the
congregation of the firstborn, my body rests in hope, and if there I
may honour my God either by doing or by suffering, I shall be most
glad.

Truly, no poor creature hath more cause to put forth himself in the
cause of his God than I. I have had plentiful wages beforehand, and
I am sure I shall never earn the least mite. The Lord accept me in His
Son, and give me to walk in the light, and give us to walk in the light,
as He is the light. He it is that enlighteneth our blackness, our
darkness. I dare not say, He hideth His face from me. He giveth me
to see light in His light. One beam in a dark place hath exceeding
much refreshment in it. Blessed be His name for shining upon so
dark a heart as mine! You know what my manner of life hath been.
Oh, I lived in and loved darkness, and hated the light. I was a chief,
the chief of sinners. This is true; I hated godliness, yet God had
mercy on me. O the riches of His mercy! Praise Him for me, pray for
me, that He who hath begun a good work would perfect it to the day
of Christ.

Salute all my good friends in that family whereof you are yet a
member. I am much bound unto them for their love. I bless the Lord
for them; and that my son, by their procurement, is so well. Let him
have your prayers, your counsel; let me have them.

Salute your husband and sister from me. He is not a man of his
word! He promised to write about Mr. Wrath of Epping; but as yet I
have received no letters. Put him in mind to do what with

conveniency may be done for the poor cousin I did solicit him about.
Once more farewell. The Lord be with you; so prayeth
Your truly loving cousin,
OLIVER CROMWELL.
Ely, October 13th, 1638.
[P.S.] My wife's service and love presented to all her friends.[34]

This enables us to shorten the timescale fairly considerably. The writer comments 'You know what my manner of life hath been'. Elizabeth was twenty-two when Oliver wrote to her. Since she can scarcely have been in a position to understand and pass judgement on her cousin's former lifestyle before her mid-teenage years this suggests a date no earlier than about 1630 for Oliver's conversion and locates it within the years he spent at St Ives.

There are two less direct pieces of evidence which support this conclusion. Bishop Burnet reported having heard that the transformation came over Cromwell's life 'about eight years before the wars' which, as John Morrill points out, puts the event between 1631 and 1634, depending on whether Burnet was reckoning from the Bishops' Wars or the Civil War.[35] Secondly, we have Heath's lampoon of Cromwell the incompetent farmer so preoccupied with spiritual exercises that he neglected his St Ives land and stock (see above pp. 192). It seems that Cromwell came under some influence at St Ives which brought on that cataclysm which was to have so profound an effect not only upon him but upon the whole of English history.

As soon as we enquire into the religious life of the little town we discover that – at the precise time that Oliver and his family moved there – it was a buzzing, clamorous hive of intense spiritual activity; a centre of what we would now call charismatic evangelicalism, which attracted like-minded believers from a wide area and exercised a profound (and, in the eyes of the authorities, a disturbing) influence over the countryside. Radical, fringe Christianity has always existed and survived by networking: stirring preachers attract disciples and establish cells and from these highly motivated congregations divinely anointed proselytisers go forth to strengthen the outlying faithful and to replicate the pattern of spiritual intensity. Just such a network was operating in and around St Ives in the middle decades of the seventeenth century.

In 1630 the parish of All Saints had been under the leadership of its vicar, Job Tookey, for seventeen years. Tookey was regarded by at least one observer who was not of his following as 'a reverend and holy man'. In matters of Church order he was a Puritan who favoured simplicity and the minimum of ceremonial in worship. In pastoralia he encouraged the development of spiritual gifts among his lay people and that personal devotion and closeness of fellowship which was symbolised by the gathering of the Lord's people seated around the Lord's table set in the body of the church. Many were attracted to this spiritual powerhouse and, inevitably, many others were repelled by it. Parishioners who favoured a more formal and 'seemly' worship as well as neighbouring clergy were scandalised by the 'going-on' at All Saints. Doubtless a growing volume of complaint had been directed to patrons and to the diocesan but it was not until 1629 that a situation developed which was noted in ecclesiastical records which have survived.

In the spring of that year Bishop Williams intervened suddenly and decisively. He rode unannounced into St Ives to put a stop to a disturbing exhibition of religious frenzy, which centred around a certain Jane Hawkins who,

> . . . having fallen into a rapture of ecstasy, has uttered strange things in verse which she could not confess she could ever make before or can do now in matters of divinity and state. She is a witty, crafty baggage. Feigning herself in a trance, she began to preach in verse, magnifying the ministry of Mr Tookey, the vicar . . .

Williams described how, over a period of three days and nights, nearly two hundred people had stood around Jane's bed and observed her performance:

> . . . the vicar and Mr Wise, his curate, and another scholar sitting at the bed's feet and copying out the verses which the poor woman (she is but a pedlar) did dictate, which amounting to some thousands, they had transcribed fair with intent to print them, when, coming suddenly, the bishop seized on the copy and originals.

Williams demanded that the clergy should acknowledge to their parishioners that the whole thing was a sham. This they could not or would not do. Faced with such obduracy, the bishop suspended Tookey and sent the curate packing. Then he attempted to impose his authority on the congregation. On Sunday, he preached a denunciatory sermon and afterwards rode away satisfied that 'the people have quite forsaken this rhyming preacheress'.[36]

Either the bishop grossly overestimated his influence or he was indulging in a monumental piece of wishful thinking. Jane Hawkins's manifestation of charismatic gifts (or religious delusion) can have been no isolated incident. It flourished in an atmosphere of spiritual intensity which had been created over several years and was not to be dissipated by a few stern words from the diocesan. After some months Williams considered it safe to allow Tookey to resume his duties but this leniency produced no change in the vicar's attitude and he was finally deprived in 1631.

The parish of All Saints, St Ives, was now in a state of complete turmoil. Someone had to be installed there who would restore peace and unity. It would have to be a man of firm resolve but one who would be reasonably acceptable to the wilder elements in the parish. It would also have to be a cleric who enjoyed the approval of the more important local families, for Tookey and his disciples were not without substantial support in the area. The ex-vicar and his curate were still living and active nearby under the protection of powerful friends and, in 1634, were hauled before the Court of High Commission for continuing to incite religious discord.

Among the influential leaders of society who were sympathetic to or actively supported the zealots were the Desboroughs of nearby Eltisley. The Desborough brothers were dyed-in-the-wool religious radicals. John became a leading official in the parliamentary army; Samuel emigrated to New England in 1639; James remained in Cambridgeshire to fight the cause of the Gospel. According to the family chronicler, he was 'remarkably disaffected to the monarchical as well as episcopal government and he rendered Eltisley . . . memorable for being an asylum for the most extravagant fanaticism'. If we move forward a few years we find James presenting to the living at Eltisley one Henry Denne, a charismatic extremist who had actually received adult baptism, who attracted considerable fame and notoriety as an itinerant preacher in the Home Counties and who set up several gathered churches including ones at Fen Stanton and St Ives. Denne

to please his patron and the lowest of the rabble, fell in with all the ridiculous folly that so much disgraced the era of liberty. Psalm-singing

231

was as heinous a sin at Eltisley as bending the knee to Baal, and it was then as much noted for the devout exercises practised there, as any other canting place in the kingdom.[37]

From this it appears that Denne believed in unstructured, Spirit-led worship unhampered by human regulations and customs, and his behaviour was so extreme that he was imprisoned by Parliament in 1644.

A radical network which could resist both episcopal and Presbyterian efforts to regularise its activities and attach it more firmly to the national Church was obviously very resilient. The confusion and division it created in and around St Ives had, by 1630, been in evidence for several years and would continue for many more. Several dissenting congregations came into being before and after the outbreak of civil war. Ranter, Quaker and Baptist conventicles sprang up, and something similar to the Jane Hawkins affair repeated itself in 1651 when some members of the Baptist church in Fenstanton were excommunicated for claiming 'manifestations of the Spirit above the Scriptures'.[38]

However, to return to the events of 1631: the man presented to the living of St Ives on Tookey's removal was none other than Oliver Cromwell's old friend from St John's and godfather to his son, Richard, Dr Henry Downhall. As a clergyman of moderate Puritan sympathies whose influence and connections extended far beyond Cambridge, Downhall might well have appeared to be the ideal person to sort out the mess in St Ives with firmness and sensitivity. He was installed by the King on the recommendation of the bishop (whose chaplain Downhall had once been). As well as enjoying Williams's patronage, he had other friends at court. Between 1622 and 1625 he had attended Sir Edward Herbert as chaplain on the latter's appointment as ambassador to the French court. In 1626 he supported Buckingham in the controversial election to the university chancellorship and he was a friend of the Earl of Holland who succeeded the duke.

However, those well acquainted with Henry Downhall might have doubted his qualification as a peacemaker. He was, in fact, a man of principle with a turbulent disposition who was, for several years, at the centre of controversies which, according to no less a judge than Archbishop Laud, did 'a great deal of hurt to that university, and I am afraid will do more'.[39]

The trouble began under the lax rule of Owen Gwyn, who was Master of St John's for over twenty years until 1633. Downhall took it upon himself to campaign against the corruption of some of his colleagues. This created a rift in the fellowship which was not closed when the Downhall party was vindicated, in 1630, and the offenders were obliged to make grovelling submission (the St Ives appointment may well have been intended to demonstrate Williams's support for his protégé). Storms were still rumbling in the St John's teacup. When Gwyn died in 1633 the fellows were divided on the choice of a successor. Some supported Dr Robert Lane while others, including Downhall, championed the cause of Richard Holdsworth, 'a man of much greater worth and sometime fellow of the same society ... but ... suspected as puritanically inclined'.[40] Holdsworth was a noted scholar and preacher and, though given to rigorous exercises of personal devotion, he was certainly not a religious extremist. In fact he was currently involved in an ill-fated bid, sponsored by Archbishop Abbot, to reconcile all shades of mainstream Protestant opinion by drawing up an *Instrumentum Theologorum Anglorum*.[41] Lane's supporters hastened to the royal court and acquired Charles I's mandate but Downhall refused to concede victory. He did not spare himself throughout the nine-month feud which followed. He complained to the university authorities and his court friends about Lane's 'heinous crimes' and his enemies countered by branding him a 'sinister influence'. At length the King became involved once more and resolved the conflict by appointing a neutral candidate to the mastership.

The new vicar of St Ives and his circle were moderate Puritans but men concerned for discipline and order. They were not Laudians but had strong establishment connections and were generally royalist in their allegiance. The man charged with restoring order and decorum to All Saints, St Ives was no despotic Arminian but nor was he a charismatic extrovert who believed that ecstatic excesses were inspired by the Holy Spirit and, therefore, not to be questioned. His first move was to appoint as curate one John Reynolds with instructions to establish his authority by reversing innovations introduced by Tookey. John Reynolds replaced the communion table at the east end of the church and railed it off. Given the strength of feeling in the town this demonstration of clerical power could not fail to provoke opposition. Several members of the congregation simply refused to come forward to receive the bread and wine in the sanctuary. They insisted that what was being required of them was unlawful, unscriptural and 'disturbed their meditation'. Besides, as they pointed out, they could see perfectly well from where they were. Similar protests were going on all over the country as Laudians strove pigheadedly to bring the Puritans to heel but the situation in St Ives was particularly nasty. Parishioners insulted the vicar and curate and enlisted support from powerful sympathisers in London. Stalemate resulted when, one Sunday morning, the leader of the dissidents, William Covell, advanced to the chancel steps and called out to Reynolds, who was waiting to administer, 'We are all here present to receive the sacrament, according to the laws of our kingdom and the Church of England and, therefore if you will give it to us you may. However, we intend not to come any nigher.' Several church members attached themselves to irregular conventicles. Neither side would yield. The dispute dragged on year after year and it was in 1640 that Covell and others were summoned before the High Commission.[42]

That was the year that the Archdeacon of Huntingdon tried to settle the issue. He was none other than Richard Holdsworth, Downhall's friend and now Master of Emmanuel, Vice-Chancellor of the university and about to be appointed a royal chaplain. Holdsworth was no Laudian. Indeed, the contemporary diarist, Sir Simonds D'Ewes, represented him as 'most ready to further a reformation of the church'[43] and, as we have seen, some regarded him as being 'puritanically inclined'. The archdeacon was in a difficult position. St Ives had become a test case. The altar controversy was raging throughout the country and was certain to be a major issue when Parliament met in the spring. He tried to be fair to all sides; he consulted with the erstwhile disciples of 'Mr Tookey . . . a reverend and holy man', with the clergy of neighbouring parishes and with the 'better sort' in St Ives. In his report to Sir John Lambe, ecclesiastical lawyer and one of Laud's most hated lay agents, he insisted that he was personally disposed to leniency but that weakness would send a disastrous signal to others. He ordered Downhall's parishioners to conform.[44] But by now power at the centre was changing hands; the Long Parliament was in session and it was the turn of reactionary clergy to be under investigation. Eventually, Downhall, Reynolds and Holdsworth were all deprived and, in 1644, Parliament presented Job Tookey's son (also named Job) to the church at St Ives.

Even this was not the end of the disturbances to church life in the area. It was almost inevitable that a place which had seen so much party dissension for over ten years should experience further fragmentation. The radicals were triumphant and, as we have seen, were not to be brought under ecclesiastical control for many years.

It was when the religious temperature at St Ives was approaching white heat in 1631 that Oliver Cromwell moved his family to the town. The timing cannot have been coincidental. He was fully aware of the conflict which had been raging for two years and must have known of Downhall's appointment. The decision to liquidate his assets and become a tenant farmer in St Ives was obviously deliberate but what motivated it? The opportunity was provided by Oliver's friend and close contemporary Henry Lawrence whose career at Cambridge and the Inns of Court closely paralleled his own. The man who offered the Cromwells a lease on his house and farm in St Ives was known to the authorities as a religious radical. In 1638, he removed to the Low Countries to avoid persecution and in later years he entered into theological conflict as well with wilder fanatics as with defenders of the old ways. The extreme piety of Lawrence's household made him the frequent butt of ribald comment by the enemies of Puritanism but it was probably his marriage, in 1628, to Amy Peyton which drew him, especially, to the attention of the establishment. His wife's father, Sir Edward Peyton, was a violent opponent (sometimes literally so) of Laud and the royal court. In 1627 he was deprived of the office of principal Justice of the Peace for Cambridgeshire for displaying intemperate religious zeal, a punishment which in no way chastened him. Peyton's growing extremism later proved as much an embarrassment to the parliamentary leaders as an irritation to their enemies. Lawrence, by contrast, won the respect of fair-minded men as diverse as Sir William Davenant and John Milton who, in a sonnet to his friend Edward Lawrence, wrote of 'Lawrence, of virtuous father virtuous son' and in *Defensio Populi Anglicani* praised the older man's learning and prudence. That Cromwell always held Lawrence in high regard is evidenced by the various positions of trust to which he appointed him, culminating in the Lord Presidency of the Council.

With such influences working upon him Oliver Cromwell was, we are driven to conclude, drawn irresistibly towards what the intellectual fence-sitter, Sir Edward Dering called, 'that new-born bastard Independency'. In 1630–1, at odds with authority at all levels and seeking a new direction for his life, he saw in the holy congregation at St Ives a radiant people who possessed a conviction, a certainty and a commitment that he envied; a troubled but untroubled elect whose manifestation of spiritual activity suggested that they enjoyed divine approval. He wanted to be a part of them; wanted to discover what it was that they had and he lacked. Perhaps it was represented to him by Lawrence that Oliver's friendship with Downhall might enable him to act as an intermediary between Tookey's set and the new vicar. Whatever the precise circumstances that led him to St Ives seldom was convert more willing for a complete change of life and within weeks or months of his arrival that spiritual crisis occurred which gave his life an exciting new meaning and sent him back to the Bible and to the pulpits of fervent preachers with a ravenous hunger to feed on the word of the Lord who had had mercy on 'the chief of sinners'.

Without specific evidence this re-creation of the events leading to Cromwell's conversion must remain speculative but so many facts that we do possess point in the same direction. As well as his connection with Henry Lawrence, Oliver was close to the Desboroughs, and his sister, Jane, married John Desborough in 1636. Within a few years he was deeply committed to sustaining the ardent, disruptive ministry of Henry Denne. When the preacher fell foul of Parliament in 1644 it was Cromwell who obtained his release and, five years later, he bailed him out of far greater troubles. When Denne became involved in an army mutiny at Burford, he and his accomplices were sentenced to death. Of the mutineers Denne alone received a last-minute reprieve – by order of Major-General Cromwell. Oliver shared Denne's theological outlook, especially the concern for universal toleration which the preacher advocated in some of his publications.[45] Whatever his motives, it seems that Cromwell became a part of the charismatic evangelical network whose rapid expansion was directly related to the attempts of the Laudians to stamp out all manifestations of congregational independency.

This suggestion receives some support from Sir Philip Warwick who recorded in his memoirs that Cromwell had become 'civilised' by his conversion 'he joined himself to men of his own temper, who pretended unto transports and revelations'.[46] The exact words are significant; they by no means describe all the sects thrown up by the religious tumult of the mid-seventeenth century. Like all ages of spiritual upheaval it was one in which 'untrained minds . . . were grappling with the problems of their society, problems which called urgently for solution, and . . . using the best tools they knew of. More solid Puritan divines had cited the Bible against bishops, against persecution, against tithes. The [less educated] studied it very carefully, if less skilfully and more selectively, in order to understand and so be able to control what was going to happen.'[47] Christopher Hill's succinct analysis of the plethora of non-academic religious groupings ('sects' is a question-begging term) thrown up by the crises at home and abroad describes a phenomenon oft repeated throughout the Christian centuries. Men and women, seeking 'a religious outlook on life', grappled with issues of spiritual authority, personal holiness, mystical experience, ritualism, freedom of conscience, sacramentalism, biblical exegesis and the exercise of charismatic gifts. They came to a variety of conclusions. Few of them went in for the ecstatic brand of religion which obviously gripped some of the St Ives brethren.

If evidence were needed of Cromwell's emotional involvement in the affair of Tookey and its aftermath it is to be found in the parliamentary trial of poor Richard Holdsworth. Holdsworth, that man of wise and moderate courses, lived in an age when wisdom and moderation only aroused the antagonism of extremists on both sides. His mild Puritanism debarred him from preferment under Laud and his opposition to radical change brought down upon him the wrath of the Long Parliament. In 1641 he delivered a university oration against the decay of learning and in favour of the existing state of the Church. This was interpreted as an attack on Parliament, which set up a committee to enquire into his activities. The chairman of this committee was Cromwell and it was noted that he spoke 'somewhat bitterly' against Holdsworth. A decade before Oliver would have been found among those who approved the stance of the Downhall-Holdsworth group but his spiritual crisis and the persecution of the brethren in St Ives had completely changed his outlook. It is ironical that on the issue of toleration Cromwell and Holdsworth still had much in common. The archdeacon was a reluctant disciplinarian who believed in freedom of religious expression. One of his colleagues in drawing up the *Instrumentum Theologorum Anglorum* was Walter Wells, the lecturer at Godmanchester of whom Cromwell so much approved.[48]

It has always been difficult to account for Cromwell's move to St Ives. Historians have assumed that this socially regressive descent into the ranks of tenant farmers was forced on the Cromwells either by economic necessity or by Oliver's making too many enemies in Huntingdon. Now we can consider another motive and one that agrees completely with Oliver's impulsive nature. It is entirely in keeping with what we know of him that he would have given priority to his quest for a 'religious outlook on life', persuaded his mother to sell up (although he could not talk her into leaving home) and, for five years, thrown himself into the exciting little world of Job Tookey. There, overwhelmed by the thrill of his newfound faith, he would have spent much of his time 'devouring' the Bible, listening to sermons, sharing in charismatic activities and discussing religious truth with other members of the group. Such behaviour is entirely typical of many evangelical Christians who pass through a traumatic conversion experience. It may be that only when his spiritual preoccupations led to the deterioration of his worldly affairs did he try to lay hold prematurely on his expected Steward inheritance.

It is clear from his letter to Elizabeth St John that he did not enjoy the move to Ely. Whatever the material advantages of his situation in the fenland town, spiritually he felt the place to be a wilderness. 'I live in Meshech . . . in Kedar,' he writes, 'yet the Lord forsaketh me not.' The reference is to Psalm 120, 'Woe is me, that I sojourn in Meshech, that I dwell among the tents of Kedar. Too long have I had my dwelling among those who hate peace.' In the Old Testament Meshech and Kedar are synonymous with barbarity. Oliver's daily life was closely involved with that of the dean and chapter of Ely: several of his properties were held on lease from the cathedral; he acted as steward of other ecclesiastical holdings; and with the clergy he administered certain trusts and charities. It must have been hard for a man of Cromwell's temper to sit on committees with the clergy who ruled the roost in this little town and who were dedicated to the maintenance of ornate patterns of worship. Small wonder that he found it hard to bear the Lord's 'prolonging' him in that place. Yet, only six months before the writing of this letter, the situation had worsened; Matthew Wren had arrived in Ely as the new diocesan. He was one of the most hated of the Laudian bishops and on account of an inflammatory diatribe against him the pamphleteer William Prynne had but recently suffered the savage punishment of being fined £5000, imprisoned for life and branded on both cheeks. Hot from his persecuting career in Norwich diocese, where he had imprisoned scores of Puritans and forced others into exile, Wren went on an authoritarian rampage in his new see, enforcing episcopal discipline, Prayer Book services and ornate ritual. For the time being Cromwell had to 'rest in hope' and 'honour my God either by doing or by suffering'. He willingly endured whatever persecution came his way, knowing, as a fellow believer said, that it was 'impossible to have true peace with God and not wars with men . . . [If] he shall profess to fear God and to make a good conscience the rule of his actions . . . let him be sure he shall have wars with . . . almost all his neighbours. For all of them in a manner will term him a Puritan and perhaps the best of them will tell him that he marreth all with his preciseness.'[49] If he learned patience during those Ely years it must have been for him a very hard lesson.

However and whenever it occurred, Cromwell's conversion experience, described in the biblical imagery of passing from darkness to light, is a classic of evangelical metamorphosis: 'You know what my manner of life hath been . . . I hated godliness, yet God had mercy on me.' The sinner is smitten with guilt because of his offences, then becomes aware that divine pardon is unconditional; salvation is his for the asking. This was the burden of any number of evangelical sermons and lectures:

I know that though I have committed all the sins of the world, yet they shall not prejudice my pardon; but I must do something to qualify me for it. No, not any thing as antecedareous and precedent to the pardon; it is only required of thee to come with the hand of faith, and receive it in the midst of all thy unworthiness, whatsoever it be, lay hold on pardon, and embrace it, and it shall be thine midst.[50]

Oliver's was no gradual move from a moderate Protestant position to a more radical conviction. It was sudden, cataclysmic, like walking from a darkened room into the dazzling light of God's love. It was not a surge of emotion nor was it rational enlightenment, though feelings and mental processes were involved. Cromwell had heard the way of faith expounded hundreds of times, had even helped to set up evangelistic lectureships but never had the truth penetrated the shutters of worldly preoccupation, self-assertiveness and self-doubt – until the moment when God's light shone upon 'so dark a heart as mine'. Then he received assurance that the Lord accepted him in his Son. Then he realised that he was among 'the congregation of the firstborn', the elect. Then he knew beyond a peradventure that his life had a purpose – 'to put forth himself in the cause of his God' – and that he who had begun a good work in him 'would perfect it to the day of Christ'. Only when we understand the suddenness of this experience do we realise that to seek in his family upbringing, his childhood training and his education, for 'Puritan influences' misses the point.

Indeed, in this letter Cromwell virtually tells his cousin that, in his former life, he rejected those who espoused the more extreme manifestations of evangelical religion. For whatever else the phrases about being 'the chief of sinners', 'hating light', 'loving darkness' and 'hating godliness' might or might not have meant in terms of moral depravity, what they meant above all to Puritans was rejection of the Gospel and the people of the Gospel. The words of Scripture that Oliver deliberately cited were from I Timothy: 1, 12–17, where Paul called himself the chief of sinners because, as Saul of Tarsus, he had 'blasphemed and persecuted' Christ, by insulting and harrying Christians. Oliver may have exaggerated by putting himself in the same category as the Apostle but his offence was similar in kind if not in degree. He had held in contempt those who, in modern parlance, are known as 'born-again Christians'. Now he was one of them.

However, 'evangelical Christianity' was not (and is not) a monochrome, blanket expression adequately describing all whom it covers. Cromwell's faith was unique to him; a compound of the man he was before conversion, the experiences he went through afterwards and the mentors who instructed him in his new beliefs. The raw material of his nature had a 'rough-hewn' quality; he felt passionately about things and spoke his mind. These characteristics were reinforced during the St Ives years when he enjoyed the fellowship of those who shared a simple faith, ardently expressed. There must have been about Tookey and his uncultured colleagues a compelling, blunt earnestness, a burning conviction that demanded attention. These were precisely the traits that impressed Cromwell's parliamentary colleagues in 1640–1: here was a rough-and-ready fellow who spoke without eloquence but yet compelled others to listen. He was still subject to outbursts of temper and impulsiveness and men were genuinely shocked by the violence of his unbridled tongue and impromptu acts. He had scant respect for the gentlemanly conventions of Parliament and, in February 1641, soon after his reappearance in the Commons, he was ordered to apologise to the House for intemperate language. Nor was it only the gentlemen and burgesses of the debating chamber who were so struck by this strange, new phenomenon; from the beginning of his military career Cromwell took to preaching and leading prayer meetings and using language and paralanguage that his soldiers readily understood. Bulstrode Whitelocke referred to Cromwell's subtle arts in praying, preaching, groaning and howling'.[51] There must have been occasions when this was an act intended to put heart into his men but that is not proof of insincerity or hypocrisy. Cromwell believed totally in what he was about and used the most effective methods to ensure success. He knew that 'he that prays and preaches best will fight best'. In that combined activity of praying, preaching and fighting and in leading his 'godly, precious men', he found his destiny.

Election was a doctrine that had profound meaning for Cromwell. It was a truth all good Calvinists believed but for a man who had undergone a dramatic conversion and who knew that God had chosen 'even him' it took on a more penetrating reality. He claimed for himself the promise of Jesus that the Holy Spirit would lead him into all truth. That Spirit worked by imparting inner conviction, arranging the circumstances of his life, intervening miraculously and imparting 'charisms', gifts of grace. In every situation Cromwell 'sought the Lord' in prayer and when he had received his answer he would not allow himself to be deflected from the course of action to which he believed he was being directed. His consciousness of divine guidance had incalculable impact on both friend and foe. In battle it inspired his soldiers with the certainty that their cause was God's and that they were under his protection:

I can say this of Naseby, that when I saw the enemy draw up and march in gallant order towards us, and we a company of poor ignorant men, to seek how to order our battle . . . I could not (riding alone about my business) but smile out to God in praises, in assurance of victory, because God would, by things that are not, bring to naught things that are. Of which I had great assurance; and God did it. O that men would therefore praise the Lord, and declare the wonders that He doth for the children of men![52]

To his enemies Cromwell's religious certainty inevitably smacked of cant, hypocrisy and spiritual pride. Oliver's reply was simple: God was with him; God had spoken; he could do no other than obey. His conviction, although the grounds for it were different, was as unshakeable as Charles Stuart's.

In large measure Cromwell's belief that he knew the mind of God came from his study of Scripture. He steeped himself in holy writ. For example, in his letter to Elizabeth St John there are no less than a dozen allusions to or quotations from different Bible passages. Cromwell had become a man whose mind was soaked in the word of God, which was central to the devotion of all literate Puritans. Listening to sermons was not enough, the Christian householder was 'to retire himself every day into secret and there betwixt God and himself, first, to lay open his heart and confess his sins. Secondly to call on God and give him thanks for his mercies. Thirdly to read God's word' and then to instruct his household in divine mysteries.[53] So William Crashaw, fellow of St John's, Cambridge and one of the day's leading preachers, summarised the responsibilities of those who truly sought to live a holy life. We know from the taunts of enemies that Cromwell took very seriously the task of instructing his family and workers and that he often entertained preachers in his home. From his correspondence it becomes obvious that prayerful meditation on the Bible was also part of his daily routine. Yet he did not go overboard about it – either in ramming texts down unwilling throats or in devising fantastical interpretations. His approach was common-sensical: appealing to the authority of the word of God when writing to those who shared his convictions but not unctuously heaping Scripture upon those with whom he had plain business to contract. In an age when eschatological speculation was rife and wild prophets were everywhere predicting the imminent return of Christ and the rule of the saints, Cromwell eschewed such fancies. He lived in the 'now'. If he looked to the future it was to accomplishing God's will in the land, not to ushering in the New Age, as he told the army council at Putney in 1647: 'The end is to deliver this nation from oppression and slavery, to accomplish that work that God hath carried us on in, to establish our hopes of an end [i.e. accomplishment] of justice and righteousness in it.'[54]

Nor, as his faith 'settled down' after the first exciting years, did he overemphasise dramatic charismata. He was not given to ecstatic prophecy. The one gift he did exercise was that of preaching. He had always supported Puritan lectures and his commitment to the proclamation of the word increased after his conversion, as is evident from his letter to Mr Storie at the Sign of the Dog. George Storie and his friend Mr Busse (or Basse) have been identified as members of the Mercers' Company,* with which Cromwell had contacts, as we know from the controversy over the Fishbourne bequest.[55] 'Dr Welles' is almost certainly Dr Walter Wells, the scholar engaged in ecumenical projects under the aegis of Dr Holdsworth. He had studied in Leiden, had close ties with continental Protestants and held a lectureship in Godmanchester and, possibly, another in St Ives in the early 1630s. It may be that he was a rival attraction to Dr Beard, for both men lectured at the same time. Wells's preaching was, then, another evangelistic enterprise sponsored by members of the Mercers' Company and Cromwell, who now signs himself 'Your loving Friend in the Lord', urges its continuance out of personal commitment to the Gospel.

In common with all separatists Cromwell was not prepared to believe that God restricted the proclamation of divine truth to those who were ordained to the ministry or had undergone academic training. It is not difficult to deduce from Cromwell's speeches what his sermons may have sounded like – specimens of expository passion – but one satirist has left us a wicked parody of Cromwell the pulpiteer, which to be effective must have been recognisable:

ROM. xiii. I.
'Let every soul be subject unto the higher powers; for there is no power, but of God: the powers, that be, are ordained of God.'

. . . the main question is, Whether, by higher powers, are meant kings, or the commoners? Truly, beloved, it is a very great question amongst those that say they are learned; but, I think verily, they make more stir about it than needs: for may not every body that can read observe that Paul speaks in the plural number, 'the higher powers?' Now, had he meant subjection to a king, he would have said, 'Let every soul be subject to the higher power;' that is, if he had meant one man but, by this you see he intended more than one; for he bids us 'be subject to the

* The Dog in Royal Exchange was 300 yards from the Mercers' headquarters in Ironmongers' Lane.

higher "powers",' that is, the Council of State, the House of Commons, and the Army. I hope I have cleared this point. So now, then, I will come closer to the words themselves, and shew you truly and plainly, without any gaudy rhetoric, what they signify unto us, that you be not decided and I tell you, this is not to be done by every spirit, but only by such who are more than ordinarily endowed with the spirit of discerning.* I confess there are many good men and women amongst you that intend well and speak well and understand well but yet cannot apprehend well all things that lurk in scripture-language, for lack of a sufficient measure of the Spirit.† They must be inwardly called thereunto, or else they are subject to errors and mis-constructions.

Well, then, you see who are fittest to interpret and I presume you believe God hath abundantly supplied me. I do not boast of it but I speak it to his glory that hath vouchsafed to take up his lodging in so vile, contemptible, unswept, unwashed, ungarnished a room, as is this unworthy cottage of mine. But it was his will, and I am thankful for it . . .[56]

This wicked lampoon, presenting Cromwell as a Uriah Heep whose feigned humility was a cover for spiritual pride, would not have amused the Protector if he ever read it, not because he had no sense of humour but because he retained, to the end of his days, a self-questioning, self-doubting streak. He would have been distressed to know that others thought him hypocritical and arrogant because these were traits he had always loathed in others, whether courtiers, bishops, local councillors, Presbyterians or class-conscious country gentlemen. Anyone who was so sure of his own position that he despised the opinions of others and was bent upon imposing his own will roused his ire. His later heartfelt entreaty to the Scottish Kirk's General Assembly has become Cromwell's most oft-quoted remark: 'I beseech you, in the bowels of Christ, think it possible you may be mistaken.' That plea for a show of Christian humility takes us very close to the heart of the man. For many years, as a member of a once influential family in decline, he had been on the receiving end of the opposition and taunts of others. His responses had alternated between outbursts of anger and bouts of depression. One who knew him well explained how, when Oliver had come to a deep personal

* Note the spiritual discernment and charismatic gifts.
† Ditto.

faith, he was able to come to terms with his earlier experiences by interpreting them as examples of divine discipline:

> This great man is risen from a very low and afflicted condition; one that hath suffered very great troubles of soul, lying a long time under sore terrors and temptations, and at the same time in a very low condition for outward things; in this school of afflictions he was kept, till he had learned the lesson of the Cross, till his will was broken into submission to the will of God . . . [Religion] was laid into his soul with the hammer and the fire.[57]

He had, as a result, a sympathy for all men who were honestly struggling to find their own faith.

In March 1643 he came to the defence of a dismissed officer. The Presbyterian Major-General Crawford asserted that the man in question was an Anabaptist. 'Are you sure of that,' Cromwell demanded.

> Admit he be, shall that render him incapable to serve the public? He is indiscreet? It may be so, in some things, we have all human infirmities. I tell you, if you had none but such indiscreet men about you, and would be pleased to use them kindly, you would find them as good a fence to you as any you have yet chosen.
>
> Sir, the state, in choosing men to serve them, takes no notice of their opinions, if they be willing faithfully to serve them, that satisfies. I advised you formerly to bear with men of different minds from yourself; if you had done it when I advised you to it, I think you would not have had so many stumblingblocks in your way. It may be you judge otherwise, but I tell you my mind. I desire you would receive this man into your favour and good opinion. I believe, if he follow my counsel, he will deserve no other but respect from you. Take heed of being sharp, or too easily sharpened by others, against those to whom you can object little but that they square not with you in every opinion concerning matters of religion.[58]

Cromwell made a point of enrolling in his own troop godly officers and men and he formed them into a fighting congregation, a literal 'church militant' with its own preachers and acts of worship. This, in effect, meant drawing his strength from and coming to rely on recruits from that amorphous mass of religious rebels, the separatists or Independents. These were the hottest fighters because they had the most to lose. If the Royalists triumphed there would be no place in the ensuing religious settlement for gathered churches. As Cromwell crafted his formidable fighting unit he grew to love his 'russet-coated captains who knew what they were fighting for' (to paraphrase one of his letters). They were semi-literate and illiterate fellow evangelicals who, as he frequently argued, were for the most part free of those vices usually associated with fighting men. He was well aware – and fellow officers certainly reminded him – of the consequences of upsetting the social balance of the countryside. 'Gentlemen,' he wrote to members of the Suffolk Committee, 'it may be it provokes some spirits to see such plain men made captains of horse. It had been well that men of honour and birth had entered into these employments, but why do they not appear? Who would have hindered them? But seeing it was necessary the work must go on, better plain men than none, but best to have men patient of wants, faithful and conscientious in the employment . . .'[59] Had Oliver grown up firmly on the 'master' side of the master-servant divide he would have been less sanguine about the ambitions and motivations of his 'rude mechanicals' but the modest landowner of Huntingdon and the yeoman farmer of St Ives had never been among the shire-ruling gentry into whom was inbred the prerogative of preserving the social order.

Yet for all this Oliver was not a sectary. For all his sympathy with the separatists there is no evidence that he became a permanent member of a gathered congregation. He maintained his links with the church of St John's, Huntingdon. He attended his parish church in St Ives and we may assume that he continued the same practice in Ely where he had very close business connections with the ecclesiastical establishment. Any failure to do so would certainly have been remarked upon by his opponents then or after 1660. In fact, Oliver's continued support of the Church of England was a circumstance which later detractors had to perform somersaults to turn to his discredit:

And that this conversion might seem true and real, he manifested it with the publican first in the temple (the church) which he devoutly and constantly frequented, affecting the companies and discourses of orthodox divines, no way given to that schism of *Nonconformity* into which *Oliver* soon after fell.

246

Thus wrote the malicious Heath.[60] A less hostile witness recorded that Cromwell for a while adhered to the Church of England with greatly increased devotion but that 'in a short time he began to associate himself with the Puritans and to entertain their preachers at his house'.[61] None of this offers any evidence of Cromwell's adherence to a known conventicle. Had he been an open member of an independent Church it is as inconceivable that his enemies would not have exulted at being able to prove his association with those who 'pluck up the hedge of parish order'[62] as it is that the members of his sect would not have laid claim to him.

Cromwell's preference in the externals of religion was for simplicity. No less than the Laudians was he ready to give his cultural predilections spiritual sanction. Back in the Huntingdon days Dr Simcott reported that his patient 'had fancies about the cross' in the market square, by which we may assume that he objected to the edifice on grounds of idolatry. The image of Cromwell as the 'ultra-Puritan', unsophisticated boor who tried to enforce on others his own loathing of beauty and refinement has become set in the aspic of national mythology. It is worth looking closely at the impact he made on contemporaries who were not committed to misrepresenting him.

The stories of the impression he created when he entered the arena of national politics in 1640–1 are well known. Hampden reputedly said of him, 'That slovenly fellow . . . who hath no ornament in his speech . . . if we should ever come to have a breach with the king (which God forbid) . . . will be one of the greatest men in England.' And Sir Philip Warwick always remembered clearly his first sight of Cromwell:

I came into the House well clad and perceived a gentleman speaking (whom I knew not) very ordinary apparelled, for it was a plain cloth-suit, which seemed to have been made by an ill country tailor; his linen was plain, and not very clean; and I remember a speck or two of blood upon his little band, which was not much larger than his collar; his hat was without a hatband, his stature was of a good size, his sword stuck close to his side, his countenance swollen and reddish, his voice sharp and untunable, and his eloquence full of fervour; for the subject matter could not bear much of reason; it being in behalf of a servant of Mr. Prynne's who had dispersed libels against the queen for her dancing and suchlike innocent and courtly sports; and he aggravated the imprisonment of this man by the council table unto the height, that one would have believed the very government itself had been in great danger by it. I sincerely profess it lessened much my reverence unto that great council; for he was very much harkened unto.[63]

Such is the image of the man that has survived and it is generally assumed that the outward appearance of the middle-aged Cromwell accurately projected the inner man as he had always been and always would be. But this is the kinsman of the refined Sir Oliver who grew up familiar with the courtly splendours of Hinching-brooke, who was a student at Cambridge, who was related to and friendly with several of the more exalted members of East Anglian society and whose in-laws were members of a wealthy, rising mercantile family. This was the man who later showed himself to be an accomplished (if not an elegant) orator, who delighted in the Latin motets of Richard Dering and had an organ installed at Hampton Court, who was the hero of Milton and Marvell and who appeared 'of great and majestic deportment and of comely presence'. Clearly, there was much more to Cromwell than the bluff countryman.

Oliver responded to aural stimuli but was not tuned in to the visual arts. His reported carelessness of dress, his brusque address and his reputation for iconoclasm have combined into the common perception of him as a joyless boor. This stereotype has to be firmly rejected. His vandalism of churches is a fiction (see below pp. 288f). His roughness of speech and apparel was in part affected as he identified with simple believers and in part the result of that impatience and passion which impelled him to be always 'doing'. However, he certainly had a blind spot when it came to appreciating representational art and its relation to the life of the spirit. Basically, he had had no opportunity for an aesthetic education. Men and women of modest means simply never came into contact with beautiful paintings and sculptures. The only places where these had ever been available to ordinary people was in churches and from these buildings, they had been banished three generations before. Artefacts which were not understood often became objects of suspicion, especially when they were associated with Roman heresy and the vices of the rich.

Cromwell shared this widespread attitude and he had an additional reason for doing so: he had witnessed the Jacobean court at close quarters. It was a world of twin poles that attracted and repelled; a world he had once been drawn to and had come to reject. We obtain a hint of this from his connection with Prynne and Lilburne, alluded to by Warwick above. John Lilburne was a printer who had published some of Prynne's works (he was not a servant of Prynne's as Warwick suggested) and it was for this that he was arrested, imprisoned, pilloried, whipped and fined. In 1640 he sent a petition urging Cromwell to take up his case, which indicates that he was already acquainted with the new MP and expected from him a sympathetic response. His case was referred to a parliamentary committee and it was when Oliver addressed that committee in support of Lilburne that Warwick took notice of him. The Commons Journal records that the House concluded that the printer's treatment had been 'bloody, wicked, cruel, barbarous and tyrannical' and his punishment 'illegal and against the liberties of the subject'.[64] Cromwell may well have lived to regret the part he played in the enlargement of this vitriolic political agitator but the interesting point for the moment to notice is that in his speech Oliver attacked 'dancing and suchlike innocent and courtly sports'.

It was Prynne in his *Histriomastix* who had so criticised the behaviour of the court as to provoke his persecution at the hands of Archbishop Laud. In the exuberantly extravagant denunciations of Prynne and the ferocity of the royal response we can discern that culture clash which lay at the heart of the troubles of the 1640s. Prynne was nothing if not comprehensive in his condemnation. Almost the first third of *Histriomastix*'s over one thousand pages is an indignant exposé of the Stuart court. Among the activities that roused the author's all-embracing ire were:

> . . . effeminate mixed dancing, stage plays, lascivious pictures, wanton fashions, face painting, health drinking, long hair, love locks, periwigs, woman's curling, powdering and cutting of their hair, bonfires, New Year's gifts, May games, amorous pastimes, lascivious effeminate music, excessive laughter, luxurious, disorderly Christmas-keeping, mummeries, with sundry suchlike vanities . . .[65]

Prynne connected all such luxurious excesses with immorality and Roman Catholicism, which all alike emanated from the Queen's circle. In its hysterical blanket condemnation of court life *Histriomastix* expressed a resentment at the arrogance, extravagance, exclusiveness and detachment from the lives of ordinary people which Puritan killjoys were not alone in feeling. Nor was the connection Prynne made between these abuses and an alien religion mere, unsubstantiated prejudice. Henrietta Maria, her ladies, priests and cavaliers deliberately projected an image which contrasted with what they considered as the boorishness of native Protestantism. 'The Queen's cult of love, its exaltation of woman, and its connection with Catholicism, may be seen as the defiant gesture of a minority group – élitist, feminist and Catholic – whose existence in the 1630s was being threatened by forces outside the court.'[66] Cromwell, who had no reason to admire or envy the life of the Stuart court, broadly went along with Prynne's analysis.

He also shared the author's attitude to the plastic arts:

. . . since our late renowned Sovereign King James, and our own homilies against the peril of idolatry . . . do absolutely condemn, as sinful, idolatrous, and abominable the making of any image or picture of God the Father, Son, and Holy Ghost or of the Sacred Trinity, and the erecting of them, of crucifixes, or, such like pictures in churches . . . so they, likewise condemned the very art of making pictures and images, as the occasion of idolatry, together with all stage-portraitures, images, vizards, or representations of heathen idols, etc as gross idolatry . . .[67]

For all Prynne's close reasoning, his citations of Scripture, and his appeals to classical writers and the Fathers, his was at root an emotional reaction to those things which, rightly or wrongly, he associated with the Caroline court – wanton expense, remoteness from the people, arrogance, corruption, frivolity and false religion.

In the House of Commons Cromwell aligned himself with that protest. But whereas the rabid pamphleteer rejected a world of which he knew next to nothing, Cromwell spoke as one who had seen the court. Throughout his early years he had watched the Stuarts and the gorgeous creatures with whom they surrounded themselves. He had seen his proud uncle taken up, used and then dropped by the Stuarts. If he declined to hold the King in awe and if he affected a rough, very *un*courtly manner, he had reason.

The Cromwell of 1640 was a man who wanted nothing to do with the King's household or the King's religion but that is not to say that he was intent upon war with either. Ironically he esteemed himself, as Charles considered himself, to be a man of peace. In September

1645 he wrote a report to Parliament on military affairs in the West Country. The yearnings and convictions he expressed in it will fairly round up this study of Cromwell's faith.

It may be thought that some praises are due to these gallant men, of whose valour so much mention is made: their humble suit to you and all that have an interest in this blessing, is, that in the remembrance of God's praises they may be forgotten. It's their joy that they are instruments to God's glory, and their country's good; it's their honour that God vouchsafes to use them. Sir, they that have been employed in this service know that faith and prayer obtained this city [Bristol] for you. I do not say ours only, but of the people of God with you and all England over, who have wrestled with God for a blessing in this very thing. Our desires are, that God may be glorified by the same spirit of faith by which we asked all our sufficiency, and having received it, it's meet that He have all the praise. Presbyterians, Independents, all had here the same spirit of faith and prayer; the same pretence and answer; they agree here, know no names of difference: pity it is it should be otherwise anywhere. All that believe, have the real unity, which is most glorious, because inward and spiritual, in the body, and to the head. As for being united in forms, commonly called uniformity, every Christian will for peace-sake study and do, as far as conscience will permit; and from brethren, in things of the mind we look for no compulsion, but that of light and reason. In other things, God hath put the sword into the parliament's hands, for the terror of evil-doers, and the praise of them that do well. If any plead exemption from it, he knows not the Gospel. If any would wring it out of your hands or steal it from you under what pretence soever, I hope they shall do it without effect. That God may maintain it in your hands and direct you in the use thereof is the prayer of
Your humble servant
Oliver Cromwell[68]

'We look for no compulsion', 'real unity is inward and spiritual' – such expressions mark out the religious territory occupied by Oliver Cromwell and his colleagues from the enemy terrain claimed by the King and his Laudian bishops. The differences between the two men were those which lay at the very heart of the Reformation confrontation. On one side was an affective, interiorised Christianity, whose adherents responded to the Word and the Spirit, who set little or no store by visual and aural stimuli and who looked to their ministers as proclaimers and interpreters of the saving Gospel. On the other, an institutional religion for which 'Church' was a concept at once mystical and tactile, something to be beautifully adorned as befitting the gateway of heaven, whose priests mediated divine grace through the living symbolism of sacraments and who possessed a divinely bestowed authority, not to be questioned. Oliver and Charles were men of profound personal faith in the same God but their differences of character and upbringing meant that they nurtured their beliefs according to different theories of spiritual husbandry. Both men believed ardently in religious toleration but extended it in opposite directions. Charles would embrace Roman Catholics because he saw them as part of the historic Church. Cromwell's heart was wider. 'I have waited for the day to see union and right understanding between . . . godly people (Scots, English, Jews, Gentiles, Presbyterians, Independents, Anabaptists and all).'[69] King and gentleman both espoused the principle of order but Charles could only conceive of this in terms of a society led by nobility and clergy under the Crown while inherent in Oliver's position, though he never formulated it so starkly, was the separation of Church and state.

A secular age may look with little comprehension on the arcane issues of doctrine and Church order which separated the two sides in the Civil War. Some historians have assumed that such religious disagreements cannot possibly have lain at the heart of the conflict; that we must look for 'real' social and political dislocations in our quest for the causes of that upheaval. Yet, passionately held beliefs were primal in motivating the two major players, determining their moral attitudes and providing them with the justification for the shedding of blood. In obedience to the will of God, as he perceived it, Oliver Cromwell took arms against his King to safeguard true religion. In obedience to God, as he perceived it, Charles Stuart lied, cheated and broke his word to preserve the true Church.

SIX

RELIGION

THE YEARS 1629 TO 1640 when Charles governed without Parliament have been called the 'eleven years of personal rule' and the 'eleven years of tyranny'. It is more helpful to think of them as a period during which the King tried to make the existing organs of central and local administration serve the ends of absolutism – an absolutism he certainly regarded as benevolent. There was nothing new about a monarch not summoning Parliament: all Charles's predecessors had preferred not to be bothered with the assembly as long as they could get by without increased tax revenue or achieve their objectives without the sanction of statute law. Charles resolved to rule by edict and to make the Crown financially independent under normal, peacetime conditions, and he set out with a high heart to achieve this in 1629. Whether or not he envisaged keeping the nobility and the representatives of town and county away from Westminster permanently and thus becoming an absolutist monarch in the French or Spanish sense is a matter for debate. He certainly believed that he could so impress his people with the blessings of firm and wise royal government that there would be little support for parliamentary troublemakers who only had themselves to blame for their exclusion from government.

To a considerable degree he was successful. He oversaw the elaborate strict guidelines for the offices of state, issued a Book of Orders to clarify the duties and responsibilities of justices and magistrates, tightened up the financial administration, exploited to the full prerogative sources of income without provoking too vociferous an outcry, sold off or modernised Crown estates, attempted to improve the training of the militia and kept the nation at peace. It was not only by contrast with the holocaust that followed that the 1630s were looked back on by many subjects as halcyon days. For his part Charles basked in immense self-satisfaction. He was playing his role with conviction and following with apparent success the script of divine monarchy written by his father. His court was a glamorous living museum in which images, tableaux, sounds and ritual presented a convincing assemblage descriptive of the viability and benefits of autocracy. It was almost inevitable that he should have become convinced that he could push his authority beyond the limits of what many of his subjects considered acceptable.

The King's problem was that for the success of his policies he relied on the efficient collaboration of the gentlemen of the shires and the burgesses of the towns, the unpaid agents of government. These men found themselves under pressure to work harder implementing edicts to which there was increasing hostility and which they could not fully justify to themselves.

> These men had borne the brunt of the most ambitious experiments in governance that the nation had ever seen . . . In them was the frustration that men in command felt who had struggled with the growing hostility which had dogged every step taken to advance the King's service. Each had known the misery of seeing his neighbours' enmity turned against him personally . . . What they had seen, and more, what they had intimately experienced, raised in them contempt for the system of government and the instruments of that system. For ten years they had had a grandstand view of 'personal rule'. If the members of the Long Parliament were convinced 'not that a few things had gone wrong, but that everything had gone wrong', certainly those among them who had been local governors knew just how wrong everything was.[1]

It was in the localities; in the county assizes, the magistrates' courts and the parish churches that Charles's experiment failed. And one might say *especially* in the parish churches, for it was here that royal impositions were brought home, not just to those of moderate means, but to all sorts and conditions of men and on a regular, Sunday by Sunday basis. The reforms carried out by William Laud in the Church mirrored those being enjoined upon the secular administration but they were carried out with a greater degree of insensitivity often by clergy who inspired no respect and – what was worse – they were carried out in the name of God.

'Orthodoxy is my doxy; heterodoxy is another man's doxy.' Conflict is inevitable, as the eighteenth-century Bishop Warburton succinctly observed, when men of influence and power project their

256

own concepts of truth on to the regulated life of religious institutions. But the aphorism has a more pointed application to the Caroline Church. Soon after his accession Charles asked Laud to advise him on clergy who merited preferment. The resulting list had a letter beside each name: 'O' for Orthodox, 'P' for Puritan. A national church only survives when it make allowance for a wide diversity of pious expression and even of doctrinal definition. England's medieval *ecclesia* had contained within it numerous variants, reflecting regional, local, familial and personal predilections as well as differences of theological emphasis. Each parish church was a worship centre in which devotion was offered to a profusion of saints, and focused at shrines and altars tended by families, confraternities, chantry priests, religious orders and beguinages. In a country not given to heresy-hunting, unorthodox views were tolerated except when their supporters deliberately drew attention to themselves or when a particularly zealous bishop went on visitation.

Profusion entails confusion and the Reformation was an attempt to clear the weeds from the border so that the flowers of faith could grow more strongly and be seen more clearly. After the vigorous hoeing of the 1530-60 generation, the English Church slowly found its way back to something of the old comprehensiveness or, rather, tried to work out a new comprehensiveness, one in which, for example, Catholics, like the Lollards of old, were allowed their beliefs as long as they did not make nuisances of themselves. Reformation historians have too often tended to be obsessed with how far England ever was truly 'Protestant' or truly 'Catholic'; with the extent to which innovations in belief and practice were welcomed or resented by 'the people'. It is more helpful to ask to what extent the inevitable variety of religious expression was able to find comfortable lodgement within the Church of England. The religious aspect of the mid-century upheaval was all about whether a national church had any meaning and, if so, what that meaning was. Elizabeth had the wit not to pry into men's souls or impose too rigid an ecclesiastical discipline, and James, though a martinet in theory, was pragmatic in practice. Two factors upset this balance in the 1630s: the Counter-Reformation throughout Europe and, in England, a king who inherited his father's authoritarianism without his father's wisdom.

It is fashionable to eschew the term 'Counter-Reformation' and to substitute for it the more positive 'Catholic Reformation'. The arguments are that on both sides of the divide protagonists were labouring for the purification of life, worship and doctrine and that, when the grime of persecution, scurrility and mutual anathematising has been wiped away, the actual theological differences do not seem so great. For the historian enjoying the luxury of detached analysis this may well be valid but realities looked very different to those who were living through them. The Council of Trent marked out rigid ideological boundaries; the Inquisition and committed heads of state dragooned troubled consciences; Catholic gold bought mercenary generals charged with reconquering territory from heretical rulers; above all, the Counter-Reformation attempted to re-establish a dictatorial, hieratic church from which there could be no appeal to temporal rulers, Bible or individual inspiration. There was a perceived conflict of religious and cultural attitudes which, after 1618, projected itself as what James I called 'the miserable and torn estate of Christendom, which none that hath an honest heart can look on without a weeping eye'.[2] James was, frenetically, a man of peace who believed he had a mission to bring people together and dampen passions. It was a naïve vision and one not shared by his son; Charles could see no further than his own need to establish firm government. With that in view he set William Laud and his episcopal storm troopers to bring the Counter-Reformation across the Channel.

Charles embarked on the years of personal rule with a high heart and an advantage that Catholic sovereigns much to their frequent chagrin did not possess in their realms: he was, by law, Supreme Head of the Church of England. This divinely bestowed authority he was resolved to exercise to the full. The religious aspect of his kingly *potestas* featured in the propaganda which he now generated for himself.

And what propaganda! So effective was it that it created an image of the King and his court which has persisted ever since. Today, when we think of Charles I we see in our minds those public relations projections of the 1630s – the monarch bravely mounted on a magnificent dapple-grey, a pose borrowed from antiquity sym-bolising imperial power; the dismounted sovereign with an aura of natural hauteur, elbow thrust towards the viewer bidding him keep his distance; the close-up portraits of that narrow, elegantly bearded face with its air of melancholy that later ages saw as presaging tragedy; the affectionate and affecting family groups rendered poignant for us because we know how violence sundered this husband from his wife and children. Where the King led, his fashionable courtiers followed. Society's leaders clamoured to be immortalised by the flattering brush of the royal artist. For the remarkable gallery of Van Dyck portraits of Caroline beautiful people is a stunning example of sycophancy in paint. The Flemish master made his fortune by representing his subjects as they most wished to be represented. When the Countess of Sussex was shown Van Dyck's picture of her she noted that it was 'too rich in jewels, I am sure, but it is no great matter for another age to think me richer than I was'.[3] And when Sophia, daughter of Charles's sister, saw her aunt Henrietta Maria for the first time she had quite a shock: 'Van Dyck's fine portraits had given me such a magnificent impression of all the ladies of England that I was astonished to observe that the queen, whom I had regarded from her picture as so beautiful, had long, lean arms, crooked shoulders and teeth protruding from her mouth like defence works.'[4]

No one better understood than Charles I the importance of art as an aspect of statecraft. One of his first appointments on becoming king was that of Daniel Mytens as court painter. He tried unsuccessfully to persuade the great Rubens to settle in London for a long stay and honoured him with a knighthood in 1629 but it was Rubens's pupil, Anthony Van Dyck, who succeeded Mytens in 1632. He was promptly knighted and awarded a pension of £200 per annum, and the King was so involved in the artist's work that he had a landing stage built before Van Dyck's Thameside premises to facilitate his frequent visits. All the painters who worked for the King were contributing to a great and complex statement. The products of their genius were presented to foreign dignitaries and a cohort of copyists was kept constantly busy making replicas for favoured subjects. But the finest works were designed for specific settings within the royal palaces. As ambassadors and supplicants waited to be admitted to the royal presence they were subjected to a static 'warm-up act' to put them in the right frame of mind. Thus, at St James's Palace there was a gallery lined with eleven portrayals by Titian of Roman emperors. As the visitor strolled past these masterpieces he could scarcely take his eyes off the large canvas confronting him on the end wall: Van Dyck's equestrian portrait of Charles as an armed conqueror, emerging from beneath a triumphal arch.

Portraits conveyed simple, powerful images but allegorical

pictures offered almost limitless scope for interpretation. In 1629, within weeks or months of his dismissal of Parliament, an exultant Charles commissioned from Rubens a painting which would express the new, happy epoch upon which the kingdom was entering. In *Landscape With St George and the Dragon*, the artist places the King and Queen at the centre of an English idyll. The sun breaks through upon a broad arcadian vista and angels smile from heaven as dark storm clouds roll back. Beneath the King's feet the dragon lies slain, while women and children, its erstwhile prey, give way to expressions of relief and joy. In the centre of the large canvas Charles, as St George, the patron saint of England, hands a bridle to Henrietta Maria, the rescued maiden. In the most obvious reading of this dramatic piece the dragon represents discord – at home and abroad. Charles has disposed of a fractious parliament and cut through years of fruitless diplomatic wrangling by making a treaty with Spain. On top of these achievements the succession has been secured by the birth of a healthy heir to the throne. Well might the sun of peace and harmony be seen to bathe the nation in its healing warmth.

But what are we to make of the central act in this painted drama in which the Queen, serene and smiling, accompanied by a lamb – the symbol of Christ – is the dominant figure? The bridle she receives from her champion is a traditional symbol for control of the passions. There may be a biblical allusion here: in the Epistle of James the writer urges the necessity of restraint. As a horse needs bit and bridle so do men and nations, for 'what causes wars and what causes fightings among you? Is it not your passions that are at war in your members?' (James: 4, 1). Whether or not this direct reference is intended, the point remains the same: the trophy Charles hands his Queen is his control of the 'unruly wills and affections of sinful men', as the Prayer Book called them. Since the chief cause of discord is religion one aspect of the painting's message seems to be that the realm will rest at peace as long as Protestant King and Catholic Queen can restrain their more aggressive co-religionists. Only England's reformed Catholicism can achieve this.[5]

It is quite clear from Charles's actions in the religious sphere that he saw himself in this light. Paintings, masques and the whole elaborate ritual of the court supported and enhanced a fantasy world; an idealised vision which, like court portraits, sacrificed realism to the enhancement of the desired image. Part of Charles's misfortune was that he made the mistake of believing his own publicity.

'Enhancement' is the operative word in this business of visually representing Stuart kingship. Wherever he turned in his palace he saw some aspect of his life and philosophy apotheosised. Of nothing was this more true than of his marriage. Relations between Charles and Henrietta Maria had improved since the early tempestuous days. The Queen was maturing from a petulant, self-obsessed girl into a young woman aware of her responsibilities, and after the dismissal of her attendants she no longer lived in a Gallic enclave of the court. However, it was the death of Buckingham which brought the royal couple together in a more intimate way. In his intense emotional upheaval Charles turned to the only close companion he had left. His wife did not fail him. The comfort she brought enabled him to overcome his grief and also awake within him a new love. Within two months of his friend's assassination Henrietta Maria was pregnant. If any other incident was needed to bind Charles and his Queen more closely together it occurred the following April. Henrietta Maria fell badly while alighting from her barge and this brought on a premature and difficult birth. The Queen became critically ill and her husband was distraught, tearfully beseeching the doctors to save her and spending long hours at her bedside. After the Queen's recovery all observers noticed the change which had come over the royal couple. Very simply, they had become lovers, kissing and exchanging looks and gestures in public and unable to bear long absences from each other. Their feelings for each other endured throughout their remaining years together and were extended to embrace their children. In August 1647, when Charles was a prisoner at Hampton Court, he had brought from Whitehall a copy of the group portrait of himself and Henrietta Maria with Prince Charles and Princess Mary, made by Van Dyck in 1632, the first family painting he had commissioned.

Artists no less than masque makers took this happy example of conjugal contentment and enlarged it into the perfect model for a whole range of virtues. Domestic harmony became a pattern for the relationship between monarch and people. For example, in the Van Dyck family group already mentioned the Crown and the Parliament House are displayed in close proximity, suggesting that the trouble-some legislators can learn something from the loving care lavished by a husband on his wife and the loving obedience she renders in response. Poets and dramatists produced a new code of courtly love similar to that which had prevailed in Elizabeth's day. Chastity, faithfulness and platonic affection were extolled. Such images had a didactic intention within a court where young men and women were thrust together in an atmosphere of pleasure and luxury, and their most obvious messages reinforced by masque, drama and song were to do with fidelity and the blessings of Christian family life based on pure love.

Religion was central to all Stuart propaganda because the ultimate justification of the regime lay in the will of God. It was daily affirmed in the elaborate worship of the royal chapel. It was assumed in all the court masques, whose praising of the King's virtues would have been exposed as syrupy sycophancy had they not rested on the belief that the blessings of Charles's person and reign were divinely bestowed. Though the entertainments traditionally featured the inhabitants of Mount Olympus and their emissaries (thus provoking cries of 'atheism', 'idolatry' and 'paganism' from Puritans) these were mere conventions linking the demi-paradise of Stuart palaces with the throne room of God. Painting also bridged this gap and the commissioned canvases were replete with allusions to the holy recognised by all who shared the King's esoteric passion for art. Thus, for example, Van Dyck's *Charles I on Horseback with M. de St. Antoine* echoes Tintoretto's *Flight into Egypt*, the King substituted for the Virgin and the adoring stable master for Joseph.

Such sacred allusions were lost on all but the initiated; elaborate propaganda seldom protruded beyond the narcissistic court. Whereas Henry VIII and Elizabeth I had mastered the art of self-presentation for the adoration of their subjects, Charles had inherited the more cameral style of Stuart kingship. He occasionally sanctioned the public performance of masques but it never occurred to him to authorise the kind of pageants and riverain spectacles which had helped to form the common perceptions of Tudor subjects. In the 1630s there was very little government window-dressing to counteract the multifarious grumbles in which private citizens always indulge. The gap between 'court' and 'county' widened in these years. The Council exercised a deliberate and fairly successful censorship over the publication of domestic news (From 1628 Laud, as Bishop of London, controlled the printing presses of the capital.). The abandonment of parliament diminished the two-way traffic of gentlemen and burgesses between the capital and the shires. Since provincial conformity was, almost by definition, quiescent this often left the rhetorical initiative with evangelical preachers, lecturers and pamphleteers. The Laudian camp produced tracts and published sermons for popular consumption aimed at exposing the overt and covert activities of the 'enemies of godly order'. In one such, Christopher Down complained that the insidious behaviour of the precisionists had a long history. For many years they had kept their heads down. They concentrated their activities in lectures which were under lay protection or outside episcopal control while installing 'conformable curates' in their parishes who dutifully observed the prescribed rituals

> 'Thus saving themselves, and maintaining their reputations with the people, they gained the opportunity to instil into them their principles, not only of dislike of the Church-government and rites, but also of the doctrine established.[6]

It may be that Laud would have made more use of religious controversialists had his hand not been stayed by the King. Charles's natural distaste for disputation was accompanied by a very practical rationale: contentious sermons and writings provoked riposte and kept debate alive. The way to bring dissidents back into the fold with maximum expedition was by force and not persuasion. The disciplinary framework of diocesan bishops backed, where necessary, by the Church courts, lay ready to hand and this the King was resolved to use. In a set of instructions issued to bishops in 1626 he explained the support that they could look to from him in words reminiscent of the Elizabethan apologist, Richard Hooker:

> Church and State are so nearly united and knit together that though they may seem two bodies, yet indeed in some relation they may be accounted but as one . . . This nearness makes the Church call in the help of the State to succour and support her . . . and . . . the State call on for the service of the Church both to teach that duty which her members know not, and to exhort them to, and encourage them in that duty they know.[7]

Laud's mission closely matched that of his sovereign, which is why it has always been difficult to be certain which of them initiated policy. The archbishop had a purely clericalist agenda on which there were two items: freeing the Church from lay control and exterminating evangelicalism. He did not underestimate the difficulty of attaining his first objective.

To one who wrote to congratulate him on his appointment to Canterbury he replied,

> . . . I must desire your Lordship not to expect more at my hands than I shall be able to perform . . . for as for the Church, it is so bound up in the forms of the Common Law that it is not possible for me, or for any man, to do that good which he would or is bound to do. For your Lordship sees (no man clearer) that they which have gotten so much power in and over the Church will not let go their hold. They have indeed fangs . . .[8]

The other objective he was able to pursue with unstinted relish. Institutionalists hate what they cannot control or fit into an ordered pattern and Laud's loathing of the Puritans was total. Unimaginative, tidy-minded administrator that he was, the archbishop looked across the Channel and saw or thought he saw, a monumental Church, under the rule of a priestly hierarchy, its altars and shrines adorned by the offerings of the faithful, its liturgy performed in identical words from village to village and town to town. This was the bride of Christ as she should be, pure and unspotted by disfiguring blemishes of ritual variation, unconventional spirituality or unseemly enthusiasm. By contrast *Ecclesia Anglicana* had been allowed to get into a parlous state. The Reformation had set the state's seal of approval on the open Bible, experiential religion and greater lay involvement in the formulation of doctrine. The results had ranged from evangelical revival to peasant unrest and violent apocalyptic sectarianism. By 1625 the alarming signs were everywhere to be seen: the neglect of church buildings, the rejection of traditional liturgies, simple laymen challenging their parish clergy, uncontrolled preaching, theological disputation and the majestic salvation ship of the Church abandoned for the bobbing boats of self-defining holy huddles. Laud believed that, old though he was (he became archbishop at the age of sixty) he had been raised to his eminent position to set all to rights. This would entail unscrambling much of the Reformation, taking back for the Church hierarchy that share of national government that had been usurped by civil lawyers and raising the profile of the parish clergy. He believed, doubtless sincerely, that this change in the socio-political structure could be achieved without a drift back to full-blown Catholicism, with or without the Pope. Against the backdrop of the bloody confessional war sporadically raging on the continent it was difficult for many to share this optimism or to believe Laud's oft-repeated claim that he was committed to 'the Protestant religion here established'. As the Earl of Northumberland observed of him, 'To think well of the reformed religion is enough to make the archbishop one's enemy.'[9]

Charles had no such elaborate schema. What was indelibly inscribed on his conscience was that the good governance of the Church was his *personal* responsibility. He was, therefore, determined to set his own stamp upon it. This meant much more than imposing his prejudices about order, decorum and obedience. Because he was the apex as well of the spiritual as the temporal hierarchy, every parish church was a focal point of royal authority. For this reason irregular practices and recalcitrant clergy had to be suppressed. Thanks to the fears and suspicions he had taken over from his father and his chaplains he identified Puritanism as a subversive force within the realm which must be crushed. In this campaign the bishops were his field generals and he appointed men he knew and trusted personally, even at times rejecting Laud's nominees. Once they were in place, as he had promised, he supported them to the hilt. He took in hand several major issues himself, such as the beautification of St Paul's and the appointment of Buckingham as Chancellor of Cambridge University. The King issued directives on his own volition, such as the instruction to all theologians in 1628 as to how they were to interpret and expound the Thirty-Nine Articles. Whenever he was really fired by a religious issue Charles took it up with enthusiasm. But in this, as in other areas of policy, his attention span was limited and, having a zealous and efficient archbishop whose ideas dovetailed with his own, he left most of the day-to-day decisions to him.

He wrote affirming marginalia on Laud's reports, permitted the draconian enforcement measures which made full use of the courts of Star Chamber and High Commission and, on one occasion, he even summoned before the Council disputants in a local clash between parish and archbishop over the placing of the communion table. When families fled to the Netherlands and the New World Charles shared his primate's rejoicing that the realm was being rid of 'troublemakers'.

The real objective of this collaboration was power, although that word had different resonances for each party. When Laud insisted that the altar was more important than the pulpit because one offered people the Saviour's very body, the other merely his word, he was making a sacerdotal claim: the priest by virtue of his ordination possessed *exousia*, the authority which empowered him to mediate between God and man. Evangelicals were outraged at this selling of the Reformation pass and saw it as the reintroduction of transubstantiation and the priestly miracle of the Mass. Laud denied such Roman doctrines but without them the representation of the clergy as a separate caste to whom reverence and obedience were done by divine mandate, irrespective of moral uprightness and soundness of character lacked any rational basis. For Charles the imposing of unity and the disciplining of Puritan dissidents was a much-needed buttress for royal authority – an authority handed down from the throne of God. These two types of power were fused together in a bimetallic strip but each had its own distinct properties and would react differently to the applications of political heat. Yet fused they were and could not avoid sharing the same destiny. As James I had warned, 'No bishops, no kings.'

This particular King and bishop started out on their purgative campaign with a very big advantage. 'Laudianism' was an idea whose time had come. There was throughout the country and at all levels of society an irritation with the disorder and divisions fostered in parish life by Puritan zealots who denounced Sabbath-breaking, public entertainments, drunkenness and gaudy apparel and who insisted that only members of their exclusive coteries were saved. When Charles reissued the *Book of Sports*, which countered Puritan criticisms of Sunday sports, holidays and entertainments, he was tapping into a public mood of discontent and demonstrating that *his* Church supported age-hallowed customs and the harmless fun and games of traditional town and village life. King and bishop were on the side of 'cakes and ale'. However, it was not only citizens who were inclined not to take their religion too seriously who resented Puritan excesses; there were many clergy and theologically informed laymen who were concerned about the separatist drift of English Protestantism. The conflict of the 1630s cannot be told as a trial of strength between 'Laudianism' and 'Puritanism'. English religious life of the period was much more fragmented and dynamic and 'Laudianism' could not have captured many hearts and minds had it not been so. The archbishop had a certain amount of support from Calvinist divines who were reassessing their own concepts of 'Church' in the light of the tendency towards exotic and ill-conceived fringe Christianities.

What suddenly happened in 1625 was that all those who were prejudiced against evangelical Calvinism on emotional, intellectual or spiritual grounds were provided with determined leadership. A new political correctness became fashionable backed by law. It became possible to question assumptions which had, for decades, been sacrosanct. The situation was not dissimilar to the sudden dominance of Thatcherism in the 1980s. Britain's first woman prime minister did not invent right-wing Conservatism and millions who voted for her party were not of her extremist stamp. What she did was tap into a widespread disillusion with liberal, left-of-centre politics and provide a broad consensus of people with aggressive, charismatic leadership. Her government waged war against a panoply of evils conveniently bundled together and labelled 'Socialism'. 'Thatcherism' was just as much a vague, catch-all title as that allocated to its opposing 'philosophy'. Ultimately it failed because the consensus fell apart. The more extreme the government's legislation and polemic became, the more supporters it lost and eventually not even the minority who had achieved power and wealth through Tory policies could shore it up. The parallel with the rise and fall of 'Laudianism' is remarkably close.[10]

What the ecclesiastical programme of the 1630s lacked was a considered theology. 'Laudianism' appears in inverted commas above because, like 'Puritanism', it would be erroneous to think of the word as identifying a coherent set of doctrinal propositions. A document issued in London diocese by Juxon in 1635 shows just how mixed were the theological, disciplinarian, and economic considerations which made up the programme he was following in obedience to King and archbishop.

Certain articles propounded to ministers and lecturers in and about London to be consented unto:
1. That every one that is baptized is regenerated. 2. That a minister cannot with a safe conscience administer the sacrament to any but those that kneel. 3. That a canonical man may possess more than one benefice. 4. That clergymen have right to temporal goods in God's Church. 5. That ministerial power in forgiving sins is not merely declarative. 6.

That the order of bishops is by the law of God. 7. That bowing at the name of Jesus is a pious ceremony. 8. That bowing before the altar is lawful. 9. That the voice of the people is not required in the election of a minister. 10. That Christ descended locally into hell. 11. That the Church of Rome is a true Church, and truly so called.[11]

The ingredients of the stew doled out by ordinaries and incumbents varied from place to place and time to time. All the people in the pews had to do was swallow it. Both King and prelate were intellectual lightweights who were by nature not disposed to explain their actions to others, but even had they been brilliant theological expositors they would have been unable to win widespread intellectual support. What Charles may not have grasped but what Laud would certainly have understood was that no convincing *Protestant* apologia could be presented for their programme. Protestant theology stood four-square upon the word of God and the availability of divine grace apprehended by faith. On the continent men were dying in defence of these fundamentals. In England their co-religionists would never accept a belief system based on sacramental grace and which played down the importance of the Bible. Laud could not even carry all the bishops with him. Thus, John Williams of Lincoln on the positioning of the communion table:

> . . . The proper use of an altar is to sacrifice upon, the proper use of a table is to eat upon . . . a communion is an action most proper for a table, as an oblation is for an altar. Therefore, the Church in her liturgy and canons calling the same a table only, do not you now call it an altar . . . That it should be there fixed, is so far from being the only canonical way, that it is directly against the canon . . . And so is the table made removable, when the communion is to be celebrated to such a place as the minister may be most conveniently heard by the communicants . . .[12]

Not all critics of the government's ecclesiastical policy could be silenced, punished in the courts or driven into exile. Though reluctant, the King and the archbishop were obliged to provide some doctrinal justification for their policies. The answer seemed to lie in a subdivision of Calvinism. In the words of Nicholas Tyacke, 'King Charles became the architect of an Arminian revolution.'[13]

'Arminianism' though a swear word in the mouths of evangelicals was also a name adopted by some of Laud's fellow travellers because it gave their cause a degree of Protestant respectability. For several decades Church of England theology had meant Calvinist theology. There had always been churchmen uneasy with aspects of the French reformer's schema but since the only other dogmatic edifice of any size in the landscape was Roman Catholicism and any serious departure from core doctrines was stigmatised as 'popery', the development of any dissenting movement was inhibited. Then, in the early years of the century, a split appeared within Calvinism when the liberal Jacob Harmensen (known in the academic fraternity as Jacobus Arminius) came down on the free will side of the old predestination and free will argument. From his chair of theology at Leiden he propounded an understanding of salvation which allowed greater play for divine mercy and human response than the irresistible grace, unconditional election and total depravity of orthodox Calvinism. After his death, Arminius's views were discussed at the Synod of Dort (1610) and rejected by the majority of delegates from all the European centres of Calvinism. However, the new doctrines commended themselves to some who considered themselves in all other respects good Calvinists, and would continue over the centuries to attract adherents whose evangelicalism was above suspicion – notably John Wesley.

The Laudians did not come into this category. It was the freedom to question that appealed to them in Arminianism. It gave them the opportunity to attack the exclusivism of the godly, their tendency towards sectarianism and their 'disorderly' worship, while not departing from the Protestant camp. The conviction that Christ died potentially for all was a willing horse which could be made to carry several riders – good works, sacerdotalism and parish discipline (for there was, arguably, no room for a gathered church in the Arminian dispensation). In England Arminian theology took on a distinctive form. Its champions plucked predestination from the throne and raised on their shields sacramental grace: men were saved, not by the inscrutable will of God, but by believing reception of the Church's means of grace administered by God's priests. Arminians approached ecclesiology from a diametrically opposed direction to that followed, not only by Puritans, but by the majority of Protestants. The starting line for reformed Christians was individual salvation; 'Church' in the wider sense was something which, as Wycliffe had urged, only existed in the mind of God, and in the narrower sense was an expression of how the elect chose to organise themselves during their common pilgrimage to glory. The Catholic fundament was the sacramental reality of the Church as a visible organisation through which alone divine grace was mediated and which was to be clearly recognised by its established hierarchy and its liturgy. In the latter part of James's reign the adherents of the new ideas committed themselves to gaining power and harrying evangelicals. The campaign had its theologians, prepared to engage their opponents from pulpit and printed page, but it was essentially cultural in ethos and political in methodology. In their zeal to denounce the hypocrisy, vandalism and sacrilege of the party which 'defaces pictures and rifles monuments, tortures an innocent piece of glass for the limb of a saint in it, razes out a crucifix and sets up a scutcheon, pulls down an organ and advances an hour glass and so makes an house of prayer a fit den for thieves'[14] they convinced themselves that they could dismantle and rebuild in a decade what had been erected over a century. This could never be achieved by scholarly debate or pulpit and pamphlet polemic. Thus, as we have seen, they deliberately infiltrated the royal court. As ideological battle was joined between Laudians and the defenders of religious freedom so theological labels became mere indiscriminate terms of abuse. In the words of the parliamentarian, Francis Rous, 'an Arminian is the spawn of a Papist', while in a Latin-English diction-ary assembled by Francis Holyoake believers in predestination were defined as 'a kind of heretics'.[15] These were among the more polite exchanges. This calls in question the validity of 'Arminianism' and 'Puritanism' as descriptions of the groupings opposing each other during the eleven years of Charles's personal rule.

A question more pertinent to this study is: 'Were Laud and Charles Arminians?' At his trial the archbishop disavowed the title and he actually preached against the teachings of Arminius in 1632. He had a genuine abhorrence of pulpit pyrotechnics and precise definitions of things which he believed should remain divine mysteries. Though he was far from even-handed in banning con-troversialists, his veto certainly extended to Arminians as well as their enemies.

No better example can be cited than that of Richard Montagu whose treatment at the hands of Parliament had provoked the royal edict against theological disputation. The controversial bishop suffered as much from the restrictions placed on his pen as he did from the diatribes of his detractors. His earlier arguments had been with 'Romanisers' but the grounds he chose for his defence of the Church of England had not pleased Puritans and this led to his having to fight a pamphlet war on another front and to his summoning before Parliament. In February 1626, at the suggestion of the Earl of Warwick, a two-day debate was held at Buckingham's house. The opposition was led by John Preston, and the fashionable and curious flocked to hear the great academics in action. It was the kind of occasion James had loved. Not so his son. Charles, observing as Thomas Fuller later noted, 'that none returned Arminians thence save such as repaired thither with the same opinions'[16] and that battle raged as fiercely after the debate as before, issued his interdict.

This, of course, did not stop the underground radical press hurling its primed anathemas but it did inhibit Montagu from defending himself. He protested to Laud but was advised to suffer in dignified silence. At the same time another academic was labouring at a monumental treatise against predestination. When this prodigious work was finished in 1630 he offered to show it to Laud, who agreed to read it – if it 'be not too long'. However, Laud pointed out, it was unlikely to receive a royal licence because the King did not want 'to have these controversies any further stirred, which now . . . begin to be at more peace'.[17] The archbishop may or may not have been speaking in his master's name; there is no doubt that the verdict was one he fully concurred with.

Laud was an administrator and not a theologian and his occasional attempts at apologetic indicate that he was more at home in the world of externals than in that of ideas. 'It is true,' he wrote, when trying to justify the submission of conscience to institutional control, 'the inward worship of the heart is the great service of God, and no service acceptable without it, but the external worship of God in his Church is the great witness to the world that our hearts stand right in that service of God.'[18] Taken at face value the sentiment was unexceptionable but it was the kind of apophthegm upon which he built a programme of Church reform, which set him at odds, not just with separatists, but with many thinking contemporaries. In 1625 Francis Bacon observed, 'it is noted by one of the Fathers, "Christ's coat, indeed, had no seam but the Church's vesture was of divers colours", whereupon he said, "*Investe varietas sit, Scissura non sit*". They be two things, unity and uniformity.'[19] Such wisdom was well beyond the reach of William Laud. Where the philosopher recognised healthy diversity, the ecclesiastical bureaucrat recognised only unholy muddle. All Laud could display was that consistency which is the 'hobgoblin of little minds': 'unity cannot long continue in the church where uniformity is shut out at the church door.'[20] Uniformity, authority, discipline – these were what mattered: the doctrinal nitty-gritty came a poor second in his order of priorities.

Charles was even less of a theologian than his archbishop. Matthew Wren was undoubtedly correct in 1623 when he observed that the prince lacked James I's grasp of issues of divinity. However, when pressed by Laud for a more detailed verdict of where the heir stood in matters ecclesiastical, his carefully weighed response was revealing: 'for upholding the Doctrine and Discipline, and the right Estate of the Church, I have more Confidence of him than of his Father.'[21] What Wren understood, having observed the prince acting independently away from the court, was that Charles had a simple and straightforward devotion to the Church of England. For James religion had been one strand of statecraft, amenable to compromise and subtle changes of emphasis when necessary – a political realism he had developed during the hazardous days of his youth. His son's mental categories were much more compartmentalised. Wren adjudged him to be a young man unlikely to bargain with religious truth. He was right. By the time Charles became king, he was secure in his own faith and that very security, coupled with his own disinclination for intellectual inquiry, predisposed him not to probe religious mysteries or argue nice points of doctrine. He believed what the Church of England taught and he expected all his subjects to do the same.

The implication of this for his governance of the Church was that he was acutely aware of his responsibilities but at the same time confident in his bishops. As a result he was, by turns, passionately involved and very relaxed. He poured considerable energy into the showcase project of St Paul's. He insisted that bishops should reside in their dioceses so that every region should have its symbol of royal authority. But he by no means appointed only Arminians to episcopal and other senior posts. Moreover, the royal chapel was certainly not closed to Puritan preachers. Like his father, Charles made his own personal judgements of men worthy to serve in the court and upper echelons of the Church and there is no evidence that he did so on party lines.

The King and the archbishop were closely in agreement on policy but each had his own special interests and priorities. The initiative on the *Book of Sports* came from Charles, as did the insistence on the railing in of altars. Laud was particularly concerned to enhance the prestige of the clergy.

'Let me say,' he expostulated in Star Chamber, 'to such as slight the ecclesiastical laws and persons, that there was a time when churchmen were as great in this kingdom as you are now and let me be bold to prophesy, there will be a time when you will be as low as the church is now.'[22] In the vast majority of cases it is impossible to disentangle the involvement of the King in whose name instructions were issued and the archbishop who fine-honed them and was responsible for their implementation. In October 1629, Charles provided the Church reformers with a powerful weapon, the 'Proclamation for Preventing the Decay of Churches and Chapels'. Its wording is very revealing: To arrest the lamentable deterioration noted in many places of worship all those who had responsibility for such buildings were to inspect them personally, 'not relying on churchwardens' reports'.[23] This refinement seems to reflect the suspicious and pernickety attitude of William Laud, who was always setting his agents to check on the diligence of church officers.

To be fair to the archbishop, he probably had little alternative if his programme was to stand any chance of success. Since he did not have complete control of royal decision-making and since he had to work with diocesans who varied in their industriousness and their commitment to reform, he had to maintain a good private information service – and to colour his reports to the King. Recent research suggests that he deliberately exaggerated the 'scandal' of neglect in parish churches. Despite the alarming information he presented, few ecclesiastical structures had suffered abuse at the hands of ultra-Protestant clergy or parishioners. The confusing and dispiriting changes of 1530–70 were far in the past; a new generation of guardians cared, by and large, responsibly for the simplified churches with which their families had long been connected.[24]

One advantage that Charles enjoyed in having so zealous a minister for religious affairs was that the unpopularity of the government fell upon the shoulders of his subordinate. The constant 'interference' by Laud and his more active diocesans was an ongoing source of irritation to parish officers. Commissioners were sent out on circuit to discover where changes were necessary and to enforce their implementation. At Puddletown, Dorset, the people were ordered 'to remodel the interior to divide the nave from the chancel, to adjust the position of the pulpit and reading place, to establish a new communion table with "a frame about it", to erect a gallery at the west end, to provide a new font cover, and establish uniform seating throughout the church'.[25] The cost of all this was £130 for a church whose normal annual expenditure was probably less than £20. The task of overseeing the work and raising the revenue fell on the churchwardens. Small wonder that the visitors' approach met with great apprehension in parishes throughout the land or that the churchwardens of Axbridge plied the commissioners with strong drink in the hope of blurring their vision. The bishops' men were no respecters of persons: the churchwardens of Holy Trinity, Micklegate, York were ordered 'to cut Sir Henry Goodriche's stall and likewise Mr Alderman, Micklethwaite's and make them uniform to the rest of the stalls'.[26]

It was not just 'difficult' towns and villages like St Ives where the ecclesiastical agents encountered resistance. So determined were the King and his archbishop to have the Church throughout the realm conform to their idealised image that, by the financial and administrative burdens they pressed upon them, they needlessly made enemies of congregations not in the least tainted with Puritanism. Laud achieved the remarkable feat of giving many loyal church members a regime which they came to loathe more than that of the canting precisionists. Even when the government sanctioned policies which should have been popular with the majority they ran into resentments. The reissue of James's *Book of Sports* was certainly not received with universal rejoicing. Clergy were required to read it to their congregations and those who failed to do so were punished. This 'probably did more to outrage Puritan sensibilities and turn Somerset against Laud, Pierce, and the whole ecclesiastical establishment than any other single act of the King and his advisers'[27] and there was a similar response in other parts of the country where the deprivation of non-compliant ministers actually boosted separatism as the ejected clergy gathered their sympathisers around them.

Few individuals have earned the title 'most hated man in England'. Thomas Cromwell was one such, because he interfered with local customs, imposed policies devised at the distant centre of power and wielded the law in all its ferocity against sincere, ordinary folk. The same label was attached to William Laud and for much the same reasons. By the end of the 1630s he was being frequently attacked in scurrilous pamphlets and broadsheets. Anonymous protagonists posted libels on church doors like the one which ran, 'So odious is he grown in the eyes of men that we believe he stinketh in the nostrils of Almighty God.'[28] Another, pinned up in St Paul's Cathedral while the work of refurbishment was still in progress, suggested, 'the government of the Church of England is a candle in the snuff, going out in a stench.'[29] Incognito graffiti was one way of expressing anger. Open disobedience was another, braver response. All over the country ministers resigned or were ejected for refusing to comply with episcopal instructions. And where clergy did conform there were often parishioners or patrons who made life difficult for them. One Middlesex vicar who bewailed his lot to Juxon was typical of many: 'I find many of them very averse and some to whom I am obliged . . . if I should [make an example of them] would much impeach my estate . . . Hope of preferment from my patron I have none, because I cannot [conform] with him . . .'[30]

Where there were ten who made some kind of protest we may be sure that there were a hundred who suffered in silence. Diocesan and court records reveal cases of attempted evasion and procrastination by churchwardens charged with expensive and unpopular refurbishment schemes, but most finally submitted with a bad grace. Episcopal visitations discovered clergy performing moral and spiritual contortions to get round the regulations. Thomas Wakefield of Horseheath when questioned could not 'remember' whether he had read the *Book of Sports* and the vicar of St Michael's, Cambridge, 'doth not exactly pray according to the canon but doth add something of his own'.[31] And, of course, there is the familiar and oft-described diaspora of Puritan families to European havens and the New World.

There were, to be sure, clergy who enthusiastically supported episcopal initiatives designed to enhance their own standing. One Huntingdonshire vicar was later denounced for railing in the altar and denouncing Puritans from his pulpit as 'the Pharisees of the times'. He raged against members of his congregation who preferred the preaching of other men to his own, comparing them to 'dawes that did fly from steeple to steeple'.[32] When the churchwardens at Little Wilbraham, near Cambridge, did not promptly comply with their priest's instruction to put up an altar rail, he soundly berated them and when they constructed a modest barrier costing 31 shillings, he pulled it down and demanded something more elaborate, 'to the great charge of his parishioners who are very poor'. The wardens did manage to defray some of the cost by selling the rejected rail to the church at Little Shelford.[33] Such clerical arrogance did little to commend the Laudian programme at the local level.

All the scarcely suppressed resentment erupted in 1640, as soon as Laud and his reforming bishops came under attack from a parliament which the Scottish crisis had forced the King to summon. It was a time for settling scores and turning tables. Clergy who had simply 'followed orders' were denounced; a mob attacked Lambeth palace; in Cromwell country hundreds of people signed a petition to complain about Bishop Wren, who soon found himself in the Tower with his archbishop.

Charles was completely behind the policy of compelling outward conformity while allowing considerable freedom of individual belief. It was a policy which quite misread the mind of the nation; to most churchgoers externals mattered. Anyone with experience of parish life would have been able to point out that the people in the pews were much more sensitive about church furnishings and liturgy than about points of doctrine. Unfortunately, the King had no contact with such advisers. His knowledge of the Church in the provinces came from bishops and preachers and the reports of troublemakers brought to his attention by Laud. And Laud was careful to tell the King what he wanted him to know.

The Stuart court had its medieval chivalric idyll and the Laudian brotherhood attempted to match it by appealing to a romanticised, golden age *societas Christiana*. In their vision of England the King's Council would be re-stocked with ecclesiastics. Some confiscated lands and sources of income would be restored to the Church, which would use the revenue to improve the quality of the clergy and establish educational and religious foundations. Parish churches would be beautified and the people would gratefully gather in them on Sundays and saints' days dutifully to receive communion at the hands of their much-loved priests and to pray for their saintly king.

This understanding of pre-Reformation English society was as distorted as the image presented by Foxe of a persecuting and morally lax religious establishment, upon which most Englishmen had been brought up. Charles loathed this anti-Catholic myth but the nation's religious ills could not be solved by replacing it with another.[34]

King Charles was unable to prevent Laud's arrest, trial and execution but there is no evidence that he felt great grief at his archbishop's death, nor that he wrestled with any guilt over the issue. He certainly did not question the rightness of the religious campaign which had cost Laud his life. On the contrary, he regarded the shedding of the old man's blood as some sort of expiation which, once made, would persuade a just God to look favourably upon his cause, 'having passed through our faults'.[35]

No man who cared about his Church could be indifferent to the ideological battle raging in the parishes. Certainly not Oliver Cromwell. As he reacted to various aspects of the Laudian reform, defining those things he found objectionable, he was, by that process, building up in his mind a picture of the Church as he believed it should be. As far as we know, he never set down his ideal on paper, nor would it be reasonable to expect of him the degree of consistency such an exercise would imply. No less than the ritualists, his concept of the Church Militant was a patchwork of Scripture, tradition and reason, sewn together with cultural and emotional threads. To reconstruct it we must bring together the fragments revealed in his actions and writing.

He showed a keen interest in issues of Church order. Given his personal history it could scarcely be otherwise. His conversion had brought him into contact with an evangelical network of like-minded Christians, the 'elect', who were very conscious of having been buried with Christ and raised with him to righteousness. He attended the sermons of 'sound' preachers; he entertained 'spiritual brethren' in his own home and discussed matters of faith and practice with them; he wrestled with the word of God in his own devotions and expounded it to his household. But all this activity was over and above his membership of and, presumably, fairly frequent attendance at his parish church and his involvement in the life of the cathedral clergy at 'Meshech', activities demanded by social status as well as economic pragmatism.

Even before his conversion the strong streak of anti-establishmentarianism in Oliver Cromwell had shown itself in criticism of the episcopal bench. In his first, brief, contribution to parliamentary debate he had attacked Bishop Neile's interference with Beard's preaching. Since then he had encountered the repressive actions of Williams and his subordinate at St Ives and the oppression of two successive Bishops of Ely.

Francis White was obnoxious to Puritans as a turncoat. He had entered the lists of theological controversy in pre-Laudian days with attacks on popery but, or so it was widely believed, he had changed his stance in the early days of the new reign in order to obtain preferment. Men said he had sold his library so that he could restock it with popish propaganda. After his consecration as Bishop of Ely he associated himself with a little coterie of Cambridge arch-ritualists, prominent among whom were Matthew Wren and John Cosin, successive Masters of Peterhouse. Wren was responsible for erecting a new chapel which was an embodiment of Laudian liturgiology and acted as a red rag to Puritans of town and gown. Cosin further embellished it with 'a glorious new altar . . . mounted on steps, to which the master, fellows, scholars bowed and were enjoined to bow by Doctor Cosin . . . There were basins, candlesticks, tapers standing on it and a great crucifix hanging over it.'[36] This deliberately provocative building, consecrated by White as college visitor in 1632, was a symbol throughout the reign to the Romeward tendencies of the Laudian regime. White added to his unpopularity by entering into controversy with the harmless eccentric, Theophilus Brabourne, who urged the restoration of Saturday as the true sabbath. White made such an issue of Brabourne's views that the unfortunate man was hauled before the High Commission and spent a year in Newgate. It was one of a growing number of instances of insensitive over-reaction by the establishment.

When White was succeeded in 1638 by Matthew Wren, who was already unpopular in the region, this must have been seen as a deliberately provocative act and the new bishop was not slow to confirm such suspicions. He immediately embarked on a diocesan visitation inaugurated by a questionnaire sent to every parish consisting of a hundred and forty-seven questions. It became clear from the tenor of the interrogation and the orders for reformation issued to clergy and churchwardens that Wren was intent on repeating the Peterhouse pattern throughout the diocese. Not surprisingly, the bishop's activities were particularly resented in Cambridge.

Cromwell was by now well known in the area as one of the fairly substantial gentlemen who was not afraid to voice his opinions about matters ecclesiastical. It may have been this which was at least one reason for his election to the House of Commons by the burgesses of Cambridge in 1640. Existing records yield no satisfactory explanation for their choice. He was not a political figure in the town and he was a landholder of only modest means. Yet he was made a freeman of the borough in January 1640, was subsequently elected unopposed and took his seat at Westminster in April. The Short Parliament lasted little more than three weeks but by September even Charles was forced to concede that his personal rule was unsustainable. A Scottish army was in possession of Newcastle; his own force was evaporating like autumn mist on the moors; there were disturbances throughout the country and riots in the capital (particularly directed at the courts of Star Chamber and High Commission); and several of his own peers were pressing for a new parliament. When fresh elections took place in October Oliver had to fight for the Cambridge seat but he and his Puritan colleague defeated the two candidates nominated by the court.

The good men of Cambridge elected someone who they believed would represent their interests and who would have influence. Cromwell had friends in the university and the town and his views were known. The electoral majority must have believed that in him they had someone firmly on their side against Laudian innovation and someone who would fearlessly speak for them. We have already seen how passionate Oliver could be in debate on religious issues and his reputation for outspokenness must have influenced the votes. There is no reason to doubt that he was any less impressive on the Cambridge hustings than he was on the floor of the Commons chamber. They were probably also impressed by his contacts. The Earl of Warwick, through his extensive East Anglian network (his brother was still Chancellor of the university), was unflagging in his attempts to secure the election of radicals. He was one of the leaders of society behind petitions such as the following urging voters to back candidates opposed to the government:

we have been unusually and insupportably charged, troubled and grieved in our consciences, persons and estates by innovations in religion, exactions in spiritual courts, molestations of our most Godly and learned ministers, ship-money, monopolies, undue impositions, army-money, wagon-money, horse-money, conduct-money, and enlarging the forest beyond the ancient bounds, and the like; for not yielding to which things, or some of them, divers of us have been molested, distrained, and imprisoned.[37]

It is a comprehensive list of those issues which mostly concerned men of substance and which Mr Cromwell MP might be expected to support in Parliament. There is one late document which links Oliver very specifically with the activists who were campaigning for a new parliament:

. . . the true cause of the calling the Long Parliament thus: at the dissolution of the former Short Parliament the members both Lords and Commons had a great opinion that the king's affairs ere long would necessitate him to call them together again, therefore such as resided about London met together frequently and gave intelligence by Mr Samuel Hartlib and Mr Frost to those in the country of affairs. Ere long, they gave a more general summons to come all up, who not only came themselves but brought up also such country gentlemen as they could confide in, amongst the rest Mr Oliver St John brought with him Mr Oliver Cromwell, the first public meeting this gentlemen ever appeared at. They agreed to send down a petition to the King at York, subscribed by twenty Lords and above 40 Commons to pray him to call a parliament, that 2 Lords and 4 Commons of their number should carry it down, the Lords pitched upon the earl of Essex and Lord Howard of Escrick, the names of the Commons I have forgotten but Cromwell I am sure was the last & Essex plainly refused to go.[38]

This connection of Cromwell with the petition of twelve peers (including Warwick and Saye and Sele) conveyed to Charles in August, if reliable, certainly suggests a degree of prominence that would make the Cambridge burgesses take Oliver's candidacy very seriously.

They knew of his widespread kith-and-kin connections but particularly impressive were his relationships with the two heroes of the hour, John Hampden and Oliver St John, the ship money champions. One of the more grandiose schemes Charles had embarked on was a necessary refurbishment of the navy. He commissioned several capital ships with the object of defending the Channel and enhancing the country's maritime prestige. To pay for these expensive items of royal shopping he fell back upon an ancient tax called ship money. In 1634 it realised £40,000 collected from coastal towns and shires. Encouraged by this, the Council chanced their arm the following year by extending collection throughout the realm. The King's legal advisers were jittery. By custom, ship money was only levied on seaboard shires and ports and in times of national emergency. There was also the possible argument that its levying needed to be endorsed by Parliament. It was Oliver's cousin, John Hampden, who decided to bring a test case by refusing his £20 contribution (a sum he could well afford). To fight his case he engaged the services of his friend and relative, Oliver St John. For several weeks in the autumn of 1637 he and the Crown Counsel made their submissions before the Court of Exchequer. Their arguments, urging points from musty ancient documents, were arcane, dry and not such as to set the blood racing but 'middle England' followed them with fascination. More important than ship money or the fate of the defendant were the legal principles raised about the rights of Crown and people. St John became famous overnight for his insistence that private property was sacrosanct and could not without consent be appropriated by the King. The verdict of the judges, delivered the following spring, though less important, made abundantly clear that royal exactions were, at the very least, questionable. The Crown's seven-to-five majority was the smallest possible. The whole Hampden case suggested to most people with little knowledge of the law that all the disturbing changes being forced upon the nation might be open to legitimate legal challenge. And the only area for such a challenge was Parliament.

When Oliver took his Commons seat alongside eighteen of his relatives and more of his friends he threw himself energetically into the work of the House but it was in attacking the Laudian church establishment that he showed most passion. In December he was appointed to a committee considering complaints against Matthew Wren. After six months' deliberation Cromwell and his colleagues brought in nine articles of impeachment against the bishop. The Commons voted him unfit for office and sent him to the Tower. The Long Parliament applied itself as a matter of urgency to the religious state of the nation and set up a major committee for the purpose but so great was the number of petitions and complaints presented to it that a working sub-committee had to be appointed. Cromwell was a member. For the next few months he and his colleagues examined the cases of 'scandalous' incumbents. During the next three years hundreds of parish clergy were deprived. In Cromwell country the numbers were approximately twenty in Huntingdonshire and over fifty in Cambridgeshire. The committee's work was not purely negative: wherever possible they filled vacancies with 'sound' men who could be relied upon to perform a preaching ministry.

In May 1641 he was found enthusiastically backing the 'Protestation'. This was, in essence, a parliamentary manifesto or justification of the members' opposition to the government policies of the previous eleven years. Each signatory affirmed,

I, A. B., do in the presence of Almighty God promise, vow and protest, to maintain and defend as far as lawfully I may, with my life, power and estate, the true reformed Protestant religion, expressed in the doctrine of the Church of England, against all popery and popish innovations, and according to the duty of my allegiance to his Majesty's royal person, honour and estate: as also the power and privileges of parliament, the lawful rights and liberties of the subject; and every person that maketh this protestation in whatsoever he shall do in the lawful pursuance of the same. And to my power, as far as lawfully I may, I will oppose, and by good ways and means endeavour to bring to condign punishment, all such as shall, by force, practice, counsel, plots, conspiracies or otherwise, do anything to the contrary in this present protestation contained.

And further I shall, in all just and honourable ways, endeavour to preserve the union and peace betwixt the three kingdoms of England, Scotland and Ireland; and neither for hope, fear nor other respect, shall relinquish this promise, vow and protestation.[39]

Cromwell would have gone further: he wanted to bind, not just members of the legislature, but all leaders of local society into an association of common purpose by requiring them to swear this oath. It was a pledge that could have been taken by everyone except Roman Catholics and the more convinced separatists. Even Archbishop Laud could have signed the Protestation.

However, at the same time that Cromwell was affirming 'the true Protestant reformed religion, expressed in the doctrine of the Church of England', he was plotting the overthrow of its constitution. Over the previous months he had been working with Oliver St John and Sir Henry Vane the Younger on what came to be called the 'Root and Branch Bill'. In the first heady days of the Long Parliament, radical suggestions had poured in from all over the country. Hundreds, perhaps thousands, of petitioners had allowed their anger and frustration at Laudian antics to boil over in a demand for the total abolition of episcopacy. Cromwell's small sub-committee – a strange combination of the no-nonsense countryman, the ice-cool lawyer and the much-travelled courtier – tried to turn these aspirations into policy. St John drafted a measure which was presented to the Commons as 'A Bill for the utter abolishing and taking away of all Archbishops, Bishops, their Chancellors and Commissaries, Deans and Chapters, Archdeacons, etc.'. It was a breathtaking piece of totally negative procedure. No account of Cromwell's speeches on the Bill has survived but Vane denounced episcopal government as 'rotten and corrupt from the very foundation to the top' and St John claimed that right back as far as Augustine, bishops had been potential traitors whose very existence threatened monarchical authority – Laud and his cronies, so far from supporting royal power, had been working for its overthrow.

If the proponents of this draconian measure had really intended to force it into the statute book we would be obliged to question their political acumen or even their sanity. They did not; they knew that, whatever happened in the Commons, the Bill would never get through the Upper House. A recent attempt to limit episcopal power had recently been thrown out by their lordships. The Root and Branch Bill was window-dressing. It provided an opportunity for the angrier members of the assembly to let off steam and it demonstrated to radicals throughout the country that their MPs were on their side. Parliament had to ride the wave of Puritan reaction rolling over the country and already channelling itself into outbreaks of iconoclasm and violence. To the Laudians and their sympathisers it sent a strong warning signal. And it played an important part in short-term politics. The Scottish army was still on English soil and demanding the acceptance of Presbyterianism as part of the price for withdrawal. Oliver Cromwell was learning some lessons in practical politics.

As for his own opinions on Church government, he had scarcely had time to formulate what might be practicable. That he was studying all the options we know from a note written in February to a merchant friend who was in touch with the Scots:

> Sir,
>   I desire you to send me the reasons of the Scots to enforce their desire of uniformity in religion, expressed in their 8th article; I mean that which I had before of you. I would peruse it against we fall upon that debate, which will be speedily.[40]

It was clear to him that episcopal power in its present form could not be tolerated. Might Presbyterianism offer a better system? Was it more scriptural? Would English people accept it? How did it square with what he and his separatist friends had already experienced of Christ? These were the sort of questions with which Cromwell was wrestling in 1641 – and coming to no answers if we believe Philip Warwick's report that he admitted, 'I can tell you . . . what I would not have; though I cannot what I would.'[41] Yet, there may be even in the brief note above a hint of his attitude: 'their desire of uniformity in religion'. It was not so much the system to be applied that he questioned but the need for a system at all. Laud's crime had been his attempt to enforce outward uniformity. Should the English Church exchange one form of bondage for another? Ten years later he was quite clear on that score when he challenged the Scottish Presbyterian leaders with the offence of claiming divine authority for their own polity and seeking to impose it on Christians not of their persuasion:

> Are we to be dealt with as enemies because we do not come to your way? Is all religion wrapped up in that or any one form? Doth that name or thing give the difference between those that are members of Christ and those that are not? We think not so. We say faith working by love is the true character of a Christian.[42]

Milton has already made the point more elegantly though with no greater passion.

> Because you have thrown off your prelate lord,
> And with stiff vows renounced his liturgy
> To seize the widowed whore, Plurality,
> From those whose sin ye envied, not abhorred,

Dare ye for this adjure the civil sword
To force our consciences that Christ set free . . .[43]

Cromwell could never accept the fiction of Thomas Hooker, the apologist of *Ecclesia Anglicana*, that an Englishman and a Christian are the same animal seen from different viewpoints but neither could he escape from the fact that the Church of England was part of the framework holding society together and could still, potentially, provided a valuable means of reaching all parishioners with the Gospel. There were, within its ranks, godly preaching ministers whom he had no desire to silence. Yet he had no sympathy with those who were afraid of disorder. Thomas Coleman, a London minister who sometimes preached to the Long Parliament spoke for many when he said of the Independents, 'I do here profess I reverence their persons . . . [yet] under this notion of Independency weavers and tailors may become pastors . . . so that one may bind his son prentice to a cobbler and at seven years end he may go out free a minister.'[44] To which Cromwell might well have shouted a hearty 'Amen!' What was needed, in his view, was a structure sufficiently fluid to allow for a wide variation of emphasis and an acceptance of separatists whose consciences would not permit them to remain even within a very liberal regime.

Cromwell's passionate concern for maximum freedom in the conduct of worship and the governance of the Church stemmed from his charismatic background at St Ives. Jesus had compared the Holy Spirit to the wind which 'bloweth where it listeth'. Those who were overly concerned about Church order were often guilty of trying to steer this unpredictable, dynamic force into man-made channels or even of putting up wind-breaks. His study of I Corinthians and other New Testament passages reinforced his experience in the loosely structured assemblies of some of the separatists, that God gave his gifts to individual Christians without benefit of human organisation. He was particularly sensitive on the subject of preaching (a gift he believed himself to have been given). In 1650 he demanded of the Scottish kirk leaders:

Where do you find in the Scripture a ground to warrant such an assertion, that preaching is exclusively your function? Though an approbation [ordination] from men hath order in it, and may do well; yet he that hath no better warrant than that, hath none at all. I hope he that ascended up on high may give his gifts to whom he pleases . . . You know who bids us *covet earnestly the best gifts*, but chiefly *that we may prophesy* [I Corinthians: 14, 1]; which the Apostle explains there to be a speaking to instruction and edification and comfort, – which speaking, the instructed, the edified and comforted can best tell the energy and effect of, 'and say whether it is genuine' . . .

Indeed you err through mistaking of the Scriptures. Approbation is an act of conveniency in respect of order; not of necessity, to give faculty to preach the Gospel. Your pretended fear lest error should step in, is like the man who would keep all the wine out the country lest men should be drunk.[45]

Yet rules and order of some kind there must be and that raised the question of exactly who and what could be tolerated within a broadly based Protestantism. Just as much as Charles and Laud, Cromwell had his orthodoxy, beyond which all else was heterodoxy. Catholicism, it goes without saying, did not even come within the latter category; it was anti-Christian. In May 1641 Cromwell urged the Commons to consider expelling papists from Dublin. This was not so much a sectarian attack as an expression of mistrust. The Protestant colony in Ireland was always vulnerable to attack from the majority population, never more so than at a time when the English and Scots were preoccupied with their own squabbles. Cromwell was concerned that, in a crisis, Catholics in the Irish capital and garrison would make common cause with their co-religionists. Such a crisis might occur at any time and Cromwell was not alone in fearing it. Much of Europe was convulsed by religious warfare in which all manner of atrocities were excused by reference to Old Testament precedent or papal decree. The Stuart dominions had so far been spared this but the weak spot was always Ireland. It was not many years since the last great rebel leader, Hugh O'Neill, Earl of Tyrone, had died in Rome a pensioner of the Pope and, though the Ulster plantation was growing, there were several other clan leaders whose loyalty could not be relied upon. In an atmosphere vibrant with rumours of international Vatican plots Cromwell was not the only Englishman to be nervous about the possibility of the neighbouring island being used as a base and arsenal for a Catholic assault. It was this apprehension that exaggerated the rising when it did come, five months later, from a catastrophe into a holocaust. The rebellion of 1641 was a fearful explosion of looting, burning and slaughter but far worse was the exaggerated legend which immediately circulated in England and poisoned relations between the two countries for centuries:

While the king was in Scotland, that cursed rebellion in Ireland broke out wherein above 200,000 were massacred in two months' space, being surprised, and many of them most inhumanly butchered and tormented; and besides the slain, abundance of poor families tripped and sent naked away out of all their possessions; and, had not the providence of God miraculously prevented the surprise of Dublin Castle the night it should have been seized, there had not been any remnant of the protestant name left in that country.[46]

For a Protestant nation brought up with Foxe's *Acts and Monuments* and tales of the Armada and the Gunpowder Plot no perfidy or act of violence was considered to be beyond the forces of Antichrist. It does not fall within the scope of this book to evaluate Cromwell's behaviour in Ireland but it is important to stress the gulf of incomprehension which lay between him, together with thousands who thought like him, and Charles I and his court sophisticates who could contemplate the possibility of an accommodation with Rome.

The most dramatic evidence of Puritan determination to rid the English Church of every vestige of Romanism was the alacrity with which local and central authorities stripped out the Laudian accretions from churches and often went much further in destroying objects of superstition. Cromwell's name has been firmly tied to this 'sacrilegious vandalism' for no better reason than that the events of 1640-60 became telescoped in popular imagination until it was assumed that the Protector must have been responsible for all the evils of those years. The truth, as ever, is more complex.

On 10 February 1641 Oliver was appointed to yet another parliamentary committee. With his friends Barrington, Masham and over sixty other MPs he made up a group to consider 'An Act for the Abolishing of Superstition and Idolatry and for the Better Advancing of the True Worship and Service of God'. The end result was a parliamentary ordinance of August 1643 which appointed commissioners in every country to oversee a 'blessed reformation' of worship by removing from churches 'all monuments of idolatry and superstition'. We know nothing of Cromwell's contribution to the ensuing debates and we only have one piece of clear evidence of him as an abolitionist. In 1642 he was appointed military governor of Ely and in this capacity he wrote to Mr Hitch, one of the cathedral canons.

> Lest the soldiers should in any tumultuary or disorderly way attempt the reformation of your cathedral church, I require you to forbear altogether your choir-service, so unedifying and offensive; and this as you will answer it, if any disorder should arise thereupon.
>
> I advise you to catechise, and read and expound the Scriptures to the people not doubting but the parliament, with the advice of the Assembly of Divines, will in due time direct you farther. I desire the sermons may be where usually they have been, but more frequent.
>
> Your loving friend,
>
> Ely, January
> 10, 1643   OLIVER CROMWELL.

When the cleric persisted with his unauthorised worship the governor acted promptly and with a demonstration of his old hot temper:

> Cromwell, with a party of soldiers attended by the rabble, came into the church in time of divine service, with his hat on; and directing himself to Mr. Hitch, said 'I am a man under authority and am commanded to dismiss this assembly.' Upon which Mr. Hitch made a pause; but Cromwell and the rabble passing up towards the communion table, Mr. Hitch proceeded with the service; at which Cromwell returned; and laying his hand on his sword in a passion, bid Mr. Hitch leave off his fooling and come down; and so drove out the whole congregation.[47]

The services Cromwell found 'unedifying' and 'offensive' were sung Matins, Evensong and Holy Communion. They were offensive for their ritual, and for the ornate music which obscured rather than extolled the plain words of Scripture. They were unedifying because, although Bible passages were read, there was rarely an exposition and, so, the congregation was not instructed. The governor's action in stopping this worship in his home town was forthright yet the tone and content of his letter exude no vicious zeal or unseemly triumphalism. His reason for urging Mr Hitch not to proceed with the traditional offices was so as not to provoke the militia to precipitate action. It could be argued that his subsequent

288

appearance at the head of a troop was in order to prevent just such a violent eruption by the soldiers. No act of vandalism attended or followed this visit and everything we know about Cromwell the general tells us that he was jealous of the reputation of his men and severe upon breaches of discipline.

Exactly what could happen when troops got out of hand was revealed at Peterborough Cathedral three months later:

Notwithstanding all the art and curiosity of workmanship these windows did afford, yet nothing of all this could oblige the reforming rabble, but they deface and break them all in pieces, in the church and in the cloister, and left nothing undemolished, where either any picture or painted glass did appear; excepting only part of the great west window in the body of the church, which still remains entire, being too high for them, and out of their reach. Yet to encourage them the more in this trade of breaking and battering windows down, Cromwell himself (as 'twas reported) espying a little crucifix in a window aloft, which none perhaps before had scarce observed, gets a ladder, and breaks it down zealously with his own hand.[48]

'Cromwell the iconoclast,' as Margaret Aston has observed, 'helped by this minor and poorly authenticated incident, was already launched on his legendary career.'[49] It is not just the giveaway parenthesis – (as 'twas reported) – that casts doubt on this account: the passage in question is a later interpolation into Simon Gunton's *History of the Church of Peterborough* (1686) by an editor determined to expose 'the more than Gothic barbarity' of Cromwell and his men. That Gunton, who spent most of his life in or near Peterborough, did not include this story in his narrative is significant, as is the fact that this report conflicts with other stories which reveal Cromwell restraining his men from hooliganish behaviour.[50]

If Oliver Cromwell did authorise or personally carry out the 'purification' of churches we would expect him to have done so in his own locality. As we have already seen, a considerable number of Huntingdonshire and Cambridgeshire clergy were removed from office during the 1640s and the concentration of deprivations was particularly strong in the country around Huntingdon, Kimbolton and St Ives. It was a region also that suffered at the hands of William Dowsing who embarked with such devastating zeal on the 'blessed reformation' enjoined by Parliament. In 1643–4 this, otherwise obscure, East Anglian yeoman farmer visited 243 churches in Suffolk and Cambridgeshire, including the chapel of Peterhouse, to carry out the parliamentary injunctions against altars, rails, chancel steps, crucifixes, stained-glass images of saints and other offending paraphernalia. Two interesting factors emerge from his account of his destructive tours. The first is that much of the offending material had already been removed by parishioners. Thus, he only had to order the dismantling of seven altar rails. Clearly local people themselves had reversed the hated innovations imposed by the Laudians. The second point is that Dowsing's patron was the Earl of Manchester.

Edward Montagu had determinedly turned his back on his father's allegiance to the King and associated himself with those Puritan nobles and gentlemen who headed the opposition to royal policies. He was an opposition leader in the House of Lords, and in 1642, the year that he succeeded to the earldom, he was appointed Lord-Lieutenant of Huntingdonshire and Northamptonshire. Cromwell was soon to be very closely connected with Manchester in military matters but it was the earl, and not the gentleman, who commissioned Dowsing to purge East Anglian churches and who appointed a committee of eleven men to examine 'all ministers and schoolmasters . . . that are scandalous in their lives, or ill affected to the parliament or fomentors of their unnatural war, or that shall wilfully refuse obedience to the ordinances of parliament . . .'[51] The purge of the eastern counties was organised from Kimbolton, not Ely.

Even if he had had the inclination personally to oversee the spiritual disinfection of the Church Cromwell would not have had the time. The enormous industry he devoted to parliamentary work suggests that he believed that he had found his calling. The frustrations of life at Ely were behind him. He could now advocate and help to formulate those policies that would reverse the ills visited upon England over the last decade and earlier. God had appointed him, as a Christian and a simple patriot, to play his part in reshaping the nation. He gave himself without stint. When the Irish revolt broke out he donated £500 of his own meagre capital towards the country's pacification, and as the crisis at home deepened he gave anxious thought to the defence of the realm. On top of this he still had his responsibilities in Ely to attend to. And he was the father of a large family. His youngest daughter, Frances, was born at the end of 1638 and she brought the tally to eight. Five months later his eldest boy, Robert, died suddenly at Felsted at the age of seventeen, leaving Oliver and Elizabeth devastated. Like Charles and Henrietta Maria, they werc fond parents, devoted to each other and their children. Like the royal couple, they were soon to experience tumultuous events that would overshadow family joys and griefs. As for Oliver, he would discover that God had endowed him with a gift whose existence he had never suspected.

SEVEN

WAR

'WHAT KING, GOING to meet another king in war, will not sit down first and take counsel whether he is able with ten thousand to meet him who cometh against him with twenty thousand?'[1]

One answer to the Gospel question might well be King Charles I. When he went to war against his Scottish subjects he either did not calculate or miscalculated both the mood and the military capability of his opponents. It was he who began the civil wars when, in 1638, he decided to impose his will north of the border by force of arms. If, for the moment, we leave aside Ireland – always a special case – we have to go back a hundred and two years to find a parallel. In 1536 Henry VIII sent an army to the north of England to put a stop to the Pilgrimage of Grace. The comparison between the two events is close: in both a king involved in creating strong, centralised government confronted malcontents far from the centre of power who disliked the drift of royal policy, particularly the intrusion into their traditional religious practices. The major difference is that the Tudor king won and the Stuart king lost. Charles I was no more autocratic than Henry VIII but much had changed in the intervening century: Parliament was no longer overawed by the Crown; the mainland territory ruled from Whitehall had doubled in size; decades of religious conflict and propaganda had created a polarised and well-informed populace; and Crown finances could no longer be bolstered by confiscations and appropriations on the scale of the Dissolution of the Monasteries. Faced with what he regarded as a rebellion in Scotland, Charles lacked the economic, political and moral resources to deal with it ruthlessly. On the other hand, he had manoeuvred himself into a position which offered little or no room for compromise. How had the situation come about of which one consequence would be the turning of the King and the gentleman into generals?

In 1633 the aged and very distinguished ex-diplomat, Sir Henry

Wotton wrote, 'We know not what a rebel is; what a plotter against the commonwealth, nor what that is which grammarians call treason; the names themselves are antiquated with the things.'[2] As Provost of Eton the cultured sixty-five-year-old was no longer at the centre of affairs, a fact which may add even more weight to his verdict. In the mid-1630s it seemed to many people that the King's personal rule was working. The country was at peace, local administrative reform, though burdensome to the magistrates, was grappling with such ancient problems as vagrancy and care of the parish poor, trade was buoyant and there had been a run of good harvests. The liturgical and financial implications of the re-ordering of parish churches were only slowly becoming apparent and the majority of the King's subjects were, in any case, prepared to do no more than grumble in the tavern and the marketplace. Such was the general impression in the country at large.

Within the court this lack of active discontent was, inevitably, magnified into a chorus of popular acclaim for the King and his golden vision of a happy and harmonious realm, a 'British Heaven'. *Coleum Britannicum* was, indeed, the title of a masque presented in 1634 which drew on ancient Roman and national legends.

> A curtain flew up at the very opening revealing 'the ruins of some great city of the ancient Romans or civilised Britons. An anti-masque of Picts, Scots and Irish, who performed a grave Pyrrhic dance, was banished by the apparition of a vast mountain on which the three kingdoms 'all richly attired in regal habits' and the masquers, including the king, were discovered as British Worthies 'attired like ancient heroes' with their flanking torch-bearers 'apparelled after the old *British* fashion'.[3]

Charles, unable by now to believe anything other than what he wanted to believe, was impatient to accomplish that truly united empire which had been the Stuart dream ever since the conjoining of the crowns. This meant imposing Englishness on the Scots and the Irish. Not surprisingly they resented this.

It was part of the King's tragedy that, either by accident or design, there were no politicians among the small group of advisers to whom he actually listened. After Buckingham's death he never had at his right hand the kind of shrewd manipulator who might have imparted to him something of the art of survival. He had his coterie of sophisticated friends – Toby Matthew, George Conn, Endymion Porter, et al. – among whom the Queen was the chief. With them he freely discussed affairs of state, knowing that they would agree with him and share his attitudes. He had councillors and government officers but the only ones he took fully into his confidence were the members of an inner circle whom he could rely on to carry out his will. In effect, that meant men of either too little or too great principle. The contrast is excellently pointed up by the men he trusted with the affairs of Ireland and Scotland.

Thomas Wentworth, who became Lord Deputy of Ireland in 1632 at the age of thirty-nine, was a hard Yorkshireman whose unyielding nature was not made more amenable by frequent attacks of gout. His constitutional principles were as strong and sharp-edged as well-honed steel. 'The authority of a king,' he once announced, 'is the keystone which closcth up the arch of order and government, which contains each part in due relation to the whole and which, once shaken, infirmed, all the frame falls together into a confused heap of foundation and battlement of strength and beauty.'[4] Wentworth was a narrow-minded patriot, not so much attached to the King as devoted to efficient, effective government and, like Laud, he was a man with a personal agenda, who forced his way into royal service to achieve the things he believed in. His objectives in secular government paralleled what the archbishop was striving for in matters ecclesiastical. In their correspondence they even coined a term – 'Thorough' – to describe the uncompromising style of government they advocated. It was inevitable that they should be allies and that the names Laud and Strafford (Wentworth became Earl of Strafford in 1640) should become joined together in the parliamentarian mantra of hatred.

Charles had no more personal affection for Wentworth than he had for Laud. The blunt Yorkshireman was as hard on government corruption and waste as he was on potential stirrers of sedition. He had begun his political life among the ranks of royal critics and it was many years before the King felt that he could trust him completely. But Charles recognised in Wentworth a man strong enough to enforce the royal edict in the wilder and more remote parts of his realm. With servants like Laud and Wentworth the King could stay aloof from the sordid business of contesting with 'fanatics' and 'barbarians'. He could keep his hands clean and even persuade himself that the iconic nature of monarchy demanded it.

Amidst the Roman Catholic natives of Ireland and the Puritan settlers Wentworth was very much at the sharp end of the Stuart reform movement. He applied even-handed justice and won few friends in the process. He induced the Dublin government to vote generous supplies. In return he set in train valuable economic and judicial reforms, dealing firmly with Irish Sea pirates and introducing new crops such as flax, which gave rise to the Northern Ireland linen industry. But there was no concealing the government's Anglicising intentions, nor did the Lord Deputy bother to conceal them. If Presbyterially inclined Scottish settlers co-operated with Wentworth it was only because they feared the majority population. As for them, spurred on by their priests, they clung obstinately to their ancient faith. Such stubbornness only made the King's representative more determined. 'I plainly see that so long as this kingdom continues popish, they are not a people for the crown of England to be confident of; whereas if they were not still distempered by the infusion of these friars and Jesuits, I am of belief they would be as good and loyal to their king as any other subjects.'[5] The principle which Charles and his deputy were applying was the one which applied throughout most of Europe and which was regarded as a sensible one for resolving Reformation discord within states: *cuius regio, eius religio*. This had, theoretically, settled the matter within most states of the Holy Roman Empire and was the basis on which Louis XIII, with the blessing of James I, had sought to bring his Huguenot subjects to heel. If Charles failed to grasp that many people had higher loyalties than those to their sovereign he was not alone among the princes of western Christendom in his self-deception.

History proved the 'Irish Problem' to be intractable and it is inconceivable that even with enlightened policies uncharacteristic of the seventeenth century the country could have been moved peacefully towards meaningful union with the rest of Britain, but the behaviour of Charles I towards those whom he held in contempt ensured that reaction would be swift as soon as the strong hand of Wentworth was removed. Two royal traits, in particular, gave unnecessary aggravation and provide insights into just how the King compounded his own difficulties: he loathed parliaments and he could not keep his word. Wentworth, who believed in the Tudor practice of creating and working with a biddable popular assembly, wanted to keep the Dublin legislature in being. Charles, who regarded it as only a necessary evil for the raising of revenue, insisted on its dissolution in 1635 as soon as it had served its purpose. The compliance of the Dublin members over taxation had been secured by the promise of further sessions to deal with their grievances, a ploy which English parliamentarians had long since learned to recognise. In carrying out his master's policy Wentworth was obliged to be both forthright and devious. What particularly infuriated landowners in both communities was Crown impropriation of property. Charles wanted land which could either be sold to new settlers or used to bolster the authority of the bishops and their independence against lay interference. Wentworth had his officials probe title deeds and rake up ancient laws in order to provide the King with the necessary leverage.

Seven years later, after Strafford's death, Charles wrote to James Hamilton, 'the failing to one friend hath, indeed, gone very near me; wherefore I am resolved that no consideration whatsoever shall ever make me do the like.'[6] Wentworth was not a 'friend' in the same sense as the marquis. Hamilton had been many years at court and, as we have seen, was one of the King's sophisticated intimates. Charles always treated him affectionately and he was one of those who scandalised court-watchers by his accumulation of valuable monopolies. James Hamilton was a pleasure-loving and impulsive young man with no depth of character. Charles decided he was just the person to be his commissioner to Scotland.

Since leaving the land of his birth at the age of three and a half Charles had visited it once. That was for his coronation in 1633 and the expedition did nothing to endear the 'North Britons' to a distant, foreign king. James I, who understood well the Scottish power blocs, got his own way – principally over bishops – by playing off the nobles against the ministers of the Kirk. Charles I, who did not understand the political situation in Scotland, managed to unite the leaders of Church and state against him. As in Ireland, he began with an attempted land grab. By an Act of Revocation he reclaimed all former ecclesiastical property which had been alienated by his father and grandfather. Since most of the wealthier families had profited from the post-Reformation re-allocation of Church land much of which had been parcelled and re-parcelled, sold, resold and let out on tenancy, the Act was as impracticable as it was unpopular. When the King sent the Earl of Nithsdale to Edinburgh to explain his intentions a mob fell upon the coach carrying his lordship's papers and personal effects as soon as it crossed the border, hacked it to pieces and killed the horses. After this Charles settled for a compromise and adopted his father's policy of letting sleeping dogs lie. He did not venture his royal person among his northern subjects until 1633. Then it was the turn of the Calvinist clergy to take offence. Members of the royal train literally turned up their noses at the grubby capital and its 'sluttish', 'nasty' people. At the coronation service and other occasions of communal worship the Scots were horrified to see that Laud and his associates had set up richly decked altars, around which they flounced and genuflected in 'popish' garb, and when the archbishop preached on the benefits of uniformity and the use of reverent ceremonies their worst fears were realised.

Yet there was no uproar, no organised protest. On the surface everything was quiet – as it was in England and Ireland. Until the summer of 1637. That was when the plaster began to fall from the walls of Stuart autocracy, revealing the damp patches and structural defects beneath. Oblivious to the mounting grievances his subjects were experiencing, the King proceeded with his plans to create, from three diverse nations, one people, one Church under one Crown. He had set the Scottish bishops to work to produce a service book for use north of the border. When it was delivered in 1637 it was seen to be little different from the Book of Common Prayer. Laud approved it and Charles by proclamation ordered its use throughout Scotland. The reaction has become a major part of Scottish folklore: the riot in St Giles' Church when stools, sticks and stones were hurled at the minister; the street disturbances, the petitions; the Bishop of Brechin obliged to lead worship with a brace of pistols on the prayer desk; and the Covenant.

When the people of Edinburgh queued up on 28 February and 1 March 1638 to sign a document pledging themselves to resist, not just an alien form of worship, but government by decree, the news winged its way throughout the kingdom. The Prayer Book controversy coincided with the ship money trial and signalled to all that resistance to unpopular government measures was possible. In law-abiding Somerset, where a hundred and fifty parishes had mutely accepted altar rails, the people of Beckington rioted over the issue. The citizenry of Yeovil assailed the court house when a local brewer was prosecuted by one of the King's friends; at St Cuthbert's, Wells, the parishioners threw out a clerk imposed upon them by their Laudian bishop and throughout the county the archbishop was made the butt of vulgar jokes.[7]

Charles was unaware of these stirrings but he was very aware of the Scottish situation and he was seen to be visibly shaken. Vigorously he asserted that he would be obeyed, that the Covenant must be withdrawn, that to yield would mean that he ruled by consent of the people and not by the will of God. Then, fresh news arrived that all classes of people in Scotland were united and determined. Charles faced the astonishing reality that he might have to use armed force to crush a rebellion. That was when he hit upon the idea of sending Hamilton to Edinburgh to reach an accommodation.

Hamilton was no Wentworth nor did he have an army at his back. He was confronted by threatening and suspicious delegates who demanded a complete royal climbdown while being urged at the same time to firmness by messages from the King. He was alarmed – both by the total irreconcilability of the two positions and by the threat to his own standing in the country where he had considerable property. For five months he shuttled back and forth between the two capitals but all his feeble efforts at diplomacy achieved was to convince the Covenanters of the weakness of the King's position. In November Hamilton presided over a newly convened assembly. He was quite unable to control it and when the members launched an attack on episcopy he declared it dissolved. The representatives simply ignored him and went on to pass measures such as the re-establishment of Presbyterianism and the removal of bishops, which effectively undid all that James I had achieved. Charles could not avoid taking up the gage. He gathered together a ramshackle army and marched at its head to the border.

The King turned to Wentworth for advice and from him he received counsel quite contrary to Hamilton's whingeing despair. From his perspective of success in dealing with a subject people the Irish deputy advocated harsh measures. Charles should deal firmly with the Scots and he would send £2000 for the war chest. Although he could not in time muster and transport a military force to invade Scotland, he would gather such a force at a suitable embarkation point as a bluff which would distract the Covenanters. Wentworth shrewdly advised that Charles was not ready for armed confrontation with the rebels; the best he could hope for was to frighten them into negotiation. This would give the King time to raise and train an efficient army. He went on to suggest that with troublemakers around like Hampden who, as he notoriously opined to Laud, deserved to be 'whipped into his right senses', there should be a standing royal army. Without such a national guard Charles would never be master in his own house. Whether the King followed Wentworth's advice about the Scottish campaign or was simply the victim of events, the first Bishops' War ended without a shot being fired. Hamilton led a small contingent which failed to invest Aberdeen and Leith and hurried to the royal camp where he besought the King to agree terms. The Covenanters were no more intent on armed confrontation and met with Charles at Berwick in June 1639 to sign a treaty putting an end to hostilities and submitting points of dispute to a new Scottish parliament and Kirk assembly.

Charles's experience of Parliament did not encourage him to feel any confidence about the provisions of the Berwick treaty. His apprehension was fully justified. When the results of the Scottish deliberations were reported to him he raged against their 'insolency'. The Scots had reinforced all their previous claims, formally banished episcopacy, obliged all their countrymen to sign the Covenant and set up machinery for the levying of taxes and the administration of the nation. It was virtual independence. By no means all North Britons shared these extreme aspirations but the radicals were far more vociferous. Preachers thundered against the popish English king, there were outbreaks of iconoclasm and numerous public demonstrations.

Charles was in no doubt that he had to restore his authority, 'whereupon depends not only the keeping of this unhappy kingdom, but both the other two, who will not fail to bestir themselves, when they see such beggarly snakes dare put out their horns; besides (that which a generous prince should prize most) the hazard of his reputation all Europe over.'[8] The object was clear, less so the means. His treasury had, with difficulty, coped with ten years of peace; there simply was not enough money for a sufficient demonstration of military might to overawe the rebels. He retained Hamilton in Edinburgh as an intelligence gatherer and he sent secretly for Wentworth to return from Dublin, not 'openly at my summons but pretend some other occasion of business'. The two men now came to symbolise the dual elements of policy that Charles was henceforth to follow: forthrightness and deviousness. The King now, and apparently quite suddenly, identified the irascible Yorkshireman as his saviour. As a delicate plant requires a stake, so Charles always needed someone beside him to rely on and in the new situation the Queen could not fulfil this function. Wentworth was firm and wise in council and commanded valuable resources in Ireland. He was the man to be the public face of the monarchy, to confront opposition and firmly enunciate policy. But Hamilton was not abandoned, despite his proven ineffectiveness. His task was to insinuate himself into the counsels of the Scots and deploy all the arts of subterfuge – false promises, misinformation and bribery – to undermine the rebels' cause. Such men can never be fully trusted even by their employers and Hamilton was soon playing the role of double agent.

Both these alter egos ultimately shared the King's fate and it was fitting that they should do so. Charles's enemies loathed both his assertion of autocratic power and his duplicity. In the end it was the latter that brought about his downfall. Throughout the 1630s and 40s, as his problems multiplied and he was obliged to enter into various agreements, Charles demonstrated over and again that he could not be trusted. His PR experts presented an image of the King as the epitome of chivalric virtues, among which honour bore the palm. Inigo Jones said of him, he 'transcends as far common men as they are above beasts, he truly being the prototype to all the kingdoms under his monarchy of religion, justice and all the virtues joined together'.[9] Charles *did* possess many admirable qualities and sustained them through his adamantine self-control and sense of duty. The serious flaw of his dishonesty, therefore, needs explanation.

He was virtually incapable of discerning the real opinions, convictions and apprehensions of those who opposed him largely because he closed his mind to them. His own shyness and diffidence prevented him entering into any dialogue that was likely to prove confrontational. Sir Philip Warwick identified the difference between the way Charles debated with friends but kept at a distance disputants who wished to raise matters of substance.

His way of arguing was very civil and patient; for he seldom contradicted another by his authority, but by his reason. Nor did he by any petulant dislike quash another's argument and he offered his exception by this civil introduction, 'By your favour, Sir, I think otherwise on this or that ground.' Yet he would discountenance any bold or forward address to him. And in suits or discourses of business he would give way to none abruptly to enter into them but looked that the greatest persons should in affairs of this nature address to him by his proper ministry or by some solemn desire of speaking to him in their own persons.[10]

Public figures then, as now, were bombarded with advice. Charles's way of dealing with it was to isolate himself from it. Important decisions were arrived at in one of two ways: they were left to a very small band of trusted deputies or they emerged, like Anadyomene, from the waves of the King's unconscious. Charles's later considered advice to his heir was, 'Never repose so much upon any man's single counsel, fidelity and discretion in managing affairs of the first magnitude, as to create in yourself or others a diffidence of your own judgement, which is likely always to be more constant and impartial to your crown and kingdom than any man's.'[11] It was part of a king's dignity that he be seen to be his own man. It followed that it was undignified to change his mind or even to appear hesitant. Thus diffidence led to dogmatism. Thus wrong decisions once made were followed through regardless.

The myth that the King was of a different order of being to other mortals was an invaluable brace to Charles's character defects. It absolved him from the need to explain his decisions to anyone. Charles made clear to his first parliament that it was no part of their responsibility to question his actions or call him to account and he later tried to throw the same blanket of non-responsibility over some of his ministers. Total self-containment is too much of a strain for most people and Charles always had to have someone to whom he could unburden himself, in whose private presence he could emerge from his protective shell, weep, rage and share his hopes and fears. The only person who completely filled this role after 1628 was Henrietta Maria. She played an increasingly prominent part as the crisis grew more grave – offering advice, raising money at home and abroad, liaising with foreign courts and, in every way open to her, shoring up her husband's confidence. But she understood the English even less than Charles and she understood the Scots and the Irish not at all. When she urged Catholic gentlemen to stand firm for the King or negotiated with the Pope for mercenaries or brought in a boatload of weapons from the continent, the adverse publicity outweighed any good she did for the royalist cause. All her instincts were focused on the preservation of her family and their position and she did not shrink from urging Charles to use whatever deceptions and lies might be necessary for his survival.

Charles was far from being a cynic who considered dishonesty a conventional tool of government. He did question his conscience. He agonised, for example, over war with the Scots and over his desertion of Strafford. The results of such inner debate were far from consistent but there was always one prior claim, one dominant consideration to which Charles submitted. When he asked Juxon's advice about making a false promise to the Scots to introduce Presbyterianism he wrote,

> The duty of my oath is herein chiefly to be considered; I flattering myself that this way I may better comply with it, than being constant to a flat denial, considering how unable I am by force to obtain that which this way there wants not probability to recover.[12]

At his coronation Charles had sworn to uphold the Church and Commonwealth. Then, and on every anniversary of his accession, he and such of his subjects as were loyal to the Prayer Book had besought God, 'Give us grace seriously to lay to heart the great dangers we are in by our unhappy divisions. Take away all hatred and prejudice and whatsoever else may hinder us from godly union and concord.' Charles was, by divine appointment, the focus of national unity. That was his prime responsibility to God and his people. He would risk anything, do anything, say anything to keep to the spirit of his oath. This was the 'higher honesty' that excused what other men regarded as lies and deceit.

It was Wentworth, now unofficial chief counsellor, who, in the autumn of 1639 devised the main stratagems for dealing with the Scottish crisis. He would convene a Dublin parliament which, by voting supply, would send a signal to all the King's loyal subjects. He would raise an Irish army. The members of the Council would personally contribute to a war fund and encourage corporate bodies such as the City to follow suit – and an English parliament was to be called. It was an expedient Charles accepted with the greatest reluctance. Sir Francis Windebank, one of the King's conciliar inner table, indicated what was expected of the assembly. His Majesty, he said, summoned it,

> so that he might leave his people without excuse and have wherewithal

to justify himself to God and the world that in his own inclination he desired the old way.

But the councillor added a stern warning:

> if his people should not cheerfully, according to their duties, meet him in that, especially in this exigent where his kingdoms and person are in apparent danger, the world might see he is forced, contrary to his own inclination, to use extraordinary means, rather than by the peevishness of some few factious spirits to suffer his state and government to be lost.[13]

Since Charles began with this attitude the Short Parliament was undermined before it started. It was opened on 13 April 1640 and dissolved on 5 May 1640 and its peremptory dismissal was one of the King's major blunders. Gentlemen and burgesses who had campaigned for weeks, gone through the electoral process, travelled to London, leaving their home affairs in the hands of others, obtained lodgings in the capital and come together to debate the burning issues of the day felt affronted at being sent home so contemptuously. It was the King's decision entirely: both Strafford and Hamilton were among those counselling patience. All that Charles could see was a re-run of earlier assemblies which became deadlocked because the government asked for supply before discussion of grievances, and Parliament insisted on discussion of grievances before voting supply. Strafford won over the Upper Chamber and proposed some minor concessions which might have induced the Commons to grant him at least some of the money he needed for the campaign. At the last moment Charles decided to reject this compromise. To yield would be to demonstrate weakness: if he could not command the English Parliament how could he bring the Scottish one to heel?

Reaction throughout the country was immediate. In and around the capital: Laud fled Lambeth Palace on the approach of a 2000-strong, stone-throwing mob; hundreds more citizens gathered angrily at St George's Fields; placards and pamphlets circulated freely; someone scratched insults on a window at Whitehall, which the King smashed in person. Such behaviour, which served to confirm Charles's opinion that those who opposed him were an ignorant, boorish rabble, set the atmosphere in which the Council's panic-stricken measures of the summer must be seen. In the desperate quest for money and victory over the Scots they set off a frenzy of tax collecting, confiscated bullion in the Tower mint, hijacked a shipload of pepper at the docks, proposed Spanish matches for the royal children, contemplated debasing the coinage and mustered troops in the North and the Midlands. And, fatally, a patent licensing Strafford to raise an Irish army authorised him to employ it in 'any of the king's dominions, with power to suppress rebellion or commotions within any of the three kingdoms'.[14]

The Scots did not wait for Charles to sort out his problems. They had for months been in contact with sympathisers in London and, on 20 August, their army crossed the border. They swept aside a force sent to intercept them and when news of this English defeat reached London people actually celebrated. For the first time ever an invasion of England was welcomed by a substantial part of the population. Within days the Scots were in Newcastle. Militarily Charles and Strafford, with their dispirited and dwindling army, could do nothing. They had already received the petition for a recall of Parliament. Humiliated, the King returned to London to face it.

No parliament had ever met with such a lever on the executive. There was a foreign army on English soil that would not go away until it was paid and it could not be paid until Parliament had voted the necessary taxes, and Parliament would ensure that other matters preceded finance on the agenda. Charles knew that, for the time being, his plans for the realm had suffered a setback, but they had become so much a part of him that he could not abandon them. In all the wheeling and dealing that necessarily went on over the next two years there is no evidence that he ever contemplated genuine compromise, ever countenanced a permanent diminution of his prerogative power. He simply practised the arts of survival – patience, dissembling and intrigue. His immediate preoccupations were threefold: to maintain his dignity; to preserve, as far as he was able, those who were closest to his person and policies, and to help his disparate enemies to fall out among themselves.

In fact, there was very little the King could do to protect his chief advisers from an assembly bent on revenge. Strafford, Laud, a couple of Council members and a clutch of bishops were soon in prison. Windebank and others fled. About his family Charles was torn; he was anxious to see them reach safety but at the same time he could not bear to be parted from them. An opportunity soon presented itself to get some of them out of the country. The Prince of Orange proposed a marriage between his son, William, and the King's nine-year-old daughter, Mary. It was not a prestigious match but it would bring in much-needed money and it had the advantage of linking the Stuarts with an impeccably Protestant royal house. The wedding took place on 7 May 1641, a very subdued affair by the standards of seventeenth-century princely nuptials, and over-shadowed by more sombre events. In February 1642 Henrietta Maria and her daughter sailed for Holland. The intervening eleven months had been a period of high tragedy.

Five days after the wedding, which was marked by little more than conventional public rejoicing, an immense crowd, variously estimated at between 100,000 and 200,000 gathered on Tower Hill to cheer the execution of 'Black Tom' Wentworth. It was the culmination of six months of bizarre legal proceedings which had touched the King deeply and during which he had done everything he could think of to keep his minister from the block. He remem-bered Buckingham and the stratagems that had been necessary to save him. So, unfortunately, did John Pym, the 'king' of the Commons, and other veteran MPs who had been disappointed of their prey in 1626. Attacking the King through the minister was a venerable proceeding but Strafford was particularly obnoxious to the parliamentarians because he was a turncoat and an outspoken advocate of absolutism who had treated the people's representatives with contempt. His enemies threw the book at him – extortion, cruelty, provoking war between England and Scotland, advising the King to rule contrary to law, advocating the employment of an Irish army to overthrow the liberties of Englishmen; every charge was rolled up into one accusation of treason. Moreover, they were published in detail in order to stir up the London mob – an early example of trial by media.

In the end the Commons almost tripped over their trailing legal arguments. Wentworth defended himself strenuously and it became apparent that his impeachment for treason might fail. It was a desperate moment for Pym and his friends. Strafford at liberty would be a dangerous animal, capable of re-energising and resourcing the King's cause and turning the tables on his enemies. The answer was to proceed by Act of Attainder. If such a motion passed both Houses and received the royal assent the law could take its course. The proposal for a Bill of Attainder seems to have come from Sir Arthur Haselrig who was an intimate of Cromwell and St John and involved with them, around the same time, in setting forth the Root and Branch Bill.

Charles stood by the earl at every stage of the proceedings. He attended the impeachment hearings in the House of Lords. He tried to bribe Pym with the offer of the Chancellorship of the Exchequer. He offered £20,000 to the Lieutenant of the Tower to connive at Strafford's escape. When that official proved to be beyond corruption, Charles attempted a rescue bid by infiltrating some of his own guard among the yeoman warders. He was even party to a wild plot to bring down the remnants of the northern army to overawe the capital. At the very last he sent a personal letter to the House of Lords by the hand of his elder son begging for clemency. And when the Bill passed its final reading in the Upper House – by a meagre seven votes – the King could not bring himself to sign his assent for twenty-four hours and eventually did so with tears in his eyes. All this was more than he had ever done for any other human being. This was not because of a deep affection for the stricken servant. Charles felt an obligation because of his oath. He knew how much Strafford had done for him and he, in return, had given his word that he would not allow the earl to suffer in life, limb or estate. When he made the promise he doubtless believed that he could deliver it; it was inconceivable to him that Parliament could destroy a man because of his faithfulness to his sovereign. At the last he had failed Black Tom, who received the news of his condemnation by quoting Psalm 146: 'Put not your trust in princes.' Charles carried the shame of his desertion to his own dying day.

In the emotional confusion Charles now experienced his wife became the strong member of the partnership. He had been genuinely shocked by the rage displayed against Strafford by so many of his subjects. He might try to convince himself that the malcontents were a mere rabble set on by malicious and traitorous spirits but such rationalisation could not entirely banish self-doubt. But Henrietta Maria was unwavering in her determination that the King should regain the splendour and unquestioning obedience he had so long enjoyed. When he faltered she was at his side to comfort and, when necessary, cajole. 'Would'st thou have that which thou esteem'st the ornament of life, and live a coward in thine own esteem, letting "I dare not" wait upon "I would", like the poor cat in the adage?'[15]

In the summer of 1641 the Queen's mother, Marie de Medici, found the English situation too distressing to be endured and returned to the continent, where she died (in Cologne) a year later, an exile to the end. This left Henrietta Maria, so much her mother's daughter, free to devote all her energies to fighting her husband's cause.

In August Charles, having sent his family to Oatlands to be away from the London rabble, travelled north again to attend personally to the treaty and pay-off concluded with the Scots. That, at least, was the official reason for his journey. In fact, he was also furthering Hamilton's latest intrigue, which involved playing on Scottish divisions and promising to establish Presbyterianism in England in return for an army to help him restore his power. He fell over backwards to make himself agreeable to his subjects beyond the border even to the extent of joining in Presbyterian worship and enthusiastically singing metrical psalms. The Earl of Argyll (raised to a marquis by Charles) was not deceived. He accepted all the concessions the King made and yielded nothing in return. In fact, as Clarendon observed, all Charles did was 'make a perfect deed of gift' of Scotland to the Covenanters. He did manage to make his own soundings of the rivalries among the Scottish nobles but for the time being this availed him nothing.

Meanwhile the gilt was wearing off the parliamentary gingerbread. The rapid dismantling of the machinery of personal rule had given many members all that they desired. The fact that others wished to go further opened up divisions. Tension between the two houses came to a head at the end of the year when, frustrated by the opposition of the Lords to endorse their ever more draconian measures, the Commons asserted they were the representative body of the whole kingdom and their lordships but of particular persons and that when necessary the Upper Chamber might be bypassed.[16] The mood was also changing outside Westminster. When Members returned to their constituencies they discovered what all politicians discover eventually, that popularity is a fickle jade. People liked the programme of the radicals but they did not like paying for it. There is a familiar ring about the protest of one Yorkshirewoman: 'They promised us all should be well if my Lord Strafford's head were off, and since then there is nothing better, but I think we shall be undone by taxes.'[17] Others were concerned that the nation had exchanged a lion for a tiger. There were the beginnings of a Laudian/royalist

backlash. A 1641 pamphlet *The Protestants' Protestation* lambasted
by name Pym, Hampden, Haselrig, St John, Warwick and 'Saye the
Anabaptist' as 'perpetrators of a conspiracy against the king, crown
and posterity'. They had sold England to the Scots, destroyed free
speech and encouraged 'ignorant and licentious sectaries and
schismatics to stir up sedition, to bring in atheism, discountenance
all reverend ministers and take away the Prayer Book'.[18] From
Charles's point of view there were shreds of blue sky to be observed
through the dark clouds.

That was the moment when another and more terrible storm
broke. The Irish revolt of October 1641 opened up all the old fears
of popish plots, foreign invasions and the Queen's intrigues.
Protestant unity was reforged in the heat of anti-Catholic fury. The
opportunity of creating a royalist party from the more moderate
lords and commoners seemed to have passed. It was probably this
that precipitated Charles into his most headstrong and foolhardy
action to date.

The radicals, helped by reaction to the Irish revolt, rushed ever
onward in their work of constitutional revolution. On 1 December
they presented to Charles the Grand Remonstrance, a wide-ranging
document which had been months in the making. It listed scores of
complaints against the King's government, announced ecclesiastical
reforms and demanded new rights for Parliament such as military
control and approval of royal advisers. The Grand Remonstrance,
the distillation of years of discontent and anti-monarchical prejudice,
came close to achieving parliamentary self-destruction. The debates
were angry and on one occasion swords were brandished in the
Commons chamber. In its final form the measure passed by a mere
ten votes in the Lower House. There was no way that the King could
accept this document, which was only a skip and a jump away from
being a republican manifesto.

Charles sat brooding and indecisive at Whitehall weighing the
conflicting advice of his councillors and trying to judge the mood of
the people. Despite the Irish scare his return to his palace through
London had been almost a triumphal procession. That the radicals
had overreached themselves was clear. The questions were how and
when to expose their treasons to the best advantage. Charles's
agents had gathered information against five of the Commons
leaders which proved – or could be made to prove – that they had
colluded with the Scots to invade England. Charles nursed the idea

of poetic justice: how fitting that those who had condemned Strafford for allegedly projecting the use of an Irish army on English soil should go to the block for actually carrying out a similar crime. However, he delayed, torn between the advantages of confrontation and seeming compliance. Only at the beginning of January when a rumour reached him that Pym's vengeful eyes were now trained on the Queen did he send the Lords a notice of impeachment of Pym, Hampden, Haselrig, Denzil Holles and William Strode. The peers hesitated, unwilling to take sides in the conflict between King and Commons. Charles sent the sergeant-at-arms to arrest the accused but he returned to Whitehall empty-handed. Not for the first or last time the King had manoeuvred himself into a corner. His enemies had called his bluff and he had to respond. Even now, it was only with Henrietta Maria's taunts of cowardice ringing in his ears that, on the morning of 4 January, he took 500 pikemen to Westminster and burst into the Commons chamber to arrest the 'traitors' in person. The flight of the five birds before the trap could be sprung immediately became the stuff of democratic legend. At a stroke Charles had humiliated himself, put himself in the wrong and undermined what was left of his negotiating position.

For the next two months while uncertainty vibrated in the political air, rival mobs roamed the streets of the capital and individual parliamentarians weighed carefully where their interests lay, Charles temporised, delaying endorsement of parliamentary appointees to key positions, signing some Bills, stalling on others, now yielding to pressure, now resisting. But this seems to have been policy rather than indecision. The royalists had several irons in the fire. Catholic magnates were supplying the King with funds. Negotiators were attempting to raise a force in Ireland. Plans were afoot to seek aid abroad. When Henrietta Maria sailed for Holland with her daughter on 23 February, a fortune in jewels was concealed in her baggage. They were to be pawned to raise foreign troops and diplomatic influence. Charles accompanied his wife and daughter to Dover and their parting was tearful. Afterwards the King rode along the clifftop to watch the diminishing sail reach the horizon. Once again he was on his own. Brother, sister, mother, father, Buckingham, Strafford – so many whom he had loved and relied on were gone from him for ever. Now his wife and daughter had joined their ranks. Those about him in the ensuing days noted his melancholy and loneliness.

Yet there was work to be done. On 3 March, with his sons safely at his side, Charles left his troubled capital behind to make a leisurely progress northwards. Parliament was alarmed but had no right or means to stop him. Most worrying of all to the King's enemies was his complete refusal to include a Militia Bill among those measures which he reluctantly signed. Both parties realised how vital it was to control the shire levies and when Charles would not allow military authority to pass from the Crown to Parliament, Parliament took this power by passing an ordinance. It now rested with the Lords-Lieutenant and the muster masters to decide whom they would obey. If divided allegiance manifested itself in rival citizen armies England would have slithered down the final few yards of the muddy slope into the mire of civil war.

Whether or not it was wise for Charles to desert his capital, it was an action which was bitterly resented. In the light of later events the King was presumed to have deliberately distanced himself from Parliament in order to wage war upon the representatives of the people. It was a charge Charles, or someone writing in his name, felt the need to rebut:

> Who can blame me or any other for withdrawing ourselves from the daily baitings of the tumults, as not knowing whether their fury and discontent might not fly so high as to worry and tear those in pieces who as yet they but played with in their paws? God, who is my sole judge, is my witness in heaven that I never had any thoughts of going from my house in Whitehall if I could have had but any reasonable fair quarter. I was resolved to bear much and did so, but I did not think myself bound to prostitute the majesty of my place and person, the safety of my wife and children to those who are prone to insult most when they have objects and opportunity most capable of their rudeness and petulancy.[19]

And the writer claimed that the King's withdrawal was prompted by 'shame rather than fear'. Self-justification after the event must be treated with caution and we shall never be able to fathom the depths of Charles's thoughts and feelings when he made his dignified exit from London.

As he made his way first to York and then into the Midlands he was gratified and, probably, surprised by the support he received. Noblemen joined him with bands of retainers. Town and city corporations yielded up their plate for conversion into coin.

Alarmed now at the prospect opening up before them, the parliamentary leaders kept up the attempts at negotiation but Charles was no longer interested. He sensed, probably correctly, that if the King of England raised his standard and called upon loyal subjects to support him against the monstrous prospect of rebellion the response would be overwhelming. On 9 July he appointed the Earl of Lindsey as his Commander-in-Chief. On 22 August on a windswept Castle Hill at Nottingham, he unfurled his pennant while a herald read out a summons to all loyal Englishmen to muster for the defence of the realm.

> . . . his whole carriage was so tempestuous and his behaviour so insolent that the chairman found himself obliged to reprehend him and to tell him that, if he proceeded in the same manner, he would presently adjourn the committee and the next morning complain to the house of him.[20]

Clarendon's recollection of Cromwell the parliamentarian may have been coloured by the later experiences of both men but there is every reason to accept the essence of his pen portrait. The behaviour of which Clarendon complained was displayed in July 1641 during a debate on the thorny issue of fenland drainage, about which Cromwell had long felt strongly. Certain commoners of Huntingdonshire and the Isle of Ely had taken the law into their own hands by pulling up the fences with which Edward Montagu, Lord Mandeville, had enclosed certain areas of land, and the case had been referred to a Commons committee of which Cromwell was a member and Hyde the chairman. The Member for Cambridge vociferously took the part of the poor tenant and his language at times became distinctly unparliamentary. It was less than six months since he had offended colleagues by his intemperate words on the position of bishops. Clearly, he still had a chip on his shoulder about what he considered the misuse of authority and social position.

This unfashionable man from an unfashionable shire who was unschooled in the niceties of parliamentarian convention believed passionately in Parliament and its ability to put an end to what he considered as the abuse of royal power. Nothing indicated this more clearly than his enthusiasm for the Grand Remonstrance. He expressed impatience when debate on it was briefly postponed and

11. An allegory of the eleven years' personal rule. Charles I slays the
dragon of discord and offers Henrietta Maria a kingdom at peace.
Landscape with St George and the Dragon by Sir Peter Paul Rubens.

12. For royalists Cromwell was the barbarian who destroyed the golden age
by hacking down the royal tree with all its splendid fruits.
The Royall Oake of Brittayne – contemporary propaganda.

13. *Charles I with M. de St Antoine*
by Sir Anthony Van Dyck.

OLIVARIVS CROMWELL EXERCITVVM ANGLIÆ REIPVBLICÆ DVX GENERALIS LOCVM TENENS ET GVBERNATOR HIBERNIÆ OXONIENSIS ACADEMIÆ CANCELLARIV

Cernimus hic ornat Caput admirabile Mundo: Regibus Hic Fratres Populis Pater: Hostis, inditam Nobilis: Ille Imet quám Solum Numinis armis Quæ dubiat: Sicut hoc si progate hoc e Viel

14. *Oliver Cromwell with London in the Background*
Artist unknown.

15. The ultimate flattery. Nothing could more graphically display the distance between the court and ordinary mortals. Buckingham is displayed as the messenger of the gods presenting the liberal arts to the royal deities while crudity and barbarism are driven from the land.
Apollo and Diana receive the Homage of the Liberal Arts by Gerrit van Honthorst.

16. Cromwell, by contrast, was in royalist eyes the arch-patron of all the crude and barbarous factions besetting the realm.
O. Cromwell, the Chief Head of the Fanaticks – contemporary propaganda.

17. Fairfax, a Yorkshire gentleman – 'the man most
beloved by the rebels in the North' – became the
Commander-in-Chief of the Parliamentary forces.
Thomas, Baron Fairfax
Artist unknown.

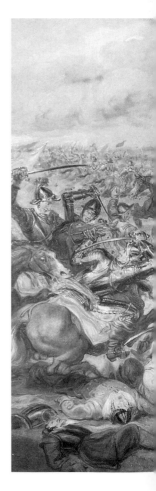

19. At the battle of Marston Moor Cromwell first came to
prominence as a brave and brilliant field commander.
Marston Moor by James Ward.

18. The country split into two snarling factions – contemporary cartoon.

20. The event which stunned Europe. The execution of the King sent a
shock wave throughout the continent as well as Britain. Pictorial representations
of it were rapidly being circulated from royalist cells in the Low Countries.
Cromwell and Fairfax shared the blame for the tragedy.

21. *The Entombment of Christ* by Titian (see caption to plate 1).

afterwards he confided to Lord Falkland that if the measure had failed he would immediately have emigrated. The Member for Cambridge, an earnest, unsophisticated, outspoken man, provoked indulgent laughter among the more 'knowing' who understood the subtleties and compromises of English politics – a laughter which gradually gave way to a mixture of irritation and grudging respect. Few members of the Lower House were more industrious. The glimpses afforded of his activities in the Commons Journal and private chronicles show us a busy Member interesting himself in enclosures, the removal of prisoners from London in time of plague, appointments to the army in Ireland, paying off the Scottish army, the King's 1641 visit to Edinburgh (of which he strongly disapproved), business matters to be referred from the Westminster to the Dublin Parliament and the disarming of recusants. His interest in ecclesiastical matters continued when he spoke against the Prayer Book and for the expulsion of bishops from the House of Lords. He moved a Commons motion urging the guardianship of the Prince of Wales to be vested in the safe hands of the Lords Saye and Bedford. Cromwell supported the radical managers in both chambers who were working for godly reformation but he was just as often a voice in the wilderness, and his rough-and-ready advocacy which sometimes did more harm than good to a measure made his usefulness to the anti-court party at best questionable.

What did make an impression on Oliver's colleagues was his forcefulness and clarity of vision in military matters. From early on in the life of the Parliament he advocated the need for a loyal army to protect English liberties. He showed concern for the speedy return of the Scottish army across their own border, watched events in Ireland carefully and expressed concern that the King might have military designs in Scotland. Before many of his colleagues were prepared to think the unthinkable, Cromwell's mind was focusing on the real possibility of armed struggle. In May we can detect the first glimmer of the idea which would eventually blaze forth as the New Model Army. Cromwell urged the creation of a Bond of Association whereby lords and gentlemen would provide for the armed defence of Parliament and Protestantism. Six months later he tried to deprive King Charles of the military means for mischief. At the beginning of the year Charles had appointed the Earl of Essex to his Council and showed great favour to him in the hope of winning him over to the royalist cause. Essex was a firm opponent of the court but the King, accustomed since childhood to buying loyalty, failed to grasp the fact that the earl was a man of principle. In July he named Essex Commander-in-Chief of the forces south of the Trent during his absence in the North. On 7 November it was Cromwell who moved a motion, 'that we should desire the Lords that an ordinance of parliament might pass to give the Earl of Essex power to assemble at all times the trained bands of the kingdom on this side Trent for the defence thereof till further order were taken by parliament.' This was the first suggestion that the supreme authority in military matters should be removed from the King to Parliament. The Upper House was not ready to endorse so revolutionary a proposal and it was another eight months before Essex was appointed General of the parliamentary forces.

By then the dogs of war were straining at their leashes and could scarcely be restrained – the more so since Cromwell had further loosened their collars. In January 1642, within days of the King's attempts to arrest the five members, he rose to his feet in the Commons to urge the creation of a committee which would organise the country's defence. It was this committee whose Militia Ordinance finally challenged the Crown's control of the local levies and so forced a showdown.[21]

Cromwell was one of the few men in the crisis ready to turn from words to resolute action. While Charles and the leaders of the opposition felt their way like blind men from obstacle to obstacle until the pit yawned at their feet, he moved decisively within his own limited sphere of responsibility. Even before the general militia ordinance was issued he had spent £100 of his own money to buy arms for the Cambridgeshire train bands and, on 15 July 1642, he obtained permission to raise and equip two companies of volunteers in Cambridge. At the same time he was busy on the parliamentary committee overseeing the reinforcing of Irish garrisons. As well as his personal contribution to the defence of Ireland he gave another £500 for military organisation in England as a signal of how urgent it was to put the nation in a state of military preparedness. Within days he was in Cambridge mustering recruits, training them and nerving them for action, as his grandfather had done with the Huntingdonshire levies in '88. It was not long before he and his men saw action.

In his native territory, as in the rest of the country all was confusion during the first weeks of actual warfare. Authorities did not know whether to muster troops for King or for Parliament. Most decisions rested on local allegiances and in Cambridgeshire and Huntingdonshire these could not have been more divided. Parliament appointed Lord Mandeville (who, in November, succeeded to the earldom of Manchester) Lord-Lieutenant, and he set about the military organisation. Meanwhile his brother, Sidney Montagu, at Hinchingbrooke, refused to swear allegiance to Parliament, was arrested in his house and taken to the Tower. The Cromwells were just as split. Sir Oliver sent money to the King and urged his sons to fly to arms in the royalist cause. His eldest, Henry, wasted no time; he was soon on the road to Cambridge with a contingent of fifty men. Cambridge was split between town and gown; burgesses for Parliament, masters and fellows for the King. Charles had asked for contributions from the colleges and these were collecting together chests of plate for despatch to the royalist headquarters at York. Henry Cromwell and his men had come as part of a diversionary tactic to prevent the enemy getting hold of the university's treasures. But Henry's cousin was too quick for him. Aided by his brother-in-law, Valentine Walton, he seized the magazine at Cambridge Castle, then with a brave show of force marched to King's College and confiscated plate to the value of £20,000 for the parliamentary cause. When a royal troop approached the town to collect the Cambridge contribution they were ambushed and seen off.

Oliver rode on to Huntingdon to raise his own troop. This was no straightforward matter. Only three weeks before, Valentine Walton, charged by Parliament with raising 200 men, had managed to recruit a mere handful. The major landowners were either for the King or unwilling to commit themselves either way. A colleague of Walton's wrote to Lord Mandeville, 'I know no way at this present to fetch up the spirit of our freeholders but either to appear in your person or send someone among them whereby they may receive encouragement.'[22] That 'someone' was Oliver Cromwell. This was the first test of his leadership and it gives us a fair glimpse of just why men followed him. He gathered a large group of young men in the market square – men whose families he had known for years – and he spoke to them plainly, almost brutally. He would trouble them with no high-flown nonsense about fighting for 'King and Parliament' against Charles's evil advisers – the official line of the opposition. Let there be no mistake; as things stood they were going to war with their sovereign. If the King persisted in taking arms against his people and if Cromwell encountered him in battle he would 'discharge his pistol at him as at any other person'.[23] No one who followed Captain Cromwell's colours could claim that he had been enlisted under false pretences.

Oliver went on to face what may well have been a more difficult meeting. He rode to Ramsey to confront his uncle. They had a long and probably emotional conversation. Oliver tried to persuade the seventy-nine-year-old ex-courtier to come over to the parliamentary cause and warned him of the consequences for himself and his family once the King had been brought to a settlement, but the aged knight was not prepared to break the habits of a lifetime. The conference ended with Oliver confiscating all his uncle's arms and armour plus a 'contribution' of plate. The following year the two men met again 'on the bridge at Ramsey'. This was probably in the wake of a parliamentary ordinance for the sequestration of delinquents' estates and marks a final attempt by Colonel Cromwell, as he now was, to save the head of the family from further distress. He looked to his uncle for supplies for his newly raised regiment and provided the old man with the opportunity to demonstrate support for the 'people's cause'. Once again Sir Oliver was adamant. The difference was that by now the supplicant was one of the leading men in the country with a sizeable military contingent at his back. He threatened to bombard Ramsey if his relative did not see reason and with this persuasion Sir Oliver provided his nephew with forty saddle horses for his cavalry. But Sir Oliver never swerved from his allegiance to King Charles – stubbornness was, perhaps, a family trait. As a result his lands *were* sequestered. But not for long – in 1648 Oliver got the order lifted.

The first major engagement of the Civil War, at Edgehill, in October was valuable only for what the participants learned or failed to learn from it. For Cromwell it was a particularly educative experience. Some of the officers had seen service abroad but the majority were novices and no one knew what it would feel like trying to kill fellow Englishmen on English soil. The battle plans were simple: King Charles was heading for London; the Earl of Essex intended to stop him. The result was a 'draw' because, although Charles's army was not cut off from the capital it was too demoralised to press on and had to divert to Oxford to recoup. The carnage and suffering during the battle and the bitter night which followed made emotional inroads on all the commanders. The following day neither side had the heart to renew the conflict and both drifted away from the corpse-littered ground dazed and subdued.

Cromwell, it seems, was an exception. Bringing his troop across country from Cambridge, he had arrived late and it is not clear what part he took in the fighting but he was able coolly to appraise what he saw. He observed the frightening dash of the royalist cavalry led by Prince Rupert, son of Elizabeth of Bohemia. They were capable of scattering raw infantry but were too idiosyncratic to be as effective as they might have been in the overall tactics of a battle. They lacked the discipline for swift regrouping and tended to exhaust themselves following up a fleeing foe. As for the parliamentary soldiers they also wanted discipline and training if they were to stand firm against the awesome charge of mounted cavaliers. There was, Oliver realised, a social element in all this: the man on horseback represented the ruling class in the shires, the hunting man who was – literally – looked up to by his forelock-tugging tenantry. If Parliament's recruits were to overcome a built-in sense of inferiority they would need not only inspiring leadership and effective training, but a real conviction about their cause. Such was the burden of his conversation with John Hampden after the battle:

> Your troopers are most of them old, decayed serving men and tapsters and such kind of fellows; and their troopers are gentlemen's sons, younger sons and persons of quality. Do you think that the spirit of such base and mean fellows will be ever able to encounter gentlemen that have honour and courage and resolution in them . . . You must get men of a spirit that is likely to go on as far as gentlemen will go or you will be beaten still.[24]

During the following non-campaigning season Oliver was busy in his own country and only able to apply there the ideas and principles that were forming rapidly as his agile mind cross-referenced his religious beliefs, his social prejudices and his battlefield experience. In December Parliament set in hand the military and financial organisation of the territory under its command. They appointed committees for each county and banded counties into associations. Cromwell became one of the leaders of the Eastern Counties Association comprising Norfolk, Suffolk, Essex, Cambridge, the Isle of Ely and (after May 1643) Huntingdonshire. He made his headquarters at Cambridge and from there expanded his troop into a regiment. Now that the early months of confusion were past and East Anglia had been successfully claimed for Parliament, recruiting was easier. In his quest for the 'right kind' of soldiery Cromwell had a communication network ready to hand in the loosely interconnected separatist churches of the region. The evangelical subculture to which he had belonged for a dozen years provided exactly the raw material he was looking for: men who believed profoundly in the Old Testament God of Battles and were ready to fight and die for him. By September he had more than six hundred men under his command, the nucleus of what would become the New Model Army. These were, as he told his friend, St John, 'a lovely company . . . honest, sober Christians'.[25] Among them Cromwell was in his element. At last he had discovered the vocation for which God had prepared him when he marked him for his own.

To analyse Cromwell's greatness as a general, which has so often been done, in a sense misses the point. One might understand better the workings of an intricate watch by taking it to pieces but to appreciate the beauty of its smooth and accurate motion it is only necessary to observe it in action. Carrington wrote of him 'he loved his soldiers as his children'[26] and that emerges from his correspondence and from every description of his military activity. If Oliver had ever been known to have attended a performance of *Henry V* it might almost be possible to believe that he had modelled himself on Shakespeare's pious hero with the common touch. Like the idealised warrior-king, Cromwell appeared to his men as a firm disciplinarian who fined them for swearing, put them in the stocks for getting drunk and dismissed with dishonour any soldier who insulted a comrade, but also as a commander who would sit with them round the camp fire, share their jokes and not be offended by their bawdy songs. He preached to them with a rough eloquence, prayed with them and for them in rolling cadences of fervent supplication and was – in a way that Charles never was for his people – a link with the God who would vindicate their cause. His convictions became their convictions, and never for a moment did he doubt that his cause was the Lord's.

> O God, thy arm was here!
> And not to us, but to thy arm alone,
> Ascribe we all . . .

320

Come, go we in procession to the village;
And be it death proclaimed through our host
To boast of this or take that praise from God
Which is his only.[27]

Oliver loved his men and he loved his work. All his aggression, all his ebullience he poured into planning and executing his tactics. Many who saw him in the thick of battle saw a man intoxicated with excitement. 'He did laugh so excessively as if he had been drunk; his eyes sparkled with spirits,'[28] one of them reported. Such exuberant courage conveyed itself to the troops who followed him.

Commanding his soldiers was one thing; dealing patiently with the 'gentlemen in England now a-bed' was quite another. Like field officers in all ages he had to cope with politicians and their friends who relied on their troops to make sacrifices but indulged in the luxury of arguing among themselves and were dilatory in supplying the necessary support. Throughout the early part of 1643 divided counsels seriously hampered the deployment of men and Cromwell took the initiative of requesting the appointment of a commander who carried respect and authority. His recommendation was the Earl of Manchester. This generous suggestion is evidence of Oliver's tendency to look for the best in people. He had known Montagu for many years and clashed with him on more than one occasion, sometimes angrily. Moreover, Manchester represented the family who had displaced the Cromwells from their position in county society. On the other hand, Oliver respected the earl's sincerely held religious views: he was a convinced evangelical, Presbyterially inclined. He was also the man who stood at the pinnacle of the local social pyramid and commanded widespread allegiance. As such he was the obvious choice for someone who would be a focus of unity and Cromwell suppressed whatever reservations he had in recommending him. In response Manchester made him one of his four cavalry colonels.

While the war in the west was going badly, not helped by that other war – the faction war – at Westminster, Cromwell's most debilitating running battle was over finance. Most seventeenth-century wars, as Cromwell knew, were decided on the regular and efficient flow of funds. Lack of payment spawned a variety of ills – inadequate arms, looting, desertion, dispirited troops and mutiny. Colonel Cromwell could not raise and maintain an effective, well-disciplined fighting unit without the means to pay and equip his men. Over and again he had to appeal, badger and cajole Parliament and the money men of the Eastern Association for funds which were promised but not promptly delivered. He wrote, with some embarrassment to friends like St John and Thomas Barrington, to whom he could express himself with greater frankness than formal correspondence permitted.

Of all men I should not trouble you with money matters, did not the heavy necessities my troops are in, press me beyond measure. I am neglected exceedingly!

I am now ready for my march towards the enemy; who hath entrenched himself over against Hull, my Lord Newcastle having besieged the town. Many of my Lord Manchester's troops are come to me: very bad and mutinous, not to be confided in; they paid to a week almost; mine no ways provided for to support them, except by the poor sequestrations of the county of Hunt . . .

If [I] took pleasure to write to the House in bitterness, I have occasion. [Of] the £3,000 allotted to me, I cannot get the part of Norfolk nor Hertfordshire: it was gone before I had it. I have minded your service to forgetfulness of my own and soldiers' necessities. I desire not to seek myself; I have little money of my own to help my soldiers. My estate is little. I tell you, the business of Ireland and England hath had of me, in money, between eleven and twelve hundred pounds; therefore my private can do little to help the public. You have had my money: I hope in God I desire to venture my skin. So do mine. Lay weight upon their patience; but break it not. Think of that which may be a real help. I believe [£5,000 is due].

If you lay aside the thought of me and my letter, I expect no help. Pray for

Your true friend and servant,
OLIVER CROMWELL.

[P.S.] There is no care taken how to maintain that force of horse and foot raised and a-raising by my Lord Manchester. He hath not one able to put on [that business.] The force will fail if some help not. Weak counsels and weak actings undo all. [Send at once or come] or all will be lost, if God help not. Remember who tells you.[29]

This letter, written to St John in September, is a clear indication of those aspects of military command which soaked up huge amounts of Cromwell's time and energies and from which the excitements of battle must have come as something of a relief. Financial worries and personality clashes also go some way to explaining the impatience he showed when dealing with a recalcitrant canon of Ely and his own stubborn uncle.

Over and again, Cromwell raised with anyone who would listen the importance of attracting the right sort of men to the parliamentary forces and by 'right sort' he meant 'godly'. Oliver never lost sight of the fact that he was engaged in a holy war and he never lost his contempt for social barriers. God only divided humankind into two categories, the elect and the reprobate, and it was impossible to fight the Lord's battles with sons of darkness. His preference for 'plain russet-coated captains' over 'what you call gentlemen' has often been quoted. In the same letter, to the Suffolk committee, he referred contemptuously to a batch of recruits recently sent from Essex who were, in his view, worse than useless and asked them, by contrast to give their support to a Mr Ralph Margery.

> I understand Mr. Margery hath honest men who will follow him: if so, be pleased to make use of him. It much concerns your good to have conscientious men . . . I beseech you, give countenance to Mr. Margery. Help him in raising this troop; let him not want your favour in whatsoever is needful for promoting this work; and command your servant. If he can raise the horses from malignants, let him have your warrant; it will be of special service.[30]

Margery was a zealous young man and obviously a rough diamond after Cromwell's own heart. Within days he upset the Suffolk committee by commandeering horses from countrymen who were not, or claimed not to be, 'malignant'. Accordingly the committee declined to commission him. Oliver was furious and responded by commissioning Margery on his own authority. On the comfortable committee members Cromwell vented his sarcasm:

> If these men be accounted troublesome to the country, I shall be glad you would send them all to me. I'll bid them welcome. And when they have fought for you and endured some other difficulties of war which your honester men will hardly bear, I pray you then let them go for [i.e. consider them] honest men.[31]

323

It might seem that Cromwell the anti-establishmentarian was well on the way to becoming Cromwell the social revolutionary; that he was prepared, in pursuing the divine re-ordering of the nation's life, to hold all authority and convention in contempt. To reach this conclusion would be to underrate the pressures of the wartime situation. If he mistrusted the reactions and motives of 'what you call gentlemen' he had reason.

The tumultuous, if brief, career of John Hotham makes the point. He was a hot-headed, arrogant Scarborough gentleman who served the parliamentary cause in Yorkshire valiantly in the early stages of the war, but he was always a law unto himself and he responded badly to discipline. Added to this was the fact that there was a feud between his family and the Fairfaxes, who were the military leaders of the Northern Association. The loyalty of the Hothams was first and foremost to themselves and they were almost certainly in contact with the Queen when John was ordered in May 1643 to place himself under the command of Cromwell and Lord Grey to march northwards from Nottingham. This was too much for the young man's hubris. Cromwell, he believed, was nothing but a patron of low-born sectarians – and he was presuming to give orders to Hotham via a certain Colonel White who, before the war, had been a mere yeoman. The conceited young man proceeded to make a nuisance of himself. He allowed his men to plunder friend and foe alike and when taken to task responded that he thought the parliamentarians were supposed to be fighting for 'liberty'. Shortly afterwards he showed his respect for Cromwell by training two pieces of ordnance on him. Hotham was precisely the kind of arrogant young pup that Oliver loathed and for whom he could find no use in the army of the new order. He had the young man arrested and charged with misconduct and desertion in battle (for not coming to his superiors' aid when summoned). His behaviour would have been sufficient to ensure severe punishment but he put his own head on the block by escaping and vigorously intriguing with the enemy. From captured correspondence it transpired that he proposed to change allegiance in return for £20,000, a viscountcy for his father and a barony for himself. He was re-arrested, tried and beheaded in January 1645. Motives, ambitions, political principles, class and family loyalties and allegiances were mixed on both sides. Cromwell never for a moment underestimated the magnitude of what he and his colleagues were undertaking and was only prepared to put his trust in the pure-hearted.

Cromwell was now beginning to emerge as one of the granite strata in the parliamentary cause which became more and more exposed as softer rock was worn away by the difficulties of sustaining the war. Optimists on both sides had hoped for a quick victory. When this failed to materialise commanders found it difficult to keep their forces together and an increasing number of parliamentary leaders were swinging behind the policy of reaching a compromise agreement with Charles. But others knew that if the King was restored to power they could expect no mercy. Manchester was among those afflicted with despondency. 'If we beat the king ninety-six times,' he told Cromwell, 'he is king still and so will his posterity be after him. But if the king beat us once, we shall be all hanged and our posterity be made slaves.' This defeatist talk drew from the earl's cavalry commander the response, 'Then why did we take up arms in the first place? Let us hasten to make peace, however humiliating it may be.'[32] Oliver, who had entered the fray out of conviction and with his eyes wide open understood that boats had been decisively burned. There could be no stopping until the King was forced to a settlement he was powerless to abandon. Such a situation would be brought about by victory on the battlefield and not at the conference table.

That was why he reluctantly signed the Solemn League and Covenant. One of the last services performed by John Pym, who died at the end of 1643, was reaching an agreement with the Scots. His representatives had not exaggerated when they claimed, 'If ever a poor nation were upon the edge of a most desperate precipice . . . we are that nation.'[33] The Scots agreed to come to the aid of their friends by sending troops back across the border but the price demanded was the same as they had asked before: a unified, Presbyterian, church structure. Vane, who brokered the deal, managed to insert a get-out clause: the system to be imposed on the Church of England was to be 'according to the word of God and the example of the best reformed churches'. Despite the qualification the Solemn League and Covenant was not to the liking of men of Cromwell's religious stamp. He had come thus far to escape a straitjacket religious uniformity and he hesitated to sign, doubtless agonising long in prayer before reaching his decision. But the realities of the military situation were too compelling. Parliament desperately needed the 20,000 well-trained troops the Scots could provide.

Their appearance turned the tide of war in Parliament's favour and came close to destroying the parliamentary cause. The Battle of Marston Moor on 2 July 1644 was the only major engagement in which the allies fought side by side. In what was one of the bloodiest battles of the war some 5000 men were slain during two hours in the dwindling light of a summer's evening. There was nothing about the man-to-man hacking of flesh and bone that could be called glorious, but Cromwell and Rupert confronted each other as cavalry commanders and the parliamentary leader showed that he had learned his tactical lessons well: after chasing the royalists from the field Cromwell regrouped his men in order to attack the King's infantry in the rear. Charles's defeat at Marston Moor lost him the north of England but victory was almost as disastrous for the parliamentary army.

Manchester's contingent had recently been joined by Colonel Lawrence Crawford, a veteran of wars in Europe and in Ireland, and he was appointed the earl's second-in-command. That alone brought him into rivalry with Cromwell but personal animosity was soon underscored by religious differences, for Crawford was an ardent Presbyterian. The two colonels were already at daggers drawn before the battle but afterwards Crawford charged Cromwell with cowardice and Cromwell countercharged with accusations that his rival had disobeyed orders and had also dismissed a valuable officer on grounds of pure religious prejudice. Both combatants were men of fiery temper and when Manchester failed to reconcile them he accompanied them to London where the war committee patched up a truce between them. The Commons, at Oliver's request, even set up a committee to explore ways of enabling Presbyterians and Independents to work together harmoniously.

But this contretemps was more than just a private spat between two officers whose differences had become influenced by battle fatigue. What lay behind it was fear – fear of Cromwell and fear of the King. The nobles and gentlemen of the officer corps had come to realise that war had thrown up a dangerous phenomenon: a people's champion with a highly effective private army. Cromwell had at his back a corps of sectaries officered by men of humble birth whose loyalty to their commander was unquestioned. This coupling of religious enthusiasm and military might was potentially disastrous. If men like the Ironsides (the nickname had been given to Oliver at Marston Moor by Prince Rupert and the epithet, conveyed to

Cromwell's men, was, in itself, a recognition that a new force had appeared in the land) came to rule the roost after the war then social order could break down; anarchy and anabaptism (a catch-all term for any kind of peasant rabble) might be let loose. The sight of servants on horseback, wielding swords, was anathema to the traditional ruling class. Essex who, after a disastrous campaign in the South-West, was also vulnerable to parliamentary criticism, commented, 'Our posterity will say that to deliver them from the yoke of the King, we have subjected them to the yoke of the common people.'[34] The wildest rumours began to fly about. Cromwell, it was alleged, had been heard to say there would never be a good time in England till we had done with lords. He had made Ely into a 'little Amsterdam', a personal enclave where only his writ was law and where common soldiers abused the pulpits to promote their own weird heterodoxies. The Scots also turned against Cromwell after Marston Moor, though on rather more rational grounds: they had come to see the force of his opposition to Presbyterianism. By the autumn all the factions which felt threatened by the 'King of the Fens' had begun meeting in Essex's London house to plot the downfall of their *bête noire*.

Manchester and his friends were nervous of the King because, if the Cromwellian rabble were thwarted, then an accommodation with Charles would have to be found and if they were tarred with the radical brush then their position in the post-war order of things would be problematical in the extreme. But these were men of England's ruling class, conscious of their position in the established and eternal order of things, accustomed to wheeling and dealing with kings and dynastic rivals to maintain those political realities in which they all had a vested interest. Therefore, in the aftermath of Marston Moor, Manchester and Fairfax advocated accepting Presbyterianism and opening negotiations with Charles Stuart.

The immediate military result of all this was that Manchester became extremely lethargic. The last thing he wanted was a decisive battle. While Cromwell urged him to follow up his advantage and strike at the royalists in the South who were still demoralised, the major-general dawdled and dallied and hundreds of his men drifted back to their homes to harvest their crops. Not until 28 October did he come to an engagement with the enemy (the second Battle of Newbury) and then he bungled it so badly that the royalists were easily able to slip away to winter quarters. Within the month Cromwell laid a formal complaint before the Commons. He exposed the earl's 'continued backwardness to all action, his averseness to engagement or what tends thereto, his neglecting of opportunities and declining to take or pursue advantages upon the enemy, and this (in many particulars) contrary to commands received, and when there had been no impediment or other employment for his army'.[35]

Manchester, supported by Essex's faction, countered with a well-trained volley of damning accusations and was supported by the moderates in both Houses. But the Cromwell who was now under attack was not the inept MP of three years before. Battle honours crowded his brow and gave him a new stature in the lower chamber. He was too great an asset to be cast aside and those who believed that the war could be decisively won rallied to his support. For several days the supporters of Cromwell and Manchester grappled with each other using all the subtle techniques of seasoned cabalists, and the urgent practical objective of securing an enduring peace was threatened by messy clashes of personality and power rivalries. In the end it was the aristocrat generals who were outflanked – by the stratagem of the Self Denying Ordinance.

On 9 December, after what was described as 'a general silence for a good space of time', Lieutenant-General Cromwell rose in his Commons seat and urged his fellows to consider the real issues at stake:

> . . . what do the enemy say? Nay, what do many say that were friends at the beginning of the parliament? Even this, that the members of both houses have got great places and commands, and the sword into their hands; and, what by interest in parliament, what by power in the army, will perpetually continue themselves in grandeur, and not permit the war speedily to end, lest their own power should determine with it. This 'that' I speak here to our own faces, is but what others do utter abroad behind our backs. I am far from reflecting on any. I know the worth of those commanders, members of both houses, who are yet in power: but if I may speak my conscience without reflection upon any, I do conceive if the army be not put into another method, and the war more vigorously prosecuted, the people can bear the war no longer, and will enforce you to a dishonourable peace.[36]

From the following deliberations sprang the Self Denying Ordinance.

This measure, which had, of course, been the subject of careful planning prior to the December debate, was projected as a major purge of the military hierarchy. It enacted that 'no member of either house . . . should during the war enjoy or execute any office or command, military or civil'. When carried through Parliament, it ended at a stroke the wrangling within the high command and, by separating the military from the legislature it disposed of allegations of corruption. It removed the aristocratic dead wood from the control of the army and paved the way for promotion by merit. The conservatives were induced to accept it because the law removing Manchester also deprived Cromwell of his commission.

However, Cromwell remained in post, his command being regularly renewed until the end of the war. Inevitably, his enemies and later historians alleged that he was party to a subtle plot to pave the way for his own pre-eminence. If that was the case it was a very risky manoeuvre. Cromwell did not have so many friends in the house that he could bank on their making an exception in his case. Nor does such deviousness square with what we know of his character. Cromwell was a plain, outspoken (sometimes too outspoken) man. He lacked both the inclination and the intellectual equipment to be a subtle schemer. And he believed in Providence. He had proved over and again that God moves in mysterious ways; his own life had taken several unexpected turns since he had yielded it to the control of the Holy Spirit. His friends might scheme on his behalf but it seems more likely that the man who lacked personal ambition and who lived one day at a time would, if it was for the common good and in obedience to the inner voice, lay down his baton.

What was more important in his eyes was that the Self Denying Ordinance paved the way for that re-organisation of the army for which he had long campaigned. Local militias and forces raised by individual commanders had proved totally inadequate over the previous two years. Troops did not like fighting far from home and agitated to get back to their land at important times of the agricultural year. Training and standards varied from contingent to contingent. What was needed was a new military machine paid for by a special levy and not dependent on piecemeal contributions. The force which emerged from the debates of the next few weeks was the New Model Army – 22,000 men based largely upon the Eastern Association contingent that Cromwell had done so much to train and inspire. He must have been saddened to think that he would no longer be a part of it but there is no evidence that he intrigued to remain at the head of his 'lovely company'.

Charles found his first experience of battle distressing. He spent the night after Edgehill by a camp fire unable to sleep for the sights he had witnessed and the sounds he had heard – and could still hear, for the groans of those who were dying or tormented by their wounds continued through the hours of darkness.[37] What degree of self-doubt, one wonders, did the King permit himself as the statistics of the carnage were brought in from different parts of the field? It is unlikely that he faced up to the inadequacies of his own generalship or that, if he did, any candid self-appraisal survived the dawning of the new day. When it became obvious that Essex had no more stomach for fight Charles's officers told him that he had won a great victory and that the road to London lay open before him. Yet he rejected Prince Rupert's advice for an immediate advance on the capital and turned instead towards faithful Oxford. On 11 November a not-very-convincing foray towards London by Rupert led to the brief capture of Brentford but, after that, the King buttressed himself in the university city with freshly dug defence works, established at Christchurch a fair imitation of the Whitehall court and eagerly awaited the arrival of his wife. There was something instinctive about this retreat into the comforting familiarity of court rituals and luxury.

Thus, the war drifted on through the lack of any clear will to bring it to an end. Edgehill could have beaconed peace – by showing the way to royalist victory or signalling the opportunity for negotiated settlement. Either way the initiative lay with the King. In the autumn of 1642 he held an impressive hand of cards. He possessed a secure base of operations and to it loyal Englishmen were still resorting. Henrietta Maria's coded letters brought encouraging news of the Prince of Orange's support and her accumulation of over a million pounds and a shipload of arms. Parliamentary moderates were assuring him of their support for a meeting. And Edgehill had provided him with a moral victory, for the appalling reality of armed rebellion had shocked many previous malcontents into sympathy with the King.

Possibly it was the awfulness of battle which stunned Charles into inactivity. Edgehill cost him the lives of friends and faithful followers. Among the brave supporters who had heroically hurried to the royal cause and were now numbered in death was George Stuart, son of Esmé, Duke of Lennox, who fell while leading the three hundred horses he had raised for the King. The poignant tale of Sir Edmund Verney is told whenever the Battle of Edgehill is recounted. The fifty-two-year-old knight was a man of fierce principle – a Protestant who loathed Laudianism and a monarchist who literally beggared himself in unstinting service to the King. At the outbreak of war Verney did not hesitate to go to his master's side. Charles was very fond of this forthright courtier and had good reason to be grateful to him. He made him the royal standard bearer at Edgehill, a duty Verney accepted with both pride and foreboding. According to Edward Hyde, the old soldier was very depressed and doom-laden throughout the early days of campaigning. 'My condition,' he once told Hyde,

is much worse than yours, and different, I believe, from any other man's; and will very well justify the melancholic that, I confess to you, possesses me. You have satisfaction in your conscience that you are in the right; that the king ought not to grant what is required of him; and so you do your duty and your business together: but for my part I do not like the quarrel, and do heartily wish that the king would yield and consent to what they desire; so that my conscience is only concerned in honour and in gratitude to follow my master. I have eaten his bread, and served him near thirty years, and will not do so base a thing as to foresake him; and choose rather to lose my life (which I am sure I shall do) to preserve and defend those things which are against my conscience to preserve and defend: for I will deal freely with you, I have no reverence for the bishops, for whom this quarrel [subsists].[38]

In the thick of battle the royal standard was lost and subsequently recaptured. Verney's body was not found in the mound of sixty corpses piled around the King's pennant but his hand was discovered, still tightly clutching the staff.

More significant is the death of the Earl of Lindsey. Robert Bertie, ennobled in 1626, was a veteran of many land and sea campaigns who had first served during the reign of Elizabeth. Having raised the counties of Lincolnshire and Nottinghamshire for the King he was appointed Commander-in-Chief of the royal forces. Within days

Prince Rupert arrived from Holland and it was very soon clear that he and Lindsey did not see eye to eye in military matters. It was a case of caution versus panache; tried and tested methods versus novel ideas; a young prince of the blood versus a royal servant of almost fifty years' standing. Theirs was the sort of personality clash that often occurs between field officers under the pressures of active service. A good general should be able to deal with such conflicts. Rupert and Lindsey both had valuable qualities which could have been complementary: the prince was a bold and formidable cavalry commander and rapidly became the most feared of all Charles's officers; the nobleman was a highly respected leader in the shires who had a large personal following. But Rupert was Elizabeth's son and much loved by Charles for his mother's sake as much as for his own ebullient nature. The prince became just the latest of those intimates in whose judgement Charles reposed complete trust. With his wife gone from his side he needed someone to rely on. Thus, for the time being, he gave Rupert his head and defended him against all rivals. The King gave his nephew overall charge of the horse and exempted him from obedience to the orders of the commanding officer. When Lindsey, understandably piqued, protested that Charles paid more attention to Rupert and his swaggering cavaliers (the royal horsemen defiantly appropriated this continental word which appeared to give them more panache than their stolid opponents) than to himself, the King handed the ordering of the Edgehill formations to Patrick Ruthven, Earl of Forth, a soldier older than Bertie and renowned for hard drinking. The disgruntled Lindsey told his friends that since he had been effectively demoted he would march into battle at the head of his regiment as a mere infantry colonel and that he fully expected to be killed. In the event he was carried from the field bleeding profusely and died of his wounds for want of a surgeon.

Charles could not afford the loss of such men. He grieved for them and, if there were moments when he was honest with himself, he must have acknowledged his share of the blame for their sacrifice. The mesmeric effect of the sight of Englishmen hacking Englishmen to death cannot be overemphasised. It sapped the resolution of generals on both sides; Essex no less than the King retreated, chastened, from Edgehill. One way of coping with the horrors of battle was to put up mental shutters and plunge into the fray. Charles was not lacking in courage and refused (or, perhaps, could not bear) to watch the carnage from hilltop safety. Twice he went into the thick of the infantry engagement, wearing a black cloak lined with crimson, brandishing his sword and shouting encouragement to his men. Openly and enthusiastically he commended bravery in others. He had a supply of gold medals cast which he handed out to deserving recipients (and to less deserving friends). When John Smith, the captain who retook the standard at Edgehill, was brought to him Charles immediately dubbed him a knight bannaret, an ancient and by then rare honour. Smith, a taciturn, plain soldier and ardent Catholic (in many ways a counterpart to Cromwell) became one of the great heroes of the King's army and an examplar held up to recruits until his death at the battle of Cheriton, eighteen months later.

On the field of battle Charles projected an image of kingly splendour and total disdain for his enemies. Addressing his troops at Shrewsbury in September before moving eastwards he told them that they were fighting for 'your religion, your king and the laws of the land' and that the only people who would come against them would be 'traitors, most of them Brownist, anabaptists and atheists . . . who desire to destroy both church and state'.[39] In the council chamber, also, he maintained a posture of magisterial aloofness. There was no escaping the imperatorial self-concept inculcated by every aspect of his upbringing. Mixed with his innate indecisiveness this created a very unstable alloy. His civilian advisers, like his military commanders, were frequently in despair of a sovereign who would not consult them at all, or agreed with them and subsequently changed his mind, or took advice in secret from others, and always gave his final verdict with an hauteur that silenced further discussion. The months following Edgehill were given over to diplomatic overtures and military entractes. Commissioners came to Oxford from Westminster where Charles and his advisers spent days in discussion with them over the terms of a possible treaty. The two sides were as far apart as ever but, as in any political deadlock, peace did at least have a chance as long as all parties were talking. Such was the counsel offered by the King's moderates, such as Lord Falkland, Lord Dorset, Sir John Culpepper and Sir Edward Hyde (recently appointed Chancellor of the Exchequer). At the same time both combatants continued with their preparations for the next campaigning season. They had locked themselves into obduracy and thrown away the key as soon as they had committed the vindication of their causes to military might. For either side to disband its army would open its leaders to reprisals. Pym and his colleagues knew that a king back in power would renege on all promises exacted under duress. The King knew that a throne retained on Parliament's terms would be very unstable and insecure. There seemed to be no alternative but to press on to victory, but given the unique 1643 situation what did the word 'victory' mean?

At Oxford the doves, with justification, felt that their endeavours were always being undermined by the hawks. The Earls of Bristol and Newcastle were the Council members who were the most insistent advocates for pursuing the war to a swift and glorious conclusion. Indeed, throughout the winter Newcastle worked assiduously to strengthen the royalist position in the North. And Rupert and his friends always had the King's ear and were ever ready with dashing and devastating strategies.

However, the most effective sabre-rattler, though far away, was the Queen. In fact, Henrietta Maria seemed to exercise even more influence in her absence. She wrote frequently and Charles hungered for her letters, in which she constantly urged him to stand firm. She was a wife and mother fighting for her family with every ounce of her strength, and determined, above all else, that they should not be deprived of their positions. Hyde believed that before her departure she had extracted a promise from her husband that he would take no major decisions before consulting her and this is borne out by the tone and content of the correspondence which has survived. Early in the war when a rumour reached Paris that the King was contemplating a return to London rather than bending all his efforts to military triumph and the chastisement of rebellious subjects, her reaction was uncompromising. If the news was true she would have nothing more to do with him; she would retire to a convent there to spend her remaining days in prayer for her erring husband. 'You have already learned to your cost,' she chided, 'that want of perseverance in your designs has ruined you.' Her tirade continued:

> . . . I can never trust myself to those persons who are your directors, nor to you, since you would have broken your promise to me. If you had wished to make an accommodation you could have done it as well at York and more to your advantage than near London. As you had decided on this at my starting, I cannot believe any other, although I confess I am troubled almost to death for fear of the contrary; and I have

cause, for if you have broken your resolutions then there is nothing but death for me . . .[40]

Though often distressed or driven to distraction by his wife's threats, Charles continued to dote on her and to regard reunion with her as the highest form of earthly bliss. 'Make my acknowledgement to the Queen of England,' he writes to her in one of his lighter-hearted letters, for it is only 'her love that maintains my life, her kindness that upholds my courage, which makes me eternally hers.'[41] Charles nevertheless drew great encouragement from the uncompromising tone of her letters and the aid they promised. Unfortunately, when they fell into enemy hands they confirmed just how wide the gulf was between the royal couple and many of their people. Hyde later lamented,

> . . . it was her majesty's and the kingdom's misfortune that she had not any person about her, who had either ability or affection, to inform and advise her of the temper of the kingdom or humour of the people or who thought either worth the caring for.[42]

At Oxford it was known in February that the Queen would be embarking for England with her precious cargo as soon as wind and wave allowed. Charles played for time. At the second attempt Henrietta Maria crossed the North Sea and landed at Bridlington on 22 February. Two weeks later she reached the royalist stronghold of York, where she immediately began intriguing with local leaders and successfully won over such opposition supporters as the Hothams. On 23 May she was impeached by the House of Commons. She had willingly placed her life in danger. For the King her courage was both an inspiration and a cause for anxiety; her condemnation the final turn of the screw of his defiance of Parliament. He was more than ever concerned to have his wife safely back at his side. For this he had to wait until 13 July when he met her riding towards Oxford at the head of a small army and 150 wagons of matériel. Two days later they entered the university city through roads lined with cheering people.

The conduct of the royalist war in 1643 followed a pattern that was rapidly becoming familiar: the King started from a position of strength, following a well-considered strategy, abandoned it as a result of hubris and divided counsels, and ended up fighting an important battle which was inconclusive in itself but lost him the initiative. The tide of success was set in motion by Rupert's capture of Bristol at the end of July. This was a shattering blow to Parliament: Bristol was the second port in the realm, a potential gateway for military support from Ireland and the continent. So disturbed were the leaders of the parliamentary party that they lashed out at Nathaniel Fiennes (Lord Saye and Sele's son), the garrison commander, who was court-martialled and sentenced to death. He was pardoned but had to wait two years for full exoneration from Cromwell and Fairfax who, 'upon a view of the place, comparing the present strength of it with what it was when he delivered it . . . freely expressed themselves as men abundantly satisfied concerning the hard misfortune that befell that noble gentleman.'[43]

Since the royalists were now strong in the West, the North and the Midlands, common-sense strategy suggested a rapid three-pronged advance on London, and this Charles set in hand. Then he changed his mind. His more cautious advisers recommended assaults on the major provincial enemy strongholds – Hull, Gloucester and Plymouth – to prevent surprise flanking attacks. All three sieges eventually had to be abandoned and, by this time, valuable weeks had been lost. Charles personally commanded the army investing Gloucester and the failure of the enterprise must be laid at his door. Very simply, he lacked the stomach for it. Faced with storming one of his own cathedral cities and seeing its inhabitants – his own subjects – put to the sword, he held back. Frantically, Rupert urged an immediate, determined assault but the King attempted negotia- tion with the military governor, promising to spare lives if the city surrendered. When his overtures met with defiance Charles did what he so often did when faced with resolute opposition: he walked away. Leaving Ruthven in charge at Gloucester he went back to Oxford to be comforted by the Queen, now ensconced in her own court at Merton College. Nine months later their fifth and last daughter was born. In September 1643 the Earl of Essex raised the siege of Gloucester.

This was not the only occasion on which Charles was inhibited from that decisive and ruthless action which war frequently makes necessary. At Hull earlier and Plymouth later he spared strategically placed towns which could not be persuaded to yield peacefully. In the collected meditations of his last days, published as *Eikon*

Basilike, these words were found: '[It is] a hard choice for a king that loves his people and desires their love either to kill his own subjects or be killed by them.'[44] There is no doubt that he felt a genuine responsibility for the people God had entrusted to his care but solemn calculation entered into his thinking also. In a quick victory against 'rebels', casualties would have been accepted by the country as a regrettable necessity. But as the war dragged on people became less indulgent. Charles knew of the mounting anger rising against his arrogant cavaliers for their pillaging, requisitioning and rape. Even that might be forgiven in the interests of securing a speedy peace. But for an English king to take his own cities by storm and put their citizens to the sword would be long remembered as unprecedented barbarity. Even when the Queen urged him to make examples of his disobedient subjects, Charles would not do it. Compassion, calculation and, perhaps, chivalry also played a part in weakening Charles's generalship. The masques, the flattering verses, the tiltyard rituals had portrayed him as a descendant of King Arthur and the epitome of gallantry. In living up to this he had to be seen to be merciful and magnanimous, as when he permitted a defeated parliamentary force to march away from Lostwithiel with colours flying and heads held high.

As Essex fell back towards London after relieving Gloucester, the King resolved to cut off the earl's retreat. When the two armies confronted each other at Newbury, the royalist leadership was, once again, disastrously divided. This time it was the King who wanted a pitched battle and Rupert who urged delay. The prince had surveyed the ground and knew that it was not good for cavalry. His staff officers also informed him that the musketeers were short of ammunition. Charles overruled him and the first Battle of Newbury ran its inconclusive course. As at Edgehill there was no resumption of conflict on the morrow, for during the hours of darkness Charles led his force back towards Oxford. Once again the combat was costly. This time among the slain was Lord Falkland, one of the few idealogues on the King's side, a man who hated the war and died, as his friend Hyde observed, 'as much of the time as of the bullet'.

The rift between Charles and his nephew was a by-product of the Queen's return. She was jealous of the influence Rupert had gained in her absence and set out to undermine his position. Inevitably factions formed about these two strong characters. That was the way the court worked. It was Henrietta Maria who blocked the appointment of Hyde as Secretary of State in succession to Falkland. Charles had a high regard for Sir Edward's political wisdom but the Queen trusted no one who advocated a negotiated peace and it was on her insistence that the position and a Council seat were awarded to George Digby. There could be no more damning indictment of the system of court patronage nor of the King's judgement of character than the admission of the Earl of Bristol's son to the ruling junta at Oxford. Clarendon, who admittedly disliked the man, described him as 'having an ambition and vanity superior to all his other parts and a confidence peculiar to himself, which sometimes intoxicated and transported and exposed him'.[45] Digby was too much governed by his passions to have the intellectual stability necessary for a royal councillor. He had entered the Long Parliament as a bitter opponent of the court but raised a troop of horse for the King in the outbreak of war. He had bayed for Strafford's impeachment, then opposed his condemnation. He had championed parliamentary privilege, then supported the arrest of the five members. He had been impeached for treason by the Commons and fled to Holland. He had served gallantly under Rupert, then fallen out with him. Anyone who had anything to do with George Digby learned not to trust him – except, it seems, the King and Queen.

Another favourite Charles persisted in trusting against all the odds was James Hamilton. He was still shuttling between Edinburgh and the court and still playing a double game. The few facts which were visible to him through the swirling mists of Anglo-Scottish politics were that Argyll was all-powerful, that he was in negotiations with Westminster to send an army to Parliament's aid, that the Covenanters' principal enemy was James Graham, Earl of Montrose. In the spring of 1643, while Hamilton was steeped in political intrigues, Montrose came to the Queen at York to warn her of the emissary's duplicity and of the impending Scottish invasion. The information was passed to the King but he refused to believe anything that questioned the integrity of his old friend. He even raised Hamilton to a dukedom to signify his confidence. To Montrose's plea to let him raise a loyal force in the Highlands which would distract Argyll from a cross-border expedition he turned a deaf ear. Only in September did the volume of intelligence reaching the King at last persuade him of the true situation in Scotland. The next time Hamilton showed his face in Oxford he was arrested and sent under guard to Pendennis Castle (and subsequently to St Michael's Mount).

In 1644 the King's war lost all pretence of intelligent strategy. The presence of Lord Leven's Scots in the North forced the royalists on to the defensive and further exposed the weaknesses in their command structure. The shortcomings of local forces following their traditional local leaders had come home to Charles's military advisers as it had to Cromwell and his colleagues, but where Parliament set in hand (in 1645) the raising and training of a professional army, the King could see no further than the appointment of more experienced field commanders to lead his motley levies: Rupert was made captain-general in the North and West and his brother, Prince Maurice, lieutenant-general south of the Thames. This seemed an intelligent division of responsibility but the realities of the situation obliged Charles to make a series of ad hoc decisions as Commander-in-Chief and to fight engagements in various parts of the country, sometimes taking over from his appointed generals. The law of averages determined that he got some things right and some wrong. As ever, personal considerations affected his judgement. In 1644 his major concern was the condition and safety of his wife. It is not surprising under the circumstances that the Queen's pregnancy was not going well and it was necessary to get her to a place of comparative quiet for the delivery and, on 17 April, the royal couple made another tearful farewell at Abingdon whence Charles had come to set his wife on the road to Exeter. They never saw each other again.

Once more the King was alone in the sense that – with the exception of his two sons, Charles (fourteen) and James (ten) – he was deprived of the company of those he loved and to whom he could unburden himself. Rupert had been despatched northwards to deal with the Scottish menace. His advice to the King was to consolidate his position in Oxford while he halted Leven's advance and Prince Maurice campaigned in the South-West. But only days after this strategy had been agreed upon, the approach of parliamentary troops to within a few miles of Oxford sowed panic among the King's Council. Charles marched to Worcester, then fearful again for his wife's safety, menaced by the westward advance of Essex, he hastened into Devon. Henrietta Maria, meanwhile, having given birth on 16 June, abandoned her child two weeks later and took ship for France. Charles continued into Cornwall to aid a hard-pressed Maurice. These weeks saw the King militarily at his best. He deployed to the full the charisma of royalty to rally the traditionally loyal South-West and was able to exult in battlefield victories which owed more than a little to his own tactical decisions. But the disaster of Marston Moor set him scurrying eastwards again to confront the Earl of Manchester where, once again, the fighting season ended inconclusively at the second Battle of Newbury.

1645 was the year that astute political observers in England soon afterwards recognised as the turning point. From then onwards the King's cause waned and the gentleman's waxed. Before we consider the train of events marking Charles's ruin and Oliver's rise we may remind ourselves of what each man was fighting for. They both had many opportunities and much cause to examine their own consciences as they led their followers through the hellish smoke and clangour of civil war towards goals more clear to them than to the grieving families of the dead. But Cromwell and the King *did* know what they were fighting for and why they had to go on fighting.

In April Oliver reported to Parliament on several days of mixed military fortunes and concluded:

> This was the mercy of God, and nothing more due than a real acknowledgement; and though I have had greater mercies, yet none clearer; because, in the first God brought them to our hands when we looked not for them; and delivered them out of our hands, when we laid a reasonable design to surprise them, and which we carefully endeavoured. His mercy appears in this also, that I did much doubt the storming of the house [Bletchingdon], it being strong and well manned, and I having few dragoons, and this being not my business; and yet we got it.
>
> I hope you will pardon me if I say, God is not enough owned. We look too much to men and visible helps: this hath much hindred our success. But I hope God will direct all to acknowledge Him alone in all.[46]

Very simply, Cromwell's cause was God's cause; he looked for and saw the divine hand in every success and every failure. His conviction that the Christian was under a special daily providence was that of the Psalmist:

340

> The enemy shall not outwit him,
> The wicked shall not humble him.
> I will crush his foes before him
> And strike down those who hate him . . .
> If his children forsake my law
> and do not walk according to my ordinances . . .
> then I will punish their transgressions with the rod . . .
> but I will not remove from him my steadfast love . . .[47]

Charles was no less sure of his calling and responsibility. In July he wrote to Rupert rejecting the prince's despairing counsel that he should make peace on the best terms available. His resolve might have taken its inspiration from the same Scripture:

> . . . if I had any other quarrel but the defence of my religion, crown and friends, you had full reason for your advice. For I confess, that speaking as a mere soldier or statesman, I must say, there is no probability but of my ruin; yet as a Christian, I must tell you that God will not suffer rebels and traitors to prosper, nor this cause to be overthrown: and whatever personal punishment it shall please him to inflict upon me, must not make me repine, much less give over this quarrel; and there is as little question that a composition with them at this time is nothing else but a submission, which, by the grace of God, I am resolved against, whatever it cost me, for I know my obligation to be, both in conscience and honour, neither to abandon God's cause, injure my successors, nor forsake my friends.[48]

For those caught up in the thick of the conflict the eventual outcome was by no means certain nor its composition clearly defined. In a very real sense Cromwell's position was more precarious than the King's. He was dependent, for the periodic renewal of his commission, not only on battlefield victories, but also on the successes of his parliamentary friends, daily involved in faction fighting at Westminster. In his relationship with the legislators he was walking on eggshells and this explains his conscientiousness in making frequent reports on the campaign and also his careful avoidance of contentious issues. It also illuminates his developing disenchantment with the fixers and compromisers who struck their deals in panelled rooms far away from the blood and smoke of battle. Cromwell had originally taken to the field secure in the conviction that Parliament, once its rights and privileges were safeguarded, would define and uphold the liberties of the subject. Now he was less sanguine.

Nothing better illustrates Cromwell's mounting unease than his failure to impress on the Commons the need for religious toleration. Many of the young men he was ordering to face the enemy's cannon, pikes and muskets were Independent brothers in Christ, fighting for freedom of worship. Yet, when he pleaded on their behalf the general was constantly rebuffed. After Marston Moor and again after Naseby he urged Parliament to find a place within a Presbyterian polity for those of a congregational persuasion. His requests were ignored. When the Commons published Cromwell's report on the triumph of Naseby, they deleted the passage containing his plea for toleration and it was left to Lord Saye and his friends in the Lords to order its reinstatement.

Cromwell did now have a valuable ally in the Lower House in the person of Oliver St John, who had emerged as one of the leaders of the war party. Cromwell and St John, long united in friendship, evangelical faith and the complex interrelationships of the Barrington-Masham circle, walked similar career paths. Each established his proficiency in his own sphere and earned the respect of his peers. Each stepped into the shoes of others. In the same way that Cromwell emerged as the finest parliamentary general once the Self Denying Ordinance had removed Essex, Manchester and other commanders, so the deaths of Pym and Hampden cleared the way for St John in the Commons.

In the spring and summer of 1645 St John's tactics at the negotiating table were as clever as his friend's in the field and just as crucial. As well as clearing the dead wood from the officer corps he had to outmanoeuvre the peace party and their supporters, the Scots. All revolutions are initiated by temporary coalitions of interest groups. They are unstable compounds of factions which either disintegrate in mutual recriminations or undergo violent change from which the most ruthless group emerges as dominant. In the delicate situation which prevailed in the early months of 1645 the Covenanters were the party which had to be handled the most carefully. They set the agenda for fresh talks held at Uxbridge and were prepared to render allegiances to whichever side seemed likely to establish a Presbyterian church polity. They disliked Cromwell and St John as Independents, resented

Cromwell's failure to credit them with the victory at Marston Moor and feared the emergence of a more efficient military machine which, in the hands of generals like Cromwell, might be directed across the border.

St John and his war party colleagues wanted the Uxbridge talks to use up time – valuable for the restructuring of the army – and then to fail. Their chief concern was that Charles would agree to the abolition of episcopacy in order to swing the Scottish army to his side. St John's cool legal mind devised two demonstrations which were, in part, for the benefit of Parliament's wavering allies. He drew up the Self Denying Ordinance which opened a gap between the legislators and the generals, and relieved Cromwell, the Covenanters' *bête noire*, of his command. His other initiative was to drag Laud out of the Tower to face a state trial. The archbishop's inevitable condemnation for treason was intended to signal to the Scots that episcopacy in England was at an end. The strategy worked and, in order to avoid his policies being too closely scrutinised, St John maintained a low profile in the Uxbridge debates. However, all his scheming could still be undermined by the King's duplicity, for Charles was likely to promise anything in the interests of suppressing the rebellion.

In the event the King either could not or would not match St John's subtlety. Although he was prepared to make all manner of promises he had no intention of keeping, there were two matters on which he refused to yield because they touched 'the duty of my oath': control of the army and the abolition of episcopacy. Over the ensuing months Charles wrestled with the doctrinal and pragmatic consequences of abandoning, or seeming to abandon, the traditional ecclesiology of the Church of England but on this point he could never give way. His position at Uxbridge was the same as that which he explained in a letter to his wife at the beginning of the following year:

> The difference between me and the rebels concerning the church is not bare matter of form or ceremony, which are alterable according to occasion, but so real that if I should give way as is desired, there would be no church, and by no human probability ever to be recovered; so that, besides the obligation of mine oath, I know nothing to be an higher point of conscience . . . This I am sure of, which none can deny, that my yielding this is a sin of the highest nature.[49]

343

Thus once again jaw-jaw came to nought and war-war continued on its devastating way.

Devastating it certainly was, especially for those places still in royalist hands. On both sides there were bullies – soldiers who ruthlessly exploited the civilian population for food, horses and provender, particularly when their pay was in arrears, as it usually was. The better commanders were tough on looters and jealous of the reputation of the men under their authority. Cromwell put his weight behind the creation of a professional, adequately and efficiently remunerated army in order to prevent military disorder as well as to bring the war to a speedy end. 'I wish to be of the faction that desires to avoid the oppression of the poor people of this miserable nation,' he wrote to his superiors. 'Truly it grieves my soul our men should be upon free quarters as they are.'[50] But on the King's side desperation was now producing atrocities which increasingly alienated even traditionally loyal areas. Whatever the strategic advantages for replacing local gentry and noble leaders with experienced officers, the severing of links encouraged the abuse of non-combatants. Prince Rupert had a bad reputation for cruelty and plunder which became worse when he was put in charge of the defence of Bristol in the summer of 1645. Even more reprehensible was the conduct of George Goring. This son of James I's carousing partner, and favourite of the Queen, was a licentious and unprincipled carpet knight and a bosom companion of the equally disreputable George Digby. He was a courtier for whom Clarendon reserved some of his most concentrated vitriol. Goring, the chronicler recorded,

> would, without hesitation, have broken any trust or done any act of treachery, to have satisfied an ordinary passion or appetite; and, in truth, wanted nothing but industry (for he had wit, and courage, and understanding, and ambition, uncontrolled by any fear of God or man) to have been as eminent and successful in the highest attempt in wickedness of any man in the age he lived in, or before. Of all his qualifications, dissimulation was his masterpiece . . .[51]

Goring and Rupert shared a mutual loathing and it might have been evident to any close observer that they were incapable of working together. Yet this was the man to whom Charles now entrusted the command of his western army. His unruly troops so alienated the country between Southampton and Exeter that 'liberating' parliamentary forces were subsequently welcomed with open arms.

Overall command of those reformed forces was entrusted to Sir Thomas Fairfax, a brave, intelligent and modest general totally lacking in personal ambition. To the more cautious Parliament leaders this courteous Yorkshire gentleman seemed a safe choice: a man who lacked Cromwell's troublesome exuberance and could be relied on to carry out the orders of his parliamentary masters. In the event, they could not keep Oliver out of the action. Everything was confusion and improvisation throughout the spring. Parliamentary intelligence was at a loss to know what the King intended: would he fortify Oxford; march northwards to link up with forces raised by Montrose in Scotland; move the bulk of his army to the West Country and consolidate there; or would he turn eastwards to confront the New Model Army, of which he was openly contemptuous, in their own heartlands? Charles considered and partially acted upon most of these alternatives, as usual a prey to divided counsels. His enemies, therefore, had to keep small, mobile armies in the field employed on marches, countermarches, skirmishes and sieges. For their part, the politicians, whatever their personal feelings or their apprehensions about Scottish reactions, realised that they could not do without their most effective cavalry commander. Cromwell was allowed to serve out the forty days' grace permitted under the Self Denying Ordinance and this was then renewed for a further forty days. Throughout all this time Parliament failed to provide Fairfax with a cavalry lieutenant-general and it may be that one can see St John's hand in this omission. Certainly Cromwell's allies at Westminster were pulling strings on his behalf and were in touch with General Fairfax.

Just as his parliamentary friends emerged into leadership rather than leaping up to grasp it, so Cromwell performed his duties in a low-key fashion, while making sure that his masters knew what he was about. He marched back and forth through the English heartland and was conscientious and respectful in the reports he made to Parliament and to Fairfax. In February he served under Sir William Waller in Somerset and Wiltshire, who was certainly no admirer and who disagreed profoundly with Oliver on religious issues. Sir William gave his subordinate a commendation from which one would scarcely recognise the Cromwell of earlier years:

he at this time had never shown extraordinary parts; nor do I think that he did himself believe that he had them; for, although he was blunt, he did not bear himself with pride or disdain. As an officer he was obedient, and did never dispute my orders, nor argue upon them. He did indeed seem to have great cunning; and whilst he was cautious of his own words (not putting forth too many, lest they should betray his thoughts) he made others talk, until he had, as it were sifted them, and known their most intimate designs.[52]

The impression we gain of Cromwell in these crucial months is of a man on his best behaviour, biting his tongue when necessary and striving never to put a foot wrong. Indeed, he claimed as much when writing to the sequestration committee in Ely: 'I have studied to deserve the good opinion of honest men.'[53] He knew that his destiny was in the hands of God but it was also in the hands of highly critical politicians who, from the comfort of their London residences, passed judgement upon their military servants.

Eventually it was the Commander-in-Chief who nudged the politicians in the direction of the inevitable. Pointing out that he needed Cromwell to command his cavalry, his urging could scarcely have been stronger:

The general esteem and affection which he hath both with the officers and soldiers of the whole army, his own personal worth and ability for the employment, his great care, diligence and courage, and faithfulness in the service you have already employed him in, with the constant presence and blessing of God that has accompanied him make us look upon it as a duty we owe you and the public to make our suit.[54]

Nor did Fairfax wait for Parliament's response but summoned Cromwell to join him immediately.

The need was urgent. On 31 May Rupert had overrun Leicester in one of the most vicious assaults of the war. The royalists massacred prisoners of war, cut down civilians, killed women and children and plundered the city, street by street, in a furious orgy of spoliation. Over seven hundred citizens were killed and scarce a family in Leicester was spared grief and distress. The location of the King during this vindictive mayhem is not recorded but he was certainly with the army and could have exercised a restraining influence on his troops. After Leicester any claim of tenderness for his 'poor subjects' could only have a hollow ring and it was to prevent any further acts of barbarity that Fairfax marched to intercept the royalist army and bring them to open battle.

The Battle of Naseby brought the King and the gentleman into direct conflict for the first time. Neither can have known that two hours of fighting on a wet June morning would decide his ultimate fate. Yet it was so: Naseby finally established Cromwell as a great leader of men and, by shattering Charles's military capability, it destroyed his cause. It is instructive to consider how each man approached his destiny. While Cromwell was covering the ground from Cambridge to Kislingbury (near Daventry) at the head of 4000 men in three days, Charles was hunting on the captured estate of a parliamentary supporter. It was a way of relaxing and also of demonstrating his kingly sang-froid. Another method of avoiding stress was to delegate tactics to his field commander. Charles still discussed overall strategy with his war council but he completely gave over day-to-day decisions to Rupert, who, now that the Queen had departed, once again enjoyed his confidence. Oliver, by contrast, took a keen interest in his general's battle plans and a last-minute change he suggested at Naseby significantly affected the outcome. On the evening of 13 June New Model scouts had located the royalist rearguard. There was time to organise the army for a dawn start and 'seek the Lord in prayer' before turning in. Charles had to be roused at midnight from his bed in the village of Lubenham with the news that the enemy was only a few miles off and had to hurry to a hastily convened high command meeting.

Rupert must have known that he was outnumbered by the enemy though he probably did not know that the odds were 14,000 to 9000. Orders had been sent to Goring to bring his army up from the West but he had not come. Fairfax knew, through the interception of a letter, that Goring was bogged down in the siege of Taunton. Rupert, we may imagine, put the worst complexion on his subordinate's failure to appear and was, in any case, happy to do without him. He was faced with the choice of withdrawing to Leicester, harassed by Cromwell's cavalry along the march, or standing to fight. He decided on a tactical retreat – and was overruled by the King. What was going through Charles's mind we can only guess. It is fully in character that he would disdain to run away. His contempt for the 'New Noddle Army' and his belief that his own presence on the field was worth a thousand men disposed him to stand up to the enemy.

He had never personally experienced a major defeat and, a year before, had led his own men in a very creditable victory over Sir William Waller at Cropredy Ridge.

If Charles came to the battlefield wrapped in stately confidence, Cromwell mounted up on the morning of Saturday 14 June 1645 in a mood of euphoria. He was always on a high before a clash of arms; mind alert, adrenalin pumping, laughter and earnest prayers coming equally readily to his lips as he rode among his men. Excitement and anticipation were features of his hyperactive nature, though he was always ready to put a spiritual gloss on his feelings and never more so than on the morning of Naseby.

> When I saw the enemy draw up and march in gallant order towards us, and we a company of poor ignorant men, to seek how to order our battle – the General having commanded me to order all the horse – I could not (riding alone about my business) but smile out to God in praises, in assurance of victory, because God would, by things that are not, bring to naught things that are. Of which I had great assurance; and God did it. O that men would therefore praise the Lord, and declare the wonders that He doth for the children of men![55]

So he wrote to a House of Commons friend a month later.

The day was won by Cromwell because of his acute sense of tactical advantage and the excellent discipline and training of the men under his personal control. The confronting armies were drawn up along ridges on either side of a rain-sodden depression called Broadmoor. Surveying the ground, Cromwell noted that a small movement to the left would make problems for the royalist cavalry by giving them a steeper incline up which to charge. Fairfax agreed and gave the necessary orders. It was the re-organisation of the parliamentary ranks which encouraged Rupert to start the action. The royalist line advanced, infantry in the centre, cavalry on the wings. Despite the unfavourable conditions, Rupert's horse, on the right, turned the parliamentary line, driving Henry Ireton and his mounted troops from the field and sweeping on to secure Fairfax's baggage train, more than a mile behind the battle zone. The hand-to-hand infantry fighting, meanwhile, was going bloodily and turgidly against the New Model ranks. Only on the right of the parliamentary line was there any encouragement for Fairfax. Cromwell allowed Sir Marmaduke Langdale (one of the King's most committed and disinterested supporters who was eventually ruined in the royal case) to charge his position uphill. Then, as the royalists' impetus slackened, he swept down upon them. As soon as Langdale's scattered horsemen were fleeing back towards the reserves where the King was stationed, Cromwell reined in his cavalry and turned them upon the infantry mêlée in the centre of Broadmoor. Caught between the New Model foot and mounted regiments the King's men were either cut down or surrendered. At this point the King spurred forward from his vantage point at the rear to throw his reserves into the fray. A story to which Clarendon gave credence has Charles bravely thrusting into the battle shouting to his men for 'one more charge' until one of his staff officers grabbed his bridle to turn his horse away from danger. Seeing their sovereign apparently leaving the field, others wheeled around to follow and the last possibility of reversing the tide of battle was lost. The episode, if true, presents one of the intriguing 'might have beens' of history. Without the intervention of the solicitous officer Charles and Oliver could have come face to face on the field of Naseby with possibly fatal results for one of them.

The royal army that had marched out to do battle in the morning by the afternoon was no more. The dead, wounded and prisoners amounted to over 5000. From this point onwards the majority of Charles's advisers were urging him to come to terms with his enemies. Yet, still he forced himself to hope. There remained Goring's army in the South-West; loyal friends in Wales would raise more men; Bristol, the essential link between the two, was still secure; Montrose was labouring on his behalf north of the border; and Henrietta Maria assured him of French help. Over the remaining summer weeks all the props on which he leaned broke one after another. His Welsh subjects did not rush to his standard. On 10 July, Goring, who for days had avoided an engagement, was trapped by Fairfax and Cromwell at Langport in Somerset. He fled through the town, firing it behind him, but this did not prevent pursuit and most of his force was annihilated. Thereafter, he reclined in Devon in a state of supreme inactivity until November, when he took himself off to France.

Yet it was Rupert who added the final ingredient to the bitter cup of Charles's disappointment. He was sent to hold Bristol and he ruthlessly dragooned the inhabitants into working on the city's defences. But when Fairfax and Cromwell arrived to invest it in

September he found, like Fiennes before him, that his garrison was too small to guard four miles of wall. Before delivering the city up he set fires in three places and the invaders could only watch in horror 'to see so famous a city burned to ashes before our faces'.[56] Fairfax allowed the prince and his men to withdraw honourably but he made his feelings very clear. Rupert's behaviour, he told him, was not only barbarous; it was ungrateful bearing in mind all that his uncle's countrymen had done for his unfortunate parents over the years:

> Let all England judge whether the burning its towns, ruining its cities and destroying its people be a good requital for a person of your family, which has had the prayers, tears, purses and blood of its parliament and people.[57]

Rupert received even shorter shrift from the King. Like Fiennes, the prince had to pay dearly for the loss of Bristol. When Charles learned of the surrender he poured out all his bitterness in a letter of blistering reproach.

> Though the loss of Bristol be a great blow to me, yet your surrendering it as you did is of so much affliction to me, that it makes me forget not only the consideration of that place, but is likewise the greatest trial of my constancy that hath yet befallen me; for what is to be done? after one that is so near me as you are, both in blood and friendship, submits himself to so mean an action (I give it the easiest term) such – I have so much to say that I will say no more of it: only, lest rashness of judgment be laid to my charge, I must remember you of your letter of the 12 Aug., whereby you assured me, (that if no mutiny happened), you would keep Bristol for four months. Did you keep it four days? Was there any thing like a mutiny? More questions might be asked, but now, I confess, to little purpose. My conclusion is, to desire you to seek your subsistence (until it shall please God to determine of my condition) somewhere beyond seas, to which end I send you herewith a pass; and I pray God to make you sensible of your present condition, and give you means to redeem what you have lost; for I shall have no greater joy in a victory, than a just occasion without blushing to assure you of my being Your loving uncle, and most faithful friend.[58]

The changes of tone and, at some points, near incoherence of that letter speak of a mind in turmoil. Over the next eighteen months,

Charles fluctuated between moments of depression, when he faced up to his impossible situation, and interludes of fantasy when he indulged in a variety of bizarre plans for recovering power. Nor was it only the harassment of enemies he had to contend with. The Queen's letters were full of reproaches. Her only chance of regaining her crown and ensuring the succession of her son lay in Charles's victory over his enemies. For the moment, at least, this was out of the question militarily. Therefore, she urged, he must use duplicity. He should promise anything that would regain him the initiative. Henrietta Maria simply could not understand that her husband was troubled in conscience over certain concessions: nothing was worth losing a throne for – certainly not a bunch of Protestant bishops. Small wonder that Charles responded in exasperation to some of his wife's taunts. 'Be kind to me or you kill me,' he had implored in January 1645. 'I have already affliction enough to bear which without you I could not do.[59] I should sink under my present miseries if I did not know myself innocent of those faults which thy misinformed judgement condemns me of . . . I am blamed both for granting too much and yet not yielding enough.'[60] After twenty years the royal couple still could not see eye to eye on Church matters and this adds point to Charles's insistence when writing to the Prince of Wales that the boy should obey his mother in all things *except religion*.

His children were another cause of anxiety for the King. In the spring of 1646 he managed to get young Charles away to the Channel Islands in the care of Edward Hyde and John Culpepper. From there he was supposed to be going to join his mother in France. This filled Hyde with alarm: to place the heir to the throne under the sole tutelage of the Queen (in whose veins flowed the domineering blood of Catherine and Marie de Medici) was to limit his chances of ever being accepted as King of England. Even if he were not openly converted to Catholicism, there would always be the suspicion that he had become a covert papist. The King disagreed, believing that his son would be able to do what he and his father had done before him: resist the blandishments of his womenfolk in matters of religion. As for the other royal children, baby Henrietta had been smuggled across the Channel to her mother and James, Elizabeth and Henry were with their father in Oxford as the parliamentary forces gradually strangled it into submission. Their safety concerned him greatly but their presence was his remaining comfort and in his distracted state of mind he left it too late to arrange for them to be conveyed away to some secret refuge.

Eventually it was Charles who clandestinely left Oxford. As soon as he knew of the Prince of Wales's escape he allowed his attendants to devise a plan to put himself beyond the reach of his enemies. At 3 a.m. on 27 April 1646 three figures slipped out of Oxford by the east gate. They were John Ashburnham, Groom of the Chamber and Army Paymaster, attended by two servants, one of whom was Michael Hudson, royal chaplain, and the other, known as 'Harry', was Charles I, King of England. As they rode through the night and watched the dawn rise Charles cannot have failed to remember that other masquerade when a young man full of excitement had set out to find a bride. The circumstances now were very different. In 1623 discovery would have meant embarrassment and agitated fluttering in diplomatic dovecotes; now it would mean arrest, confinement and the total humiliation of being at the mercy of Parliament. But the major difference between this escapade and the journey to Spain was that the latter had had an unambiguous destination. This time Charles did not know where he was going. He set off in the direction of London imagining that his sudden appearance in the capital would rouse spontaneous popular support. He had second thoughts and swung north-eastwards into Norfolk. This offered the opportunity of escape by sea should his preferred option prove impracticable. This was to hand himself over to the Scots, do a deal with them and break their alliance with Parliament. Having received a satisfactory response, the incognito trio turned inland again, rode through Huntingdon and, by various less-frequented roads reached Newark on 5 May where the Covenanters were part of a besieging army.

It is almost incomprehensible that the King should have supposed that after eight years of turmoil the Scots would be eager to compromise. Charles had angered them into armed revolt by trying to make them abandon Presbyterianism. They had resisted and not only brought the King to his knees but come very close to obliging the English Parliament to accept their form of Church government. Because the King's expectations had been all awry his treatment at the hands of the Scots came as a real shock. They moved him to moderately comfortable quarters in Newcastle and, for the first time in his life, Charles Stuart was surrounded by people who refused to treat him as a superior being. His captors did not set out to be deliberately offensive but they were rough and ready soldiers whose religion taught them to be no respecters of persons, and their lack of deference struck him as 'barbarous usage'. 'I hope God hath sent me hither for the last punishment that he will inflict upon me, for assuredly no honest man can prosper in these people's company,' he complained to his wife.[61] Every day the King was visited by earnest ministers who sought to persuade him that episcopacy was of the devil and that theirs was the only ecclesiology that had biblical sanction. George Conn and other Catholics had tried to convert Charles but always with good humour and sophisticated argument. This constant, dour assault on his conscience only served to confirm the dictum instilled into him by his father that monarchy and presbytery agreed as well as God and the devil. It was his settled conviction, as he wrote to the Prince of Wales, that Presbyterianism could not but bring anarchy into any country. Yet there was no escaping intellectual combat. Charles wanted military support from the Scots; therefore he had to bargain and argue. The man who had always silenced or walked away from religious disputations now could not escape it.

Nor could he call other protagonists to his aid. Ashburnham and Hudson had been sent away for their own safety and he had no other servants of his own to attend him. With the Covenanters demanding capitulation, and his wife and her allies no less insistent that he should agree to anything in the interest of recovering the plenitude of his power, Charles had urgent need of his most trusted advisers. It was under these circumstances that he wrote to Juxon asking whether he could in conscience make a promise which he had no intention of keeping. The reply was accommodating and might have helped the King if it had arrived in time for him to act upon it:

Considering . . . the condition your Majesty's affairs now stand in, being destitute of all means compulsory or of regaining what is lost by force, we cannot conceive in this your Majesty's condescension any violation of that oath whereof your Majesty is so justly tender, but that your Majesty doth thereby still continue to preserve and protect the Church by the best ways and means you have now left you (which is all the oath can be supposed to require) and, that the permission intended (whereby in some men's apprchensions your Majesty may seem to throw down what you desire to build up) is not only by your Majesty levelled to that end but, as your Majesty stands persuaded, probably fitted for the effecting it in some measure.[62]

The nine months that he spent as guest of the Scots was the worst episode in the tragedy that was the life of Charles I. It was vastly more taxing than the days he spent on trial for his life. By then he had come to a certainty that was unshakeable and which lifted him to a plateau of inner calm from which he could look down on his judges. He had found within himself those resources that in earlier days he had always relied on others to supply. But from May 1646 to February 1647 he was a man bereft of family, friends, counsel and comfort. There are few more heartrending cries of desolation than Charles's outburst to his wife in a letter of 10 June, 'there was never man so alone as I'. He looked forward eagerly to every written and oral message from Henrietta Maria but as often as not they brought him little relief. The Queen was going through her own brand of hell. In poor health, desperately worried about her children, short of money and supported on sufferance by her French relatives, she kept up tireless intrigues with courts in France, Holland and Rome and with royalist supporters in Ireland and Scotland – all to no avail. There were times when she became impatient with her husband's 'weakness'. When he contemplated trying to escape to the continent she replied sharply, 'I . . . conjure you, that till the Scots shall declare that they will not protect you, you do not think of making any escape from England . . . you would destroy all our hopes, besides the danger of the attempt.' Another letter, now lost, threw the King into a panic because it seemed to suggest that her patience with him had reached its limit.

> I assure thee, both I and my children are ruined, if thou shouldst retire from my business: for God's sake leave off threatening me with thy desire to meddle no more with business . . . as thou lovest me give me so much comfort (and God knows I have but little, and that little must come from thee) as to assure me that thou wilt think no more of any such thing.[63]

It would have occasioned Charles no comfort to know that during these same months Oliver Cromwell was plunged in a like depression.

EIGHT

JUDGEMENT

It's Tommy this an' Tommy that, an' 'Chuck him out, the brute!'
But it's 'Saviour of 'is country' when the guns begin to shoot.
                                        – Rudyard Kipling, 'Tommy'

A STANDING ARMY IS an awesome thing and Parliament was determined that the New Model should not become one. With the surrender of Oxford in June 1646 there seemed no further need to go on paying armed men to march around the shires disturbing the lives of law-abiding citizens and posing a potential threat to the establishment of peaceful government. There were still problems in Scotland and Ireland, and the men at Westminster could not feel really secure until the Covenanters had handed over the King and returned across the border, but it was widely agreed that the bulk of the army should be stood down and that all that required discussion was the terms of decommissioning.

Cromwell was fully in agreement with the principle. His own exemption from the Self Denying Ordinance had been regularly renewed but finally ran out in June 1646. No serving officer could have been more eager to return to civilian life and to the bosom of his family. He had seen little of his wife and children for four years and been unable to share fully in the joys and sorrows of a domestic life which ticked away remorselessly although drowned out by the commotion of war. His second son, Oliver, had died of smallpox while on army service. Contracts had been made for the marriage of two of his daughters (one to his friend and military colleague, Henry Ireton). The other boys, Richard and Henry, who had also fought in their father's regiments, now had to find civilian occupations. Richard was about to enter Lincoln's Inn and his younger brother was destined to follow him after a few terms at Cambridge. There was much for an affectionate father to concern himself with. Materially, the war had made the family's fortune. Parliament voted

357

Oliver an annual pension of £2500. Now, at last, he could leave 'Meshech' and set Elizabeth up in a comfortable London house from where he could more conveniently attend to his parliamentary duties. It must have been a matter of some satisfaction that he had rescued the Cromwells from that descent into obscurity which had seemed inevitable only a few years before. He was a man of consequence in the land – a popular hero. In the autumn of 1646 the head of the senior line of the family, Thomas Cromwell, Earl of Ardglass, who had served the royalist cause, was obliged to appeal to his distant relative for aid in making his peace with the victorious regime. Life, then, should have been very sweet for the forty-seven-year-old ex-general as he unbuckled his sword. In fact, his mind was far from easy.

In August 1646 he wrote in a letter to Fairfax:

> Things are not well in Scotland; would they were in England! We are full of faction and worse . . . Sir, I hope you have not cast me off. Truly I may say no [one] more affectionately honours and loves you. You and yours are in my daily prayers. You have done enough to command the uttermost of
> > Your faithfullest and most obedient servant
> > Oliver Cromwell[1]

The reason that Cromwell feared he might have become estranged from his old chief was that he had become trapped in a no man's land between Parliament and the army. There is no doubt that he sincerely wished to see the New Model regiments disbanded. Apart from a genuine desire for peace he wanted his 'lovely' men to be safely returned to their farms, businesses and families. Many friends and sons of friends had been killed in the recent conflict and he had had to write consoling letters to grieving widows and parents. In one of his speeches to the Commons after his return he assured the House that the army would willingly lay down its arms as soon as they were called upon to do so.

There was more of optimism than reality in that affirmation; the officers and men who had toiled and suffered much at the behest of Westminster had a strong sense that they were about to be betrayed by a bunch of ungrateful politicians who could not wait to see the back of them. Their grievances were real: their pay was months in arrears and Parliament had made no provision for the families of the dead and maimed. Moreover, they had been offered no statutory indemnity for acts of war and many feared that, once they had surrendered the protection of a uniform they would be subjected to recriminations from neighbours suffering real or imaginary grievances. Parliament for its part was in difficulties. It could not afford to pay the soldiers; it would have taken £2½ million to settle all just demands. They feared the army and suspected some of their leaders of plotting to use force to overthrow the constitution. All the old anxieties about anarchy were aired in the debating chambers, sometimes in immoderate language and not infrequently by members who had been singularly prominent by their absence during the war and now returned to dominate the peace. As months passed with no positive attempt to meet the soldiers' grievances those very developments the leaders feared began to materialise. Angry, under-occupied troops had plenty of time to listen to barrack-room lawyers, semi-educated demagogues, fiery preachers and social revolutionaries.

Cromwell had a foot in both camps. As a commander who, throughout the war, had wrestled with bureaucrats and politicians to obtain a fair deal for his men, he knew what they were suffering and how keenly they felt their rejection. He also recognised the concerns of his fellow parliamentarians about the possible misuse of military might. Much of the suspicion expressed in both houses was directed against himself and he was keen to disarm his critics. As early as April 1646 he had publicly reprimanded his future son-in-law, Henry Ireton, for an innocent action that might have been mis-construed. His younger friend had received information in Oxford that the King might be prepared to treat with the army and he, not unnaturally, passed the intelligence on to Cromwell. The member for Cambridge reprimanded the sender and took the first opportunity to read his letter to the Commons. He well understood the mischief determined opponents might cause by spreading rumours that the army was ready to do a deal with the King behind Parliament's back. In all likelihood he also smelled a royalist plot: it was no secret that the King's only hope lay in sowing mutual distrust among his enemies. Cromwell was determined to be loyal to Parliament and to be seen to be loyal. But he also had that other loyalty to his comrades-in-arms – hence his letter to Fairfax, which was only one of several keeping the general informed of affairs at Westminster.

However, his life had become much more complex and he was

now experiencing a stress that undermined his health and, in all likelihood, contributed to an illness he suffered in the opening months of 1647. When he wrote of 'factions and worse' he was describing a situation that seemed to be undermining everything that he had been fighting for since the opening of the Short Parliament. War had been a distillation process, concentrating negatives. Those who took arms against the King (and even some who took arms for him) had defined with considerable precision what they disliked about the Stuart regime. Some were incensed by arbitrary taxation and government through favourites. For others it was the unrestrained ritualism of Laud and the exercise of episcopal coercion that angered them. Many were concerned about the Romeward drift of foreign alliances and policies which encouraged English Catholics to come out of the closet. A consensus for opposition had emerged naturally. Peace, always more difficult to wage than war, demanded that the lawmakers bring positive, creative ideas to the constitutional alembic and combine them according to a formula on which the majority could agree. In 1646 what had been recognised by more intelligent observers (including the King's advisers) for a long time became obvious to everyone: that there was not the remotest chance of Lords and Commons reaching even the semblance of unanimity.

It used to be considered helpful to use the terms 'Presbyterian' and 'Independent' which contemporary commentators like Hyde and the leading Scottish theologian, Robert Baillie, employed to explain the groups contending with each other from the middle years of the war. Such neat classifications have long since been discredited. If they have any value it is to remind us that the conflict was still, at rock bottom, a religious one. In political terms the convention obscures more than it illuminates. It may be that we instinctively want to project back into the seventeenth century the concept of the peculiarly British two-party system which emerged later, though even that was, more often than not, a confrontation of uneasy alliances. The Long Parliament in 1646-7 was a cacophony of political choristers singing from a variety of different hymn books. At the extreme edge were a few covert royalists and republicans propounding their simple draconian solutions to complex problems. There were those who favoured a new king, such as the Elector Palatine or the Prince of Wales, who would be firmly controlled by Parliament. Some persisted in believing that Charles I could be brought to accept and abide by a package of compromises, though just what should go into that package was far from clear. A minority of parliamentarians would have been happy to preserve a depoliticised episcopate while others, out of genuine conviction or a desirè to work closely with the Scots, wished to install a Presbyterian system in the Church of England. Those who were for religious independency, because they were dissenters themselves or because they resented government exercising control of men's consciences, campaigned for the greatest possible toleration of Protestant groupings. Their opponents could see only political and religious anarchy emanating from such an open-handed policy.

It was inevitable that the agenda would be set by forthright politicians working by intrigue and bombast to cobble together alliances which would secure them voting majorities. The man who now emerged as the most successful parliamentary manager was Denzil Holles, a turbulent younger son of the Earl of Clare with a rare capacity for hatred. In any assessment of Cromwell's aggressive speech and behaviour it is instructive to compare him with his exact contemporary. Holles was, from the beginning of the reign, such a violent opponent of royal policies that, in 1629, he had been thrown into the Tower and subsequently spent several years in exile. As a member of the Long Parliament none was more eager than Holles to demand the impeachment of members suspected of royalist sympathies. He raised a regiment of foot and fought at Edgehill. But as the war progressed Holles transferred his spleen from the King to the King's enemies. His loathing of St John and Cromwell, 'the two grand designers of the ruin of the three king-doms'[2] was personal and he tried to have Cromwell impeached for aggravating the conflict. He later challenged Ireton to a duel. His opponents countered by accusing him of going behind Parliament's back to arrange a deal with the King. However, in the changed atmosphere after Charles's flight to the Covenanters, more and more moderates were attracted to Holles's programme of maximum co-operation with the Scots, the acceptance of Presbyterianism, an accommodation with the King and the speedy disbandment of the New Model. The factions led by St John and Holles contended bitterly against each other during the second half of 1646 and by the end of the year it was obvious that the 'Presbyterians' were winning.

For Cromwell the situation was insufferable. Parliament had betrayed him, and St John and all their friends, by being ready to negotiate away principles that had been secured by the shedding of much blood. They had betrayed the evangelical cause by agreeing to deliver the Church into the hands of an unscriptural Presbytery. They had betrayed the army by reneging on their commitments to the very men who had won for them the freedoms they were now ready to bargain away. His despondency was recalled years later by Edmund Ludlow, one of the more radical members of the House of Commons who reported a conversation which he dated to September 1646* during which Oliver opined that 'it was a miserable thing to serve parliament to whom let a man be never so faithful if one pragmatical fellow amongst them rise up and asperse them, he shall never wipe it off'.[3] It would seem that Cromwell, in his old forthright style, had told the House a few home truths and found himself snubbed for his pains. Yet he continued, right up until January, to be an assiduous and active member. He believed in the institution of parliament and could probably see the constitutional crisis to which the obduracy of Holles and his supporters was driving the country. That crisis came two steps closer in February: the Scottish army, partly paid off, retired across their border and the King was escorted to Holdenby House, Northamptonshire.

Charles very thankfully exchanged the rough hospitality of his Scottish hosts for the comfort of one of his own residences. He made a leisurely eight-day progress, staying *en route* at the homes of several of the great Northern and Midlands magnates.

> . . . through most parts where his majesty passed some out of curiosity but most (it may be presumed) for love, flocked to behold him and accompanied him with acclamations of joy and with their prayers for his preservation . . . not any of the troopers who guarded their king gave those country people any check or disturbance as the king passed that could be observed (a civility his majesty was well pleased with).[4]

At Holdenby Charles was able to establish the semblance of a court. The parliamentary commissioners, some of whom were courtiers and nobles he had known for many years, attended him respectfully, dined with him and accompanied him to Prayer Book services in his chapel twice on Sundays. The King's life now assumed a calm and

---

* Some commentators suggest, without evidence, that the incident should be located a few months later.

pleasurable routine. Each day he spent two or three hours reading. Later he would walk in the Holdenby gardens or ride over to Harrowden or Althorpe, where the owners maintained bowling greens, and enjoy a game with his companions. In the intervals of this leisured existence he continued his discussions with the Parliament men – except on Sundays, which were entirely given over to devotional exercises.

The parliamentary Presbyterians seemed now to hold all the cards: Charles was their guest and, with no foreign troops on English soil, the disbandment of the New Model could proceed apace. As soon as Holles had raised a loan in the City to fund part – by no means all – of the army's arrears of pay, the Commons ordered the decommissioning of the majority of the New Model rank and file and, to discourage them from being a possible threat, offered them employment in Ireland. The troops who did remain in England were to be under the command of Fairfax but all other officers above the rank of colonel were to be pensioned off. By such measures the Presbyterians planned to retain a reduced force for their own protection in which all Independent elements could be suppressed. Within Parliament Holles had completely outmanoeuvred his opponents. St John, Vane and their allies were virtually silenced and Cromwell, when he had recovered from his illness, seldom attended the House. Thus, the crisis became unavoidable: the effective removal of a parliamentary opposition left the politicians and the military in direct conflict with each other. As Holles's colleague, Philip Stapleton, expressed the situation succinctly, 'We must sink them or they sink us.'

Bound up with the firm handling of the army was the Presbyterians' attempt to suppress religious separatists. Respectable citizens tended to lump all non-conventional Christians together as 'anabaptists' and 'dangerous sectaries'. They were associated in the popular mind with the New Model, and Cromwell was already being spoken of as their principal patron. Inevitably, London housed a greater concentration of these enthusiasts than any other town and, in December 1646, the City fathers presented a petition asking Parliament to suppress all unorthodox conventicles. Within days an ordinance passed both Houses instructing all local officials 'to proceed against all who preach or expound the Scriptures . . . except they be ordained either here or in some reformed church'.[5] For Cromwell this struck right to the heart. It demonstrated that

Parliament, or at least a parliament controlled by Denzil Holles and Co., would set up an ecclesiastical regime just as tyrannical and narrow-minded as Laud's.

Oliver's anguish at the way events were shaping up was acute. No less than the King did he find himself 'despised and rejected of men' and oppressed by the enemies of God's truth. His distress emerges from his correspondence with Fairfax. On 21 December he reported:

> ... We have had a very long petition from the City. How it strikes at the army and what other aims it has, you will see by the contents of it; as also what the prevailing temper is at this present, and what is to be expected from men. But this is our comfort, God is in heaven, and He doth what pleaseth Him; His and only His counsel shall stand, whatever the designs of men, and the fury of the people be . . .[6]

On 7 March he expressed himself as resigned to suffer with his fellow evangelicals. There seems to have been no thought in his mind of taking up the vengeful sword of the Lord:

> ... I find this only good, to love the Lord and his poor despised people, to do for them, and to be ready to suffer with them: and he that is found worthy of this hath obtained great favour from the Lord; and he that is established in this shall (being conformed to Christ and the rest of the Body) participate in the glory of a Resurrection which will answer all . . .[7]

Patience under persecution was still the burden of a letter he wrote four days later:

> Never were the spirits of men more embittered than now. Surely the Devil hath but a short time. Sir, it's good the heart be fixed against all this. The naked simplicity of Christ, with that wisdom He pleased to give, and patience, will overcome all this. That God would keep your heart as He has done hitherto, is the prayer of
> Your Excellency's most humble servant,
> Oliver Cromwell[8]

By 19 March the politicians were growing alarmed at the intransigence of the army leaders being thrown up by the crisis. They issued an order that no body of armed men was to come closer than twenty-five miles to the capital. Oliver passed this on to Fairfax. From this letter it is clear that he was not attending the Commons himself but that he disapproved of the defiant attitudes being struck by some of the troops.

> This enclosed order I received; but, I suppose, letters from the committee of the Army to the effect of this are come to your hands before this time. I think it were very good that the distance of twenty-five miles be very strictly observed; and they are to blame that have exceeded the distance, contrary to your former appointment. This letter I received this evening from Sir William Masham, a member of the House of Commons; which I thought fit to send you; his house being much within the distance of twenty-five miles of London. I have sent the officers down, as many as I could well light of . . .[9]

While Cromwell wrestled within himself to discern how he should react to this persecution of the saints, others were not slow to offer advice. Simple soldiers and fellow evangelicals looked to Cromwell above all men to champion their cause.

> Thou great man, Cromwell! Think not with thyself that thou shalt escape in the parliament house more than all the rest of the Lamb's poor despised redeemed ones, and therefore, O Cromwell, if thou altogether holdest thy peace, or stoppest and underminest, as thou dost our and the army's petitions at this time, then shall enlargement and deliverance arise to us poor afflicted ones, that have hitherto doted too much on thee, O Cromwell, from another place than you silken Independents . . . and therefore, if you wilt pluck up thy resolutions, and go on bravely in the fear and name of God, and say with Esther, 'If I perish, I perish'; but if thou would not, know that here before God, I arraign thee at his dreadful bar, and there accuse thee of delusions and false words deceitfully, for betraying us, our wives and children, into the Haman-like tyrannical clutches of Holles and Stapleton . . .[10]

The writer was the incendiary John Lilburne, whose cause Oliver had once championed but with whose extremism he had no sympathy. Doubtless there were other more persuasive voices assaulting his ear as, day after day, he sought the Lord in agonised prayer.

There will always be an element of dispute about Cromwell's role in the events of mid-March to early June 1647. The conspiracy theory urged by Clarendon and royalist historians has long been discredited. It would have taken extremely ingenious machiavellianism to manipulate the contending parties with the objective of gaining supreme power. Whatever degree of duplicity Oliver was capable of when under pressure fell far short of that. But this still leaves the question, 'How far was Cromwell the proactive instigator of events and how far at the mercy of those events?' Beyond a shadow of doubt his answer to that question would have been that he was waiting on divine guidance and the modern chronicler must not ignore this golden thread which ran through all his responses to the alarming and rapidly changing situation. Believers who have a strong sense that God interests himself in the minutiae of their lives are extremely sensitive to 'signs from heaven'. The Lord may speak through any man-made event or human conversation and once his message is heard and interpreted it must be acted upon – wherever it may lead. At one stage during the spring of 1647 it seemed to Oliver that it might be leading across the water into Europe. Diplomats were gradually taking over from generals after thirty years of intermittent war but all the contenders wished to appear as strong as possible as the peace process gathered momentum. That included the Elector Palatine (Prince Rupert's elder brother) who hoped for the restitution of his territory. Just as, years before, Cromwell had contemplated emigration to the New World when the free exercise of his religion was threatened at home, so now he considered leading a small army for the Calvinist Elector Charles Lewis. This may have seemed desirable on two counts: it would provide Cromwell with a legitimate crusade and it would defuse the English situation by removing part of the army overseas.

However, there was to be no escape for him; he was the one man who could resolve the crisis. Parliament's leaders, though loath to admit it, needed Cromwell no less than the army. General Fairfax had the respect of all, but the wilder elements among the troops would not automatically follow him, as they were soon to show. Only old Ironsides had the necessary charisma. The army rank and file, particularly those in the major encampment at Saffron Walden, were organising themselves by electing 'agitators' to present their legitimate grievances to Parliament. But theirs were not the only voices being heard in the military ranks. More strident were those of John Lilburne and the Levellers. These London-based social revolutionaries were demanding an extended franchise, religious toleration and abolition of the House of Lords, and their leaders saw in the New Model a body which would back their programme with force. This was exactly what the politicians at Westminster and their friends in the City had claimed – and had helped to bring about: the New Model was a rabble of sectaries, fanatics and revolutionaries. Holles insisted that to such men there could be no surrender. When an army petition came before Parliament at the end of March it was summarily dismissed and the Commons went on to resolve that those who continued to resist them should be proceeded against as enemies of the state. They did, however, raise another £200,000 towards arrears of pay. It was too little, too late.

> I entreat you that there may be ways of love and composure thought upon. I shall do my endeavours, though I am forced to yield something out of order to keep the army from disorder or worse inconveniences.[11]

That appeal by Fairfax was rushed off to Westminster at the end of May and what is surprising about it is not that the crisis had deepened but that it had taken so long to do so. The army had the power to overawe the politicians, they felt that they had justice on their side and several of their officers were prepared to lead them, but they were reluctant to resort to force and for this Cromwell takes much of the credit. He had spent the greater part of the month as part of a commission operating between London and Saffron Walden to deal with the soldiers' grievances. By patiently receiving delegates from the various regiments and openly discussing their representations with them, point by point, he and his colleagues did much to calm their fears. In a speech to over two hundred officers in the church of St Mary the Virgin, Cromwell's strong voice echoed around the vault of Essex's most magnificent ecclesiastical edifice: 'Gentlemen, by the command of your major-general I will offer a word or two to you,' he began. He outlined to his audience Parliament's latest proposals for dealing with their complaints, urged them to disband and communicate the information to their regiments and to wait patiently while the politicians deliberated upon the issues still outstanding. 'Truly gentlemen,' he concluded,

> it will be very fit for you to have a very great care in the making of the best use and improvement that you can both of the votes and of this that hath been last told you, and of the interest which all of you or any of you

may have in your several respective regiments, namely to work in them a good opinion of that authority that is over both us and them. If that authority falls to nothing, nothing can follow but confusion. You have hitherto fought to maintain that duty, and truly as you have vouchsafed your hands in defending that, so [vouchsafe] now to express your industry and interest to preserve it, and therefore I have nothing more to say to you. I shall desire that you will be pleased to lay this to heart that I have said.[12]

The Commons received their commissioner's report sombrely and actually began to address themselves to the points raised. But they did so in an atmosphere of mounting panic and at the same time the Holles faction was engaged in intrigues whose discovery finally shattered the patience of the long-suffering troops. They toyed with various schemes of which the main elements were: to lodge the King more securely (possibly in Scotland), to invite the military involvement of the Scots by promising the rigid enforcement of Presbyterianism, and to set in hand the immediate disbandment of the army and, while this was being done, to disperse the regiments to different parts of the country so that they could not combine. Within days all that had been achieved at Saffron Walden collapsed, as did the commission, and a new concentration of army units gathered at Newmarket to plan drastic action.

Cromwell now had to take the initiative. He called a group of army leaders and prominent evangelicals to a series of meetings at his house in Drury Lane. There they talked and prayed and plotted with a sense of rapidly mounting urgency. Something would have to be done and done quickly to prevent the unleashing of anarchy. Nathaniel Fiennes, one of their number, explained in a pamphlet what their objectives were and dissociated their cause from Leveller radicalism: '[We] resolve . . . to keep the three estates coordinate equally to praise and blame each other . . . We need not, we will not to gain a peace be without a king, nor without this king: only he himself hath brought this necessity upon us, not to trust him with that power whereby he may do us and himself harm.'[13] It was in accord with their avowed principle of protecting the King from his enemies and from himself that they resolved to place a trusted guard around him. This was done on 3 June. The same day Parliament voted to seize Cromwell and convey him to the Tower.

*

'I believe thou wilt not think it strange that I desire to go from hence to any other part of the world,' so Charles complained in a letter to his wife while he was suffering the hospitality of the Covenanters. He might have reflected that he only had himself to blame. It was he who had decided to leave Oxford and throw himself on the mercy of the Scots. Hyde had counselled him to stay in the university city 'to the last biscuit' and then allow himself to be honourably escorted to London for negotiations with Parliament. History would certainly have been very different had this advice been followed. But Charles, unable to weigh opinions objectively, alternated between lassitude and determined activity. He was also obsessed with his image. Much as he hated his confinement at Newcastle he aborted what might have been a feasible escape attempt when he felt his dignity affronted. He donned a disguise and made his way down a servants' staircase. Then he suddenly decided that he would be sure to be spotted by at least one of the guards who would then have a great laugh at his expense. Rather than risk that he returned to his room.

The change in his circumstances in February 1647 was profound. Holdenby House was a very large Elizabethan mansion seven miles from Northampton, built by Sir Christopher Hatton as 'the last and greatest monument of his youth'[14], and subsequently bought by Anne of Denmark as a gift for her younger son. The manor was disconcertingly close to Naseby but here Charles could feel himself to be once again a real king. He had his court, his household routine, his hunting, his chapel and some of his favourite servants. Although he was guarded, the restrictions were not onerous. He was able to ride out to the estates of local magnates and to receive Northamptonshire gentry who came to assure him of their loyalty. Whenever he went abroad the curious and the devout came to stare and cheer. Clearly, Charles could reflect, his people still loved him. The strains of recent months were eased away and everything he heard about the mutual hostility of Parliament and army put him in a good humour. Negotiations with Holles and his clique were, of course, continuing and the tactics to be employed were simple and obvious: spin out the bargaining process as long as possible and wait for his enemies to destroy themselves. Charles's latest concessions in mid-May – Presbyterian government for three years, parliamentary control of the militia for ten years and a general amnesty – were less than Parliament could accept but kept open the door for further discussion. Nothing shook Charles's basic conviction that the Crown was the nation's only possible focus of loyalty and that eventually some caucus of politicians and/or generals would have to restore him to his rightful place. Then the reckoning could begin. But suddenly events took on a new momentum and, once again, Charles was powerless to prevent himself being carried along with them.

He was playing bowls on the afternoon of 2 June at nearby Althorpe when a message arrived that mounted troops were approaching Holdenby. The King's party returned to the house but it was not until much later, after Charles had retired, that a body of five hundred soldiers arrived. The ensuing events are best described in the vivid prose of an eyewitness.

> . . . about midnight came that party of horse, which in good order drew up before the house at Holdenby and at all avenues placed guards; which done, the officer that commanded the party alighted and demanded entrance. Colonel Graves and Major-General Browne* asked him his name and business. He replied his name was Joyce, a cornet in Colonel Whalley's regiment and his business was to speak with the king.
>
> 'From whom?' said they.
>
> 'From myself,' said he, at which they laughed.
>
> 'It's no laughing matter,' said Joyce.
>
> Then they advised him to draw off his men and in the morning he should speak with the commissioners.
>
> 'I came not hither to be advised by you,' said he, 'nor have I any business with the commissioners. My errand is to the king and speak with him I must and will presently.'
>
> They then bid the soldiers within to stand to their arms and be ready to fire when ordered. But, during the short treaty twixt the cornet and the colonel, the soldiers had conference together and, so soon as they understood they were fellow soldiers of one and the same army, they quietly forgot what they had promised; for they opened the gates and doors, shook one another by the hand, and bade them welcome.[15]

Joyce made his way by back stairs to the King's apartments

---

*Richard Browne was a parliamentary general of Presbyterian inclinations who had been appointed one of the commissioners. It appears that Charles secured his conversion at Holdenby and he later suffered long imprisonment for supporting the royalist cause.

demanding instant admittance. Finding the door locked he brandished a pistol before the chamber staff but all to no avail. At length, the King, roused by the commotion, sent word that he would receive the officer in the morning, and with that Joyce had to be content.

The following day George Joyce gruffly presented his credentials. He was, he announced, a cornet (junior officer and pennant carrier) in General Fairfax's regiment and he had been sent to convey the King to a place of safety beyond the reach of Parliament. When Charles enquired after Joyce's authority the soldier waved a hand towards the window through which could be seen the New Model horsemen in the courtyard. This response amused the King who was happily prepared to go with his army escort. To him this turn of events was proof of how rapidly the opposition was disintegrating. It mattered not whether Parliament or army was the agency of his return to power.

Thus Cornet Joyce appears on the stage of history for his brief and crucial moment of fame, leaving the audience to grapple with the conundrum of who wrote his script. Joyce was twenty-nine, a London tailor before the war, a soldier who spent some time serving under Cromwell's cousin, Richard Whalley, one of the more radical senior officers, and he was a zealot whose commitment had in recent months led to his becoming an agitator. He must have been in London during those first days of June when Cromwell and his friends were having their urgent meetings, though he was certainly too junior to be a party to them. The 'conspirators' felt themselves under pressure of events: reliable informants or rumour or both indicated that the Holles faction were about to follow their con-demnation of the army with drastic action. Since confrontation was now inevitable, Cromwell's group had to pre-empt their opponents' plans and two priorities were obvious: they had to secure the considerable store of munitions still in Oxford and they had to place an effective guard round the King. There was no time for setting in hand careful plans; haste and secrecy dominated all. It would have taken too long to send into East Anglia for appropriate contingents of troops and, in any case, with the army refusing to obey orders to disband, conveyed through Fairfax, it was by no means clear who was in command. Thus, a makeshift and desperate operation was cobbled together. Cornet Joyce was summoned and ordered to gather what men he could and attempt both objectives.

371

But what precisely was he instructed to do? When he reached Holdenby he had no written orders that he was prepared to show the King, yet written orders he must have received. The commanding officers at Oxford and Holdenby would scarcely have accepted the unsupported authority of a mere cornet. If the major objective was to seize the King is it really feasible that the Cromwell caucus would have sent a boy – and a hot-headed boy, at that – to do a man's job? Would not both prudence and courtesy have demanded that a senior officer should be sent on such a mission? Any moral judgement of Cromwell's action in this crisis must face the question, not whether he intended to make the King his prisoner, but why, if he did, he did not take charge of the operation himself. It would have been an act of appalling cowardice to shelter behind a young officer whose actions could be disavowed if anything went wrong. Such a yellow streak does not square with what we know of Cromwell's character nor does self-preserving dishonesty – he later rejected Joyce's claim that he had ordered the cornet to take the King into custody.

The most likely interpretation of the hasty and muddled events of 2–3 June is that Joyce was despatched with orders for the troops at Oxford and Holdenby. These orders were illegal because they did not bear the authority of Parliament or Fairfax but Cromwell was confident that his name would be sufficient to ensure compliance. So it transpired: the garrison commander at Oxford agreed to hold the magazine for the army and ignore any instructions to the contrary from Westminster. Joyce was then provided with a contingent of men with which he hastened the fifty miles to Holdenby. But there his reception was not so cordial. While the ordinary soldiers welcomed Cromwell's agent, the sympathies of Colonel Graves, the officer commanding, lay with the parliamentary leaders. He had received news of Joyce's approach (presumably from colleagues at Oxford) and made some attempt to resist handing over responsibility for his charge. Overborne by sheer force he escaped in the middle of the night and hurried southwards to report on events and excuse his own dereliction of duty. It was Graves's flight which provoked Joyce's subsequent action. The young man was out of his depth. The parliamentary commissioners at Holdenby insisted that the King was their responsibility but Joyce was under orders to prevent Parliament deciding the King's fate. Anxiously he wrote to Cromwell for fresh instructions the following morning:

Sir,

We have secured the King. Graves is run away, he got out about one o'clock in the morning and so went his way. It is suspected he is gone to London; you may imagine what he will do there. You must hasten an answer to us, and let us know what we shall do. We are resolved to obey no orders but the general's. We shall follow the commissioners' directions while we are here, if just in our eyes. I humbly entreat you to consider what is done and act accordingly with all the haste you can. We shall not rest night nor day till we hear from you.

Your and the Kingdom's
Faithful servant till death,
GEORGE JOYCE[16]

It was the letter of a man close to panic. For all his brusqueness towards Charles, care for the safety of his sovereign thrust upon him a responsibility far beyond his ability to cope. The commissioners will not have been slow to play upon the young man's insecurity and, with only five hundred men at his disposal, he might well have feared an attempt by local royalist sympathisers to storm the house and set the King free. He did not wait for a reply to his letter. Within twenty-four hours he set out with Charles for the main army encampment, which was now at Newmarket. They spent the night of 4–5 June at Hinchingbrooke, which had experienced a change of allegiance. The royalist Sir Sidney Montagu had died in 1644. His son, Edward (later to be famous as Lord Admiral and Earl of Sandwich) was another family member who rebelled against his father, becoming a friend and supporter of Cromwell. Edward was with the army but his wife, Jemima, provided Charles with a reminder of ancient Cromwell hospitality at the former family house.

Cromwell was also on the road. He fled London in the dawn light of 4 June, making for his own country and the army. He reached Newmarket that evening to find the encamped troops buzzing with the exciting news of the King's capture and Fairfax fuming. The general resented the responsibility that had been thrust upon him and wanted to know who was responsible. Cromwell disclaimed all knowledge of the King's transfer and backed the orders the general now sent to Whalley to convey Charles back to Holdenby. Clearly, Fairfax could think no further than restoring the *status quo ante*.

373

The only problem was that Charles refused to co-operate. He would not go back to Northamptonshire and he insisted on remaining a guest of the army. He revelled in Fairfax's embarrassment, he enjoyed the adulation of the crowds who turned out to cheer him wherever he went and he persuaded himself that the nearer he got to the capital the stronger his support would be. Meanwhile, the game he had been playing with Parliament he could go on playing with the army.

Charles was absolutely right in his belief, which he put quite frankly to the general, that someone would have to do a deal with him and that, in the process, they would upset those parties who were excluded from any agreement reached. The 'someone' would then be locked into an engagement of mutual protection with the Crown. If the officer corps of the New Model was that 'someone' they would be faced with the opposition of the Presbyterians, their Scottish allies, the Levellers and other radicals inside and outside the army, and also the City, whose leaders were terrified at the armed hordes stationed not a couple of days' ride from their own walls. 'You cannot do without me; you will fall to ruin if I do not sustain you,' he gleefully told his military hosts a few weeks later.

At last the King and the gentleman met face-to-face, man-to-man. It happened in the house of Sir John Cutts at Childesly, near Cambridge, whither Charles had been removed from Hinchingbrooke on the 5 June 1647, *en route* for Newmarket. It was one of those historical confrontations of which we know tantalisingly little. Cromwell was part of the reception committee headed by the Commander-in-Chief which had come to meet the King, arrange for his accommodation and set up a process of three-way negotiation between Crown, army and Parliament. The only detail which has survived of the encounter is that, while Fairfax kissed the King's hand, Cromwell and Ireton contented themselves with a slight bow. Over the next few weeks Oliver seems to have taken a subordinate position in the negotiations. Ireton, widely acknowledged as a man of 'good learning and great understanding', drafted the propositions which the army wished discussed. During these debates, which occurred as the King and his escort moved, first to Newmarket and thence, by easy stages to Caversham, on the Thames, the military men developed a political philosophy for themselves. They concluded that, 'princes have no prerogatives nor parliaments any privileges but such as are consistent with and in no way prejudicial to the common good of man'[17] and that the army was the guarantor of that common good. Cromwell would never have expressed himself in such words; he was no theorist; but in essence he agreed because, practically speaking, the leaders of the army had become the arbiters of peace.

Since Cromwell now became *de facto* the dominant member of a new army council set up on that same day, 5 June 1647, it was his relationship with the King which moved steadily to the position of centre stage in the nation's life. Fairfax was henceforth no more than a figurehead, and an unwilling figurehead, at that. He carried out his responsibility as guardian of the King while strongly resenting having this role thrust upon him, and he later disclaimed involvement in many decisions of the army council to which his name was attached.

For over four decades Charles and Oliver had occupied positions on the periphery of each other's experience. It was only during the war that 'Cromwell' had been anything more than a name to the King. The same was not true of Oliver's perception of his sovereign. From childhood he had had occasional glimpse of the prince and King. He had grown up with the knowledge of his uncle's devotion to the Stuarts and where that devotion had led him. Since those early days at Hinchingbrooke he had never been able to gaze upon James I or his son through the shimmering veil of royal mystique which the image makers interposed between the sovereign and ordinary mortals. As his own political awareness developed he had formed his own ideas about the function of the Crown and Charles I did not conform to the pattern. Any understanding the King and the gentleman had formed of each other as individuals had been largely compounded of myth, gossip, the opinions of others and occasional, brief encounters. Now, they were thrust into each other's company in conditions, if not of equality, certainly of proximity in which the traditional monarch-subject partition had become paper thin.

The relationship began in an atmosphere of mutual suspicion and mistrust but, remarkably, this soon changed, at least on Cromwell's side. Charles was adept at the tactics of the charm offensive. He had been brought up in an atmosphere in which dissembling often took the place of reasoned debate, flattery was a substitute for kindness and graciousness passed for sincerity. This is not to say that he was capable of nothing but deliberate duplicity. There was about his character, particularly in relaxed moments, a sweetness and diffidence which had nothing to do with contrivance and which won him many devoted servants. The republican, James Harrington, who was later employed as a guardian of the King, often spoke of him with 'the greatest zeal and passion imaginable' and was eventually dismissed for getting too close to his charge. But under the polished courtesies and politeness of a civilised court such *royauté oblige* mingled with studied artifice so completely that it was not always possible for Charles himself to distinguish between artlessness and calculation. He was more than a match for the plainspoken, straight-dealing Cromwell. As they met and talked in various locations during the King's southward journey Oliver was so won over that he came to regard His Majesty as much abused and was even heard to speak of him as 'the most uprightest and most conscientious man of the three kingdoms' and to call God to witness to 'the sincerity of his heart' towards the King.[18] So enthusiastic did Cromwell become to see Charles restored under an acceptable constitution that friends like St John became genuinely alarmed that he was deserting his principles.

It was in the interests of both men to establish good relations during the high summer of 1647. Cromwell had the Presbyterians and the Levellers snapping at his heels, urging their respective unyielding and unacceptable formulas for political settlement. He had not the slightest intention of overthrowing the monarchy and that meant creating a future in which he and his family could live securely under the Stuarts free from any recriminations arising out of the war. Cromwell had every reason to make his peace with the man who would, within months, be back on his throne. There was also the consideration to be borne in mind that the King was the fount of patronage. Oliver always insisted that he had no ambition and desired nothing more than to return to private life. According to Sir John Berkeley, who was appointed to mediate between Charles and the army, Cromwell insisted,

> that whatever this world might judge of them, they would be found no seekers of themselves farther than to have leave to live as subjects ought to do, and to preserve their consciences; and that they thought no men could enjoy their lives and estates quietly without the king had his rights, which they had declared in general terms already to the world.[19]

However, he would have been less than human if he had not reflected on the possible rewards that might fall to those who helped the King to 'have his rights'. So committed had Cromwell become to the King's cause and so openly did he champion it in the army council and Parliament that the radicals branded him a traitor who had abandoned his principles on the promise of an earldom. In August he claimed to be in fear of assassination at the hands of disappointed extremists. Later judges regarded his sentiments of loyalty to the Crown as further evidence of Oliver's duplicity and hypocrisy. However, it is only if we accept them as genuine that we can begin to understand the relationship between the King and the gentleman. Cromwell always respected the honest beliefs of others and wanted to stretch toleration as wide as possible to cover all shades of genuine piety. Now that he came into close contact with Charles he recognised the sincerity of his adversary's faith. He realised that he and the King shared many Protestant convictions, although they chose to express them in different ways. He came to trust the King. It was the subsequent betrayal of that trust that made Cromwell so bitter. Disillusionment, not ambition nor long-term hostility drove the gentleman to kill the King.

Charles's need for cordial relations with his captors was even more obvious. In the short term he was dependent on the army council for his daily comforts. He still had to suffer the company of parliamentary commissioners whose responsibilities did not include making life pleasant for him. His military nurses were more amenable and had it in their power to restore his favourite servants and provide him with accommodation suitable to his status. Edward Whalley had immediate charge of the King and he exercised his responsibilities with vigilance and respect. A letter to him from Cromwell of 25 June instructed him to allow some of the royal chaplains to minister to Charles and to prevent the Presbyterian commissioners from interposing themselves. By keeping negotiations going and allowing the military junta to hope for a speedy settlement the King was able to bargain for fresh concessions. He was allowed considerable freedom, enjoyed hunting and bowls and the civilised company of courtiers and friends. On 24 August the pilgrimage ended at Hampton Court where, in the extensive palace, Charles was able to feel really at home. The most moving moment of the royal travels, however, had occurred on 3 July at Caversham. The three royal children, who were under the custody of the Duke of

Northumberland at Syon House, just along the river, were reunited with their father. Cromwell was present at the touching scene and it brought tears to his eyes.

Charles's longer-term interests also depended on his reaching an accommodation with the army because only the army could guarantee him his throne. Moreover, the Grandees (as the Independent leaders were dubbed by those who resented their prominence) were prepared to make far more concessions than any of the other parties with whom the King had dealt. They were even at one stage prepared to extend the rights of co-existence and freedom of worship to Roman Catholics. This revolutionary concession was an extension of the Independents' desire for religious toleration for all shades of Protestant opinion. It also reflected the kind of settlements being reached on the continent where a generation of warfare had brought home to many people the pointlessness of confessional conflict. As for the other aspects of the proposed religious settlement, episcopy was to go but so, too, was the Covenant, and churches who wished to go on using the Prayer Book would be permitted to do so. The other major sticking point, the control of the militia, was covered by the suggestion that it should be returned to the Crown after ten years. These and several other somewhat rambling clauses made up the Heads of the Army's Proposals, which Berkeley commended to the King in the words 'never was a crown so near lost so cheaply recovered as his majesty's would be if they agreed upon such terms.'[20] So well did the discussions proceed and so graciously did Charles behave towards Cromwell and his colleagues that the Grandees believed a settlement would be reached in a matter of weeks.

Then, at the end of July Charles, with a sudden return to his old haughty demeanour, brusquely rejected the Heads of the Army's Proposals and told the negotiators to come up with 'more equal terms'. The King who claimed, correctly, that the army needed him, was incapable of understanding or accepting the corollary that he needed the army. At some stage he would have to do a deal with someone: he could not go on indefinitely playing off one party against another without losing credibility. The Queen and other counsellors who had previously urged him to come to terms with the Scots now pressed him to accept what was on offer from the army. And for the same reason: the priority was to regain power; once that was achieved concessions granted under duress could be reviewed. It was honourable on Charles's part to refuse to give ground on those principles he most believed in but folly to imagine that constant shilly-shallying would eventually enable him to dictate his own terms.

Charles's rejection was like a douche of cold water to Cromwell and his colleagues. It taught them a hard lesson about the trustworthiness of kings. However, the army leaders had more pressing problems on their hands. The reason for Charles's sudden change of stance was a popular rising in London. True to the maxim that force begets force, the Presbyterians had raised a mob which marched on Parliament. Several days before Holles and ten of his party who had been branded by the army had fled. Now their supporters in the City rallied to their defence. On 26 July, while insurgents held the Speaker in his chair, the Commons passed a resolution recalling the King to London. At the same time the anti-Independents made a forlorn effort to put the capital in a state of defence. This desperate show of defiance only achieved results which its leaders had not desired: it encouraged the King to return to his old divide-and-rule stratagem and, by obliging the army to restore order, it underlined the fact that the political initiative had passed to the military. With what ruefulness must the citizens who had grumbled at Cromwell as an instigator of anarchists have watched that same Cromwell ride through their streets at the head of a cavalry troop to restore order and receive a hasty address of welcome from the Lord Mayor.

England was now under military rule. Parliament continued to make laws and pass resolutions but Independents like St John and Vane, who were now once more in the ascendancy, occupied their positions only by courtesy of the army. This had now withdrawn in good order to quarters at Putney and it was a considerable testament to the discipline instilled into the New Model that the troops behaved responsibly – for the time being. There was no looting and there were no personal reprisals. The Grandees continued to urge a political settlement and to use their power to bring this about. The King continued to enjoy royal state at Hampton Court and to receive there those families who were now politically important. Among the more frequent guests were Oliver and Elizabeth Cromwell.

But there was no question of the King and the gentleman picking up where they had left off. The events of late July and early August had rebuilt the walls of mutual suspicion. Behind the smiles and politenesses there was a wariness. Charles had been plunged back

379

into depression by the dashing of his briefly awakened hopes. When negotiations resumed he reluctantly accepted the Heads of Proposals, but he had no confidence in the army's ability or willingness to deliver its side of the bargain. The radicals at Putney were poised for a takeover and if they were successful they would remove his crown and probably his head with it. As for Cromwell, he had come to the conclusion that he was no safer with him. One of his own aides had told him that the man was a villain who was plotting his downfall and he was inclined to believe it. By one agency or another, Charles was convinced that he faced the real threat of assassination.

For his part, Cromwell's intelligence service brought him snippets of information which assured him that the King was still playing devious games. He frankly told John Ashburnham, who had returned to his master's service,

> that the king could not be trusted and that he had no affection [for nor] confidence in the army but was jealous of them and all the officers that he had intrigues in the parliament and treaties with the Presbyterians of the City to raise new troubles [and] that he had a treaty concluded with the Scottish commissioners to engage the nation again in blood.[21]

Yet, despite his own misgivings, the suspicions within the army ranks and the mounting frustration of colleagues who urged abandonment of the King, Cromwell laboured throughout the autumn with brain-punishing intensity to concoct a comprehensive settlement that would retain the monarchy, be achieved through Parliament, take account of the army's Heads of Proposals and release the pressure of steam building up at Putney. No one saw more clearly than Cromwell just how critical the situation was: the army was becoming daily more difficult to manage; the people were desperate for peace and resentful of the continued expense of maintaining a large body of armed men; if the Scots once more intervened there was no guarantee that English troops would be prepared to face them in battle; once the army had been divided to undertake different duties the Grandees would probably be unable to maintain control. On 20 October Cromwell, reputedly, regaled the Commons with a three-hour speech in which 'he spoke very favourably of the king, concluding that it was necessary to re-establish him as quickly as possible'.

Religion was, of course, central to any permanent solution and Cromwell was a member of the group that grappled with proposals for as generous a constitution as possible for the national church. The Toleration Bill, presented to Parliament in October, advocated tithe reform, and abolished fines for absence from parish worship for all those who heard the word of God preached or expounded 'elsewhere'. Orthodoxy was defined as those points covered in the first fifteen Articles of Religion, a minimal Trinitarian test which avoided such contentious issues as predestination, election and church order.[22]

While responsible parliamentarians and army leaders were straining every mental muscle to achieve an honourable settlement, Charles was fretting in his gilded cage. He resented his imprisonment and had no confidence in any settlement dictated by the army. Reports from Parliament informed him that Cromwell had pressed for far-reaching reprisals against Charles's advisers and a severe purge of court personnel as conditions of restoring him to power. Even if he were to consent to be conveyed to his throne riding on the shields of the army it seemed far from clear that the soldiers could convey him safely thither or provide united support. The King was fully aware of the divisions within the army quartered a mere six miles away across the river and the open heathland of Richmond and Wimbledon. How could a crown be safe which came by courtesy of anarchists and republicans? Some of his attendants even suggested that Cromwell was hand-in-glove with the extremists: he had visited John Lilburne, currently in prison in the Tower, and spent more than an hour in private conversation with the arch-agitator (Cromwell had, in fact, been trying to persuade Lilburne to calm the activities of his anti-Parliament, anti-King, anti-Grandee supporters). In an atmosphere of rumours flying thick and fast Charles did not know what to believe, and he could take no initiative which might enable him to adopt a positive role in the course of events. Cooped up at Hampton Court, he received news of plots, counter-plots and assassination plans. When he demanded the right to come to Parliament in person to take part in negotiations his guardians refused to allow him to move. As the autumn advanced Charles's powerlessness to influence the course of events became intolerable.

His plotting with other parties continued. He was allowed to receive commissioners from the Scottish parliament: as the representatives of an allied nation they could scarcely be denied access to their sovereign. Hamilton was still *persona non grata*, but Charles welcomed his younger brother William, Earl of Lanark, accompanied by John Campbell, Earl of Loudoun and John Maitland, Earl of Lauderdale. Lauderdale, an arrogant schemer of the first water, took the lead in urging the King to firm and decisive action. In July he had been forcibly removed from Charles's presence on discovery of plans to bring a Scottish army back into England. At the end of the month he was again at the King's side steeling him to reject the army's peace plan. The commissioners frequently attended on the King at Hampton Court. The sticking point, as always, in negotiations with the Scots was their insistence on the Covenant. Lauderdale suggested that this problem could be got round if the King had his freedom. He even arrived with fifty mounted men one day in the park at Hampton while Charles was hunting, offering to spirit him away on the instant. He brought with him written guarantees of Scottish military intervention but Charles declined, saying that he had given his word not to escape.

He contemplated many ways of regaining his liberty during his months at Hampton Court but, as ever, he became tangled in his confused emotions and principles. He could not decide whether to go, where to go and whom to go with. Chivalry dictated that he should not break his promise. However, when it became necessary he found a way around this. The royal pledge had been given to Whalley via Ashburnham. Charles instructed the latter to tell his jailer that because Scottish influence at court was increasing he could no longer personally guarantee that efforts would not be made to carry the King off. By somewhat Jesuitical logic the King reckoned that this absolved him also from his oath.

He continued his clandestine correspondence with the Queen. Of course, his guardians knew that the King was taking every opportunity to send and receive messages and sometimes they were able to intercept them. The most celebrated piece of Cromwellian counter-intelligence was the so-called 'saddle letter'. According to an account which passed through several layers of oral tradition but which claimed to originate with Cromwell himself, the lieutenant-general personally trapped a courier at the Blue Boar Inn in Holborn. He was carrying a royal message concealed in a saddle which he was to hand to French agents in Dover. When the stitching was slit and the secret paper removed it was found to be a letter to Henrietta Maria informing her that the army and the Scots were rivals for his co-operation and that he had decided to throw in his lot with the latter. Cromwell claimed that it was this that had finally turned him against Charles Stuart. The story, which has all the signs of being considerably embroidered, provides a conveniently simple answer to a crucial question which, in reality, had a much more complex solution. Another version of the incident speaks of a letter *from* Henrietta Maria *to* Charles, informing him of the Scottish invasion. After interception it was re-sealed and allowed to reach the King. A few days later the King was asked if he knew anything about Hamilton's actions. When he replied in the negative, it is said, he forfeited the last vestiges of trust.

Cromwell supported monarchy because he could not conceive of any other kind of government being accepted. He struggled against mounting opposition to restore Charles to his throne only to be irritated by Charles's frequent exhibitions of bad faith. No less than the King, he was the victim of alarmist rumours: there were schemes to bring aid to the Stuart cause from Scotland, Ireland, France and pockets of royalist resistance in various parts of the country; Presbyterians, Scots, even Levellers were in cahoots with emissaries from the court. In such an atmosphere Cromwell must have often questioned his championing of the King, and whether such a man, once restored, could have reunited the country in peace. Doubtless there was a 'final straw' which eventually forced him to turn against the King and it may have been the saddle letter incident or something very like it. Throughout much of the autumn of 1647 he certainly had more worrying and pressing problems to cope with, problems which must have worn down his patience to paper thinness.

By the end of October the simmering discontent in the army had to be faced. Some units were close to mutiny and several high-ranking officers were infected. The Grandees decided that demonstrations of firm discipline would not answer; they would have to listen to the complaints of the men and provide them with answers that would buy their continued loyalty. Fairfax had concealed himself behind a barrier of 'illness' and it was Cromwell who, on 28 October, took the chair of the famous Putney Debates in the church of St Mary the Virgin, little more than a stone's throw from the building where his ancestor had opened an inn in the years of the first Tudor. Robert Paul called this extraordinary gathering 'the "Church Meeting" of a congregation in arms'.[23] Each day's session began with prayer and speakers buttressed their arguments with appeals to Scripture. The range of opinions ardently offered was such that no agreement was possible. Probably Cromwell was enough of a realist to recognise this from the outset. What was important was the process, not the outcome. Cromwell had two motives in his handling of this potentially explosive gathering. The first was pragmatic: the situation could only be defused if the participants knew that their views had been aired and listened to and that the leadership understood the fears and expectations of the rank and file. The chairman was scrupulously fair in allowing every shade of opinion to be expressed. He even permitted the troublesome Thomas Rainsborough to attend, even though he had been recently transferred to the navy and was, therefore, technically debarred from the Putney Debates. Cromwell's second, and overriding concern, was to discern the will of God. In his sincerely held conviction it was the Lord of Hosts who was the real chairman of the assembly. The discussions, therefore, had to take place *sub specie aeternitatis* so that kings and parliaments and soldiers could be seen in the context of the divine plan.

The Levellers had just published two manifestos: *The Case of the Army Truly Stated* and the *Agreement of the People* and these formed the basis for discussion although, despite the chairman's efforts, speakers often rambled off the point. The advocates of people power wanted parliaments accountable to all men and elected on the basis of manhood suffrage. Soldiers who had ventured their lives to achieve a just constitutional settlement thought it reasonable that they, as well as the men of property, should have a place in that settlement. Wilder spirits pressed for the abolition of the privileges of the Crown and the House of Lords. The majority declared themselves against any more treating with Charles Stuart, denounced by one of their number as a 'man of blood'. Everyone was agreed on the principle of religious toleration. Resolutions were passed concerning the frequency and duration of parliaments and the absolute supremacy of the House of Commons. Before Cromwell persuaded the representatives to disperse to their regiments on 8 November, having effectively killed the *Agreement of the People* by referring it to a committee, the constitution had been taken apart, its components scrutinised and left unassembled.

Cromwell's responses to the Putney Debates proposals, most of which had to wait at least two centuries before being incorporated

into the British political system, show him to have been no demo-
crat. He opposed extension of the franchise as anarchic, agreeing
with Ireton that it was for men of property with a stake in the country
to be involved in the government of the country. He strongly advised
against tearing down the existing political fabric; it was for
Parliament, not the army, to decide how the country should be
governed. However, this did not mean that the constitution was
sacrosanct. He bade his comrades consider the people of the Old
Testament:

> . . . They were first [divided into] families where they lived, and had
> heads of families [to govern them], and they were [next] under judges,
> and [then] they were under kings. When they came to desire a king, they
> had a king; first elective, and secondly by succession. In all these kinds
> of government they were happy and contented. If you make the best of
> it, if you should change the government to the best of it, it is but a
> [small] thing. It is but as Paul says 'dross and dung in comparison of
> Christ', and when we shall so far contest for temporal things that if we
> cannot have this freedom we will venture life and livelihood for it, I
> think the State shall come to desolation. Therefore the considering of
> what is fit for the kingdom does belong to the parliament.[24]

And, of course, over and above Parliament stood the sovereign God.
This was the voice of the liberal, rather than the radical, urging
cautious change, through the appropriate channels, and warning
against the siren song of 'Liberty'.

It was at this moment that Charles chose to display yet again what
one commentator has called 'his facility for the timely blunder'.[25]
With hotheads talking about putting the 'man of blood' on trial or even
disposing of him without that formality Cromwell took the prudent
step of instructing Whalley to double the guard at Hampton Court.
Whalley put this order into effect on 11 November and explained to
Charles why it was necessary. That very night Charles absconded. It
was like the flight from Oxford all over again: although escape plans
had been discussed, the actual breakout was an impromptu affair and
its aftermath woefully disorganised. Whether Whalley's talk of
assassins spurred the King into action or reports of the Putney Debates
convinced him that he was no longer safe in army hands, Charles
hurriedly left the palace by a side door, was rowed across the river to
Thames Ditton and there met by Ashburnham and Berkeley with

horses. The plan was to make for the Earl of Southampton's fine house at Titchfield close to the south coast which they should have reached by the following morning; however, they managed to get hopelessly lost during the night and this gave Cromwell time to despatch messengers to all the likely ports. In fact, the lieutenant-general credited Charles with better organisational skills than he possessed. Arrived at Titchfield, the King did not know what to do next. No ship had been arranged to convey him across the Channel. Lauderdale had advised him to make for Berwick from where he could contact the Scots, upon whom his salvation now rested.

It was Ashburnham who suggested the Isle of Wight as a staging post for the continent. There were royalist gentlemen there who would count it an honour to aid the King's escape. They would, however, have to satisfy themselves as to the attitude of the island's governor, Robert Hammond, who was known to the courtiers as the nephew of one of the royal chaplains and an officer who, though having fought for the enemy, had become disillusioned with the army leadership. Having so far been successful in his freedom bid, Charles hazarded all on an approach to someone whose loyalty he could not be sure of. He commissioned Ashburnham and Berkeley to cross the choppy waters of the Solent, corrugated by an autumn gale, to sound Hammond out very discreetly. He expected them to return, having spied out the situation, with information he could weigh up in deciding where to go next. What happened was that they returned with Hammond in person. Of all the mistakes made by the King and his companions since the beginning of the war this was arguably the worst. It is no wonder that Charles greeted Ashburnham with the words, 'What! You have brought Hammond with you? O you have undone me!'

Robert Hammond, who came from a distinguished line of doctors, lawyers and divines, was a twenty-six-year-old soldier of the highest integrity who was very jealous of his honour and who enjoyed the affectionate regard of most people who knew him well. Among that number was Oliver Cromwell, to whom he was distantly related (having married one of John Hampden's daughters). The Civil War had obliged him to consider carefully where his loyalty lay. His own family was one of those bitterly divided by the conflict: of his two uncles, the elder, Thomas, was a parliamentary lieutenant-general of ordnance who later took part in the King's trial, and the younger was among the most scholarly of

Laudian divines, and accompanied Charles as a chaplain throughout the latter part of the war. Robert enlisted in the parliamentary army, rapidly commended himself to the leadership and, when the New Model Army was formed, he became one of its youngest regimental commanders. However, after the defeat of the royalists he witnessed with dismay the conflict between army and Parliament, became assailed by doubts and, in the middle of 1647, resigned his commission. His friends among the Grandees respected his conscientious objections and awarded him the quiet sinecure post of Governor of the Isle of Wight. Before taking up his appointment he went to Hampton Court to call upon his uncle and Dr Hammond introduced him to the King. From their – probably brief – conversation Charles and his attendants gained the impression that the likeable young man had been converted to the royalist cause and it was on the basis of that belief that Ashburnham went to Carisbrooke Castle and blurted out the whole story of the King's escape.

But Hammond was no more a committed King's man than a supporter of the army leadership. He was still wrestling with religious, moral and political principles. What those principles were becomes clear from a remarkable letter Cromwell wrote to him a year later. It is worth a slight digression from the narrative to look at this affectionate and frank epistle, for in it the writer reveals much about the development of his own attitude towards Charles and Parliament:

Dear Robin,

   No man rejoiceth more to see a line from thee than myself. I know thou hast long been under trial. Thou shalt be no loser by it. All must work for the best.

   Thou desirest to hear of my experiences. I can tell thee: I am such a one as thou didst formerly know, having a body of sin and death, but I thank God, through Jesus Christ our Lord there is no condemnation, though much infirmity, and I wait for the redemption. And in this poor condition I obtain mercy, and sweet consolation through the Spirit, and find abundant cause every day to exalt the Lord, and abase flesh, and herein I have some exercise.

Before considering the issues of conscience Hammond has raised with him, Oliver directs him to what had become the fundamental reality of his own life – the perfect and eternal purposes of God.

If thou wilt seek, seek to know the mind of God in all that chain of Providence, whereby God brought thee thither, and that person [i.e. the King] to thee; how, before and since, God has ordered him, and affairs concerning him: and then tell me, whether there be not some glorious and high meaning in all this, above what thou hast yet attained?

As at the Putney Debates, Cromwell was insistent in relating present experiences to the higher economy of the spiritual realm.

Then he comes to Robin's central problem. It was one which he had had to confront – along with numerous dissidents ever since the beginning of the Reformation: on what grounds is a Christian justified in defying 'the powers that be'.

You say: 'God hath appointed authorities among the nations,' to which active or passive obedience is to be yielded. This 'resides in England in the Parliament' . . .

Authorities and powers are the ordinance of God. This or that species is of human institution, and limited, some with larger, others with stricter bands, each one according to its constitution. I do not therefore think the authorities may do anything, and yet such obedience [be] due, but all agree there are cases in which it is lawful to resist.

The question was whether the army found itself in such a case. Hammond had suggested that, surely, the justification for any government was the good of the people. To this the older man makes three observations:

First, whether *Salus Populi* be a sound position? Secondly, whether in [the current negotiations between King and Parliament] really and before the Lord, before whom conscience must stand, this be provided for, or the whole fruit of the war like to be frustrated, and all most like to turn to what it was, and worse? And this, contrary to engagements, declarations, implicit covenants with those who ventured their lives upon those covenants and engagements . . .? Thirdly, whether this army be not a lawful power, called by God to oppose and fight against the king upon some stated grounds; and being in power to such ends, may not oppose one name of authority, for those ends, as well as another . . .

These are no more reasoned arguments than the Stuarts' assertion of the divine right of kings. They stem from Cromwell's fundamental beliefs in a God who acts in history through his people, whose responsibility it is to co-operate with the divine initiatives. Cromwell is impatient with 'fleshly reasonings' and invites his young correspondent to assess for himself what the Lord has been doing in the land since the start of the conflict.

> My dear friend, let us look into providences; surely they mean somewhat. They hang so together; have been so constant, so clear and unclouded. Malice, swollen malice [possessed] against God's people, now called Saints, to root out their name; and yet they, by providence, [possessed] arms, and therein [were] blessed with defence and more.

What of those who insist that it is the Christian's part to suffer, rather than to meet force with force? Cromwell does not despise such 'passive' believers; he tolerantly accepts that they may be led by God to their viewpoints, but counters with the argument that those who are active do not suffer less; indeed, they are ready to risk all, even life itself. The army is made up of such active Christians and God has manifestly been with them.

> Have not some of our friends by their passive principle . . . been occasioned to overlook what is just and honest, and [to] think the people of God may have as much or more good the one way than the other? Good by this man, against whom the Lord hath witnessed [i.e. the King]; and whom thou knowest. Is this so in their hearts; or is it reasoned, forced in [i.e. has it come by spiritual enlightenment or mere human reason].
>
> Robin, I have done. Ask we our hearts, whether we think that, after all, these dispensations, the like to which many generations cannot afford, should end in so corrupt reasonings of good men, and should so hit the designings of bad?
>
> This trouble I have been at, because my soul loves thee, and I would not have thee swerve, nor lose any glorious opportunity the Lord puts into thy hand. The Lord be thy counsellor. Dear Robin, I rest thine,
>
> Oliver Cromwell[26]

Cromwell's faith was not irrational; it was supra-rational, intuitive, experiential. Changes of direction, which to others looked like hypocrisy, and harsh decisions, which critics labelled as vindictive were to him fully justified by his following of the 'mysterious ways' of God. With the man who is convinced that he is led by the Holy Spirit to do what he does there can be no dialogue. Oliver wanted to bring his young friend into this state of attending solely on divine inspiration. Hammond, who clearly shared his mentor's basic religious beliefs, had not yet learned to walk in 'freedom' from the 'tyranny' of fleshly reason.

When Berkeley and Ashburnham called on the young governor at Carisbrooke they completely departed from their brief. Instead of cautiously discerning how Hammond was disposed towards the King they revealed their mission after the briefest preliminaries. Hammond could not have been more alarmed. He grew pale and trembled and broke out into 'passionate and distracted expressions'. He was being drawn into the centre of that very conflict he had sought to avoid. He resolved this dilemma by receiving Charles at Carisbrooke and immediately informing Parliament what he had done.

The army council were furious at the King's flight. They had done everything possible to treat him with the respect due to a sovereign – allowed him to re-establish his court, permitted access by his friends and supporters, allowed him his chaplains (including Richard Holdsworth) and his preferred style of worship. Charles's response had been to break his word, claiming that all men had a right to freedom. Yet, as things turned out, the King only put the army in a stronger position. Cromwell, hearing the news from Hammond, was delighted. The King was out of danger from extremists and was in the custody of the most conscientious jailer imaginable. It was yet one more proof of the unexpected working of divine providence. What mere human agency could so have engineered events that Charles would, of his own volition, place himself securely in the hands of the army and in a place where all undesirable access to him could be prevented?

The immediate priority was still the peaceableness of the army. The radicals had dispersed after the Putney Debates but they were still far from satisfied and the King's flight was yet further proof of just how slippery a customer Charles was and how far distant any permanent settlement of the nation which would permit them all to return to their homes. They demanded further meetings with the army council and there was wild talk of seizing the Grandees and slitting their throats if they did not come out in support of the *Agreement of the People*. The first, and decisive, gathering was at Corkbush Field, near Ware, on 15 November.

Petty demagogues led by John Lilburne's brother had disobeyed orders by coming from other regiments and had been working on the troops for some hours. By the time Fairfax and his colleagues rode forth to the meeting they were confronted by a sullen body of men, some of whom had been whipped into a state of defiance, while the rest waited to see what would happen. The ringleaders had distributed copies of the *Agreement* and several soldiers now paraded with these tied to their hats. The radical Colonel Rainsborough came forward to the general brandishing a copy of the *Agreement*. It was one of those see-saw moments when order and chaos were evenly poised. Then Fairfax brushed Rainsborough aside. Other officers urged their men to support Rainsborough but their superiors acted quickly. Members of the general's bodyguard spurred forward to arrest the dissidents. Still the crisis was not over; Lilburne's followers tried to rally the mutineers. At this point Cromwell thrust himself into their midst. He snatched the papers from some of the men's hats and ordered the rest to remove the offending badges of defiance. Still there was resistance. The lieutenant-general drew his sword and he and his escort grabbed some of the dissidents. This initiative turned the situation. The assembly deserted the mutineers and allowed themselves to be formed into a square to watch the immediate court-martial of the ringleaders. Here, again, the army leaders displayed their mastery by a combination of discipline and mercy. Only three culprits were found guilty and they were allowed to decide their own fate on a throw of the dice. As a result only one mutineer went before a firing squad. This was generalship of a high calibre. It ensured that the meetings on the following two days accepted without question the guidance of the army council. From this point the Levellers were a spent force within the New Model but the day might have been theirs and their success could have unleashed bloody revolution.

Cromwell learned from all these troubled events. His own inclination, as a member of the English landowning class, was towards political and social conservatism but his mind was open to the evolution of new patterns of government and the degree of support for radical change contributed to his own developing ideas. It is impossible to determine any constitutional preference in his thinking at this time and that is because, in all probability he had none – or, at least, that he veered back and forth between republicanism and various forms of limited monarchy. He was content to wait on providence. He spoke in the ongoing Commons debates but by the end of the year Parliament and King were as deadlocked as ever and when news of Charles's latest dealings with the Scots reached Westminster an angry and despairing assembly concluded that further discussion was pointless.

The latest initiative from north of the border was set forth by Hamilton who, taking advantage of a swing in public opinion back towards the King, had gained increased support in Parliament. The terms he obtained were carried to Carisbrooke and formed the basis of the 'Engagement' which Charles agreed with the Scottish commissioners on 27 December. The latest rearrangement of *Titanic* deckchairs looked like this: in return for an army which would place him back on the throne, the King would agree to a three-year trial period for Presbyterianism after which an assembly of divines would conclude a permanent religious settlement, accept the Covenant but compel no one to sign it, enjoy freedom of worship for himself and his household and abolish religious separatism.

The Commons' response was to pass a Vote of No Addresses which finally excluded Charles Stuart from any say in the political settlement of the nation – except that, in the tumbling cloudscape of insubstantial, repetitive and evanescent resolutions, nothing was ever 'final'. In the debate Cromwell was at his most vehement. According to one account he expatiated at great length on the King's duplicity and insisted that he was 'so great a dissembler and so false a man that he was not to be trusted' and several observers noted that the Member for Cambridge spoke with his hand on his sword hilt.

Charles rapidly tired of his new place of confinement. He was, as ever, treated with courtesy by his guards and allowed considerable freedom. Yet again he daily received assurances and tokens of loyalty and devotion. There was the lady who pressed a late musk rose into his hand, the fisherman who had a boat ready at a moment's notice should Charles decide to flee, the laundress who smuggled messages in and out of his chamber, the ex-royalist officer who disguised himself as a labourer in order to carry letters and instructions off the island. And there were guards and castle staff

392

who were won over by the King's charm. Charles had so many devoted subjects on the island that it is surprising that all of the plans made to set him free came to nothing. Several were hatched during the year that Charles spent at Carisbrooke: a boat was made ready to convey him from Newport to Jersey but had to be aborted after a last-minute change of wind direction; a scheme to make a hole in the ceiling of the bedchamber was abandoned because the King feared its discovery; an attempt which involved Charles climbing through a window and down a rope to the courtyard failed when the fugitive stuck in the window frame. Some of these efforts were hare-brained improvisations but others were the result of careful planning and involved several agents pledged to secrecy. The movement of guards and traffic to and from the castle were carefully observed by a network of eager activists. In the last analysis the blame for the failure of all these attempts lies with the King himself. There is no doubting his enthusiasm for escape. He was convinced by rumours and what he considered reliable intelligence that his life was in danger. Now it was not anarchists that he feared: Cromwell had become the arch-assassin. A report in December described an army prayer meeting during which Cromwell and Ireton had pledged themselves to put their sovereign on trial for his life. Another story accredited the military leaders with a plan to send five hundred picked troops to replace the Carisbrooke guard and do away with him clandestinely. Charles had plenty of incentive to get away from the Isle of Wight but so often when the moment for action came he drew back. Sometimes it was fastidiousness that restrained him: certain disguises or stratagems were too demeaning. On other occasions he feared discovery. Other efforts were ruined by his stubbornness. The window incident, for example, occurred because Charles disagreed with his accomplice, Harry Firebrace, one of his pages. Firebrace opined that the opening would have to be enlarged. Charles insisted that he could get through. He was wrong.

Intriguingly bound up with Charles's various escape fantasies is the story of a relationship which, surprisingly, the writers of historical romance have yet to cash in on. Jane Whorwood was, in 1648, a tall red-haired woman with a round, pock-marked face (not unusual in the seventeenth century) in her early thirties. She was passionately devoted to the King's cause and was one of those employed in the chains of couriers who conveyed messages and news to and from the royal prisoner. Charles first met her when she smuggled gold to him from the London royalists and helped organise his flight from Hampton Court. He was soon very taken with this warmly loyal young woman and began treating her as one of his trusted advisers. On his behalf she consulted the astrologer William Lilly to discover the most auspicious times and destinations for the King's escape from Hampton Court and, later, Carisbrooke. At some point their relationship passed beyond that of sovereign and subject and even beyond friendship. In the letters between them Charles signed himself her 'best Platonic lover or servant' and she responded as 'Your most affectionate Helen'.

Charles was very susceptible to the charms of a sympathetic and intelligent woman whose love declared itself in the risks she took for him. He had long been denied the marital comforts of Henrietta's bed and he always sought someone 'special' in his life, never more so than during his stressful captivity. As far as his jailers could discern there were no cracks in the King's mask of rigid self-control but Jane certainly touched his need to love and be loved. His messages to 'Sweet Jane Whorwood' reveal many of the emotions of the languishing Romeo – impatience at her absence, assurances of devotion, anxiety about her feelings for him, suggestions for assignations. For her part, Jane took lodgings close to Carisbrooke in order to be able to see the King as often as possible and render such services as she was able.

How intimate those services were remains a tantalising mystery. There is no proof that Charles and 'N', as she was referred to in cipher, had a physical relationship. No tongues ever wagged about them and no scandal circulated which could be gleefully used by censorious, anti-royalist preachers. But the evidence of the letters is sufficient proof that the King was in love with Jane and that she offered him an affection which went well beyond loyalty.

One man who was not won over by the King was Robert Hammond. His responsibility weighed heavily upon him and periodic exhortations to vigilance from Cromwell made his task no easier. On top of this he was obliged to play cat-and-mouse with his prisoner, tracking down secret messages, foiling escape bids, setting spies and having to call in question the loyalty of some of his own staff. Under instructions from London, Hammond progressively tightened the security surrounding the King. Responding to instructions from Cromwell at the end of the year, in a letter warning him of the activities of Sir George Carteret, royalist Lieutenant-

Governor of Jersey – 'You have warrant now to turn out such servants as you suspect; do it suddenly for fear of danger' – he expelled Ashburnham and Berkeley. In April the King surprised Hammond searching his apartments and there was an unseemly scuffle. In May one of the King's gentlemen accused the governor of involvement in a plot on his master's life. Weeks later more of Charles's close attendants were sent packing following the discovery of acid and tools to be used for loosening the metal fittings of his chamber window. By the summer, relations between host and guest were extremely bitter and Charles was complaining about his guardian, 'the devil cannot outdo him neither in malice nor cunning'.[27]

Hammond's reaction was that he was only doing his job and that he showed the King every consideration possible within the constraints of keeping him secure. This conscientious and sensitive young man found the situation almost as intolerable as did his charge and more than once he begged to be relieved. Hammond ensured that the prisoner received whatever books he wanted although Charles either did not receive or ask for any of his precious pictures. However, the governor did send his young chaplain, Mr Troughton, to the King's apartments in an effort to convert the prisoner. Hammond also provided Charles with a summerhouse. Here he could escape from the gaunt and draughty chambers of the old castle and sit gazing across Newport to the sea and the hills of the mainland beyond. Here Charles spent an increasing amount of his time in that solitary study and prayer he had loved since childhood. He read Hooker's *Ecclesiastical Polity*, Herbert's poems or the philosophy of Bacon. Here, too, he made his own minor contribution to literature; the observations and meditations which would later be incorporated into what devoted royalists believed to be his spiritual testament, the *Eikon Basilike*.

A motto the King wrote frequently in his scraps of memoirs was *dum spiro spero* – 'while I breathe, I hope' – and, despite the frustration of his captivity, Charles had reasons for optimism. Numerous reports – always presented to him in the best possible light – told him that his people wanted him back. From all over the country the news arrived: riots at Canterbury over Christmastide; defiant celebrations of the King's accession day in March; the young Duke of York successfully smuggled out of the country; London apprentice boys marching through the City shouting the slogan

'Now for King Charles'; Welsh gentlemen mustering men and arms; demonstrations throughout the West Country; the Prince of Wales at sea with a fleet provided by his Dutch relatives; and, of course, the Scots would soon be on the march. As the fine spring weather encouraged more people to come out on to the streets and declare themselves, the momentum of dissent accelerated. In April protest turned to disaster when a Norwich crowd stormed the castle and accidentally ignited the magazine. Scores of citizens and soldiers perished beneath the rubble. In May 27,000 signatories were collected in Kent for a petition demanding an agreement with the King and the disbandment of the army. At the same time two thousand Essex men marched to Westminster with similar requests. If the King showed himself to be an incompetent escapologist, part of the reason may have been a belief that it was only a matter of time before his own people rescued him to ride in triumph back to his capital.

Charles's assessment of the mood of the nation (or, at least of the 'better sort' within the nation) was closer to the truth than Cromwell's. Although only doctored fragments of news reached his secluded eyrie he was able to interpret them better than the MP/General who was at the centre of affairs and emerging by sheer force of conviction and personality as the most influential man in England. There is here an ironical reversal of sensitivities: the King for so long isolated in his own dream world was now in tune with what the common heart was pining for; the gentleman who came from the people was now enclosed within a 'court' of fanatics and radical theorists propounding their versions of the new order which must be imposed on an unwilling populace.

That populace hankered after certainties which many of them associated with the 'good old days'. Those who now indulged the Englishman's birthright of being 'agin the government' had much to complain about. Taxes were at an all-time high. Much local government had been taken over by centralised authorities. Citizens felt menaced by soldiers still garrisoned in several parts of the country. There were rumours of a return to war. Families and communities were divided by their rival allegiances. But the dislocation of society went deeper than that. 'The impact of the revolutionary crisis on the certainties of traditional Calvinism' produced 'widespread despair and atheism'.[28] Christopher Hill has graphically described the world of the sectaries: Quakers, Ranters, Seekers, Anabaptists, millenarians and antinomians of every hue, and beyond them hundreds of self-appointed itinerant preachers and prophets. Such manifestations of experiential, lay-led religion, for which Cromwell was blamed by his opponents, would have occurred if the name 'Cromwell' had never been heard in the land and, indeed, if there had been no attempted re-organisation of the church but the collapse of episcopal discipline greatly exacerbated the trend.

In many parts one form of extreme authoritarianism had given way to another even more oppressive. The old hierarchical system had been replaced by varieties of mongrel Presbyterianism. Godly ministers had been introduced and were locally grouped in classes with lay and ordained colleagues, which worked with differing degrees of effectiveness to provide organisation and control beyond the parish. These units, with the magistrates, were charged with the reformation of manners for which the Puritan Parliament legislated. They were supposed to enforce strict Sabbatarianism, to close theatres, to stop dancing, church ales and feast days, and generally to oversee the spread of godliness. In many places they achieved little more than making godliness appear even less attractive.

The reversal of the Laudian reform did not automatically make for peace and harmony in the parishes. Just as men like Job Tookey continued to exercise influence after their deprivation, so some traditionalist clergy dispossessed by the Long Parliament had their supporters and could make life very uncomfortable for the new incumbents. One example among many can be taken from Cromwell's own locality. At Soham, near Cambridge, the Laudian rector, Mr Exeter, was ousted in 1644 and replaced by the Reverend John Fenton. On 8 August 1647 Exeter,

> did in a violent and riotous manner and by force, keep the said Mr Fenton out of the desk and pulpit, and entered therein the said Mr Exeter and one Mr Grimmer, a sequestered minister, who officiated there the same day, the said Exeter reading the book of Common Prayer, and the said Grimmer publishing a proclamation in the name of the king, and a pretended declaration from the army for reinvesting such scandalous ministers as are sequestered into their livings.

Afterwards they went to the rectory and 'cast forth out of doors most of the goods and household stuff of Mr. Fenton and settled Mr. Exeter in possession of the house'.[29] This violence obviously had considerable local support since efforts to dislodge Exeter failed completely and Fenton was obliged to appeal to General Fairfax who, in October, sent a body of cavalry to remove the intruder by force.

Parliament was not slow to sense the mood of the country. In the spring of 1648 they put the Vote of No Addresses on hold and agreed to make no change to the monarchical constitution. All except a small minority in the Commons were in favour of embarking on a new round of negotiations with the King. It is not clear at what precise point Cromwell finally broke with the parliamentary majority over this central issue. Despite his forthright rejection of further substantive talks with the King, we find him in April 1648 accompanying Lord Saye to Carisbrooke on what was supposed to be a secret mission to persuade Charles to abandon his Scottish alliance and, at the same time, sending a personal emissary to Edinburgh on a similar errand. This remarkable volte-face which, of course, did not remain secret for long, did no good at all to his reputation with the army rank and file but it did demonstrate that Cromwell was no less troubled than his parliamentary colleagues about the country's mood and that his overwhelming desire was for peace.

The rejection of Cromwell's overtures and the determination of the parliamentary majority to offer fresh concessions in order to prevent a recrudescence of war left the generals isolated. The situation had now resolved itself into a contest of principle between the army and the people. To disband the fighting men at this time of mounting instability would be to invite chaos. To allow Charles to be swept back to his throne on a tide of popular feeling would be to abandon everything Cromwell and his friends had fought for. The army council met on 29 April to do what it always did in a crisis – pray – and Cromwell urged that they should seek the Lord in earnest repentance over whatever undisclosed sin had provoked his anger against them. On the following evening the officers' meditation and discussion were interrupted by news of a major uprising in Wales. With heavy hearts they prepared, once again, for war. Yet Cromwell was not entirely downcast, for was not this latest turn of events yet one more instance of God's clear guidance? Just as he had sent prophets such as Moses and Elijah to confront recalcitrant kings who had hardened their hearts and thus brought destruction on themselves, so also Charles Stuart had been given, and had rejected, every opportunity for repentance. Now the godly army would be the tool of divine vengeance. 'Further dealing with that man is to meddle with an accursed thing,' he told his troops.

For Cromwell enough was enough. In order to maintain the shifty monarch on his throne he had wrestled in prayer, argued with recalcitrant radicals, put his reputation and even his life on the line and finally gone cap in hand to Carisbrooke to plead for peace. He had been accused of being a royal 'creature' by the Levellers and abused as a defender of anarchists in the Commons chamber. Opening doors for the King had cost Cromwell dear and every one had been firmly slammed by Charles. There could be no more attempts to reach an accommodation. The King must be *forced* to make terms, and only the army could apply the necessary pressure. What was particularly painful for Cromwell was the wedge inexorably being driven between him and old parliamentary friends who had long stood beside him in the holy struggle. While he and his soldiers were crushing the enemy and making it possible for Parliament to dictate terms the faint-hearted Lords and Commons were bargaining away the advantages being won for them.

In military terms the Second Civil War was a mere postscript to the earlier conflict. The New Model Army was still a formidable fighting machine and the royalist forces thrown into the field against it lacked unified command and strategic planning. Four months sufficed for the annihilation of those inadequate legions in which the prisoner of Carisbrooke trusted for his salvation. While Fairfax reduced the royalists in Kent and Essex, Cromwell made short work of the Welsh, then marched his men northwards to face the invasion led by the Duke of Hamilton. Poor, incompetent Hamilton! The Battle of Preston was to be his last and most spectacular failure. With twenty-four thousand fresh troops at his back and facing an English army of nine thousand, most of whom had just endured a hard march of over a hundred and fifty miles, he managed to suffer a humiliating defeat and personal capture.

The fresh effusion of blood further embittered Cromwell against the King and the triumph of Preston could only be seen by him as the crowning vindication of his godly purpose. On 1 September he wrote exultantly to Oliver St John,

I can say nothing but surely the Lord our God is a great and glorious God. He only is worthy to be feared and trusted, and His appearances patiently to be waited for. He will not fail His people. Let every thing that hath breath praise the Lord . . .

Let us all not be careful what use men will make of these actings. They shall, will they, nill they, fulfil the good pleasure of God, and so shall serve our generations. Our rest we expect elsewhere: that will be durable. Care we not for tomorrow, nor for anything. This Scripture has been of great stay to me; read it: *Isaiah* eighth, 10, 11, 14; – read all the chapter.[30]

The passage to which Oliver drew his old friend's attention tells of God's punishment of his people for their disobedience. To Cromwell it spoke precisely of the condition of England, plunged once more into war because she had wandered from the way of the Lord. The key verses he highlighted read, 'Take counsel together and it shall come to naught; speak the word and it shall not stand. For God is with us. For the Lord spoke thus to me with his strong hand upon me and warned me not to walk in the way of the people . . . he shall be for a sanctuary, but for a stone of stumbling and for a rock of offence to both the houses of Israel, for a gin and for a snare to the inhabitants of Jerusalem.' Herein lies the key to the grim course Cromwell now believed himself to be embarked upon. 'The Lord warned me not to walk in the way of this people' – Oliver now becomes the lonely prophet standing against the common will. 'Take counsel together and it shall come to naught . . . for God is with us' – continued debate with the King is not only fruitless but sinful, for it sets up human counsels in place of communion with God. These are the words of a student of the divine who has found certainty, who is following God's will and is resolved to care nothing for the opinions of men. It was also an exhortation to his friend not to touch an unclean thing.

The implications will have been crystal-clear to St John. While the generals were away the politicians had been at play. Lord Saye and Sele took the lead in making fresh overtures to the King. 'When he thought there was mischief enough done,' commented Clarendon, who loathed him, 'he would have stopped the current and have diverted further fury but he then found he had only authority and credit to do hurt [and] none to heal the wounds he had given, and fell into as much contempt with those whom he led as he was with those whom he had undone.'[31] Saye had approached St John to take part in the negotiations. Cromwell as eagerly wanted his friend to reject them. It is significant that this was the moment when St John elected to abandon politics. The lawyer, who had, ever since the ship money trial, been a leading member of the Commons and the Independent group within it and had laboured for a constitutional settlement, now realised that events were heading to a far different conclusion. He sought the post of Chief Justice of the Common Pleas and was appointed in mid-October. He disassociated himself from the course Cromwell pursued over the following weeks. Oliver craved his old friend's support and there is no evidence of a falling out between them but their political alliance was at an end.[32]

'Blessed is the man who walketh not in the counsel of the ungodly . . . whose delight is in the law of the Lord.' Blessed, yes, but also lonely. It was a loneliness that the King and the gentleman both experienced in the dark autumn days of 1648. Victory and defeat alike directed these two men into the path of holiness, *hagiasmos*, 'set-apartness'. Both knew, at a deep level of their being that they were being propelled by a power beyond themselves towards an apotheosis that was alike glorious and terrible. In their frail humanity, both had moments when they embraced, and moments when they turned from, their destiny. Never were Charles and Oliver more alike than in these days of foreboding. This is not the judgement of misty-eyed romanticism seeking to weigh down with significance the events leading immediately to the Whitehall scaffold on 30 January 1649: the words and actions of the King and Cromwell provide ample evidence of their consciousness of what was now at stake.

Charles's negotiations with the parliamentary commissioners lasted from 18 September to the end of October. They took place in the little school house at Newport and the King was brought down from the castle to be lodged with one of his supporters, Colonel William Hopkins. The participants went over all the old ground yet again – bishops, Prayer Book, Covenant, militia, power of Parliament. Little by little, fresh concessions were dragged from the King who, having nothing to bargain with, yet continued to haggle. Every night he went over the day's proceedings with his secretary, sometimes with tears in his eyes. He believed, as he informed the Prince of Wales, that he had laboured long in the search for peace. Yet, he confided to Hopkins, 'the great concession I made this day

– the church, militia and Ireland – was made merely in order to my escape, of which if I had not hope, I would not have done.'[33] Argument, counter-argument, exhortation and repetition was a tiresome process for all concerned but neither party hurried to bring it to an end; the consequences of failure were too appalling to contemplate. The black spectre of the army, now united in its opposition to a settlement, hovered over every day's discussion. The commissioners needed a royal climb-down so complete that Parliament could confront the military men with an agreement they could not, with reason, oppose. Charles knew what was in the minds of the more extreme army leaders and feared it. His only hope was to induce his enemies to believe that he would yield some new point every day and that eventually security would become lax, enabling his friends to snatch him out of danger.

Yet there were other times when Charles abandoned dreams of escape. The intermittent news he received from Paris was bad. France was in the grip of its own civil war, the Fronde. Taking inspiration from their English counterparts, the members of the parliament of Paris had earlier in the year made a stand against royal autocracy. The confrontation spilled over into riots in the capital at the end of August. As twelve hundred barricades went up in the streets, Henrietta Maria left the palace of St Germain which had been allocated to her by the queen regent, and took refuge in the Louvre. From there she could hear the tumult of the mob but she could also move easily and obtain news of England. The hated Cardinal Mazarin and Anne of Austria lost control of Paris and moved out to St Germain at the end of the year. Nine-year-old Louis XIV then had the first taste of that humiliation at the hands of his own people which he never forgave. Henrietta Maria's French relatives had no resources to spare to assist her. At times she enjoyed fewer comforts than her husband. When Cardinal de Retz, one of the frondeurs, visited her he found her shivering in a room without heat, her infant daughter wrapped up in a bed to keep warm and snow falling in the streets outside. The appalled churchman immediately arranged a delivery of fuel and food and obtained a parliament vote of 40,000 livres for her relief, not failing to make propaganda capital out of the fact that Henry IV's daughter was suffering such privations while her family refused to succour her. News that reached her from diplomatic sources told of rebellions in Portugal, Catalonia and Naples. It seemed as though the whole world was going mad. In November, writing in despair or confusion, she advised her husband not to escape and assured him that the army would not dare to harm him.

Charles did not share his wife's optimism but he was still under her spell and her opinions always weighed heavily in the balance with those of other advisers. 'I am resolved to stay here,' he told one of them, 'and God's will be done.' Providence was as great a reality for him as for Cromwell, although he did not talk so fervently about it. His resignation to the divine will carried the hope of miraculous deliverance – but also the acceptance of suffering. On 25 November in a letter to his eldest son alternating between hope and despair he wrote:

> We know not but this may be the last time we may speak to you . . . We are sensible into what hands we are fallen; and yet (we bless God) we have those inward refreshments the malice of our enemies cannot perturb. We have learned to busy ourself in retiring into ourself and, therefore, can the better digest what befalls, not doubting but God's providence will restrain our enemies' power and turn their fierceness to his praise.[34]

When Henrietta Maria heard that Charles was preparing himself for death she was distraught. She could not, would not live without him, she vowed, and would do all in her power to save him.

The general council of the army had just (16 November) issued a 25,000-word 'Remonstrance' (the last in a succession of documents with this name) in which they rejected the 'treaty' of Newport and demanded that the King be put on trial. It is unlikely that any agreement would have been acceptable to the men who now wielded *de facto* power but Charles had made things easier for them by not yielding enough. In the end, bishops remained the principal sticking point. The King had insisted, 'Episcopacy was so woven in the laws of this land, that we apprehended the pulling out this thread was like to make the whole garment ravel.'[35] Sir Edmund Verney had been right; the quarrel *was* about bishops.

In London the army leaders and the politicians had by this time locked horns. On 20 November the Commons deferred consideration of the Remonstrance and continued to communicate with the King over the minutiae of the Newport articles. The tension was rising and everyone involved felt it. Robert Hammond certainly did.

He poured out his concerns in letters to Cromwell and the latter tried to calm his fears and bade him to be 'spiritually minded'.[36] To the high command it became obvious that Colonel Hammond's conscience was too tender for the action which would soon be necessary. On 21 November Fairfax despatched orders to Carisbrooke Castle commanding Hammond to report to St Albans and to hand his responsibilities to Colonel Isaac Ewer. These instructions filled Hammond with alarm. Ewer was known as one of the army's more ardent radicals with a reputation for violence beyond the call of duty. A contemporary describes him thus: 'His look was stern, his hair and large beard were black and bushy he . . . had a great basket-hilt sword by his side; hardly could one see a man of more grim aspect, and no less robust and rude was his behaviour.'[37] Since Ewer had presented the Remonstrance to Parliament and was now chosen to take over as royal guardian his attitude to the King is very clear. Although Hammond was bound to obey Fairfax's summons, he tried to evade the rest of his orders on the basis that it was Parliament who had entrusted Charles to his care and he left instructions that the King was not to be delivered to Ewer or taken from the island. However, when Hammond arrived on the mainland it was to be confronted by his replacement who immediately detained him under custody in Hurst Castle.

Two days later the fiasco of the King's talks with Parliament came to an end. The commissioners called upon him to take their ceremonial leave before a small crowd in Newport town hall. Charles took the opportunity to make an affecting speech, designed to be copied down and widely published:

My Lords, you are come to take your leave of me, and I believe we shall scarce ever see each other again; but God's will be done. I thank God, I have made my peace with him, and shall, without fear, undergo what he shall be pleased to suffer men to do unto me. My Lords, you cannot but know that, in my fall and ruin, you see your own, and that also near to you. I pray God send you better friends than I have found. I am fully informed of the whole carriage of the plot against me and mine, and nothing so much afflicts me as the sense and feeling I have of the sufferings of my subjects and the miseries that hang over my three kingdoms drawn upon them by those who, upon pretence of public good, violently pursue their own interests and ends.[38]

On 30 November a detachment of troops sent by Ewer arrived. Two days later, in a wet and windy dawn, Charles was escorted across the water to spartan lodgings in Hurst Castle built by Henry VIII, not as a royal dwelling, but as part of his coastal defences.

In none of the autumn events in London or the Isle of Wight was Oliver Cromwell directly involved. The reason is, on the face of it, simple: he was still in Scotland and the North of England tidying up the military situation. However, that does not adequately explain his prolonged absence from the centre of action: his behaviour throughout these weeks looks remarkably like procrastination. After the rout near Preston he turned his attention to the towns of Berwick and Carlisle which had been occupied by the Scots. In the event he was not obliged to retake them by force. The royalist cause had collapsed in Scotland, restoring the Marquis of Argyll to the position of dominance. On 4 October Cromwell was enthusiastically received in Edinburgh, where he spent the next two weeks formalising the return of the two border towns and the disbandment of Scottish forces. From there he marched southwards for Yorkshire where some resistance was still sustained by reason of a royalist garrison holding out in Pontefract. He was some twenty-five miles short of the town when a messenger arrived with shocking news: Thomas Rainsborough, the radical colonel and darling of the troops, had been murdered in cold blood. He had been dispatched to take over the siege of Pontefract only to discover that the current commanding officer would not yield to him. While his superiors sorted out the dispute, Rainsborough withdrew to Doncaster. There he was surprised by a party of royalists who tried to capture him and in the ensuing scuffle he was killed. A tidal wave of anger swept through the northern army and Cromwell stayed to ensure good order, track down the culprits and try to secure the reduction of the town.

All that was at the beginning of November. A month later he was still there, despite an urgent summons from Fairfax to hasten to London. He did not leave Pontefract until 1 December and he then travelled southwards at a very leisurely pace and did not reach the capital until the 6th. Why did Cromwell deliberately absent himself from the centre of national life when such momentous events were taking place? Pontefract did not demand his presence: he reported on 17 November that the garrison was victualled for a year and in no mood to surrender. He was certainly not the man to avoid a fight, whether on the battlefield or in the Commons chamber. Quite the reverse – he was more prone to rush in where angels feared to tread.

The answer probably has three levels. The surface level concerns his membership of Parliament and the army. For years he had been like a circus rider standing astride two horses and managing, often with miraculous dexterity, to maintain contact with both. To Cromwell they were equally essential: his military command gave him a power base but his election to the Commons was the foundation of his authority and he never confused the two. Now, when the horses were pulling violently in different directions, his skill was stretched to the uttermost and it seemed he would have to abandon his parliamentary mount. The constitutionalist in him rebelled against this: a Christian country cannot be ruled by a caucus whose only mandate is military might. And yet were not God's manifold blessings to the army evidence that he had raised up this force to steer the nation into the paths of holiness and justice abandoned by the King *and now, it seemed, by Parliament*? These were the problems with which Cromwell wrestled in the autumn of 1648 and which surfaced in his correspondence with Robin Hammond, to which we have already referred. He utterly rejected the Newport Treaty which threw away most of those rights for which the war had been fought and betrayed all those 'engagements, declarations, implicit covenants with those who ventured their lives'. This being the case, he posed to Hammond the question he had posed to himself 'whether this army be not a lawful power, called by God to oppose and fight against the King upon some stated grounds, and being in power to such ends, may not oppose one name of authority, for those ends, as well as another, the outward authority that called them'.[39] Such considerations needed to be carefully and prayerfully weighed and Cromwell refused to rush southwards at Fairfax's behest until his own mind and conscience were clear.

A second level, and one at which his own pride was engaged, concerned his own supposed ambition. It was only since the Putney Debates that Cromwell had been perceived as a power in the land, because of his military successes, his popularity with the bulk of the army and the attacks of the Levellers. Joshua Sprigg, a New Model Chaplain and a protégé of Fairfax, published in 1647 *Anglia Rediviva: . . . being the History of the Motions, Actions and Successes of the Army under his Excellency Sir Thomas Fairfax*. It was largely a compilation of information culled from contemporary broadsheets and pamphlets and it provides the first written testimony of Cromwell's rise to pre-eminence among the military leaders:

> ... long famous for godliness and zeal in his country, of great note for his service in the House; accepted of a commission at the very beginning of the war; wherein he served his country faithfully and it was observed God was with him and he began to be renowned; insomuch that men found that the narrow room whereunto his first employment had confined their thoughts must be enlarged to an expectation of greater things and higher employments whereunto divine providence had designed him for the good of this kingdom.[40]

Leveller pamphleteers were not nearly so complimentary. They regarded Cromwell as a traitor to the radical cause and subjected him to a mounting bombardment of abuse (their revelations eagerly being taken up by royalist controversialists). The principal elements of these libels were that Cromwell had set his sights on sovereign power, that in his campaign to achieve it Ireton was his lieutenant and Fairfax his stooge. What these diatribes recognised was that the overall commander of the army lacked Cromwell's resolution. Cromwell also knew this and that if he hurried to London to stiffen Fairfax's resolve in the showdown with Parliament his detractors would see this as further proof of his overweening ambition. Throughout the final weeks leading up to the King's death Oliver repeatedly tried – and ultimately failed – to ensure that his commanding officer was more than a figurehead; that he would actively take the lead in doing what had to be done with Charles Stuart.

Yet there was a deeper, intuitive motion for his hesitation: Cromwell had a sense of foreboding throughout those dark, grey, autumn days. Charles was not alone in sensing that events were moving to a climax, a denouement, a catharsis. Anyone who was in any way involved in the struggle between King, Parliament and army knew that the pace was quickening towards a resolution that would be painful to all concerned. Fairfax felt it, which was why he tried to bring Cromwell to his side to share responsibility as earnestly as Cromwell avoided doing so. Men of sensitivity both looked forward to and dreaded what lay ahead. For Cromwell the post-Preston euphoria had given way to a more sombre mood. He was convinced about what must, within limits, be done; what, in the divine ordering of things, would be done, and yet,

> Between the acting of a dreadful thing
> And the first motion, all the interim is
> Like a phantasma, or a hideous dream:
> The genius and the mortal instrument
> Are then in council; and the state of man,
> Like to a little kingdom, suffers then
> The nature of an insurrection.

Cromwell felt passionately about the second outbreak of war which had produced yet more death, injury and grief. Not to punish those responsible would be an insult not only to those who had given and risked their lives, but also to God. When he learned that Sir John Owen, a royalist leader in Wales, had merely suffered banishment for his crimes he wrote to protest at the lenient treatment allowed to people guilty of 'prodigious treason' and concluded,

> Gentlemen, though my sense does appear more severe than perhaps you would have it, yet give me leave to tell you I find a sense amongst the officers concerning such things as these, even to amazement; which truly is not so much to see their blood made so cheap, as to see such manifest witnessings of God (so terrible and so just) no more reverenced.[41]

Cromwell might fume at decisions made in his absence but as long as he chose to remain in the North he could make no immediate impact on the formulation of policy. Thus he only participated at a distance in the lengthy army council deliberations which led eventually to the draconian Remonstrance. This branded Charles Stuart as 'the capital and grand author of our troubles . . . by whose commission, commands or procurement and in whose behalf and for whose interest only . . . all our wars and troubles have been (with all the miseries attending them)'. Justice demanded that the King be tried for 'the treason, blood and mischief he is . . . guilty of' and that the principal enforcers of royal policy should be executed, 'so as their exception from pardon may not be a mockery of justice in the face of God and man'.[42] This document did not spell out the need to kill the King. Indeed, the insistence on the death of royal ministers may be seen as a nod towards the traditional principle that the Crown's evil advisers were the appropriate scapegoats.

Exactly what input Cromwell made to the army's final list of demands cannot be known. It was Henry Ireton who drew up the Remonstrance and it is inconceivable that Cromwell was not in correspondence with his more extreme son-in-law. Some contemporaries believed that Ireton exercised a malign influence over Cromwell, urging him to more vengeful policies than those to which he was by nature inclined. The younger man possessed a greater passion than his father-in-law who was beginning to be mellowed by experience, and, being more intellectual, was inclined to pursue issues to their logical conclusions, whereas Cromwell preferred to wait upon divine guidance. Posts sped between Windsor, London and the North, keeping Cromwell fully apprised of developments. On 20 November he was able to respond in a letter to Fairfax, to the general principles of the Remonstrance while at the same time maintaining a moral as well as a geographical distance:

MY LORD,
   I find a very great sense in the officers of the regiments of the sufferings and the ruin of this poor kingdom, and in them all a very great zeal to have impartial justice done upon offenders; and I must confess, I do in all, from my heart, concur with them; and I verily think and am persuaded they are things which God puts into our hearts.

   I shall not need to offer anything to your Excellency: I know God teaches you, and that He hath manifested His presence so to you as that you will give glory to Him in the eyes of all the world. I held it my duty, having received these petitions and letters, and being desired by the framers thereof, to present them to you. The good Lord work His will upon your heart, enabling you to it; and the presence of Almighty God go along with you. Thus prays, My Lord,
               Your most humble and faithful servant,
                  O. CROMWELL[43]

When he received his copy of the actual document from Fairfax his response was less than overwhelming: 'We have read your declaration here and see in it nothing but what is honest and becoming Christians and honest men to say and offer. It's good to look up to God, who alone is able to sway hearts to agree to the good and just things contained therein.'[44] In this letter the writer expressed his 'hope to wait speedily upon you' but Fairfax had to send another urgent summons before Cromwell finally set out on 1 December.

There are further clues to his tardiness in these letters to the army commander. When he stressed that he had no advice to offer Fairfax and that God would lead him and that Fairfax should rely on the Lord to 'sway hearts' he was trying to stiffen his friend's resolve. He wanted Fairfax to be, in reality, the leader he was by virtue of his office – an office to which God had called him. The Commander-in-Chief needed such encouragement. He was a man who, by nature, shunned extremism. His anger at the failures of King and Parliament which had precipitated the second war had brought him into line with Ireton and the more vehement members of the leadership but there was no telling how long this degree of commitment would last; there were times in the past when Fairfax had avoided involvement when situations became potentially unpleasant. Moreover, he had a wife who was no lover of Cromwell. The army needed the credibility and the unity which only Fairfax could supply. Cromwell knew his superior well enough to realise that he would delegate embarrassing tasks to him as soon as he returned to the capital. Still wrestling in his own mind with what should happen to the King, Oliver was content to 'Wait and see, O sons of glory, what the end shall be'. Therefore, as long as he could convince himself that God had military work for him to do in the North he stayed put.

He arrived in the capital on 6 December and that date is charged with significance: it was the day of Pride's Purge, the eventual showdown between the army and Parliament. On the 1st, the day Charles was brought to the mainland, the southern army had moved from Windsor to London and camped in Hyde Park. The council had then drawn up a list of about a hundred and forty members of the Lords and Commons who were reckoned inimical to their cause. On the morning of 6 December Fairfax ordered Lieutenant-Colonel Thomas Pride to set a cordon of troops around the Parliament house and turn away all the proscribed members.

Cromwell's arrival was very carefully timed for *after* this unconstitutional act so that he could take advantage of the purification of the legislature while disclaiming involvement in the process itself. This was certainly duplicitous, though he may have excused it to himself on the grounds of his need to keep a foot on both horses. There can be no doubt that he was a party to the army council's decision. He also knew Pride and his extremist attitudes, for the lieutenant-colonel had recently served under him in Wales and at Preston. Cromwell certainly approved of the firm action which removed the 'ungodly' but in distancing himself from that action he hoped to preserve his role as a mediator between Parliament and the army.

The remaining 'rump' was now the army's tool, there merely to give some legality to the actions being set in hand to bring the King to trial. On 19 December Charles left from Hampshire to ride to Windsor Castle – comfortable but very secure.

In the grey stone confines of Hurst Castle Charles may well have reflected on the butchering of Edward II in the dungeon at Berkeley or Richard II's supposed murder by Exton in the fortress at Pontefract. He had a real fear of assassination in the gloomy and isolated castle which was enclosed by the waters of the Solent at every high tide. It would, after all, be very convenient for his enemies if he were to 'die' in captivity. It was, therefore, with relief that he heard that Thomas Harrison had arrived to convey him to Windsor.

On 19 December his last royal progress began. It was, as always, a triumphal journey. As he rode unhurriedly under heavy escort along the puddled, rutted lanes of Hampshire, Surrey and Berkshire, villagers and townsfolk crowded to wave and cheer and many pressed upon him to receive the King's touch. The mayor and corporation of Winchester came robed to the city gate to give him a formal welcome. At Bagshot he was entertained to dinner by the young Earl of Newburgh, who had been a gentleman of his bedchamber in happier days, and his wife, Catherine, former widow of George Stuart, Seigneur d'Aubigny, who had perished at Edgehill. It was they who promoted the last in a long series of rescue attempts by putting at his disposal a fleet horse on which, they suggested, he would be able to outstrip the troopers. Harrison was more than a match for such stratagems and had been well primed to be on the watch for trickery. As the party reassembled in the drizzle of a prematurely dark day the colonel pointedly drew Charles's attention to the quality of his men's mounts. The King decided not to put them to the test. By the time they arrived at Windsor the rain was sheeting down but the streets were lined with the loyal and the curious. The little cavalcade turned in at the castle gate. One of the bedraggled figures in the outer ward ran up to greet him. As the man reached up to kiss the King's hand, Charles recognised James Hamilton. The duke sobbed a greeting before being brushed aside by the soldiers. Though the two prisoners shared the same place of captivity for several days they never met again.

The month that Charles spent at Windsor could only be a time of uncertain waiting. No longer was there anything to engage his thoughts except his own fate. No more messages were smuggled to him from his wife or distant advisers. No parliamentarian commissioners came to haggle over terms. No companions spent time with him over cards or bowls. His modest entourage was progressively reduced until he was eventually taking his meals alone in his rooms. Only visits from little Henry or Elizabeth, still at Syon, brightened his days.

For Cromwell the weeks spanning the departure of 1648 and the arrival of 1649 were much busier but scarcely less bleak. What he had suspected and feared about Fairfax rapidly came to pass: the general increasingly absented himself from army council meetings and seldom appeared in the Commons. His distaste for the proceedings carried on in his name created a power vacuum into which Cromwell was sucked. The situation in London was one which was rapidly slipping out of control and there was urgent need of men able to maintain command and to steer the demands and aspirations of the people to some positive conclusion. Soldiers were swaggering the streets and boasting in the alehouses of what they would do to the King. Market women called out insults at army officers. Gangs of apprentices posted up ribald placards and picked fights with troopers. Preachers hurled holy invective from City pulpits. Many of the men of substance who might have exercised a restraining influence left town for their country estates. Those who had been ejected from Parliament had little reason to stay in the capital. Others made sure that their names were not associated with whatever the military rabble were planning. Those with more stamina who were motivated by religious zeal or the common good (or both) did whatever they could to bring matters to a conclusion. 'Honour not yourselves nor one another,' a preacher passionately urged, but God, and then the people, instead of railing upon you will honour and bless you for all the pains you have taken for them. Let him inherit all your joy. Rejoice in the Lord that he is glorified and that he is honoured and you shall see the people shall rejoice in you. You shall be those which the people shall joy in and continually make their boast of; and that all this shall be, let us turn all into the Psalmists' prayer: 'Arise, O Lord, and judge the earth; for thou shalt inherit all nations.'[45]

The fragmentary glimpses offered of Cromwell's movements in these troubled days are confusing – but may be none the less accurate for that. His appearances in the Commons were infrequent, even though that body was working out the details of the King's trial. The recorded discussions of the army council reveal more about his concern with Charles's immediate care and security than his ultimate fate. When more stringent measures for the King's confinement were proposed Cromwell dissented from the majority over refusing the prisoner private conversations. The reason for his concern about the King's security emerged in a debate on 25 December (a day of no special significance in the Puritan calendar) when he argued with his colleagues that it would be imprudent to have Charles executed, for, should royalist elements wish to continue the war, possession of the King's person would be a powerful deterrent. There are tantalising snippets of information about messages sent to Charles, and when Cromwell himself paid visits to Windsor to interrogate Hamilton it remains possible that he talked with the King. As the year drew to an end Cromwell was hurrying from meeting to meeting, group to group, clique to clique – praying, arguing and, through all, seeking the Lord's will.

It seems that by 26 December the process had brought him to an important conclusion – though not without manifest reluctance:

When it was first moved in the House of Commons to proceed capitally against the king; Cromwell stood up and told them, That if any man moved this upon design, he should think him the greatest traitor in the world; but since Providence and necessity had cast them upon it, he should pray God bless their counsels, though he were not provided on the sudden to give them counsel.[46]

Most scholars have inferred that his activities during December were largely directed towards curbing the demands of the more bloodthirsty officers and politicians. This is surely true only insofar as that objective served two others: the dictates of 'Providence and necessity'. Discerning God's will was, of course, always Cromwell's primary concern. 'Necessity' in this context must have meant the maintenance of public order. He had concluded that, with the way various factions were balanced in the capital (though not in the country at large), not to put the King on trial would create more disturbance than doing so. This would almost certainly mean the death of Charles Stuart. It was inconceivable that a court in which the army was represented would acquit the King and that, having condemned him, would demand anything other than the ultimate penalty.

What this decision cost Cromwell in terms of emotional and spiritual anguish we can only conjecture. There was no manic exuberance about his demeanour, such as he often displayed before a battle. For all that royalists later charged him with subtle scheming, there was no strategic planning involved. He had been drawn to his present opinion by the movement of events. And behind the movement of events he saw the hand of the Almighty. That being so he would suppress any feelings of pity he might experience and commit himself to the work in hand. God had hardened Pharaoh's heart and Moses must play his part in the execution of divine justice.

Although the prosecution of Charles I was a state trial and a 'guilty' verdict was the only possible outcome there was about the final stage of the conflict a frenziedness amounting almost to panic. The King and the gentleman exchanged not a word throughout the entire proceedings but, behind the confusion in the courtroom, where accusers and accused claimed to stand for the public weal and noisy partisans shouted their competing slogans, the real drama was that of two implacable wills drawn up in battle array. Cromwell threw himself into the necessary preparations for the unique proceedings which had to be made, and made quickly. Now he attended Parliament regularly and was less often seen on the army council, for it was only the representative body which could give a gloss of legality to the proceedings. To that body he brought those skills in tactical and strategic planning – that insistence on iron discipline that made him a formidable field commander. He sat on every committee – appointing judges, collecting witnesses, drafting the indictment. He bulldozed opposition. When justices, including St John, refused to participate in an illegal tribunal he brushed their objections aside. When nervous participants recommended that the public should be excluded from the trial, he vetoed the suggestion. God's justice must be seen to be done. If they had nothing to be ashamed of, their deeds should be performed in plain view. When a prolix Commons wandered off into side issues such as the abolition of the House of Lords, he brought them 'violently' back to the business in hand: were they mad, wanting at such a time to alienate the peers he wanted to know. They were not met to draft a new constitution but to end an old tyranny.

There came a time, earlier rather than later, when Cromwell knew that the course they were all embarked on had no precedent and no justification in human law. He knew that it lacked the support of the people in whose name it was carried out. Even many of the radicals were now more incensed about the tyranny of the army than the tyranny of the King. He knew that honest men like Fairfax, St John and Hammond could not walk with him. He knew that what he and the apology for a parliament were planning could only be carried through by force. All this he knew and justified in the name of Providence and necessity.

He had reached the position Charles Stuart had occupied in the 1630s. Then, what the King did – or what he encouraged Laud and Strafford and the bishops to do in his name – was done because it was the will of God and because it was necessary for the common good. Whatever the people might think, their loving sovereign knew what was best for them. Charles believed that then; and believed it still – just as Cromwell would never in afteryears deviate from his conviction that the execution of the King was right and just and good.

The King countered with the blunt assertions of his more-than-human status. No self-appointed court had the right to stand in judgement on an anointed king. That was what he believed and, this being the case, he had no need to offer any defence. On 19 January Charles was brought to St James's Palace and the following day to lodgings prepared for him in the Palace of Westminster complex. One story forming part of the embroidery of these momentous events tells of Cromwell standing at the window of the Painted Chamber and watching the King pass through the garden below. Turning to his companions he spoke words which revealed both his excitement and his anxiety. 'My masters, he is come, he is come and now we are doing that great work that the whole nation will be full of. Therefore, I desire you let us resolve here what answer we shall give the king when hc comes before us, for the first question that he will ask us will be by what authority and commission do we try him.'[47]

That was precisely the question that Charles did ask the next day as he sat in a velvet-covered chair facing the three rows of his judges in a packed Westminster Hall. Somewhere among the sixty or so men in those ranks of substantial Englishmen sat Oliver Cromwell. The King and the gentleman were at last brought into direct confrontation. The indictment was read, deposing that Charles Stuart was 'a tyrant, traitor and murderer and a public and implacable enemy to the commonwealth of England' in that he had usurped powers not granted by the laws of the land, had taken arms against his people to enforce those powers and had brought foreign armies on to English soil. All eyes turned to the King for his answer to the charge. Speaking with dignity and slowly so as not to be betrayed by his stammer, he said:

> I would know by what power I am called hither. I would know by what authority, I mean lawful . . .
>
> Remember I am your king, your lawful king, and what sins you bring upon your heads, and the judgement of God upon this land, think well upon it, I say, think well upon it, before you go from one sin to a greater . . . I have a trust committed to me by God, by old and lawful descent; I will not betray it to answer a new unlawful authority; therefore resolve me that and you shall hear more of me.[48]

Throughout three whole sessions (20, 22, 23 January) Charles refused to plead and constantly impugned the validity of the court, while his accusers became more embarrassed and aggravated. They needed to demonstrate the justice of their accusations and the best way to do that was to martial evidence and then demolish the King's effort to refute it. His austere refusal to comply with their agenda wasted time, undermined their credibility and leached away their support. Charles's most devastating weapon was his dignity and he wielded it with quiet persistence and effectiveness. John Bradshaw, presiding, and John Cook, the prosecutor shouted, blustered and argued. Behind the scenes other methods were used to break the

King's poise. In his quarters he was subjected to the noisy ribaldry of his guards. They and his accusers took every opportunity to treat him with deliberate disdain. But disdain was a quality at which the King was a past master. On one occasion Charles entered the hall to discover Cook talking with other officials and pointedly ignoring him. Having waited a few moments the King lifted his cane and prodded the prosecutor sharply in the back to indicate that he was ready to proceed.

Loss of nerve began to appear in the prosecution ranks. Judges failed to appear or, like Fairfax, having sat for the early sessions, slipped quietly away. A hundred and thirty-five assessors had been summoned from among the substantial men of the shires. No more than sixty-seven ever appeared and sometimes the number fell below fifty. Criticism of the proceedings became more open. Representatives of the Scottish Parliament disassociated themselves from the trial. It was in the worried behind-the-scene meetings that Cromwell now took the initiative. Like a battlefield commander rallying dispirited troops, he urged his colleagues onward. One of the most sinister reports about these clandestine activities peripheral to the trial, set down thirty years later by Bishop Burnet, described Cromwell as motivated by the belief that 'there were great occasions in which some men were called to great services in the doing of which they were excused from the common rules of morality'.[49] It is unlikely that Cromwell would ever have expressed himself in such uncompromising words but the proposition certainly accords with the position he had now reached. It is an ethical cul-de-sac into which many earnest souls have been driven who insist upon the priority of the inner voice of divine inspiration over 'fleshly reason' – whatever God tells them to do cannot be sin, however it may appear to men. On another occasion, John Downes, one of the more conscience-racked of the judges, interrupted the proceedings to protest at the treatment of the prisoner. The trial had to wait while Downes was taken into an antechamber and browbeaten by Cromwell and his friends. An even more embarrassing intervention was that of a masked lady in the gallery who suddenly called out, 'Cromwell is a traitor!' and 'not a quarter of the people in England' support these illegal transactions! It later transpired that the strong-willed woman was none other than Lady Fairfax, speaking not in her husband's name but undoubtedly reflecting the anxiety he felt.

The court reconvened on the 25th to hear evidence against the

417

King. Since he refused to respond to it the formalities were soon concluded and Bradshaw indicated that he was ready to proceed to verdict and sentence. Charles interrupted with another speech which indicated how well he had, in the loneliness of his chamber, prepared himself for his ordeal.

> . . . this many a day all things have been taken away from me, but that, that I call more dear to me than my life, which is my conscience and my honour: and if I had respect to my life more than the peace of the kingdom and the liberty of the subject, certainly I should have made a particular defence for myself; for by that at leastwise I might have delayed an ugly sentence, which I believe will pass upon me . . . Now, sir, I conceive, that an hasty sentence once passed, may sooner be repented than recalled; and truly, the self-same desire that I have for the peace of the kingdom, and the liberty of the subject, more than my own particular, does make me now at last desire, that, having something to say that concerns both, I desire before sentence be given, that I may be heard in the Painted Chamber before the Lords and Commons . . .[50]

This denied, Bradshaw called for the verdict of the judges, whose number had now dwindled to forty-six (the agreed quorum being forty). The vote was unanimous and the president duly passed sentence of death. But later more backroom discussions led to the conclusion that the conviction was less than convincing. Two more days passed during which an agitated Cromwell took the lead in obtaining more signatures for the warrant of execution.

After the Restoration, when regicides were trying to escape the penalty for their part in the King's death and Cromwell was no longer around to defend himself, several of the signatories accused him of obtaining their compliance by moral pressure. One story, which rings truer than others, tells of Cromwell waving the pen around in a mood of giggling boisterousness and splashing a colleague's face with ink. The incident accords well with the release of hypertension Oliver often displayed before a battle. By the afternoon of 27 January fifty-nine signatures had – one way or another – been accumulated. The deed was done and the date of execution fixed for the following Tuesday (the 30th). Charles was escorted from Westminster Hall by well-rehearsed soldiers shouting 'Justice! . . . Execution!'

Sentence had been passed but few, it seems, could bring

themselves to believe that it would be carried out. The intervening days and hours between the trial and the execution were abuzz with rumour, scurrying messengers, deputations and all manner of behind-the-scenes activity. The King's friends did not cease their efforts to obtain a reprieve. The Queen had written to Parliament, desperately imploring mercy for her husband. Her letters were discovered two centuries later – unopened. The Prince of Wales appealed directly to Fairfax and received no reply. The general himself was in a state of some turmoil – a turmoil which resulted only in inaction. He later claimed that he laboured hard to save the King but exactly what he did and how industriously he did it has never come to light. Rumours spoke of a last-minute deputation Fairfax received from some of his officers, urging him to lead a coup to snatch the royal prisoner, but recorded that the general had declined to take an action which would stir the wrath of the army.

On Monday Oliver received a surprise visitor. It was his cousin, John Cromwell. He had spent several years as a captain of foot in the service of the Elector Palatine and was now recruited by the Prince of Orange to make an appeal to his relative. He urged Oliver to spare the King's life and indicated that he was empowered to offer almost anything in return. He implored his cousin to reflect what dishonour would be brought upon the family name if he went ahead with the dreadful deed and indicated that he would be ashamed to be called 'Cromwell' (he made good this claim by later reverting to the name Williams). Oliver assured his visitor that he had 'prayed and fasted for the king' but that the army would have his blood. However, he promised to give the matter further consideration. At one o'clock on Tuesday morning he sent John this message: 'The council of officers have been seeking God, as I have also done, and it is resolved by them all that the king must die.'[51]

These events seem to dovetail with another recorded in a Leveller attack. According to this, on the night of the same Monday Cromwell and Ireton, hearing that Fairfax was being petitioned to intervene, rushed to his quarters, taking two troops of horse to back up their arguments, and managed to dissuade him. Now that all the months of denunciation and demands for blood were past; now that regicide was an imminent reality, many wanted to draw back from the deed. There was a very real possibility of an eleventh-hour reprieve. It was Cromwell who steadied the nerves of the King's executioners.[52]

We need not charge Cromwell with hypocrisy or brutality. Rather should we ask the question which he certainly asked himself, 'What would happen if Charles Stuart was pardoned or his sentence commuted?' Two things are certain. The first is that the army would have got completely out of control. They would have vented their anger on their senior officers and, led by hotheads, would have unleashed anarchy on the nation. The second inevitability is that Charles would have become the focus for all those who wished to see a return of Stuart autocracy. The death of a king was a terrible thing; the chaos that would follow his reprieve was unimaginably worse.

Would Charles Stuart, by some means restored to his throne, have returned to his old ways? On the day before his death he wrote a final letter to the Prince of Wales which indicates that he might have learned something from the terrible events of the previous ten years:

> I [would not] have you entertain any aversion or dislike of parliaments, which, in their right constitution with freedom and honour, will never hinder or diminish your greatness, but will rather be an interchanging of love, loyalty, and confidence, between a prince and his people. Nor would the events of this black parliament have been other than such (however much biased by factions in the elections) if it had been preserved from the insolencies of popular dictates, and tumultuary impressions . . .

He had seen what happened when the political nation was denied its forum. Alliance with Lords and Commons enabled the Crown to hold in check those forces which all members of the English establishment feared. A restored Charles I would, on the basis of this letter, have had no designs to establish another eleven-year tyranny:

> The next main hinge on which your prosperity will depend and move, is that of civil justice, wherein the settled laws of these kingdoms, to which you are rightly heir, are the most excellent rules you can govern by, which by an admirable temperament give very much to subjects industry, liberty, and happiness . . . Your prerogative is best showed and exercised in remitting rather than in exacting the rigour of the laws; there being nothing worse than legal tyranny . . .

There was, however, one point on which he would never have

budged and on which he counselled his son to be immovable:

> Your fixation in matters of religion will not be more necessary for
> your soul's than your kingdom's peace, when God shall bring you to
> them . . .
>
> I do require and entreat you as your father and your king that you
> never suffer your heart to receive the least check against or disaffection
> from the true religion established in the Church of England. I tell you I
> have tried it, and have concluded it to be the best in the world . . .
> keeping the middle way between the pomp of superstitious tyranny and
> the meanness of fantastic anarchy.[53]

It was precisely that middle way that had led him and his people over
the precipice.

Charles was at St James's Palace when he wrote this letter. His
last hours were spent in reasonable comfort attended only by Bishop
Juxon and his personal attendant, Thomas Herbert, who had been
appointed by Parliament to attend him in 1647 and had become
a trusted friend. After judgement was passed on him he gave
instructions that none of the many prominent men and women who
wanted to visit him were to be admitted. He took a tearful farewell
of little Elizabeth and Henry, extracting a promise from his son that
he would never allow himself to be made king while his brothers
were alive. Charles obviously feared that the boy might be subjected
to Puritan influences and installed on the throne to preside over the
dismantling of the Church of England.

The next morning Charles left the palace under guard to walk
across the frosted grass of St James's Park to Whitehall. There he
spent most of the forenoon in devotions with Juxon while he waited
for the summons to the specially erected scaffold. It came at about
two o'clock. As the King processed through the palace

> a guard was made all along the galleries and the banqueting house; but
> behind the soldiers abundance of men and women crowded in, though
> with some peril to their persons to behold the saddest sight England
> ever saw. And as his majesty passed by with a cheerful look, [he] heard
> them pray for him, the soldiers not rebuking any of them; by their
> silence and dejected faces seeming more afflicted rather than
> insulting.[54]

It was a solemn business they were all about and there was little evidence of raucous exultation. As Charles walked through the Banqueting House, the scene of so many happy memories, he can scarcely have avoided looking up at Rubens's great painting of his father, James I, being received into glory. Then he stepped through the window on to the black-draped platform, the departure point for his own apotheosis.

According to the most reliable tradition, Cromwell, too, spent the morning in prayer. He was with members of the army council at Harrison's house when the news arrived that the sentence had been carried out. The gentleman had chosen not to witness the King's death, although he was on hand immediately afterwards to give orders for the disposal of the body. This was unusual: it was the custom for government notables to be very visibly present at public state executions. But Cromwell would not be seen to be rejoicing in a triumph he did not feel. How else could he pass those solemn moments of the execution other than in prayer? There was much to pray for – above all the peaceful settlement of the nation, for the King's death did not in itself solve all problems. As Oliver joined with his colleagues in earnest supplication we may be sure that one thing he did not ask for was forgiveness.

At the end what judgement did Charles pass on Cromwell? His last letter to the Prince of Wales includes the only direct reference he ever made to Oliver. In urging that no revenge should be taken against his enemies he yet made clear his own seething anger with them.

> . . . The abused vulgar shall learn that none are greater oppressors of their estates, liberties and consciences than those men, Cromwell, Ireton, Bradshaw and Peters, that entitle themselves the vindicators of them only to usurp power over them . . . whose own sin and folly will sufficiently punish them in due time.[55]

In putting Cromwell's name first in his list of rebels the King finally recognised the one who was the major architect of his downfall. John Bradshaw, who had presided over the 'illegal' proceedings, was an obvious target for his wrath and Charles cannot have failed to hear of Hugh Peters's hysterical public sermons which had denounced him as the 'great Barabbas of Windsor'. He made no mention of Fairfax in whose name the army acted and may even have known that the general was making half-hearted attempts on his behalf. He had no direct evidence of Oliver's determination to bring him to the scaffold. Cromwell had not spoken at the trial, had deliberately retained a low profile throughout the entire proceedings. Yet from messages which found their way into his place of confinement the King was aware of the realities of the situation. He knew that Cromwell and his son-in-law were the campaign managers of the faction holding out for his death.

This is the closest we can get to bringing the King and the gentleman on stage together in the last scenes of the tragedy. The facts of history deny the romantically minded any final confrontation, exchanged glances or words between the doomed monarch and the subject who would assume his place. It was left to legend to provide the story of the nocturnal leave-taking and Cromwell gazing at the body of the King with the words 'Cruel necessity' on his lips.

We set out to tell the story of two men and, therefore, the death of one rightly concludes the narrative. It would be inappropriate to think in terms of victor and vanquished. Both combatants were, in reality, victims. Charles had certainly been brought to book and the Stuart monarchy, as far as anyone could tell, was at an end. But the events of January 1649 had not solved anything. The problems which had inflicted war and regicide on the realm remained and Cromwell was among those who would continue to suffer the consequences.

In the immediate aftermath of the King's death Cromwell was demonised and Charles canonised by royalists at home and abroad. As part of the cult of the martyr-king engravings of the execution were soon circulating on the continent. They depicted the bleeding head being held aloft in front of a large crowd of onlookers who exhibited various signs of lamentation and shock. Vignettes contained 'portraits' of Charles, Fairfax and Cromwell. Stuart propagandists, it seems, were not sure exactly where to lay the blame in the first flush of their indignation. That soon changed: prints and broadsides, such as one displaying Cromwell presiding over the felling of the 'Royal Oak of Britain' with its fair fruits – Magna Carta, the English Bible, statute law and peace – were on sale within a year.[56]

As for Cromwell, he who had so recently left the martial arena had to return to it and months of weary campaigning lay ahead first in the pacification of Ireland, then in confronting a royalist invasion from Scotland. The prospect of going home to his family was as remote as ever and he confided wearily to his wife that he felt 'infirmities of age marvellously stealing upon me'. In 1653 he stepped into that vacancy in the executive which he had done so much to create and by doing so appeared to justify all the accusations of personal ambition levelled against him.

> A Protector, What's that? 'Tis a stately thing
> That confesseth itself but the ape of a king
> A tragical Caesar acted by a clown
> Or a brass farthing stamped with a kind of a crown . . .
> A counterfeit piece that woodenly shows
> A golden effigy with a copper nose
> The fantastic shadow of a sovereign head
> The arms royal reversed and disloyal instead
> In fine, he is one we may Protector call
> From whom the King of Kings protect us all.[57]

Cromwell bore the burdens of high office and suffered the flatteries and obloquies that attend it for a little over five years. Then, by all accounts, he made a peaceful and godly end.

When the parishioners of St Ives were quarrelling with their vicar about the positioning of the altar there was much more at stake than church furnishings. The people wanted direct access to the sacrament and to the Lord of the sacrament. They claimed a familiarity with the divine which the Laudian bishops and their disciples found abhorrent. The conflict was between two concepts equally valid in orthodox Christian tradition: the transcendent God robed in dazzling majesty; and the Saviour who called his followers 'no longer servants but friends'. The one demanded an ecclesiastical hierarchy of priests mediating holy mysteries with the aid of the most beautiful sensual stimulants. The other resented any man-made clutter that got in the way of the individual's approach to his heavenly father.

The religious dichotomy had its exact counterpart in the political life of the state. On the one hand a kingly *mysterium* at the apex of a well-ordered society; on the other a sovereign people unimpressed with the mystique of monarchy. And all this in a land where the spiritual and the secular were totally intermeshed. Thus, many were convinced that episcopacy was the handmaid of tyranny while others just as firmly adhered to the opinion that separatism and anarchy were blood brothers. As long as there was no way of bridging this divide the mantra 'No bishops, no kings' would be a self-fulfilling prophecy. Devout Christians and people of goodwill would oppose each other with prayers on their lips and curses in their hearts. Understanding would be impossible.

The King and the gentleman symbolised this mutual incomprehension and yet – and it is this that makes their tragedy so poignant – they were men whose spiritual pilgrimages had followed not dissimilar routes. Charles and Oliver were both given their religious grounding by Puritan teachers who had incised into their souls the certainty and immutability of faith. Once they had found belief systems to live by they were sure to regard them as nonnegotiable. Neither was able to rest content in the formalised Calvinism which had nurtured their early years. Charles was seduced away by the sensuousness of his mother's Catholicism and found his solace in the beauty of holiness and order. Cromwell's proactive personality needed a prophetic, martial evangelism free from the constraints of fixed liturgy. The King felt himself under divine mandate to impose decorum and uniformity. The gentleman felt himself under divine mandate to resist the compelling of men's consciences. Thus they were doomed – one to embrace death and the other to shoulder the thankless burden of trying to fashion a godly nation. A cynical age might condemn their folly and their bigotry, might point out the disparity between the gospel of love professed and the deeds of hatred performed. It might go on to conclude that political leaders with religious convictions are a menace to themselves and others. We are free to draw our own conclusions based upon whatever beliefs or disbeliefs we espouse. As for Charles and Oliver, among the many attitudes they shared was a disinclination to be remotely interested in the verdict of history. Only one thing did they fear, and it was not the opinion of posterity:

Beatus vir qui timet Dominum.

NOTES

INTRODUCTION

1 Clarendon, Edward, Earl of, *The Life of Edward Earl of Clarendon*, Oxford, 1759, I, p. 289
2 E.B. Chancellor, *The Life of Charles I, 1600–1625*, 1886, Preface
3 J.C. Davis, 'Cromwell's Religion' in J.S. Morrill (ed.), *Oliver Cromwell and the English Revolution*, 1990, p. 289
4 C. Carlton, *Charles I, The Personal Monarch* (1995 ed.), p. 62
5 P. Collinson, *Godly People: Essays on English Protestantism and Puritanism*, 1983, p. 550.

1 – GENES

1 J. Craigie (ed.), *The Basilicon Doron of King James VI*, 1944, p. 67
2 W.M. Noble, *Huntingdonshire and the Armada*, 1896, p. 21
3 Shakespeare, *Henry IV, Part I*, V. ii
4 M. Noble, *Memoirs of the Protectoral House of Cromwell*, Birmingham, 1787, p. 3
5 British Library, MS Cotton, Cleop, E. iv. fo.204b
6 *Letters and Papers Foreign and Domestic of the Reign of King Henry VIII*, ix, 1009 (ed. J. Brewer and J. Gairdner 1862–1920)
7 *Calendar of State Papers, Domestic, Edward VI, 1547–1553*, 742 (ed. C.S. Knighton, 1992)
8 M. Noble, op. cit., pp. v–vi
9 *Journal of the House of Commons*, I, 142
10 J. Nichols, *Progresses of James I*, I, 1828, pp. 98–100
11 T. Fuller, *Worthies of England*, 1662, p. 97
12 T. Fuller, *History of the University of Cambridge*, 1665

13 *Calendar of State Papers, Domestic, Elizabeth and James I* (ed. R. Lemon and M.A.E. Green, 1856–72), Addenda, pp. 424, 445, 451

14 J. Nichols. op. cit., II, p. 24

15 Ibid., p. 247

16 *Cal. S.P., Dom., Elizabeth and James I*, Addenda, pp. 435–6

17 R.A. Warnum (ed.), *Walpole's Anecdotes of Painting*, 1849, i, p. 186

18 *Calendar of State Papers, Domestic, Charles I, 1625–6* (ed. J. Bruce, 1858–97), p. 527

19 J. Strype, *Annals*, II, i. c.1

20 R. Masters, *History of the College of Corpus Christi and the Blessed Virgin Mary* (ed. J. Lamb, 1831), p. 121; C.H. Cooper, *Annals of Cambridge*, 1843, II, p. 312

21 C.H. Cooper, op. cit., II, p. 313

22 A. Peel and L.C. Carlson (eds.), *The Writings of Harrison and Browne*, 1953, pp. 397–8

23 Cf. H.C. Porter, *Reformation and Reaction in Tudor Cambridge*, Cambridge, 1958, p. 150

24 W.M. Noble, op. cit., pp. 54–5

25 T. Goodwin, *Works*, 1681–1704, V, x

26 Cf. P. Collinson, *The Elizabethan Puritan Movement*, 1967, p. 237

27 Ibid., p. 279

28 Ibid., p. 285

29 Ibid., p. 400

30 From 'The Flowers of the Forest' in G.F. Graham (ed.), *The Songs of Scotland*, 1848, I, p. 3

31 Cf. J.A. Froude, *History of England*, 1856–70, xi, pp. 457–8

32 D. Calderwood, *History of the Kirk of Scotland*, 1842–8, iv, pp. 500–1

33 Ibid., v, pp. 439–40

34 J. Stow, *Annales*, 1631, p. 828

2 – KITH AND KIN

1 M. Noble, *Memoirs of the Protectoral House of Cromwell*, I, p. 97

2 Ibid., I, p. 85

3 J. Heath, *Flagellum: or the Life and Death, Birth and Burial of Oliver Cromwell the Great Usurper*, 1663, p. 5

4 Cf. R. Howell Jnr, 'That Imp of Satan' in R.C. Richardson, *Images of Oliver Cromwell*, Manchester, 1993, p. 34

5 W.C. Abbott, *The Writings and Speeches of Oliver Cromwell*, 1937, I, pp. 96–7.

6 L. Stone, *The Family, Sex and Marriage in England 1500–1800*, 1979, p. 389

7 P. Warwick, *Memoires of the Reigne of King Charles I*, 1701, p. 249

8 Cf. W.D. Henry, 'The personality of Oliver Cromwell' in *The Practitioner*, 215 (1975), p. 102

9 Cf. S. Carrington, *The History of the Life and Death of His Most Serene Highness Oliver Late Lord Protector*, 1695, p. 3. Also W.C. Abbott, op. cit., I, p. 24

10 '. . . he hath written to the Council that it is the *only* means to maintain his health, which being the health and welfare of us all, he desires them to take the charge and burden of affairs and foresee that he be not interrupted nor troubled with too much business.' Cf. A. Kingston, *A History of Royston*, 1906, 1975, p. 108

11 Ibid., p. 107

12 *Cal. S.P., Dom., James I, 1603–1610*, p. 374

13 Ibid., *1619–22*, p. 166

14 Ibid., *1623–5*, p. 96

15 Ibid., *1619–22*, p. 456

16 M. Noble, op. cit., I, p. 210

17 Ibid., II, pp. 188f.

18 J. Chandos, *In God's Name: Examples of preaching in England from the Act of Supremacy to the Act of Uniformity*, 1971, p. 429

19 Clarendon, Edward, Earl of, *The History of the Rebellion and Civil Wars in England*, Oxford, 1704, I, p. 145

20 'He may have been completely on the fringes, an obscure cousin of some close friends of great men. But, piling speculation on speculation, what has survived may just be the fragmentary remains of a more central role . . .' J.S. Morrill, *The Nature of the English Revolution*, 1993, p. 142

21 Clarendon, *History*, I, p. 145

22 *Cal. S.P., Dom., Charles I, 1640*, p. 278

23 F.H. Mares (ed.), *The Memoirs of Robert Carey*, 1972, p. 68

24 P. Warwick, op. cit., 1813, p. 62
25 J. Nichols, *The Progresses . . . of King James I*, 1828, I, pp. 153–4
26 British Library, Harleian MSS 7007, fo.316. Cf. J. Nichols, op. cit., II, pp. 265–6
27 *Cal. S.P., Venetian 1603–7*, pp. 513–14
28 E.B. Chancellor, *The Life of Charles I, 1600–1625*, 1886, pp. 13–14
29 BL, Harleian MSS 6986, fo.156; E.B. Chancellor, op. cit., p. 24
30 F. Bacon, 'Of Masques and Triumphs' in *Essays* (1625 ed.)
31 C.H. McIlwain (ed.), *The Political Works of James I*, Cambridge, Mass., 1918, pp. 271–3
32 *The Dictionary of National Biography* (*DNB*)
33 F.H. Mares, op. cit., p. 75
34 Cf. S.R. Gardiner, *History of England, 1603–42*, 1893, V, p. 317
35 John Chamberlain to Dudley Carleton, 9 November 1616, in *The Court and Times of James I* by the author of *The Memoirs of Sophia Dorothea*, etc., 1848, I, p. 434
36 Ibid., I, p. 454
37 *DNB*
38 J. Rushworth, *Historical Collections* (1721 ed.), p. 1321
39 H. Walpole, *Anecdotes of Painting*, 1849, I, p. 21
40 BL, Harleian MSS 6986, fo.83; cf. E.B. Chancellor, op. cit., p. 49
41 G. Goodman, *The Court of King James*, 1839, II, p. 12
42 E.B. Chancellor, op. cit., 1886, pp. 35–6; *Cal. S.P., Dom., 1611–1618*, pp. 487, 493

3 – MENTORS

1 J. Craigie (ed.), *The Basilicon Doron of King James VI*, 1944, I, p. 81
2 R.S. Paul, *The Lord Protector*, 1955, p. 24
3 John Morrill in *The Nature of the English Revolution*, 1993, p. 126 calls Beard a 'greedy pluralist' who held Kimbolton in addition to his other livings until 1611. However W.M. Noble's 'Incumbents of the County of Huntingdon' in *Transactions of the Cambridgeshire and Huntingdonshire Archaeological*

Society, II (1914), pp. 130, 134, 137 lists Edward Robinson MA as being appointed to Kimbolton in 1599 and Thomas Chamberlain MA in 1604.

4 BL, Cotton MSS, Julius c.III, fo.109; *DNB*

5 BL, Add MS 15665, fo.126; *DNB*

6 J.S. Morrill, op. cit., p. 128

7 T. Beard, *The Theatre of God's Judgements, revised and augmented . . .*, 1631, pp. 64–5

8 J. Calvin, *Institutes of the Christian Religion* (1960 ed.), I, 17, 1

9 W.H. Frere and C.E. Douglas (eds.), *Puritan Manifestos*, 1954, p. 19

10 P. Collinson, *Godly People: Essays on English Protestantism and Puritanism*, 1983, p. 3

11 Luke: 6, 26

12 J. Stowe, *A Survey of London* (1908 ed.), Oxford, I, p. 167

13 And, one might add, genuine piety, as many of his verses demonstrate:

> 'Upon the Ensigns of Christ's Crucifying'
> O Sweet and bitter monuments of pain,
> Bitter to Christ who all the pain endured,
> But sweet to me, whose Death my life procured,
> How shall I full express, such loss, such gain.
> My tongue shall be my Pen, mine eyes shall rain
> Tears for my Ink, the Cross where I was cured
> Shall be my Book, where having all abjured
> And calling heavens to record in that plain
> Thus plainly will I write: *no sin like mine.*
> When I have done, do thou Jesu divine
> Take up the tart Sponge of thy Passion
> And blot it forth: then by thy spirit the Quill,
> Thy blood the Ink, and with compassion
> Write thus upon my soul: *thy Jesu still.*

14 W.C. Abbott, *The Writings and Speeches of Oliver Cromwell*, I, pp. 61–2, Speech of Cromwell in the House of Commons, 11 February 1629

15 *Victoria County History: Cambridgeshire*, II, pp. 181–2

16 M. Wickes, *History of Huntingdonshire*, 1995, p. 74

17 T. Carlyle, *Oliver Cromwell's Letters and Speeches* (1905 ed.), II, pp. 134–5

18 Cromwell to the Earl of Loudoun, 18 September, 1648, W.C.

Abbott, op. cit., I, pp. 653–4

19 A Declaration of the Lord-Lieutenant of Ireland, January 1649, T. Carlyle, op. cit., II, pp. 105–10

20 Ibid., Letter to Richard Cromwell, 2 April 1650, II, pp. 134–5

21 J. Calvin, *Institutes*, I, 9.1

22 Declaration of the Lord-Lieutenant of Ireland, January 1649, T. Carlyle, op. cit., II, p. 98

23 Cromwell to Lord Wharton, 2 September 1648, W.C. Abbott, op. cit., I, p. 646

24 Cromwell to Parliament, 12 September 1654, T. Carlyle, op. cit., III, p. 53

25 Cf. R.S. Paul, op. cit., p. 30

26 T. Elyot, *The Governor*, 1531, I, xxvii

27 J. Heath, *Flagellum*, p. 8

28 P. Warwick, *Memoires of the Reigne of King Charles I*, 1701, p. 249

29 W.C. Abbott, op. cit., I, p. 97, Cromwell to Mrs St John

30 Henry Peacham, *The Compleat Gentleman*, 1622. Cf. G.M. Edwards, *Sidney Sussex College*, 1899, pp. 78–9

31 Ibid.

32 T. Fuller, *Worthies of England* (1840 ed.), II, p. 517

33 Cf. R.S. Paul, op. cit., p. 30

34 G.M. Edwards, op. cit., pp. 68–9

35 J.C. Ryle (ed.), *Sermons and Treatises of Samuel Ward*, 1862, p. 97

36 Cf. G.M. Edwards, op. cit., p. 55

37 T. Goodwin, *Works*, 1704, V, x; cf. H.C. Porter, *Reformation and Reaction in Tudor Cambridge*, 1958, pp. 408–9

38 T. Goodwin, op. cit., pp. v–x; cf. H.C. Porter, op. cit., pp. 272–3

39 W.C. Abbott, op. cit., I, p. 29

40 Ibid.

41 Ibid., I, pp. 32–4

42 S. Carrington, *The History of the Life and Death of his Most Serene Highness Oliver Late Lord Protector*, 1659, p. 4

43 H. Fletcher, *The Perfect Politician or a full view of the Life and Actions . . . of O. Cromwell*, 1660, p. 2

44 Cf. W.C. Abbott, op. cit., I, p. 33

45 Ben Jonson, *Epigrams*, LXII

46 Cf. R. Cust, 'News and Politics in Early Seventeenth-Century England' in *Past and Present* 112 (August 1986), pp. 66–7

432

47 Thomas Adams, *Works*, 1629, pp. 45–6
48 W.C. Abbott, op. cit., p. 36
49 J. Craigie (ed.), op. cit., pp. 111, 115
50 Ibid., p. 79
51 Cf. E.B. Chancellor, *The Life of Charles I, 1600–1625*, p. 12
52 *Cal. S.P., Dom., James I, 1611–18*, p. 273
53 A. Wilson, *The History of Great Britain, Being the Life and Reign of King James I*, 1653, p. 152; cf. P.E. McCullough, *Sermons at Court: Politics and Religion in Elizabethan and Jacobean Preaching*, Cambridge, 1998, pp. 110–13
54 T. Ball, *The Life of Preston*, 1628, p. 101
55 Ibid., p. 154
56 G. Hakewill, *King David's Vow*, 1621; cf. P.E. McCullough, op. cit., pp. 202–7
57 R. Perrinchief, *The Royal Martyr, or the Life and Death of King Charles I* (1727 ed.), p. 27
58 *Cal. S.P., Venetian, 1619–1621*, p. 688
59 A.W. (Sir Anthony Weldon), *The Court and Character of King James*, 1651, p. 20
60 P.E. McCullough, op. cit., pp. 194ff., has carefully chronicled and reassessed the sequence of events. Though I do not share his conclusions, I acknowledge his skilful unravelling of these complexities. McCullough observes, 'Historians have despaired at ever finding the roots of Charles I's religious convictions.' I am less pessimistic.
61 Cf. I. Macalpine and R. Hunter, *Porphyria: A Royal Malady*, 1969, pp. 27–8
62 John Chamberlain to Sir Dudley Carleton, 17 October 1617, J. Nichols, *The Progresses . . . of King James I*, III, p. 441
63 A.W., op. cit., p. 28; cf. C. Carlton, *Charles I, The Personal Monarch*, pp. 18–19
64 J. Craigie (ed.), op. cit., pp. 117–19
65 A.W., op. cit., p. 58
66 H. Greenwood, *Tormenting Tophet, or a Terrible Description of Hell . . .*, 1615
67 J. Craigie (ed.), op. cit., p. 27
68 C.H. McIlwain (ed.), *The Political Works of James I*, Harvard, 1918, p. 333
69 J. Craigie (ed.), op. cit., p. 25
70 Ibid., p. 75

71 Ibid., p. 77
72 Ibid., p. 39
73 H. Höpfl, *The Christian Politics of John Calvin*, Cambridge, 1982, pp. 160ff.
74 Salisbury MSS, Hatfield, xvii, 15
75 P. Warwick, op. cit., pp. 67–8
76 Cf. E.B. Chancellor, op. cit., pp. 55, 57
77 Cf. A.H. Matthew and A. Calthrop, *The Life of Sir Tobie Matthew*, 1907, p. 194
78 T. Cogswell, 'England and the Spanish Match', in R. Cust and A. Hughes (eds.), *Conflict in Early Stuart England*, 1989, pp. 117–18
79 Cf. E.B. Chancellor, op. cit., p. 78
80 Ibid., p. 81
81 Ibid., p. 97
82 A.H. Matthew and A. Calthrop, op. cit., p. 223
83 C. Carlton, *Charles I*, p. 58
84 Ibid.
85 Ibid.
86 F.H. Mares (ed.), *The Memoirs of Robert Carey*, Oxford, 1972, p. 77
87 Cf. T. Cogswell, op. cit., p. 108

4 – RESPONSIBILITIES

1 A. Gilbert (ed.), *Machiavelli: The Chief Works and Others*, N. Carolina, 1965, I, p. 63
2 PRO, *Digby Transcripts*, 31/8, vol. 198. 55. Cf. R. Lockyer, *Buckingham*, 1981, p. 169
3 *Cal. S.P., Venetian 1624–5*, p. 325: 8 March 1624
4 E.B. Chancellor, *The Life of Charles I, 1600–1625*, 1886, p. 116
5 R.S. Paul, *The Lord Protector*, 1955, p. 43
6 *Historical Manuscripts Commission*, 9th report, 1883, 427. Cf. R. Lockyer, op. cit., p. 232
7 R. Lockyer, op. cit., p. 234
8 J. Brown, *Kings and Connoisseurs: Collecting Art in Seventeenth-Century Europe*, Yale, 1995, p. 29
9 R. Lockyer, op. cit., p. 232
10 Isaiah: 11, 6–9

11 D. Howarth, *Images of Rule: Art and Politics in the English Renaissance, 1485–1649*, pp. 123–5; G. Martin, 'The Banqueting House ceiling: Two newly-discovered projects', *Apollo*, February 1994, pp. 29–34

12 Lucy Hutchinson, *Memoirs of Colonel Hutchinson* (1928 ed.), p. 67

13 *Cal. S.P., Venetian, 1625–6*, p. 20, 25 April 1625

14 R. Lockyer, op. cit., p. 409

15 J. Brown, op. cit., p. 45

16 D. Howarth, op. cit., p. 253

17 E.B. Chancellor, op. cit., p. 158

18 BL, Harleian MSS, 6987.211; cf. R. Lockyer, op. cit., p. 252

19 R. Lockyer, op. cit., p. 251

20 BL, Harleian MSS, 6988.11.; cf. R. Lockyer, op. cit., p. 251

21 *Journal of the House of Lords*, III, p. 436

22 Cf. R. Lockyer, op. cit., p. 309

23 P. Gregg, *King Charles I*, 1981, p. 152

24 J. Rushworth, *Historical Collections* (1721 ed.), I, p. 225

25 Cf. R. Lockyer, op. cit., p. 399

26 Cf. D. Howarth, op. cit., p. 270

27 Cf. R. Lockyer, op. cit., p. 388

28 Ibid., p. 403

29 Ibid.

30 Ibid., p. 402

31 Cf. Ibid., pp. 425–6

32 *Cal. S.P., Dom., James I, 1623–1625*, p. 561

33 *Cal. S.P., Dom., James I, 1619–1622*, p. 103

34 *Cal. S.P., Dom., Charles I, 1625–6*, p. 527

35 *Cal. S.P., Dom., Charles I, 1625–6*, p. 67

36 G. Sandys, *A Relation of a Journey Begun in 1610*, 1615, p. 99

37 P. Warwick, *Memoires of the Reigne of King Charles I*, pp. 248–9

38 For a full discussion of this controversy see J.S. Morrill, *The Nature of the English Revolution*, pp. 125ff.

39 T. Beard, *The Theatre of God's Judgements*, Dedication

40 W. Carruthers, *A History of Huntingdon*, 1824, pp. 84–7 and Appendix. Cf. J.S. Morrill, op. cit., pp. 130ff. and W.C. Abbott, *The Writings and Speeches of Oliver Cromwell*, I, pp. 66ff.

41 W.C. Abbott, op. cit., I, p. 68

42 Ibid., p. 69

43 Ibid.
44 J.S. Morrill, op. cit., p. 131
45 J. Heath, *Flagellum*, p. 17
46 W. Dugdale, *A Short View of the Late Troubles in England*, 1681, p. 459
47 J. Hacket, *Scrinia Reserata: A Memorial of the Life of John Williams, Archbishop of York*, 1693, II, p. 212
48 T. Birch (ed.), *Thorloe State Papers*, 1742, I, p. 766
49 W.C. Abbott, op. cit., I, p. 103

5 – FAITH

1 'The British Church', *Herbert's Poems*, (1903 ed.), pp. 212–13
2 J. Brown, *Kings and Connoisseurs: Collecting Art in Seventeenth-Century Europe*, p. 87
3 This description, compiled by David Howarth in his *Images of Rule: Art and Politics in the English Renaissance, 1485–1649*, 1997, pp. 70–1, is part of an excellent assessment of art and religion in the life of Charles and Henrietta Maria.
4 Ibid., p. 71
5 Eric Newton and William Neil, *The Christian Faith in Art*, 1966, p. 182
6 D. Howarth, op. cit., pp. 69–70
7 *The Works of John Milton*, New York, 1931–40, III, pt 1, p. 54
8 Cf. D. Howarth, op. cit., pp. 60ff.
9 J.S. McGee, 'William Laud and the Outward Face of Religion' in R.L. De Molen, *Leaders of the Reformation*, Susquehanna, 1984, p. 330
10 Cf. C. Carlton, *Charles I*, pp. 62–3; K. Sharpe, *The Personal Rule of Charles I*, Yale, 1992, pp. 280–1
11 J.J. Cartwright (ed.), *Strafford's Letters*, II, p. 125
12 Cf. J. Chandos (ed.), *In God's Name*, p. 412
13 J.P. Kenyon (ed.), *The Stuart Constitution*, 1969, pp. 154–5
14 Clarendon, *Life*, I, p. 26
15 J.H. Parker (ed.), *The Works of William Laud*, Oxford, 1847–60, III, p. 226
16 Clarendon, *History of the Rebellion*, I, pp. 76–7
17 H.R. Trevor-Roper, *Archbishop Laud, 1573–1645*, 1940, p. 228
18 D. Lloyd, *State-Worthies, or The Statesmen and Favourites of*

England Since the Reformation, 1670, p. 1041

19 J. Rushworth, *Historical Collections*, IV, p. 105

20 Cf. T.A. Mason, *Serving God and Mammon: Archbishop William Juxon*, 1985, pp. 145–6

21 J. Craigie (ed.), *The Basilicon Doron of King James VI*, pp. 49–50

22 J. Hacket, *Scrinia Reservata*, pp. 63–4

23 A.G. Dickens, *The English Reformation*, 1964, p. 315

24 Cf. K. Sharpe, *The Personal Rule of Charles I* and J. Davies, *The Caroline Captivity of the Church: Charles I and the Remoulding of Anglicanism*, Oxford, 1992

25 J. Nelson, *A true copy of the high court of justice for the trial of King Charles I*, 1648, p. 118

26 C.H. McIlwain, *Political Works of James I*, p. 333

27 R. Strong, *Van Dyck, Charles I on Horseback*, 1972, p. 88

28 *The Dramatic Works of Sir William Davenant*, 1872, II, p. 326. R. Strong, op. cit., p. 88

29 E. Veevers, *Images of Love and Religion – Queen Henrietta Maria and court entertainments*, Cambridge, 1989, p. 185

30 *The Works of the Great Monarch and Glorious Martyr King Charles I*, 1766, p. 27

31 C. Jung, *Modern Man in Search of a Soul*, 1962, p. 2

32 W.C. Abbott, *The Writings and Speeches of Oliver Cromwell*, I, pp. 50–1

33 Ibid., pp. 80–1

34 Ibid., pp. 96–7

35 G. Burnet, *History of My Own Times*, 1897–1901, I, p. 121, and J.S. Morrill, *The Nature of the English Revolution*, p. 135

36 *Cal. S.P., Dom., Charles I, 1628–9*, p. 530

37 M. Noble, *Memoirs of the Protectoral House of Cromwell*, I, p. 141

38 C. Hill, *The World Turned Upside Down: Radical Ideas During the English Revolution*, 1975, p. 229; see M. Spufford (ed.), *The World of Rural Dissenters*, Cambridge, 1995, pp. 20ff., for the long-standing tradition of dissent in the St Ives area.

39 Laud to Wentworth, 16 February 1633; cf. T. Baker, *History of St. John's College*, 1869, II, p. 625

40 Ibid., I, p. 214

41 Cf. T. Webster, *Godly Clergy in Early Stuart England – The Caroline Puritan Movement c. 1620–1643*, Cambridge, 1997,

pp. 256–7

42 *Cal. S.P., Dom., Charles I, 1634–5*, pp. 108, 112, 118; *1640*, p. 214

43 W.C. Abbott, op. cit., I, p. 141

44 VCH: *Huntingdonshire*, I, p. 368; for an account of the long-established history of dissent in the region see M. Spufford, *The World of Rural Dissenters*, passim. Holdsworth's reference to the 'better sort' serves as a useful reminder that neither here nor elsewhere were parishes rigidly divided between dissenters and followers of Laud. Many, probably the majority in most cases, resented the excesses of both ritualists and schismatics. In a petition to Parliament in 1641 some 2000 Huntingdonshire residents applauded the deposition of reforming bishops and went on to complain of 'the great increase of late of schismatics and sectaries and of persons, not only separating and sequestering themselves from . . . divine service, but also opposing and tumultuously interrupting others in the performance thereof . . .' Cf. J. Maltby, *Prayer Book and People in Elizabethan and Early Stuart England*, Cambridge, 1998, pp. 83–129 for an analysis of the opinions of the 'better sort'.

45 E.B. Underhill (ed.), *Records of the Church of Christ gathered at Fenstanton, Warboys and Hexham 1644–1720*, Hansard Knollys Society, 1854, p. xii

46 P. Warwick, *Memoires of the Reigne of King Charles I*, p. 249

47 C. Hill, op. cit., p. 94

48 Cf. T. Webster, op. cit., pp. 256–7

49 J.S. Morrill, P. Slack and D. Woolf (eds.), *Public Duty and Private Conscience in Seventeenth-Century England: Essays Presented to G.E. Aylmer*, Oxford, 1993, p. 151

50 J. Preston, *Eighteen Sermons*, 1630

51 B. Whitelocke, *Memorials of the English Affairs from the Beginning of the Reign of Charles I to the Happy Restoration of Charles II*, 1682, p. 173

52 W.C. Abbott, op. cit., I, p. 365

53 W. Crashaw, *Milke for Babes, or a North-Countrie Catechisme*, 1633 ed., p. 7; D.J. Lamburn, 'Petty Babylons, godly prophets, petty pastors and little churches: the work of healing Babel' in *Studies in Church History*, Vol. 26, 1989, p. 246

54 W.C. Abbott, op. cit., I, p. 44

55 John Morrill's detective work has teased out these connections.

Cf. 'The Making of Oliver Cromwell' in *The Nature of the English Revolution*, pp. 137ff.

56 Aaron Guerdon (pseudonym), 'A most learned, conscientious and devout exercise or sermon' in J. Chandos (ed.), op. cit., pp. 460–2

57 Cf. C.H. Firth, *Oliver Cromwell*, 1903, p. 39

58 W.C. Abbott, op. cit., p. 278

59 Ibid., I, p. 262

60 J. Heath, *Flagellum*, pp. 13–14

61 Cf. W.C. Abbott, op. cit., p. 65

62 C. Hill, op. cit., p. 101

63 W.C. Abbott, op. cit., I, p. 121

64 *Commons Journals*, ii. 134

65 W. Prynne, *Histriomastix, The Player's Scourge or Actor's Tragedy*, 1633, Garland reprint, New York, 1974, Preface 'To the Christian Reader'

66 E. Veevers, *Images of Love and Religion – Queen Henrietta Maria and court entertainments*, Cambridge, 1989, p. 91

67 W. Prynne, op. cit., p. 901

68 W.C. Abbott, op. cit., I, pp. 377–8

69 Ibid., I, p. 677

6 – RELIGION

1 T.G. Barnes, *Somerset 1625–1640: A County's Government During the 'Personal Rule'*, Oxford, 1961, p. 310

2 J. Rushworth, *Historical Collections*, I, p. 21

3 F.P. and M.M. Verney, *Memoirs of the Verney Family during the Seventeenth Century*, 1907, II, p. 155

4 Quoted from A. Köcher, ed., *Memoirs of Sophia, Electress of Hanover*, Leipzig, 1879 in L. Campbell, *Renaissance Portraits*, Yale, 1990, p. 247

5 Cf. D. Howarth, *Images of Rule*, pp. 72–5

6 C. Dow, *Innovations Unjustly Charged Upon the Present Church and State*, 1638; cf. L.A. Farrell, *Government by Polemic: James I, the King's Preachers and the Rhetoric of Conformity 1603–1625*, Stanford, 1998, pp. 174–5

7 Charles I, *Instructions unto all Bishops*, 1626; cf. C. Carlton, *Charles I*, p. 161

8 Cf. H.R. Trevor-Roper, *Archbishop Laud 1573–1645*, 1940, p. 147

9 Ibid., p. 376

10 Cf. J. Davies, *The Caroline Captivity of the Church*, p. 302; A. Milton, *Catholic and Reformed: The Roman and Protestant Churches in English Protestant Thought 1600–1640*, Cambridge, 1995, pp. 531f.

11 *Cal. S.P., Dom., Charles I, 1635–6*, p. 50

12 J. Williams, *The Holy Table, Name and Thing*, 1637, pp. 17–18

13 N. Tyacke, 'Puritanism, Arminianism and counter-revolution' in C.S.R. Russell (ed.), *The Origins of the English Civil War*, 1973, p. 131

14 Humphrey Sydenham, 'A Well-Tuned Cymball' (1630) in J. Chandos, *In God's Name*, pp. 325–6

15 Cf. N. Tyacke, 'Puritanism . . .', pp. 150, 152

16 T. Fuller, *The Church History of Britain* (1837 ed.), XI, i, p. 35

17 Cf. J.S. McGee, 'William Laud . . .' in R.L. De Molen, *Leaders of the Reformation*, p. 325

18 *The Works of William Laud* (ed. W. Scot and J. Bliss), Oxford, 1847–60, II, p. xvi

19 F. Bacon, 'On Unity in Religion', *Essays* (1939 ed.), p. 11

20 *The Works of William Laud*, IV, p. 60

21 C. Wren, *Parentilia, or the Family of the Wrens*, 1750, pp. 45–6; cf. P.E. McCullough, *Sermons at Court: Politics and Religion in Elizabethan and Jacobean Preaching*, Cambridge, 1998, p. 208

22 J.S. McGee, op. cit., pp. 333–4

23 *Cal. S.P., Dom., Charles I, 1629–31*, p. 75

24 Cf. K.L. French, G.G. Gibbs and B.A. Kümin (eds.), *The Parish in English Life 1400–1600*, Manchester, 1997

25 A. Foster, 'Churchwardens' account of early modern England and Wales: some problems to note, but much to be gained' in French, Gibbs and Kümin (eds.), op. cit., p. 1992

26 A. Foster, 'Church Policies of the 1630s' in R. Cust and A. Hughes, *Conflict in Early Stuart England*, p. 216

27 T.G. Barnes, op. cit., p. 90

28 Ibid., p. 388

29 Cf. J.S. McGee, op. cit., p. 334

30 T.A. Mason, *Surviving God and Mammon*, p. 62

31 VCH: *Cambridgeshire*, II, pp. 180–1

32 Cf. M. Wickes, *History of Huntingdonshire*, 1995, p. 74

33 VCH: *Cambridgeshire*, II, p. 182

34 In this analysis of the religious views and policies of Charles and his archbishop I have followed the broad consensus of contemporary thinking because I find it compelling and because weighing the arguments of rival historians would not be appropriate here. However, this issue is central to the debate between 'traditionalists' and 'revisionists' and a brief acknowledgement of the contribution of the latter should be made. Three forceful assertions have been offered: The first is that Charles I was the real motive behind the 'Laudian' reforms and that he took a close interest in the minutiae of ecclesiastical legislation and administration. The second is that William Laud has been much maligned and should be seen as one of the architects of that distinctive brand of Christianity (neither Catholic nor Protestant) called 'Anglicanism'. The third is that Arminianism was a coherent body of doctrine which, by confronting Calvinism head-on, forced Puritans into opposition and precipitated the crisis of the 1640s. (Cf. K. Sharpe, *The Personal Rule of Charles I*; N. Tyacke, *Anti-Calvinists: The Rise of English Arminianism*, Oxford, 1987; J. Davies, *The Caroline Captivity of the Church: Charles I and the Remoulding of Anglicanism*, Oxford, 1992 are the principal texts.)

35 P. Gregg, *King Charles I*, p. 391

36 W. Prynne, *Canterbury's Doom, or the First Part of a Complete History of the Trial of William Laud*, 1646, pp. 73–4

37 Cf. P. Gregg, op. cit., p. 304

38 Cf. J.S. Morrill, *The Nature of the English Revolution*, pp. 141–2

39 W.C. Abbott, *The Writings and Speeches of Oliver Cromwell*, I, p. 127

40 Ibid., I, p. 125

41 P. Warwick, *Memoires of the Reigne of King Charles I . . .*, p. 176

42 W.C. Abbott, op. cit., II, p. 283

43 'On the New Forcers of Conscience Under the Long Parliament', *Milton – Poetical Works*, Oxford, 1966, p. 175

44 Cf. J.S. Morrill, 'William Dowsing, the Bureaucratic Puritan' in J.S. Morrill, P. Slack and Daniel Woolf, eds., *Public Duty and*

Private Conscience in Seventeenth Century England, Oxford, 1993, p. 186

45 T. Carlyle, *Oliver Cromwell's Letters and Speeches*, II, p. 195

46 Lucy Hutchinson, *Memoirs of Colonel Hutchinson*, p. 75

47 W.C. Abbott, op. cit., I, p. 270

48 Cf. M. Aston, *England's Iconoclasts: Laws Against Images*, Oxford, 1988, I, p. 65

49 Ibid.

50 Cf. C. Hill, *God's Englishman*, 1970, p. 189; G.F. Nuttall, 'Was Cromwell an Iconoclast?' *Trans. of the Congregational Historical Ass.*, XII, pp. 51ff.

51 VCH: *Cambridgeshire*, II, pp. 181–2

7 – WAR

1 Luke: 14, 31

2 H. Wotton, *Reliquiae Wottonianae*, 1683, p. 151

3 R. Strong, *Van Dyck*, p. 49

4 *DNB*

5 Ibid.

6 G. Burnet, *Memoires of the Lives and Actions of James and William, dukes of Hamilton*, Oxford, 1852, IV, p. 21

7 T.G. Barnes, *Somerset 1625–1640*, p. 273

8 D. Dalrymple, *Memorials and Letters relating to the History of Britain in the Reign of Charles I*, Glasgow, 1766, p. 35

9 R. Strong, op. cit., p. 92

10 P. Warwick, *Memoires of the Reigne of King Charles I*, pp. 65–6

11 C. Petrie (ed.), *The Letters, Speeches and Proclamations of King Charles I*, 1935, p. 266

12 Cf. T.A. Mason, *Serving God and Mammon*, p. 145

13 Clarendon, *State Papers*, 1773, II, p. 81

14 *DNB*

15 Shakespeare, *Macbeth*, I, vii

16 *Commons Journal*, II, p. 330

17 Cf. W. Palmer, *The Political Career of Oliver St John 1637–1649*, Delaware, 1993, p. 69

18 Ibid.

19 *The Works of the Great Monarch and Glorious Martyr King*

Charles I (1766 ed.), I, p. 13

20 Clarendon, *Life*, I, pp. 40–1

21 Cf. W.C. Abbott, *The Writings and Speeches of Oliver Cromwell*, I, p. 142; cf. J.S.A. Adamson, 'Oliver Cromwell and the Long Parliament' in J.S. Morrill (ed.), *Oliver Cromwell and the English Revolution*, 1990, pp. 53–5

22 VCH: *Huntingdonshire*, II, p. 16

23 W.C. Abbott, op. cit., I, p. 190

24 Ibid., I, p. 204

25 Ibid., I, p. 258

26 S. Carrington, *The History of the Life and Death of His Most Serene Highness Oliver Late Lord Protector*, 1695, p. 344

27 Shakespeare, *Henry V*, IV, viii

28 Cf. D.L. Little, 'Some Justification for Violence in the Puritan Revolution', in *Harvard Theological Review*, 65, p. 579

29 W.C. Abbott, op. cit., I, p. 258

30 Ibid., I, p. 256

31 Ibid., I, pp. 261–2

32 J. Bruce (ed.), *The Quarrell between the Earl of Manchester and Oliver Cromwell*, Camden Society, 1875, p. 99

33 J. Spalding, *Memorials of the Troubles in Scotland and England 1624–1645*, Edinburgh, 1851, II, p. 122

34 *Cal. S.P., Venetian, 1643–1647*, p. 162

35 J. Bruce, op. cit., p. 79

36 T. Carlyle, *Oliver Cromwell's Letters and Speeches*, I, pp. 160–1; cf. J.S.A. Adamson, op. cit. in J.S. Morrill (ed.), op. cit., pp. 63–5

37 C. Carlton, *Going to the Wars: The Experience of the British Civil Wars 1638–1650*, 1992, p. 147

38 Clarendon, *Life*, p. 289

39 Ibid.

40 Harleian MS 7379; cf. C. Oman, *Henrietta Maria* (1976 ed.), p. 130

41 C. Petrie (ed.), *The Letters, Speeches and Proclamations of King Charles I* (1968 ed.), pp. 201–2

42 Cf. R.W. Harris, *Clarendon and the English Revolution*, 1983, p. 114

43 J. Sprigg, *Anglia Rediviva: England's Recovery, being the history . . . of the Army under his Excellency Sir Thomas Fairfax* (1854 ed.), p. 129

44 *Eikon Basilike* (1879 ed.), p. 34
45 Clarendon, *Life*, p. 85
46 W.C. Abbott, op. cit., I, p. 340
47 Psalm 89, v. 22–33
48 Cf. R.W. Harris, op. cit., p. 145
49 *Letters to Henrietta Maria*, Camden Soc. 1856, No.6; cf. R.W. Harris, op. cit., p. 149
50 W.C. Abbott, op. cit., I, p. 344
51 Clarendon, *History*, II, pp. 428–9
52 *Recollections by General Sir William Waller* (Appendix to *The Poetry of Anna Matilda*, 1788, p. 124); cf. W.C. Abbott, op. cit., I, p. 334
53 W.C. Abbott, op. cit., I, p. 325
54 Ibid., I, p. 355
55 Ibid., I, p. 365
56 Ibid., I, p. 377
57 *DNB*
58 Clarendon, *History*, II, p. 536
59 *The Works of . . . King Charles I*, I, p. 307
60 *Letters to Henrietta Maria*, Camden Society, 1856, pp. 20, 29
61 C. Petrie (ed.), op. cit., pp. 182–3
62 Cf. T.A. Mason, op. cit., pp. 145–6
63 Cf. P. Gregg, *King Charles I*, p. 410

8 – JUDGEMENT

1 W.C. Abbott, *The Writings and Speeches of Oliver Cromwell*, I, pp. 410–11
2 Cf. W. Palmer, *The Political Career of Oliver St John 1637–1649*, p. 103
3 E. Ludlow, *Memoirs*, Edinburgh, 1751, I, pp. 144–5
4 T. Herbert, *Memoirs of the last two years of the reign of that Unparalleled Prince . . . King Charles I*, 1702, p. 10
5 *Commons Journal*, V, 34
6 W.C. Abbott, op. cit., I, pp. 420–1
7 Ibid., I, p. 429
8 Ibid., I, p. 430
9 Ibid., I, pp. 430–1
10 Ibid., I, p. 434

11 *DNB*
12 W.C. Abbott, op. cit., I, pp. 445–6
13 N. Fiennes, *Vindiciae Veritatis*; cf. W. Palmer, op. cit., p. 96
14 T. Herbert, op. cit., p. 8
15 Ibid., p. 19
16 W.C. Abbott, op. cit., p. 453
17 R.W. Harris, *Clarendon and the English Revolution*, p. 161
18 W.C. Abbott, op. cit., I, pp. 473–4
19 *Memoirs of Sir John Berkeley*, 1702, p. 16
20 Ibid., p. 30
21 Clarendon, *History*, III, p. 58
22 W.C. Abbott, op. cit., I, p. 512; cf. J.S.A. Adamson, op. cit., pp. 70–2
23 R.S. Paul, *The Lord Protector*, p. 149
24 W.C. Abbott, op. cit., I, p. 540
25 W. Palmer, op. cit., p. 110
26 W.C. Abbott, op. cit., I, pp. 696–9
27 *DNB*
28 C. Hill, *The World Turned Upside Down*, p. 182
29 VCH: *Cambridgeshire*, II, pp. 184–5
30 W.C. Abbott, op. cit., I, p. 644
31 Clarendon, *History*, II, p. 162
32 J.S.A. Adamson, 'Oliver Cromwell and the Long Parliament' in J.S. Morrill (ed.), *Oliver Cromwell and the English Revolution*, pp. 76–81, is the best succinct analysis of Cromwell's changing moods and attitudes in this crucial period.
33 P. Gregg, *Charles I*, p. 248
34 Clarendon, *State Papers Collected by Edward Earl of Clarendon*, Oxford, 1767–86, II, pp. 449–53
35 R.W. Harris, op. cit., p. 179
36 Romans, 8
37 T. Herbert, op. cit., pp. 85–6
38 R. Royston, *Works of King Charles I*, 1662, p. 137
39 W.C. Abbott, op. cit., p. 697
40 Quoted by J.S. Morrill, 'Cromwell and his contemporaries' in J.S. Morrill (ed.), *Oliver Cromwell and the English Revolution*, 1990, p. 262
41 W.C. Abbott, op. cit., I, p. 692
42 Cf. S.R. Gardiner, *History of the Great Civil War*, 1904, IV, pp. 233f.

43 W.C. Abbott, op. cit., I, pp. 690–1
44 Ibid., p. 707
45 George Cokayne, 'Flesh Expiring and the Spirit Inspiring' in J. Chandos, *In God's Name*, p. 446
46 Cf. R.S. Paul, op. cit., p. 185
47 M. Noble, *Memoirs of the Protectoral House of Cromwell*, I, p. 119
48 Cf. C.V. Wedgwood, *The Trials of Charles I*, 1964, p. 131
49 Quoted in A. Fraser, *Cromwell, Our Chief of Men*, 1973, p. 156
50 C.V. Wedgwood, op. cit., p. 156
51 J. Wise and M. Noble, *Ramsey Abbey: its Rise and Fall*, Huntingdon, 1882, pp. 153–4
52 J.S. Morrill, 'Cromwell and his contemporaries' in J.S. Morrill (ed.), op. cit., p. 266
53 *The Works of . . . King Charles I* (1766 ed.), I, pp. 134–46
54 T. Herbert, op. cit., p. 134
55 *The Works of . . . King Charles I*, I, p. 146
56 I am grateful to Dr Rosalind Marshall of the Scottish National Gallery for supplying fascinating information on the various depictions of Charles's execution.
57 Quoted in D. Norbrook, *Writing the English Republic: Poetry, Rhetoric and Politics, 1627–1660*, Cambridge, 1999, pp. 321–2

BIBLIOGRAPHY

To attempt a comprehensive bibliography of the literature on Charles Stuart, Oliver Cromwell and their times would be little short of absurd; the number of books and articles devoted to mid-seventeenth-century personalities and events runs comfortably into five figures. The chapter notes above list some of the works which I have consulted and should provide starting points for readers interested in pursuing specific lines of research. What I have attempted below is a threefold categorisation of those items which, in my opinion, are basic to a study of the subject and which indicate some of the more significant recent contributions to its re-evaluation and re-interpretation.

1: Printed Primary Sources and Early Works

W.C. Abbott, *The Writings and Speeches of Oliver Cromwell*, 1937–47

T. Ball, *The Life of Preston*, 1628

Thomas Beard, *The Theatre of God's Judgements, revised and augmented . . .*, 1631

G. Burnet, *A History of My Own Times*, 1897–1901

——, *Memoirs of the Lives and Actions of James and William, Dukes of Hamilton*, 1852

D. Calderwood, *History of the Kirk of Scotland*, 1842–8

Calendar of State Papers, Domestic, 1547–1625 (ed.) M.A.E. Green, 1856–72

Calendar of State Papers, Domestic, of the Reign of Charles I, ed. J. Bruce and W.D. Hamilton, 1858–97

Calendar of State Papers Venetian, ed. R. Brown and G.C. Bentinck, 1864

Thomas Carlyle, *Oliver Cromwell's Letters and Speeches*, 1905 ed.

S. Carrington, *The History of the Life and Death of His Most Serene*

Highness Oliver Late Lord Protector, 1695

J. Chandos, *In God's Name: Examples of preaching in England from the Act of Supremacy to the Act of Uniformity*, 1971

Charles I, *The Works of the Great Monarch and Glorious Martyr, King Charles I*, 1766

Clarendon, Edward Hyde, Earl of, *The History of the Rebellion and Civil Wars in England*, Oxford, 1704

——, *The Life of Edward, Earl of Clarendon* . . ., Oxford, 1754

——, *State Papers collected by Edward, Earl of Clarendon* . . ., Oxford, 1767–86

Commons Journals

J. Craigie (ed.), *The Basilicon Doron of King James VI*, 1944

D. Dalrymple, *Memorials and Letters relating to the History of Britain in the Reign of Charles I*, Glasgow, 1766

W. Dugdale, *A Short View of the Late Troubles in England* . . ., 1681

G.M. Edwards, *Sidney Sussex College*, 1899

Eikon Basilike (1879 ed.)

M.A.A. Everett Green, ed., *Letters of Queen Henrietta Maria*, 1857

H. Fletcher, *The Perfect Politician or a full view of the Life and Actions* . . . *of O. Cromwell*, 1660

W.H. Frere, and C.E. Douglas (eds.), *Puritan Manifestos*, 1954

T. Fuller, *History of the University of Cambridge*, 1655

——, *Worthies of England*, 1662

G. Goodman, *The Court of King James*, 1839

T. Goodwin, *Works*, 1681–1704

J. Heath, *Flagellum: or the Life and Death, Birth and Burial of Oliver Cromwell the Great Usurper*, 1663

T. Herbert, *Memoirs of the last two years of the reign of that Unparalled Prince* . . . *King Charles I*, 1702

Lucy Hutchinson, *Memoirs of Colonel Hutchinson* (1928 ed.)

E. Ludlow, *Memoirs*, Edinburgh, 1751

C.H. McIlwain (ed.), *The Political Works of James I*, Cambridge, Mass., 1918

J. Nichols, *Progresses of James I*, 1828

M. Noble, *Memoirs of the Protectoral House of Cromwell*, 1787

J.H. Parker (ed.), *The Works of* . . . *William Laud*, Oxford, 1847–60

R. Perrinchief, *The Royal Martyr, or the Life and Death of King Charles I* (1727 ed.)

R. Petrie (ed.), *Letters, Speeches and Proclamations of King Charles I*, 1935

W. Prynne, *Canterbury's Doom, or the First Part of a Complete History of the Trial of William Laud*, 1646

——, *Histriomastix, The Player's Scourge or Actor's Tragedy* (1633), Garland reprint, New York, 1974

R. Royston (ed.), *Works of King Charles I*, 1662

J. Rushworth, *Historical Collections* (1721 ed.)

J.C. Ryle (ed.), *Sermons and Treatises of Samuel Ward*, 1862

G. Sandys, *The Relation of a Journey begun an. Dom. 1610, in Four Books*, 1615

J. Spalding, *Memorials of the Troubles in Scotland and England 1624–1645*, Edinburgh, 1851

J. Sprigg, *Anglia Rediviva: England's Recovery, being the history . . . of the Army under his Excellency Sir Thomas Fairfax* (1854 ed.)

J. Stowe, *Annales*, 1631

——, *A Survey of London*, Oxford (1908 ed.)

J. Strype, *Annals*

Sir Philip Warwick, *Memoires of the Reigne of King Charles I*, 1701

A.W. (Sir Anthony Weldon), *The Court and Character of King James I*, 1651

B. Whitelocke, *Memorials of the English Affairs from the Beginning of the Reign of Charles I to the Happy Restoration of Charles II*, 1682

H. Wotton, *Reliquiae Wottonianae*, 1683

2: Standard Biographies and Reference Works

Charles I

J. Bowle, *Charles I*, 1975

C. Carlton, *Charles I, The Personal Monarch*, 1983, 1995

E.B. Chancellor, *The Life of Charles I, 1600–1625*, 1886

P. Gregg, *King Charles I*, 1981

R. Ollard, *The Image of the King: Charles I and Charles II*, 1979

K. Sharpe, *The Personal Rule of Charles I*, Yale, 1992

Oliver Cromwell

M.P. Ashley, *The Greatness of Oliver Cromwell*, 1957

J. Buchan, *Oliver Cromwell*, 1934

C.H. Firth, *Oliver Cromwell and the Rule of the Puritans*, Oxford, 1900

A. Fraser, *Cromwell, Our Chief of Men*, 1973

S.R. Gardiner, *Oliver Cromwell*, 1909

P. Gaunt, *Oliver Cromwell*, Oxford, 1996

C. Hill, *God's Englishman: Oliver Cromwell and the English Revolution*, 1970

R. Howell, *Cromwell*, 1977

J. Morley, *Oliver Cromwell*, 1909

J.S. Morrill (ed.), *Oliver Cromwell and the English Revolution*, 1990

J.F.H. New (ed.), *Oliver Cromwell – Pretender, Puritan, Statesman, Paradox?*, New York, 1972

R.S. Paul, *The Lord Protector*, 1955

R.C. Richardson (ed.), *Images of Oliver Cromwell*, Manchester, 1993

I. Roots (ed.), *Cromwell, A Profile*, 1973

C.V. Wedgwood, *Oliver Cromwell*, 1939

M. Ashley, *Charles I and Oliver Cromwell: A study in contrasts and comparisons*, 1987

C. Cross, *Church and People 1450–1610: the triumph of the laity in the English church*, Glasgow, 1976

A.G. Dickens, *The English Reformation* (1989 ed.)

R.W. Harris, *Clarendon and the English Revolution*, 1983

C. Hill, *Society and Puritanism in Pre-Revolutionary England*, 1964

——, *The World Turned Upside Down: Radical Ideas During the English Revolution*, 1972

F.H. Mares (ed.), *The Memoirs of Robert Carey*, 1972

G.F. Nuttall, *The Holy Spirit in Puritan Faith and Experience*, Oxford, 1946

——, *Visible Saints: the Congregational Way, 1640–1660*, Oxford, 1957

C. Oman, *Henrietta Maria* (1976 ed.)

G. Parker and L.M. Smith (eds.), *The General Crisis of the Seventeenth Century*, 1978

J.J. Scarisbrick, *The Reformation and the English People*, Oxford, 1984

P. Seaver, *The Puritan Lectureships: the politics of religious dissent*

1560–1662, Stanford, 1970

L. Stone, *The Family Sex and Marriage in England 1500–1800*, 1977

R. Strong, *Van Dyck Charles I on Horseback*, 1972

N. Sykes, *Old Priest and New Presbyter*, Cambridge, 1956

K. Thomas, *Religion and the Decline of Magic*, New York, 1971

H. Trevor-Roper, *Archbishop Laud*, 1940

Victoria County History: *Cambridgeshire*

——: *Huntingdonshire*

C.V. Wedgwood, *The King's Peace, 1637–1641*, 1955

——, *The King's War, 1641–1647*, 1958

——, *The Trial of Charles I*, 1964

D.H. Willson, *King James VI and I*, 1956

3: Recent Writing

R. Ashton, *Counter Revolution: The Second Civil War and its Origins*, New Haven, 1995

M. Aston, *England's Iconoclasts: Laws Against Images*, Oxford, 1988

G.E. Aylmer, *Rebellion or Revolution?: England 1640–60*, 1986

J. Brown, *Kings and Connoisseurs: Collecting Art in Seventeenth-Century Europe*, Yale, 1995

C. Carlton, *Archbishop William Laud*, 1987

——, *Going to the Wars: The Experience of the British Civil Wars 1638–1651*, 1992

P. Collinson, 'A comment concerning the name puritan' in *Journal of Ecclesiastical History*, 1980

——, *Godly People: Essays on English Protestantism and Puritanism*, 1983

——, *The Puritan Character: polemic and polarities in early seventeenth-century English Culture*, Los Angeles, 1989

——, *The Religion of Protestants: the Church of English Society 1559–1625*, Oxford, 1982

R. Cust, 'News and Politics in Early Seventeenth-Century England' in *Past and Present*, August 1986

R. Cust and A. Hughes (eds.), *Conflict in Early Stuart England: Studies in Religion and Politics, 1607–1642*, Cambridge, 1999

R. Cust and A. Hughes (eds.), *The English Civil War*, 1997

451

J. Davies, *The Caroline Captivity of the Church: Charles I and the Remoulding of Anglicanism*, Oxford, 1992

I. Gentles, J.S. Morrill and B. Worden (eds.), *Soldiers, Writers and Statesmen of the English Revolution*, Cambridge, 1998

R. Grassby, *The Business Community in Seventeenth-Century England*, Cambridge, 1995

W.D. Henry, 'The Personality of Oliver Cromwell' in *The Practitioner*, 1975

D. Hirst, *Authority and Conflict: England 1603–1658*, 1986

D. Howarth, *Images of Rule, Art and Politics in the English Renaissance, 1485–1649*, 1997

R. Howell Jnr, 'That Imp of Satan' in R.C. Richardson, *Images of Oliver Cromwell*, Manchester, 1993

M. Lynch, *Scotland, A New History*, 1991

J. Maltby, *Prayer Book and People in Elizabethan and Early Stuart England*, Cambridge, 1998

T.A. Mason, *Serving God and Mammon: Archbishop William Juxon*, 1995

P.E. McCullough, *Sermons at Court 1559–1629, Religion and Politics in Elizabethan and Jacobean Preaching*, Cambridge, 1998

A. Milton, *Catholic and Reformed, The Roman and Protestant Churches in English Protestant Thought, 1600–1640*, Cambridge, 1995

J.S. Morrill, *The Nature of the English Revolution*, 1993

——, *The Revolt of the Provinces: conservatives and radicals in the English Civil War, 1630–1650*, 1976

——, *Seventeenth-Century Britain, 1603–1714*, 1980

—— (ed.), *Reactions to the English Civil War, 1642–1649*, 1982

J.S. Morrill, P. Slack and D. Woolf (eds.), *Public Duty and Private Conscience in Seventeenth-Century England: Essays Presented to G.E. Aylmer*, Oxford, 1993

D. Norbrook, *Writing the English Republic: Poetry, Rhetoric and Politics, 1627–1660*, Cambridge, 1999

W. Palmer, *The Political Career of Oliver St. John, 1637–1649*, Delaware, 1993

B. Reay, *Popular Culture in Seventeenth-Century England*, 1985

I. Roots, *The Great Rebellion, 1642–1660*, 1995 ed.

C. Russell, *The Fall of the British Monarchies, 1637–1642*, Oxford, 1991

——, *The Origins of the English Civil War*, Oxford, 1973

D. Starkey, ed., *The English Court from the Wars of the Roses to the Civil War*, 1987

R. Strong, *Henry, Prince of Wales, England's Lost Renaissance*, 1986

H. Trevor-Roper, *Catholics, Anglicans and Puritans*, 1987

N. Tyacke, *Anti-Calvinists: The Rise of English Arminianism c.1590–1640*, Oxford, 1987

N. Tyacke and P. White, 'Debate: the rise of Arminianism reconsidered' in *Past and Present*, 1987

E. Veevers, *Images of Love and Religion: Queen Henrietta Maria and Court Entertainments*, Cambridge, 1989

T. Webster, *Godly Clergy in Early Stuart England: The Caroline Puritan Movement, c.1620–1643*, Cambridge, 1997

INDEX
Compiled by Gordon Robinson